PENGUIN BOOKS

BREAKOUT

Martin Russ earned a Purple Heart when he served with the Marines in Korea. His previous books include the bestselling *The Last Parallel: A Marine's War Journal* (a Book-of-the-Month Club selection); *Line of Departure: Tarawa* (a Military Book Club selection); *Happy Hunting Ground: An Ex-Marine's Odysee in Vietnam*; and the novels *Half Moon Haven* and *War Memorial*. Martin Russ taught writing at Carnegie-Mellon University and is also the author of *Showdown Semester: Advice from a Writing Professor*.

BREAKOUT

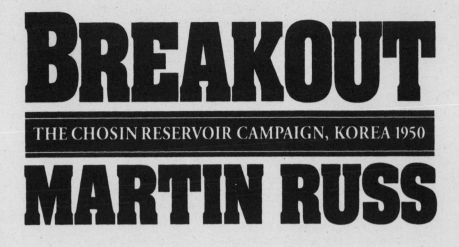

THE CHOSIN RESERVOIR CAMPAIGN, KOREA 1950

MARTIN RUSS

PENGUIN BOOKS

This book is dedicated to two foul-weather friends:
Ronald A. Clark of Coronado, California, and
Robert B. Clark of Manhattan Beach, California.

PENGUIN BOOKS
Published by the Penguin Group
Penguin Group (USA) Inc., 375 Hudson Street, New York, New York 10014, U.S.A.
Penguin Group (Canada), 90 Eglinton Avenue East, Suite 700, Toronto,
Ontario, Canada M4P 2Y3 (a division of Pearson Penguin Canada Inc.)
Penguin Books Ltd, 80 Strand, London WC2R 0RL, England
Penguin Ireland, 25 St Stephen's Green, Dublin 2, Ireland (a division of Penguin Books Ltd)
Penguin Group (Australia), 250 Camberwell Road, Camberwell,
Victoria 3124, Australia (a division of Pearson Australia Group Pty Ltd)
Penguin Books India Pvt Ltd, 11 Community Centre, Panchsheel Park,
New Delhi – 110 017, India
Penguin Group (NZ), 67 Apollo Drive, Rosedale, North Shore 0632, New Zealand
(a division of Pearson New Zealand Ltd)
Penguin Books (South Africa) (Pty) Ltd, 24 Sturdee Avenue,
Rosebank, Johannesburg 2196, South Africa

Penguin Books Ltd, Registered Offices: 80 Strand, London WC2R 0RL, England

First published in the United States of America by
Fromm International Publishing Corporation, 1999
Published in Penguin Books 2000

14 16 18 20 19 17 15 13

Copyright © Martin Russ, 1999
All rights reserved

ISBN 0-88064-231-9 (hc.)
ISBN 978-0-14-029259-6 (pbk.)

(CIP data available)

Printed in the United States of America
Set in Sabon

. . . Age shall not weary them,
Nor the years condemn.
At the going down of the sun
And in the morning
We will remember them.

—*Lawrence Binyon*

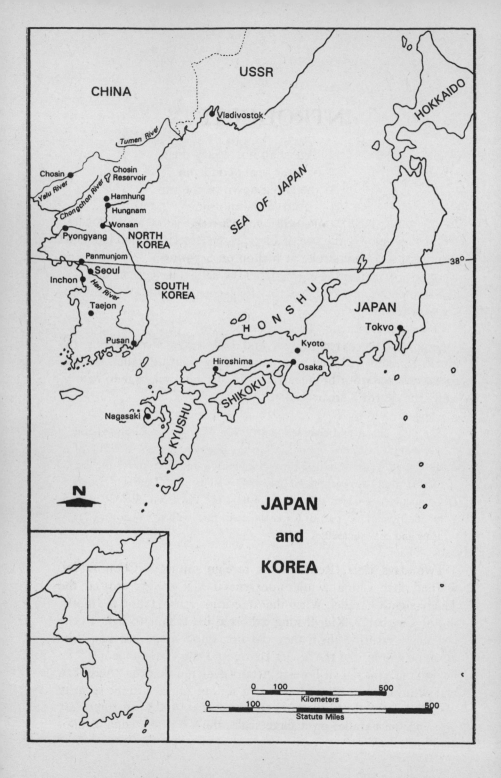

CHINA

USSR

Vladivostok

Tumen River

Chosin

Chosin
Reservoir

Yalu River

Chongchon River

Hamhung

Hungnam

Wonsan

SEA OF JAPAN

HOKKAIDO

Pyongyang

NORTH
KOREA

38°

Panmunjom

Seoul

Inchon

Han River

SOUTH
KOREA

Taejon

HONSHU

JAPAN

Tokyo

Pusan

Kyoto

Hiroshima

Osaka

SHIKOKU

Nagasaki

KYUSHU

N

JAPAN

and

KOREA

0   100   500
Kilometers
0   100   500
Statute Miles

INTRODUCTION

AFTER BEING PUSHED AROUND BY A PEASANT ARMY FOR SEVERAL weeks in a country the size of Florida, the Americans had launched a successful counterstroke at Inchon on September 15, 1950, and were now sweeping the enemy from the field. The Korean War was about to end in a splendid victory for General Douglas MacArthur. Or so it seemed.

"I shall crush them," he announced.

Seoul had been recaptured, and UN forces were driving the North Koreans pell-mell across the Thirty-eighth Parallel. On October 1, MacArthur broadcast a surrender-now message to Kim Il-sung, the North Korean leader.

> The early defeat and complete destruction of your Armed Forces and war-making potential is now inevitable. In order that the decision of the United Nations may be carried out with a minimum of further loss of life and destruction of property, I, as the United Nations Commander-in-Chief, call upon you and the forces under your command, in whatever part of Korea situated, forthwith to lay down your arms and cease hostilities . . .

Two days later, Red China's foreign minister, Chou En-lai, warned that China would intervene if UN troops crossed the Thirty-eighth Parallel. When the Americans crossed it on the morning of October 9, Kim Il-sung exhorted his troops to fight to the last man, assuring them they did not stand alone but had "the absolute support of the Soviet Union and the Chinese people." In Peking the Ministry of Foreign Affairs declared that the "American war of invasion in Korea has been a serious menace to the security of China from the very start, and now that American forces are crossing the parallel on a large scale, the Chinese people cannot stand idly by."

MacArthur's intelligence chief, Major General Charles Willoughby, issued the following statement in response: "Recent declarations by Chinese Communist Forces leaders, threatening to enter North Korea if American forces were to cross the Thirty-eighth Parallel, are probably in the category of diplomatic blackmail."

Three days later the Central Intelligence Agency delivered an assessment of the situation to President Truman. "Despite statements by Chou En-lai," it read, "troop movements to Manchuria and propaganda charges of atrocities and border violations, there are no convincing indications of an actual Chinese Communist intention to resort to full-scale intervention in Korea." At their meeting on Wake Island on October 15, Truman asked MacArthur his opinion on the likelihood of Chinese intervention. The general assured him it was unlikely, and added that North Korean resistance would end by Thanksgiving. Before the ninety-minute meeting ended, the president asked him once again what the chances were for Chinese intervention. "Very little," said MacArthur. "Had they intervened in the first or second months, it would have been decisive. We are no longer fearful of their intervention."

Four days later the 1st U.S. Cavalry Division and the South Korean 1st Division marched into the North Korean capital, Pyongyang, and the following day MacArthur watched a mass parachute drop by the 187th U.S. Airborne Regiment thirty miles north of the city. The general announced that this maneuver had "closed the gap" on the retreating North Koreans. The next day he announced from his Tokyo headquarters that the war was "definitely coming to an end shortly."

Even as great a captain as Douglas MacArthur had failed to learn the lesson that predicting victory is unwise. By the time he had assured the world the Korean War was all but concluded, major elements of Lin Piao's Fourth Field Army were swarming across the Yalu River into Korea. Advancing on foot—but only after dark—they had not yet been detected by the UN command.

Though he has since been ridiculed for it, MacArthur can be forgiven his overconfidence at that moment in history. By mid-October 1950 the North Korean army was nearly finished; all that remained were fleeing remnants. As far as the threats of Chinese intervention were concerned, no one in the Pentagon, the State Department, or the White House took them any more seriously than MacArthur did. Given the weakness of the North Koreans (Willoughby had informed his boss by memorandum that "Organized resistance on any large scale has ceased to be an enemy capability"), he can also be forgiven for dividing his force. After the Inchon landing and the recapture of Seoul in September, MacArthur had sent Major General Walton Walker's Eighth Army up the west side of the peninsula and Major General Edward Almond's X Corps around by sea to Wonsan on the northeast coast. There would be no direct communication between the two wings, which were now separated by the rugged Taebek Range.

This book concerns itself mainly with the fate of X Corps in November–December 1950, with the focus mostly on the operations of its core element, the 1st Marine Division.

The reader may find it helpful to be able to refer to the following simplified organizational chart of the 1st Marine Division and elements of the 7th Infantry Division engaged in the Chosin Reservoir campaign in November-December 1950:

The 1ST MARINE DIVISION, led by Major General Oliver Smith, was primarily composed of three infantry regiments plus an artillery regiment: the 1st Marines, the 5th Marines, the 7th Marines, plus the 11th Marines.

Each infantry regiment was primairly composed of three infantry battalions:

The 1st Marines (an infantry regiment) was led by Col. Lewis Puller. His three infantry battalion commanders: Lt. Col. Donald Schmuck (1st Battalion, 1st Marines, or 1/1), Lt. Col. Allan Sutter (2/1), and Lt. Col. Thomas Ridge (3/1).

The 5th Marines (an infantry regiment) was led by Lt. Col. Raymond Murray. His three infantry battalion commanders: Lt. Col. John Stevens (1/5), Lt. Col. Harold Roise (2/5), Lt. Col. Robert Taplett (3/5).

The 7th Marines (an infantry regiment) was led by Col. Homer Litzenberg. His three infantry battalion commanders: Lt. Col. Raymond Davis (1/7), Lt. Col. Randolph Lockwood (2/7), and Lt. Col. William Harris.

(Note: At full strength, an infantry regiment and an infantry battalion contain—roughly—3,500 and 1,000 men, respectively.)

The elements of the U.S. Army's 7TH INFANTRY DIVISION which took part in the campaign were: the 31st Infantry Regiment, led by Col. Allen MacLean, plus the 57th Field Artillery Battalion and the 31st Tank Company. MacLean's three infantry battalion commanders were: Lt. Col. Don Faith (First Battalion, 32nd Infantry Regiment, or 1/32), Lt. Col. William Reidy (2/31), Lt. Col. William Reilly (3/31).

The 1st Marine Aircraft Wing, led by Major General Field Harris, provided close air support to Marine and Army units throughout the campaign.

1. MARINES HAD ALWAYS BEEN REGARDED as shock troops, their traditional mission being to capture beachheads and hold them until occupation forces (usually Army troops) arrived. Battalion for battalion, the Marines were the most fearsomely efficient troops on either side of the Second World War—not because they were braver or had God on their side, but because Marine recruits were inspired from the beginning with the conviction that they belonged to a select and elite legion, and because of a tradition of loyalty which meant in practical terms that the individual Marine trusted in and relied on his comrades to an extraordinary degree, and that he himself was trustworthy and reliable.

Most Marines of that day believed it was better to die than to let one's comrades down in combat. The ultimate payoff of this esprit de corps was a headlong aggressiveness that won battles. Ernest Hemingway, who knew something of men at war, wrote, "I would rather have a good Marine, even a ruined one, than anything in the world when there are chips down."

It was the boot camp training these volunteers endured at the recruit depots at Parris Island and San Diego that established the foundation of this proud military attitude. For ten weeks the individual volunteer was hermetically sealed in a hostile environment, every moment calculated to prepare him to function smoothly on the edge of the abyss, subject to such harassment and confusion—very much like combat itself—that it spawned in his homesick heart a desperate yearning for order, and finally a love of that order and a clear understanding that in its symmetry lay his safety and survival.

There was an undeniable mystique about the Marine Corps, a feeling of being vastly superior to the soldiers of the U.S. Army (Marines never refer to themselves as soldiers) alongside whom they were sometimes required to campaign. By and large, Marines were a resourceful, hardy breed, readier to go in harm's way than the Army's hapless minions. The ghosts of their institutional ancestors—those who fell at Tripoli, in the Halls of Montezuma, at Belleau Wood, Guadalcanal, Tarawa, Iwo Jima, Inchon, and other hallowed sites—haunted every Marine at every base and duty station around the globe, demanding teamwork, discipline, courage, and unswerving dedication to the accomplishment of the mission, even when it required entrance into the maw of hell.

Though they were the most colorful troops in the American armed forces, there was nothing flashy about the Marines. None of their units bore names like Tropic Lightning or Screaming Eagles. The Marine uniform—aside from the "dress blues" worn on ceremonial occasions—was a simple forest green, plain and unadorned in comparison with the Army uniform with its badges, nameplates, patches, flashes, and brass buttons. Captain Michael Capraro, public information officer, 1st Marine Division: "There was a surplus of dirt-common names among the key officers of the day—lots of Browns, Davises, Johnsons, Joneses, Smiths, Williamses, Wilsons, and such. I realize that that is without significance; even so, I always thought the plainness of such names was somehow appropriate to the plainness of the Corps itself."

The division was simply the 1st Marine Division. It was composed of three infantry regiments—1st Marines, 5th Marines, and 7th Marines, each numbering about 3,200 men—and one artillery regiment, 11th Marines. Over twelve thousand strong, these were the men who would do most of the fighting during the Chosin Reservoir campaign. In the rear were ten thousand combat support troops, including the 1st Marine Air Wing.

Captain Capraro: "It was the strongest division in the world. I thought of it as a Doberman, a dangerous hound straining at the leash, wanting nothing more than to sink its fangs into the master's enemy, preferably one with yellow skin. . . . So many Regular Marine corporals and sergeants and commissioned officers hailed from the South that some folks said the division descended directly from Robert E. Lee's Army of Northern Virginia. Like the Confederates, they were volunteers and loved a good fight."

Many Americans regarded the Marine Corps as a national treasure. It was common knowledge that whenever the trumpet sounded, the Marines could be counted on as ready for action, and they had a remarkable history of winning battles quickly.

PFC Ray Walker, Able Company, 5th Marines, says he cannot recall that any of his fellow Marines resembled the handsome, square-jawed, muscular paragon usually depicted on recruiting posters. "Many of these kids had just started shaving. They were ordinary-looking teenagers, maybe a bit more hard-bitten than most. Journalists referred to them as men, but if you accompanied them on a Stateside liberty you'd notice they bought more candy and ice cream than beer or whiskey, and they were pretty bashful around girls. They would call the girls' mothers 'Ma'am.' I'm talking about the privates and privates first class [PFCs], of course, the ones who made up most of the Corps and did most of the fighting."

And they tended to strut, these youngsters. The battle record of the Corps gave them that right. But none of this explains why they were so good at what they did, or how they were able to destroy the Chinese formations sent to annihilate them in northeast Korea.

2. GENERAL ALMOND, U.S. ARMY, com-
manding X Corps, had established his headquarters in the harbor
town of Wonsan on October 20. While waiting for the Marines to
land, unopposed, he busied himself with "civil affairs." This en-
tailed conferring with local officials and granting audiences with
representatives of the population, grandly presenting all with cigarettes and candy.

The U.S. Army's 7th Division was scheduled to land behind the
Marines; the two divisions would then cut across Korea's narrow
waist and join General Walker's Eighth Army north of Pyongyang.
This would involve a march of 120 miles across the soaring Taebeks.

General Oliver P. Smith, commanding the 1st Marine Division,
read the marching order with grave misgiving. Inherent in its
crisply confident paragraphs was the dispersal and loss of operational integrity of his division. The initial zone of action measured
three hundred miles from north to south—as the crow flies—and
sixty from east to west. With the exception of the coastal route,
most of the roads between Wonsan and Pyongyang were mere
mountain trails, unfit for tanks or trucks. Studying the map, Smith
realized that he and the Army's X Corps commander were going
to have diplomatic difficulties in the immediate future.

The young men of Smith's division were divided almost evenly
between Regular and Reservist, the latter hailing from selected cit-
ies across America. For many of these young men, reporting for
active duty on short notice had been a painful experience. Captain
William B. Hopkins's case was typical. A citizen of Roanoke, Virginia, he was called up on August 8, forced to close his law office
after two years of practice.

"I lay awake every night," he recalls, "thinking about how I was
going to say good-bye."

On a Sunday morning, under overcast skies, the Roanoke Reservists assembled in front of the armory and marched down Naval Reserve Avenue to the Norfolk & Western station. The few people on the sidewalk, including a few churchgoers in front of St. John's Episcopal, watched in silence as the troops marched by, their boondockers making the characteristic crunching sound on the macadam. At the station, a photographer from the *Roanoke Times* took a picture of Hopkins shaking hands with his father. The caption would read, "Goodbye and good luck, son."

A large percentage of Reservists were veterans of the Second World War, a war that had ended only five years earlier. Corporal Roy Pearl of Duluth, Minnesota, had seen action on Bougainville, Peleliu, Guam, and Okinawa. Joining the Reserves after the war, he attended weekend drills and summer camp, drawing meager pay to supplement the income he earned servicing cars. Like most of his peers he answered the unexpected summons without complaint, but it was hard. One of his concerns was that his daughters, three years and three months old respectively, had not been baptized. "I was greatly relieved," he recalls, "when our minister agreed to stop by and take care of it in our living room."

The Duluth Reservists marched to the train station early the following morning. Helen Pearl was to meet her husband there with the girls. At first she was unable to find him among the Marines already boarding; but after a frantic search, there he was, smiling bravely. There was just enough time to present him with a keepsake ring inscribed TO ROY FROM HELEN and kiss him good-bye.

1st Lt. Chew-Een Lee's memory of leaving home remains vivid in his mind nearly half a century later. "I came from a family of limited means. My father, whose Chinese name was Brilliant Scholar, distributed fruit and vegetables to restaurants and hotels in Sacramento. He stayed home from work that morning, and my mother, whose Chinese name was Gold Jade, made a special meal. There was an awkward moment when the clock on the wall said it was time to depart. My mother was very brave. She said nothing. My father had been reading the Chinese newspaper, or pretending to. He was a tough guy, my father, and I admired his toughness. He rose from his chair and shook my hand abruptly. He tried to talk, but couldn't, and that's when my mother broke down. I was the first-born and now I was going away, probably for good. This departure was very difficult for me . . . leaving them behind like that, such hardworking people, struggling for survival."

Leaving one's family was hard enough, but leaving one's native land was painful too. Major Francis Parry, an artillery officer, recalls: "Early on the evening of September 1, 1950, we slipped out of San Diego's magnificent harbor and headed into the setting sun. It was an unforgettable experience. As the Marine band played 'Goodnight, Irene'—a favorite of the moment—hundreds of troops crowding the deck of the *Bayfield* broke into song. The families and friends swarming on the dock below began to join in. As the ship eased its way past Point Loma into the darkening Pacific, the harbor reverberated with that haunting refrain."

Fred Davidson, an eighteen-year-old infantry private, was at the rail. He recalls the black hills and twinkling lights of the city, and the song. "It was like being a member of a great choir in an enormous cathedral."

3.

PFC FRED DAVIDSON BOARDED THE troopship *Bexar* on October 11 at Inchon for the trip around the peninsula's horn. "Once we were out to sea," he recalls, "they gave us the straight scoop: the Marines were going to land halfway up the east coast and trap the few North Koreans still fighting." From the railing he watched the mountainous landmass of Korea swing slowly past on the port side as they sailed past Pusan and turned north. "Somewhere around the nineteenth I went topside and saw landfall to *starboard*. We were sailing south! Some of us took that to mean the war was over, that we were headed back to Inchon and then Stateside. But later in the day the *Bexar* made another U-turn and the mountains were back on port side. What the hell's going on here?"

D-Day for the Wonsan landing was to have been October 20, but the approaches to the harbor were mined, it was discovered, and the troopships had to be sent south and north and south again while the minesweepers performed their dangerous duty. The Marines called the laborious two-week process Operation Yo-Yo. It was, as the official Marine Corps history has it, an interlude of concentrated monotony. ("Never did time die a harder death.")

Aboard the *George Clymer* there was only one movie available, *Broken Arrow* with James Stewart. Machine gunner PFC Patrick Stingley watched it several times during Yo-Yo; there wasn't much else to do but eat, sleep, clean weapons, play cards, and read paperbacks. "There was one moment in the movie that made a lasting impression on us," recalls Stingley. "One of the Indian characters, refusing to go along with some proposal, says *I walk away*. The young Marines loved the line and adopted it. Whenever you didn't want to do something, you could always say *I walk away* like the proud Indian. The only trouble was, you couldn't actually walk away, being a Marine under oath. But it was fun saying it over and over."

Near the end of Yo-Yo the Marines aboard ship were disgusted to learn that maintenance crews of the division's Air Wing had beaten them ashore; and worse, that comedian Bob Hope, actress Marilyn Maxwell, and Les Brown's band had already performed their USO show for these support troops—Hope getting off several quips at the expense of the disgruntled Leathernecks still out to sea.

When he arrived at Camp Pendleton, the big Marine base on the West Coast, Cpl. Roy Pearl had tried to tell the assigning officer he was a trained radio operator. "I told him so three times very politely, and he told me three times not so politely that I was now a rifleman in Able Company, 7th." Pearl did not say *I walk away*. Wanting to keep his skills sharp, he practiced codes in the ship's wheelhouse during Operation Yo-Yo; one day he was discovered by a communications officer who, it so happened, needed an experienced radio operator. "Report to Lieutenant Colonel Raymond Davis," he was told.

Pearl recalls his first impression of Davis, an ordinary-looking man of average height who looked as though he would be comfortable in bib overalls. "He was from Georgia and soft-spoken. No gruff, no bluff. Never talked down to you. Made you feel comfortable in his presence." Davis, he learned, had commanded the Special Weapons Battalion on Guadalcanal and at Cape Gloucester, and was later given command of the First Battalion, 1st Marines, under the legendary Lewis B. Puller.

1st Lt. Chew-Een Lee's machine-gun platoon was quartered aboard *LST Q010*. For many Marines, sharing an LST—Landing Ship, Tank—with a Japanese crew was an eerie experience, for the Japanese had been their mortal enemy in the great Pacific campaigns, which had ended, after all, only a short time ago.

Seeking variety in his platoon's diet, Lieutenant Lee had arranged with the vessel's master an exchange of American C-rations for Japanese fare; but this turned out to be a mistake on two counts. "It was so skimpy," says Lee, "that we nearly starved." Worse, the Marines' digestive systems proved unable to handle such exotic rations. Lee—the first Chinese-American to become a Regular Marine officer—was not an admirer of the Japanese or their ways. He believed they had remained "grunting barbarians" long after his ancestors had developed their sophisticated culture.

Observing the crewmen through narrowed eyes, Lee suspected that their low standards of hygiene were responsible for the diarrhea epidemic raging through his platoon. A man of direct action utterly lacking in tact, he sent in a Marine working party with a steam hose to clean the galley from overhead to deck. Meanwhile, Corpsman William Davis ran out of paregoric and wasn't sure what to do next. He consulted the lieutenant, but the lieutenant was no help at all. "A little diarrhea isn't going to kill anyone," sniffed Lee.

A hard taskmaster, Lt. Lee had held school (as Marines say) on the weather deck of the troopship throughout the cross-Pacific voyage in September, even in the foulest conditions. Gunnery Sergeant Henry Foster told him with a twinkle in his eye that if they had been ashore, half the platoon would have gone over the hill by now. Lt. Lee, whose sense of humor was not well developed, sensed that Gunny Foster was being facetious.

Lee had been anxious to get into battle and resented it when his platoon was assigned cleanup duty aboard ship while the immortal Inchon landing was going on. "Unlike the Army," he recalls, "Marines always left their troopships in squared-away condition, and so it was a reasonable assignment; but I chafed at having to stay behind while my fellow lieutenants had the honor of being shot at by the North Koreans before I did." Once ashore, of course, there was plenty of action for all.

After the capture of Inchon and then Seoul a few days later, Lee received an unexpected visit from his younger brother. Chew-Mon Lee was a lieutenant in the U.S. Army, a blooded veteran of the fighting on the Naktong River line, recently discharged from the hospital. Their reunion was brief. Chew-Een decided that the Army-issue web suspenders his brother wore would be useful for carrying grenades, and so he asked Chew-Mon to take them off and hand them over, which Chew-Mon was only too glad to do for his revered older brother. Just then, word was passed for Baker Company, 7th Marines, to saddle up and prepare to go aboard ship, destination Wonsan. Lt. Chew-Mon Lee, U.S. Army, took a camera out of his pack and snapped a photograph of the esteemed firstborn as he crouched beside one of his machine guns. The brothers said good-bye and went their separate ways. There was hard campaigning ahead for both.

Aboard *Aiken Victory,* eighteen-year-old PFC George Crotts, a Reservist, fought off the boredom of Operation Yo-Yo by taking part in a pinochle tournament deep in the ship's bowels, where sleeping racks were stacked five high, so close above one another that it was difficult to turn over. "There wasn't much else to do but eat," he says. "The chow was horrible: greasy canned bacon, lumpy powdered milk, green scrambled eggs." No one had much of an appetite to begin with, for the murky waters of the Yellow Sea were troubled and seasickness was commonplace. "Marines like to express their comradeship through sadism," Crotts points out, "and here was a priceless opportunity. Blowing a cloud of cheap-cigar smoke at a green-gilled pal was always good for a laugh. Or you might hear a guy ask his best buddy, who was at that moment trying not to puke, 'Hey! how'd ya like a big steaming bowl of chili 'n' beans right now, haw?' I recall laying on my rack trying to ignore the stench of all the vomit in the garbage can, and then finally having to climb down myself and get in line. It was a real jolly voyage."

Crotts was assigned to Dog Company, 7th Marines, as a machine-gun apprentice, which mainly turned out to mean lugging boxes of ammunition upslope and downslope. He was told that machine gun crews have a high mortality rate, a formal way of saying a lot of them get killed in battle. Dog Company, he learned, was a hard-luck outfit. Their casualties had been heavy at Inchon and on the road to Seoul. His platoon sergeant put it this way: "D/7 is so unlucky that a half-dead gook will crawl a mile just for the privilege of taking a final shot at us before croaking." Crotts says he listened wide-eyed to this and wondered if it could possibly be true. "I was scared shitless by the time we got to Wonsan."

October 26, 1950, dawned bright and clear with a hint of frost. Soon enough the Marines would recall the hot days and warm nights on the Pusan Perimeter with something like nostalgia as the temperature dropped; but for now the weather was cool and pleasant. The administrative landing at Wonsan had gone smoothly but not without incident. Soon after coming ashore, two Marines had wandered down the beach looking for firewood; when they touched a pile of driftwood, a booby trap exploded in their faces.

The force of the blast was such that the two men, according to an official report, were "literally blown to pieces; it was impossible to identify the remains of either and they were buried in a common grave." They were the first Americans to die in the campaign in northeast Korea.

By now the Chinese Fourth Field Army—consisting of the 38th, 39th, 40th, and 42nd Armies—had crossed the Yalu, the river separating Manchuria from Korea, and were marching, mostly at night, down the peninsula's mountainous spine. There were approximately thirty thousand men in each of the four armies. X Corps was already grossly outnumbered.

4.

GENERAL SMITH WAS ANNOYED AT the X Corps commander for several reasons. During the Inchon operation, General Almond had arbitrarily taken over the division's 7th Motor Transport Battalion; now, at Wonsan, he was directed to turn over four trucks to the South Korean I Corps. For Smith it was a last straw. "We did not care to start any precedent which would establish us as a source of supply for the ROK [Republic of Korea] Army." Accordingly, he sent a dispatch to Almond asking for confirmation of the directive, pointing out that the trucks were part of the Marines' organic equipment and could not be spared. Nothing further was heard on the subject. Ill-feeling between the two services had already been reawakened during the fighting on the Pusan Perimeter, where the understrength Marine Brigade dramatically outshone the Army regiments. Time and again in August and early September, General Walton Walker had called on the Marines for emergency assistance, and during the crisis of the Naktong Bulge the Brigade had recovered a scandalous amount of weapons and equipment that had been abandoned by the Army—tanks, artillery pieces, heavy mortars, trucks, and stockpiles of ammunition.

The most serious contretemps occurred shortly before the Inchon landing. That Almond, an Army general, had been given command of the landing force was insult enough, since amphibious operations were the Marines' specialty; but then he announced that he was going to substitute the 32nd U.S. Infantry Regiment for the 5th Marines in the landing. General Smith was thunderstruck: forty percent of the 32nd's ranks were filled with Korean civilians, raw conscripts who had received no training in amphibious warfare. At this point Smith demonstrated that he was something more than the bland, pipe-puffing, white-haired gentleman he seemed by flatly refusing to go along with the scheme. Almond eventually backed

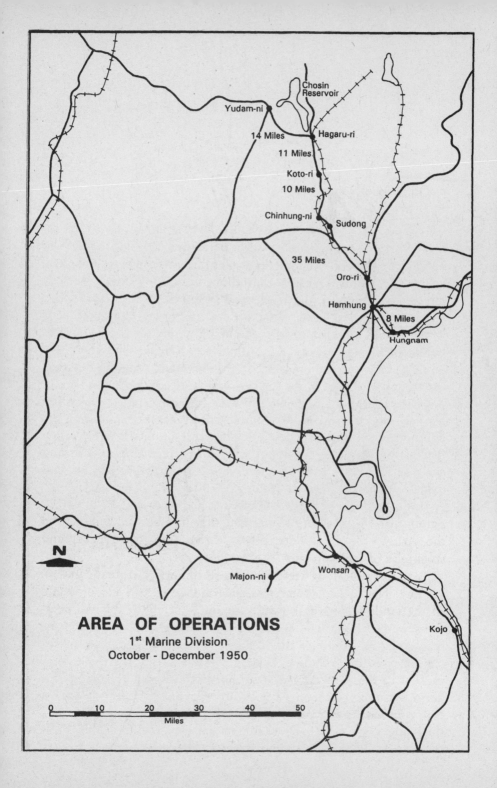

Chosin
Reservoir

Yudam-ni

14 Miles

Hagaru-ri

11 Miles

Koto-ri

10 Miles

Chinhung-ni ● Sudong

35 Miles

Oro-ri

Hamhung

8 Miles

Hungnam

N

Majon-ni ● Wonsan

Kojo

AREA OF OPERATIONS
1st Marine Division
October - December 1950

0   10   20   30   40   50
Miles

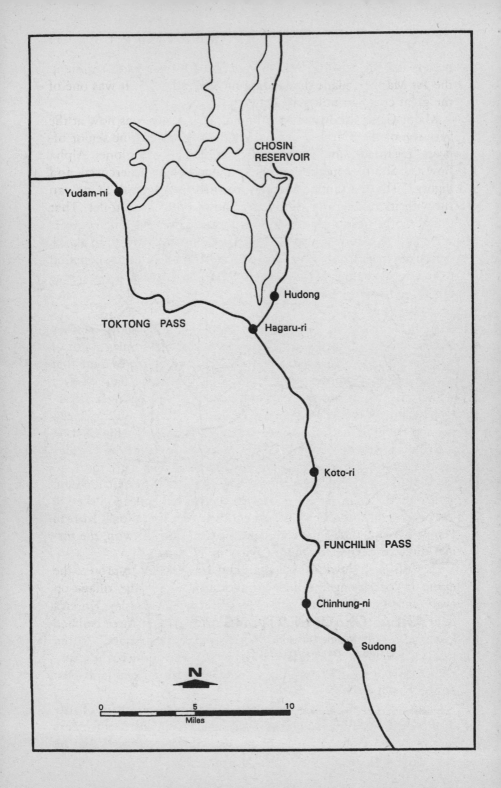

CHOSIN
RESERVOIR

Yudam-ni

Hudong

TOKTONG PASS

Hagaru-ri

Koto-ri

FUNCHILIN PASS

Chinhung-ni

Sudong

N

0   5   10
Miles

down, and the 5th Marines, in concert with their sister regiment, the 1st Marines, made the landing on September 15. It was one of the great coups of military history.

Major General Edward M. Almond, U.S. Army, was now at the very top of the Marines' always lengthy shitlist. Marine senior officers regarded him as militarily unintelligent. Colonel Alpha Bowser, Smith's operations chief, thought him "mercurial and flighty." The Spartanlike Marines frowned on Almond's living-van rig with its refrigerator, hot-water shower, and flush toilet. That the X Corps mess was provided with fine china and linen, silverware and napkin rings, with Far East Command transport planes delivering fresh fruit, vegetables, and meat daily—all this suggested to the hard-scrabbling Leathernecks that the sybaritic general was not to be trusted.

The First Battalion, 1st Marines, were in high spirits as they boarded the train for Kojo, a seacoast village forty miles south of Wonsan. Their mission: to relieve a Republic of Korea unit that was guarding a supply dump. Kojo, a fishing village flanked by a white-sand beach and sparkling blue waters, was the most attractive settlement the Marines had seen in Korea. ROK officers meeting the train assured them they would have an easy time of it. A few North Korean stragglers lingered in the neighborhood, they said, but the hapless ex-infantrymen of Kim Il-sung were more interested in surviving than fighting. The Marines thus remained unaware that a well-organized force of a thousand soldiers lurked in the nearby hills: the Tenth Regiment, 5th Division, North Korean People's Army, under the command of Col. Cho Il Kwon, the former director of the Communist Party in Wonsan.

Lt. Col. Jack Hawkins, commanding 1/1, decided to protect the dump by occupying the high ground surrounding the village on every side but the ocean side. He sent Captain Wesley Noren's Baker Company across the rice paddy to dig in on three isolated knolls two miles to the south. "With no artillery support," Noren recalls, "our neck was stuck out too far." Able and Charlie Companies dug in west of the village, with Hawkins's command post on the beach.

Captain William B. Hopkins, the Roanoke Reservist in charge of the battalion's Headquarters and Service Company, remembers that night as the first time since the end of World War II that he had to sleep on the ground, or rather tried to. "It was a crisp October night. The deck was hard and I was soft. Try as I might, I couldn't get to sleep." The following morning the Marines found the paddies glazed over with the first ice of autumn. "The old China hands among us wondered how far into the mountains they would send us before we got pulled back to the ships." The amphibian Division—not equipped to venture far from the sea—was to advance seventy-eight miles inland before the campaign was over.

Major William L. Bates, Weapons Company, was idly watching a long file of white-robed civilians—men, women, children—trudging past the railroad station. He sat up alertly when he noticed that armed men were prodding them along. A shovel-carrying group brought up the rear. Bates summoned an interpreter and strode after them. By the time he caught up, the riflemen were setting up a firing line while the shovel-carriers herded the prisoners behind a hillock. "Evidently the plan was to wait until the shooters were ready," says Bates, "then stampede the prisoners out into the open where they would become running targets."

Over near the beach, Captain Hopkins had just returned from a patrol. "I noticed the chaplain striding furiously about, clasping and unclasping his hands. When I asked him what the trouble was, he pointed to a little hill. 'Something terrible's about to happen,' he said. He explained that a youth group had weeded out the Communists in town, about seventy in number. 'When their graves are ready, they'll be shot to death.'"

Major Bates confronted the leader of the youth group and ordered the proceedings brought to a halt. The man was incensed at the American's interference. Through the interpreter he shouted that the condemned people were Communists and deserved to die. "That may have been true," says Bates, "but a summary execution without trial was foreign to my notion of justice. Besides, about fifteen of the group were children, ten and under." Despite protests from the men on the firing line, Bates took charge of the captives, marched them to the station, and turned them over to an ROK officer aboard the last train out of Kojo. Old China hands in the Marine battalion predicted that the prisoners would be shot as soon as the train pulled into the Wonsan station.

At Noren's outlying position, a squad of Marines were digging in when four Koreans carrying baskets of eggs appeared on the slope. The Marines put down their shovels and gratefully accepted the villagers' gifts. It occurred to none of them that the four might be spies, sent up Hill 109 (the number respresents the hill's height in meters) to scout out the Americans' defenses. Late in the day an old woman in white appeared on a nearby knoll and began shouting at them. The Marines asked one of the interpreters what she wanted. Smirking skeptically, he said the woman was warning them that most of the men walking about the village were North Korean soldiers posing as civilians. The squad leader expressed his gratitude for the information with a wave and a nod; the old woman turned and vanished in the gathering dusk.

The Marines settled down without anxiety for another long chilly night, a routine fifty percent watch in effect—meaning that in each two-man foxhole at least one man was awake, if not necessarily alert. They had seen bonfires in the mountains the previous night, and lantern light had been visible through the chinks in Kojo's houses; but tonight, as Hopkins recalls, "it was the kind of darkness I hadn't experienced since World War Two: no lights or fires anywhere, only the stars."

Hopkins crawled into his bag soon after nightfall and this time was able to doze off without trouble. A short while later the sleepers were jolted awake by the clatter of gunfire nearly. Amid a chaos of bursting grenades and burp guns, Marines clawed frantically at zippers to release themselves from sleeping bags, the sleeping bags turning into body bags when the zippers jammed. Seven Marines trapped in this manner were bayoneted to death early in the assault. A valiant one-man stand by Sergeant Clayton Roberts, covering the withdrawal with a machine gun, made it possible for one of Noren's platoons to withdraw; Roberts himself was then surrounded and killed. Navy corpsman Dorin Stafford had remained behind as well, refusing to abandon the wounded Marines in his care. An awestruck lieutenant showed up at Hawkins's command post to report that his platoon had been overrun; Captain Hopkins heard him tell the colonel that most of his men were dead, several bayoneted in their bags.

As soon as the action began tapering off, Lt. Col. Hawkins sent an urgent message to regimental headquarters in Wonsan.

Received determined attack from South North and West from sunset to sunrise by large enemy force. Estimated from 1000 to 1200. One company still heavily engaged. Civilian reports indicate possibility 3000 enemy this immediate area. Have suffered 9 KIA, 39 WIA, 35 MIA probably dead. Two positions overrun during night. If this position is to be held a regiment is required. Enemy now to South North and West but believe road to north is still open.

Day dawned. Hawkins was consolidating his remaining troops in a snug perimeter near the beach when some two hundred North Koreans who had been hiding in the village suddenly raced across the paddy, heading toward the hills to the west. Marines of the infantry companies and newly arrived Fox Battery of the artillery regiment combined to slaughter nearly half of them.

During the day, patrols recovered Sergeant Roberts's body and fifteen others who had died in the fight. Corpsman Stafford's body was never found, but prisoners reported that a "Marine medical man" had been captured and put to work tending wounded North Koreans. By mid-afternoon, seventeen of the missing had turned up. Helicopter pilot Captain George Parish scanned the landscape for lost Marines and was rewarded by the sight of the word HELP spelled out in straw near an isolated farmhouse. Parish set the fragile craft down long enough for a joyous PFC named William Meister to clamber aboard.

As the troops were digging in at their new positions, the youth group leader paid a call at battalion headquarters to express his displeasure at the Americans' interference with yesterday's planned execution. Through an interpreter he complained that he had lost so much face it was necessary for him to go into exile. Hawkins and Hopkins watched without sympathy as he turned and began his long journey southward.

By now the revised casualty list indicated that twenty-three Marines had been killed, forty-seven wounded, with four still missing. An estimated 250 North Koreans had died in the fight. Eighty-three prisoners were marched off under guard, to be turned over to the tender mercies of the South Korean Army.

Colonel Lewis B. Puller, the 1st Marines regimental commander, arrived by helicopter an hour before sunset, accompanied by his taciturn bodyguard, Sergeant Bodey. Puller had already decided to relieve Lt. Col. Hawkins, whose Marines had been unready to repel boarders the night before. As the shadows of the hills began to stretch across the paddy, Puller noticed the glint of fear in the eyes of his young Marines as they wondered if the night would bring another assault. Puller strolled from hole to hole, chatting with the troops, encouraging them. Hopkins recalls a couple of the simple but effective comments the colonel made in his rounds: "Let them get in close before you open up. . . . You can't stop them unless you hit them." Puller sat down near Captain Hopkins, opened a can of beef stew, and began spooning it into his mouth. "So—Roanoke!" he said. "How's it going."

The captain and the colonel chatted about one thing and another, including the beauty of Virginia, as Puller ate his cold supper. Hopkins mentioned that he had served with the colonel's brother Sam in the early days of World War II.

"He died on Guam, you know."

"Yes, sir."

"I miss him."

There was a pause and Hopkins changed the subject. He told Puller he couldn't understand the strategy behind the Wonsan landing—couldn't understand why the Division, after taking Seoul, hadn't been sent north to help Walker's Eighth Army capture the enemy capital, Pyongyang. Puller began his explanation with a question: "Who's in charge of this whole deal?"

"Why, General MacArthur."

"An Army officer. The Marines captured Seoul, didn't they? If you were MacArthur, would you let the Marines capture Seoul *and* Pyongyang?"

There was no attack that night. Many of the Marines were disappointed. This time they had been ready.

5. ON THE LAST DAY OF OCTOBER,

Puller sent Lt. Col. Thomas L. Ridge and his Third Battalion, 1st Marines, to a village thirty miles west of Wonsan called Majon-ni. Astride a natural escape corridor for North Korean Army stragglers, the village's outstanding feature was a schoolhouse with an onion-shaped dome in the Russian manner. (From the official history: "An incongruous and pretentious structure for such a small peasant community, it had been erected not for the instruction of children as for the indoctrination of adults in Communist principles.")

Ridge set up his command post in the building and proceeded to carry out his mission, which was to defend the strategic road junction and screen all travelers who came along. Among the refugees was a surprising number of soldiers trying to pass themselves off as civilians. The screening of adult males was a simple three-part business: if the man's hair was close-cropped, his neck tanned in the V-line of the regulation North Korean Army shirt, his feet calloused from miles of marching in military footwear, he was arrested and thrown into a stockade the Marines erected next to the schoolhouse.

Ridge would not make the same mistake Hawkins had made at Kojo when he spread his units too widely apart. Seeing that the dominating terrain was too far from the village for company outposts, Ridge set up a perimeter defense and was thus able to fend off several probing attacks over the following few days.

On November 4 a truck convoy bringing ammunition and supplies, escorted by Captain Robert Barrow's Able Company, ran into a formidable roadblock halfway between Wonsan and Majon-ni. With night coming on, Barrow decided it would be wise to return the convoy to Wonsan and try again tomorrow. The next day he initiated a new tactic, sending Lt. Donald Jones's platoon a mile ahead of the convoy, the idea being that the enemy would wait to hear the trucks grinding up the grade before bothering to get into their ambush positions and might not notice the quiet approach of the riflemen on foot. The tactic paid off: PFC Robert Kozelska's four-man fire team came around a sharp bend in the road, saw a platoon of North Korean soldiers eating and resting on the slope, and cut many of them down before they could escape.

By now the stockade was jammed with over six hundred North Koreans. After the trucks were unloaded, the prisoners were crowded aboard and covered over with tarpaulin so the cargo would not be identified by enemy observers and prompt a rescue attempt. Though Barrow and his two hundred Marines suffered some anxiety over being outnumbered threefold, the convoy reached the prison at Wonsan without interruption.

The industrial city of Hamhung and its adjoining coastal twin, Hungnam, seventy miles up the coast from Wonsan, were no one's idea of good liberty towns; both were unlovely conglomerations of empty warehouses, railroad yards, abandoned factories, and nervous civilians trying to stay out of the foreign soldiers' way. For Colonel Homer Litzenberg's 7th Marines, encamped in Hamhung's ruins, time hung heavy, and the young Marines were inclined to mischief.

Corporal Robert Kelly was regarded by his mortar platoon commander, 1st Lt. Joseph Owen, as a fellow with a talent for acquisition; in other words, he was a good scrounger. In Hamhung there wasn't much left to scrounge, but Kelly spotted an old steam locomotive in the railroad yards and claimed he could run it. He was offended that no one in the platoon believed him.

"I'm telling you guys I can operate that thing," he said, and stomped off, determined to show them.

Lt. Joseph Owen: "Next thing we knew, it's a *toot-toot* here and a *puff-puff* there, and make way for Engineer Kelly and his one-man railroad line. [Kelly had worked for the Illinois Central Railroad as a locomotive fireman before joining the Corps.] The upshot was that Colonel Litzenberg asked Captain Wilcox if it was true that Baker Company was choo-chooing around the city of Hamhung, and when he found out it *was* true the captain made life miserable for Kelly because the colonel didn't find it as funny as we did."

*   *   *

In accordance with Almond's incomprehensible plan, the Marines' three infantry regiments—the 1st, 5th, and 7th Marines—were moving farther apart every day. When General Smith pointed out that his division was spread out over something like 170 miles, Almond agreed to redraw unit boundaries slightly, and gave Smith permission to bring Lt. Col. Raymond Murray's 5th Marines back from a wild goose chase near Sinhung.

On October 30 the 7th Marines operations officer, Major Henry J. Woessner, attended a briefing in which General Almond, standing beside a large easel-borne map, announced that Major General David Barr's 7th Infantry Division, and Major General Oliver P. Smith's 1st Marine Division, would now push northward, while the 3rd Infantry Division, under Major General Robert Soule, would hold the rear. "When we have all this cleaned out," said Almond, sweeping his hand across the map, "the ROKs will take over and we'll pull out of Korea."

Colonel Edward H. Forney, a Marine officer attached to Almond's staff, arranged for Woessner to make a reconnaissance flight over the Marine division's proposed route to the Chosin Reservoir, a distance of over seventy-eight miles from the beach. Looking down from an Air Force T-6, Woessner could see no sign of enemy troops but noted the formidable character of the terrain and the narrowness of the road that snaked its way from the alluvial plain up sweeping slopes to the high plateau.

On the last day of October a three-jeep patrol from Baker Company, 7th Marines, drove thirty miles inland to Sudong to pay a call on the 26th Republic of Korea Regiment, the unit Litzenberg's 7th Marines was scheduled to relieve on November 2. Captain Wilcox radioed word to Litzenberg that the South Korean troops were quite anxious to depart the area. *Many many Chinese,* was the refrain. The ROKs had captured sixteen prisoners, all members of an ammunition platoon of the 370th Regiment of the 124th Division, 42nd Army, Ninth Army Group, Fourth Field Army. The prisoners said that the rest of the 42nd Army, supported by North Korean tanks, were in the mountains to the north, blocking the road to the Chosin Reservoir.

General Almond inspected the prisoners the following day, noting in his diary that they wore "the typical Manchurian quilted winter uniform. . . . Though not intelligent, they were willing to discuss what they knew of their operations. They stated that they had crossed the Yalu River at Manpojin on the 16th of October and proceeded south on foot with their equipment carried by pack-horses and mules." Almond radioed MacArthur in Tokyo that the presence of a regular Chinese Communist formation had been verified. MacArthur sent his intelligence chief, General Charles Willoughby, across the Sea of Japan for a closer look. There had already been reports of Chinese troops in the Eighth Army's zone of operation in the west, but Willoughby preferred to believe these were diplomatic "volunteers"—token troops sent by Mao Tse-tung to fulfill a political commitment he had made with North Korean leader Kim Il-sung.

On the evening of October 31, Major Francis Parry heard someone rap on the door of his command post. Looking out, he saw one of his artillerymen standing there with a jack-o-lantern, the flame of a candle flickering through the cut-out grin. The sight and smell in the crisp autumn evening brought back Halloweens of boyhood, a memory of burning leaves, and a wave of homesickness. Far to the northeast, glowing in moonlight, Parry could see the wall of mountains, sharply shadowed. With a sense of foreboding, he realized that the division would soon be heading into them, venturing far from its natural home: the beach, the ships, and the sea.

Next morning, the first day of November, General Smith received word that the Army's 1st Cavalry Division had run into large formations of Chinese and had been badly mauled. Walker's Eighth Army, at that moment roughly sixty miles to the southwest, was no longer advancing. "There was now nothing on our left flank," Smith recalled, "except the division's Reconnaissance Company, yet there was no relaxation of pressure on us by X Corps to make rapid progress in the direction of the Chosin Reservoir."

The 7th Marines, soon to be the first American unit to defeat Chinese Communists in battle, were commanded by Colonel Homer Litzenberg, a burly man of middle age who in a double-breasted suit might be taken for a bank president. There was no doubt in Litzenberg's mind that the Chinese were present in force. Assembling his officers on a knoll near his tent, the regimental commander told them this could well be the opening engagement of World War III. "It's important that we win the first battle," he said. "The results will reverberate around the world. We want the outcome to have an adverse effect on Moscow as well as Peking."

An hour later the 7th Marines were marching north in column. On this cool forenoon the foothills, draped in a purple haze, bloomed into autumn colors as soon as the sun burned through. The veterans of the fighting in the South took note of the different character of the landscape. The mountains were much bigger and steeper now, and there were more trees on the slopes.

2nd Lt. Patrick Roe, Third Battalion intelligence officer, recalls in detail the transition from urban to rural. "The brick buildings, paved streets, and open sewers of the city gave way to the usual collection of makeshift tin-wood-cardboard dwellings you found on the outskirts of any Asian city; then suddenly it was boondocks—the narrow rutted road crossing flat paddies, the occasional mud-and-thatch hut with oxcart beside it, the bleak mountains in the distance."

The young Marines of Captain Wilcox's Baker Company, 7th, were maintaining an interval of ten to fifteen yards along the road, with Lt. Chew-Een Lee in front, as usual. "I always needed to be at the very cutting edge," he says today. "My main worry at this time had to do with the prospect of getting wounded too early and not being able to discover what I was capable of in battle." Lee had seen action in the fighting around Seoul, but not enough to satisfy his desire for a formal, dramatic baptism of fire. In one engagement north of Seoul he had spotted some North Koreans peering over a ridge and impulsively dashed around their flank, hurling grenades and spraying the reverse slope with his carbine— only to discover that the enemy had departed before he launched his one-man assault. "I felt rather foolish and so forth."

Lee did not expect to survive the war. "I wanted to leave my parents something tangible, something that would benefit them, and I was very glad to have the ten-thousand-dollar National Service Life Insurance. . . . Yes, my attitude was fatalistic. To this day I don't know why, but I expected to die young."

In the open country beyond Oro-ri, Lee gazed admiringly at the cultivated paddies, rows of persimmon trees, and an unexpected stretch of vineyards that bordered the now-ascending road. Raised in California's Sacramento River Valley, he was sensitive to agricultural cycles and the balance of nature; he knew that the peasants whose huts they were passing had cut just enough wood to last until spring. The Marines in Lee's platoon were looking forward to making camp before dusk and building fires to warm C-rations and ward off the chill. Up ahead a farmer stood in his field and watched helplessly as the foreign soldiers began tearing down the slats from his vineyard trellises to use for kindling. When Lee saw what was happening, he shouted, "You! Put those back! All of you!" Though he was one of the smallest men in the division at five feet, six inches and 130 pounds, Lee was not a man to trifle with, as his troops knew by now; and so those few who had scrounged the slats now hastened to replace them, as the lieutenant glared fiercely.

"Pass the word," he shouted. "You will touch *nothing*."

And so the men of Baker Company passed by, leaving behind a lone figure whom Lee recalls as "a classic Papa-san in a white robe, with the wispy beard, bowing repeatedly in gratitude."

A few minutes later Lee happened to glance back from the top of the grade and saw that the troops of the company behind Baker were even then in the process of destroying the centuries-old pattern of trellises. There was no practicable way to stop them. The farmer stood in the field below, watching stoically. Lee turned away, resuming the march.

The point of the regiment was now entering the Sudong Gorge, where the mountains began. It was ambush country. Litzenberg would later observe that the campaign in North Korea "was novel as far as the Marines were concerned. It was mountain warfare, and we had not been particularly trained for that. The hills on either side of the road averaged a thousand to fifteen hundred feet above the valley floor. There was usually a rocky stream bed in the valley, fordable almost anywhere. Beyond each hill lay another hill, and that one always seemed higher. We had to struggle against the impulse to take the high ground, which would have overextended us. We had to accept the fact that we were always under enemy observation. What we were, at that time, was basically a moving perimeter, ready to defend ourselves from any point on the compass."

The passage of lines took place around noon, November 2, south of the village of Sudong, twenty miles inland from Hamhung. Corporal Roy Pearl: "The ROKs came down the slopes grinning and waving at us and pointing to the north. *Many Chinesu!* they said. They were moving more smartly than any South Korean outfit I saw before or since." Lt. Chew-Een Lee: "The ROKs got out of there so fast they left a couple of prisoners behind. Captain Wilcox called me over and asked me to question them. I quickly established that they were shitbirds, longtime privates with nothing to offer by way of information. I was resentful at having to interrogate them, by the way, because it raised the possibility of being transferred to the intelligence staff, which would have been a natural assignment for one who spoke Chinese; but I wanted no part of the comparatively soft life of a staffer."

Lt. Col. Raymond Davis sent a patrol north of the village to see what kind of trouble it could stir up. Soon a firefight erupted, and when the smoke cleared, the bodies of several Asians lay twitching on the ground. Corporal Frank Stockman, a machine gunner with Able Company, recalls: "We searched the bodies, looking for souvenirs. I personally explored the contents of a dead man's haversack and there was no doubt he was Chinese. The stuff was brand new: a towel with Chinese ideographs in red along the border, a green shirt and a pair of green trousers, a pair of shoes, a tube of toothpaste. It got pretty cold that night, so I pulled on the shirt and pants over my Marine utilities. I've wondered ever since what the gooks would have thought if I had been captured."

6.

WHEN THE COLUMN HALTED ON THE afternoon of November 2, it stretched four miles along the dirt-and-gravel road in the cool shadow of the Sudong Gorge. General Almond was not pleased to learn how short a distance Litzenberg had traveled that autumn day—only a little over a mile.

Hill 698—or Yondae-bong, as the Koreans call it—rose west of the road, its crest dominating a bridge and a railway tunnel which, if controlled by the enemy, meant that the Marines' supply route would be severed; in that constricted terrain there were no bypasses or secondary roads. At the base of the hill, 1st Lt. John Yancey, Easy Company, was giving orders to his squad leaders. Sergaent Rugierre Cagliotti's squad was to ascend the right side of the slope with Corporal Lee Phillips's squad on his left. Yancey himself would operate from the center position. "When we get within grenade range," he said, "I'll give the word and we'll each toss one. As soon as it explodes, get up and rush the fuckers before they can react." He snapped the bayonet on the end of his carbine, pulled back the cocking-slide on his .45 automatic, and said, "Let's take this damn hill, boys. Here we go!"

(A member of Carlson's Raiders in World War II, Yancey's face had been badly pitted from a mortar explosion during the 1943 Makin raid. One of Easy Company's former corpsmen, James Claypool, says that Yancey—with his black mustache, perfect posture, and tight little smile—reminded him of a maître d'. "Either a maître d' or a character actor who played Italian gigolos.")

Yancey and his men crossed a saddle and began the perilous ascent of the southeast slope. Machine-gun fire from the summit began crisscrossing the ground in front of them, and Yancey saw Marines falling on both sides. The rest of the platoon hesitated. "Run through it," he shouted. "Just follow me."

Volleys of potato-masher grenades came arcing down on them,

each trailing the cloth strip of its fuse. Yancey: "There were flights of them, like flocks of blackbirds." A round cut through the sleeve of his field jacket as the dwindling platoon climbed on, spurred by Yancey's hoarse barks. Sergeant Cagliotti went down hard, shot in the chest. Private Stanley Robinson—whom Yancey called the platoon delinquent—took charge of the remaining five members of Cagliotti's squad. More than half the platoon had fallen by the time it reached the crest, but there was enough firepower left to drive the Chinese down the reverse slope.

Yancey: "Robbie was the first one to reach the crest. I saw that gangly kid silhouetted on the skyline, engulfed in smoke from the potato mashers, cranking off shots at the gooks as they tried to find cover. It was a great thing to watch, except that he was sure to get himself killed if he kept it up."

PFC Arvid Hultman went down on Yancey's right, a bullet in his groin, and lay there writhing in the loose shale. Yancey scooped up Hultman's Browning automatic rifle (BAR) and began firing it from the hip at the Chinese who were now gathering down below for a counterattack. Changing magazines, Yancey paused to assess the tactical situation. The platoon runners, PFCs Rick Marion and Marshall McCann, were still able-bodied and full of fight. Off to the left, only three men from Corporal Phillips's squad were still in action. Private Stanley Robinson stood alone on the right, the rest of his squad dead or wounded. Hultman, despite his painful wound, crawled over to Yancey and began passing BAR magazines to him from his pocketed belt; when the belt was empty, Hultman crawled down the slope a few yards to fill empty magazines with rounds from M-1 rifle clips handed to him by other wounded Marines.

"McCann," said Yancey, "call down below and tell them we've took the fuckin' hill."

A few moments later the radio operator held out the little SCR-563 to the lieutenant. The company executive officer, 1st Lt. Raymond Ball, wanted a word with him.

"Good work, Yancey. How's things?"

"Not so good. There's about six of us up here, and the gooks are fixing to counterattack. We need a hand."

"Okay, hold on a sec."

In the command post beside the road, Ball and the company commander, Captain Walter Phillips, tried to decide whether to send reinforcements that would probably arrive too late to make any difference, or to pull the handful of survivors off 698 and call it quits for the day and try again tomorrow. At this point Yancey's staticky voice sounded in the earpiece: "If you get some folks up here real quick, I think we can hold."

"Can't do it," said Phillips. "There's too much fire on that slope."

"Hell," said Yancey, "*we* came through it."

"*Six* of you did."

The leader of the third platoon, 1st Lt. Leonard Clements, listening in on the exchange, decided on a bold tactical move of his own. Leaving half his platoon to protect the command post, Clements took advantage of a lull in the action and led seventeen men up the western slope of 698 just as the Chinese were launching their counterattack with the strident blast of a bugle.

"Here they come, boys," yelled Yancey. "Stand fast and die like Marines."

The men in the thin semicircle were almost out of ammunition. Hultman was now too weak to gather more M-1 clips. Robinson had two fragmentation and one white-phosphorous grenade left. McCann and Marion lay on either side of Yancey, bayonets at the ready. Corporal Phillips crouched behind a pile of rocks he had gathered into a fort. On the left flank Platoon Sergeant Allen Madding sighted along his M-1.

Robinson lobbed the white-phosphorous grenade far downhill, shouting, "Come on, you sons of bitches," and the Marines watched the soft explosion that showered orange sparks against a cloud of heavenly white. Yancey: "That grenade wiped out a few shambos, but there was no question we were about to get kicked off that crest."

At this moment of crisis a short, squat private named James Gallagher came running up the slope behind them, cradling in his arms a fifty-pound load of machine gun with tripod and a can of belted ammunition. (Corpsman Claypool had this to say about Gallagher later: "He was a young man of limited potential in the world at large, but a brave and daring Marine in combat. Five and a half feet tall, with a leprechaun's face, he was powerful and pugnacious.") The gun was ready to fire, with one end of the ammo belt clamped into the receiver. Gallagher set it up in a spot with a good field of fire, pulled the trigger, and began knocking Chinese

down the slope. Soon Gallagher was out of ammo, along with
Yancey's survivors, and it looked as though they were about to be
overrun.

It was at that moment that Clements and his half-platoon appeared, catching the Chinese by surprise with a sudden burst of
firepower from the flank. "It was the most beautiful thing I ever
saw in my life," said Yancey. "They arrived in the middle of the
counterattack and met them fuckin' shambos *head-on.*"

Dusk ended the action on Yondae Mountain, and silence settled
over the smoky scene. The Chinese Communist Army had met the
U.S. Marines for the first time in history and were the worse for
it.

7.

CORPORAL ROY PEARL WAS STANDING watch around midnight, alert to his surroundings but thinking of home. "I was yanked out of my reverie by the god-awfullest sounds—bugles and shepherds' horns and whistles—then saw the glow of flares descending in a neat row across the river. Because of the sheer walls of the gorge, the echoes rang back and forth for several seconds. Then there was absolute silence, until we heard Colonel Davis's voice: 'Listen up, Marines! The enemy is hitting the companies on the other side of the river. We are expecting an attack on this side momentarily. Get your weapons and ammo squared away and stand by. Good shooting."

Around 2 A.M. Lt. William Davis heard the characteristic clanking and metallic squeaking of a large tracked vehicle approaching from the north. Like most of the Marines within earshot, he assumed it was a Marine bulldozer.

"Tank!" It was the voice of Lieutenant Davis's mortars section-chief, Staff Sergeant Donald Jones.

"How the hell could a tank get by us?" asked Davis. "It has to be a dozer."

"Lieutenant, these old ears have heard lots of Jap tanks in the middle of the night, and that is definitely not a dozer."

A hundred yards up the road, Staff Sergeant Clayton Vondette and two privates were stringing communication wire north of the command post when the tank rounded the bend, one headlight leading the way. Vondette decided it was a Marine tank whose driver was unaware of the blackout order. Vondette jumped behind the wheel of the company jeep, started it up, and drove straight to the tank, blocking its way. "Turn that fuckin' light off," he shouted uselessly against the engine's roar. Vondette: "What happened next was: a steel hatch flew open, an Oriental face appeared, and a machine gun began firing wildly in all directions. I had time to slam the jeep into reverse and scoot while my two helpers scrambled out of sight."

The tank went trundling heavily down the road until it came to the headquarters tents, located up a draw. Lt. William Davis and Staff Sergeant Jones, paralyzed in their stocking feet, stood staring at the thing. "If there's a more futile feeling than facing a tank with a carbine," says Davis, "I don't know what it is." The huge vehicle halted, engine idling, creating the impression of a one-eyed monster looking over the platoon's 60-mm tubes. It then moved farther down the road for a look at the 81-mm mortar position. After firing several booming main-gun rounds over the heads of the astonished mortarmen, the tank turned around and headed back the way it came. Corporal Pearl could hear the wire chief screaming in rage: "You're tearing up all my fuckin' phone lines!"

By now the Marines were recovering from their shock and antitank crews were going into action, but not very efficiently. One 3.5–inch rocket set on fire the cloth of the sandbags used by the tankers to augment their armor-plating. The flaming hulk, trailing sparks, clanked around the bend and disappeared among the thatch-roofed houses of Sudong. The tank, a Russian-made T-34, belonged to the 344th North Korean Tank Regiment, a unit that was all but destroyed in the action following the battle for Seoul. Four other tanks and crews, all that remained of the regiment, were waiting three miles up the road, on the other side of the village.

At around four o'clock in the morning Staff Sergeant Jones heard shuffling sounds in front of his position. "Here come the bastards," he said. Lt. Davis ordered Corporal J. D. Farrell on the Number 2 gun to fire an illumination round, more or less straight up in the air. Davis: "The shot gave away the mortar tube's position, but that tear-shaped beauty soared about two hundred fifty feet and floated down under its little parachute, blazing with a hundred and ten thousand candlepower." There in the glare for about ten seconds stood four armed Asian soldiers in mustard-colored padded quilt. Three rifles cracked and three men went down. The fourth, eyes big as saucers, raised his hands, letting the strapped-on submachine gun flop against his chest. Lt. Davis, accompanied by his runner, PFC B. V. Halverson, went out for a look. There was one survivor. He stood frozen with his arms in the air, waiting to be taken prisoner.

"Hal, they're *Chinamen*."

"Sir?"

The company's executive officer appeared on the scene. 1st Lt. Eugene Hovatter peered at the bodies in the light of a distant flare and ventured the opinion that they were probably North Korean stragglers. Davis insisted they were Chinese.

"What makes you think so?"

It was hard to explain. Davis, who had commanded an embassy guard in Nanking, could only say he knew a Chinaman when he saw one. Another China Marine examined the corpses and seconded Davis's opinion.

Word spread fast. Pearl: "We were all pretty surprised. Only the day before we heard scuttlebutt that crowds of Chinese had been seen massing along the Yalu River, poised to prevent MacArthur from crossing into Manchuria; but here we were looking at some Chinese soldiers a hundred miles south of the Yalu."

8. ACROSS THE RIVER IN BAKER COM-
pany's sector, rumor had become reality. Lt. Harrol Kiser: "We
were afraid to close our eyes. We were looking for Chinese behind
every rock, every bush."

Staff Sgt. Archibald Van Winkle was making the rounds of his
platoon's position. "We had a small outpost about a hundred yards
out front—four Marines in a shallow hole. They were just kids,
and a bit clutched over the rumors, so I stayed with them longer
than planned."

One of Chew-Een Lee's section leaders, Sgt. Sherman Richter,
was waiting tensely for the assault to begin, when a Marine in a
nearby hole turned to him and whispered hoarsely, "Sergeant,
someone's coming this way."

The password that night was *Deep Purple*. Richter said aloud,
"Deep." The shadow on the skyline did not say "Purple." "Okay,"
said Richter, "Shoot the fucker."

And that is how the battle opened in Baker Company's sector.

Van Winkle and the four young Marines heard bugles and whistles on the other side of the skyline. "They were so close we
could've tossed a pebble at them," said Van Winkle. "I said to the
four kids, 'It's time to go,' and believe me, I didn't have to say it
twice."

Lt. Kiser was on the phone to Captain Wilcox when the Chinese
hit the lines in groups of thirty or so. Kiser: "The captain, down
in the command post, heard all the racket and hollered, 'What the
hell's going on up there!' I told him there were gooks all over the
place and they'd be in his lap in two shakes." Van Winkle: "I knew
we were in trouble when I looked around and saw more Chinese
than Marines."

Baker Company's mortar officer was a tall lieutenant named Joseph Owen. Two of his 60-mm tubes were in battery halfway up

the hill; the third was at the bottom, supposedly ready to support Lt. William Graeber's platoon. "The gooks came at us en masse," he recalls, "bouncing off Hank Kiser's platoon, then swarming past the lone gun at the bottom. I was too busy to notice we were hearing no action from that tube, but then one of the crewmen materialized out of the gloom and said the gooks had taken the gun and killed everyone but him. Holy shit! My first real battle and already I've lost a gun.

"I rounded up some volunteers and we started downhill to recover the tube. Kelly and Winget and me went ahead of the others, spraying everything in sight with our carbines. We heard gooks running away from us, so I guess we surprised them with our little counterattack. We found the gun. It hadn't even been set up; it was lying on its side, minus the bipod. By this time there was a lot of fire coming from the railroad tunnel, so we set the tube up with the idea of firing on the gooks over there.

"The first round was a misfire—it didn't come out of the tube. Dealing with a misfire is scary enough in broad daylight. One man raises the base of the tube very slowly until the round comes sliding out; another man has his hands cupped at the mouth of the tube to catch it. I was the one who caught the round. We dropped another in the tube. A second misfire. Same scary sequence.

"Someone suggested we get the hell outta there: there were gooks all around now. Just then I had the idea to see if there was some obstruction in the tube, and by God I found a cleaning rag in there. We didn't bug out: we stayed where we were, pumping rounds at the gooks down by the tunnel. A bit later the sergeant in charge of that tube showed up and explained how the gooks had taken him by surprise and overran the position. His excuse for this sorry state of affairs was that I had detained him so late in the day that it was dark when he brought the hardware to the spot and didn't have time to set it up properly. 'Bullshit,' I told him. 'You fucked up.' Next day he was on his way back to division. They made a mail clerk out of him."

On the left flank Baker Company's forward positions had been overrun. Lt. Lee could hear men murmuring to each other in Chinese at the top of the long slope. He was surprised at how deeply the enemy had penetrated. Lee and Gunnery Sergeant Foster reorganized the dispersed Marines, formed a line, and got the men settled down. "There was an almost palpable sense of fear in the air," says Lee. He decided it was necessary to force the enemy into action to determine his exact location and perhaps learn his intentions as well. Lee: "Was he going to continue his attack down that spine? Was he infiltrating under our collective nose at that very moment? I decided to make a solo reconnaissance. Of course it was dangerous, but on the other hand, there were dips and folds in the slope that kept me in defilade part of the way."

On his daring ascent he tried to draw fire by shouting, firing his carbine, and hurling grenades. "What did I shout, you ask? I don't recall. Basically I was just making noise, trying to spread confusion." He replenished his ammunition by lifting carbine magazines from the belts of dead Marines that were sprawled about. At one point he took a Browning automatic rifle out of a dead man's hands and fired a couple of bursts with it. "I realized with a shock how close I was to the enemy, and I knew I had passed the point of no return; going back would have been more dangerous than going forward.

" 'Don't shoot,' I said in Chinese. 'I'm not the enemy.' They opened up anyway, and I had no choice but to attack them. I lobbed grenades in the direction of the muzzle flashes, then ran to the right and emptied another magazine at them. As I started forward I saw three or four dead Chinese propped up against rocks, their weapons still clutched in their hands. When I reached the top I could see, since the moon was out, that the enemy was withdrawing down the reverse slope. At that point I was about a hundred yards in front of my men. Certainly I had taken a risk, but it was a calculated risk.

"All at once I realized that I had captured the spur of the hill— had actually driven the enemy off it. It wasn't that they were afraid of me, one man; they assumed I was several men. As I took a moment to catch my breath, I noticed how quiet it was in the immediate area, with furious firefights going on in the surrounding hills. Tracer rounds were skipping off the slopes, crisscrossing— the red tracers of the Marines, the green tracers of the enemy, and at one point I thought I saw blue North Korean tracers. After I was sufficiently rested, I turned around, cupped my hands, and shouted for my men to come up."

To this day Lee remains upset about the dead Marines he found along the slope and atop the knob. "Over there was Private Timmons, a curly-headed blond boy of eighteen. By the light of the moon it was like looking at a little Greek boy in marble. Over here was Platoon Sergeant Long, who died while trying to claw his way out of his bag. And there were others equally unready, caught by surprise. Totally inexcusable! Quite frankly I felt we had not performed up to Marine Corps standards. I assure you, this was the last time you would ever find me in the company rear for anything but a briefing. I had learned a lesson: I would remain at the forward positions so that nothing like this could ever happen again."

Dawn was breaking as Lee returned to the spot where he had left his pack. He was looking forward to sitting by himself and making a cup of coffee. ("I always kept myself apart. You could say I wanted to maintain a certain mystique. Oh, I was willing to engage in a cordial exchange or two after a briefing, but I never hung around for purposes of bullshitting and so on and so forth.")

Reaching his foxhole, Lee removed the belt-suspenders his brother had given him at Inchon and was just reaching up to hang them on a tree branch when "*Wham*—something hit me on the right arm like a sledgehammer. It lifted me off the ground and spun me around and I rolled down the hill a few feet, paralyzed and in great pain. I must say, it was touching the way my men showed up so swiftly to help me. I tried to talk, to convey an urgent message, but I couldn't find my voice. 'Make sure the belt-suspenders go with me' is what I wanted to say. 'Don't let them get lost.' "

Item Battery, 11th Marines, had been pouring high-angle shots into Chinese positions throughout the night, but at dawn enemy snipers found the range and began threatening the priceless howitzers. Major Francis Parry directed the battery commander to withdraw the guns down the road, deeper into the perimeter, and then jeeped back to tell the regimental commander what he had done. The stocky, square-jawed colonel was standing by his tent.

Major Parry: "After I told him, he fixed me with a look and said, 'I want that battery to remain in place. There is to be no hint of a retreat in this first meeting between Marines and the Chinese Communists.' "

9.

DAY WAS DAWNING OVER YONDAE Mountain. There was fog everywhere, but Lt. John Yancey didn't need good visibility to know that Easy Company was surrounded. Yancey's men had exchanged volleys with the Chinese throughout the night without much damage to either side. "Those shambos were conversing in a casual manner, as if they were sitting in rocking chairs on the front porch. They knew we were there. We knew they were there. *They* knew *we* knew they were there. So why bother to whisper?"

The muffled *blat* of a bugle came through the fog. There were so few Marines on the knob that Yancey didn't have to shout to be heard by everyone.

"Heads up. Don't shoot till you have a target."

They leaned forward, squinting, trying to see the enemy before the enemy saw them. "We could hear them shuffling toward us, and the first thing we saw were their tennis shoes and socks. Then the fog seemed to lift as the shambos emerged and we got in our licks first. We bowled them over in rows. Neatest thing you ever saw."

A breeze sprang up, and when the fog began to clear off, the Marines in the hills saw something alarming: Chinese formations occupied the ground between them and their command posts beside the river. Sergeant Carl Winslow: "There were Chinese all over everywhere." Major Webb Sawyer: "We were in a dickens of a mess."

Lt. James Stemple's platoon of Able Company had been holding off aggressive skirmishers east of the road. "We thought they were on drugs, the way they kept coming at us. I shot this one charging soldier four times in the chest and saw the white padding fly out the back of his jacket, but he didn't drop until he had thrown his grenade. Our little carbine didn't have nearly the stopping power of the M-1 rifle. A direct hit with an M-1 round would knock anybody on his ass. Still, four carbine rounds! Kept coming!"

Sometime around eight o'clock that morning the Chinese decided they had had enough.

PFC Vincent J. Yeasted, a BAR man, called Stemple over to his position on the left flank and pointed across the river. Through his binoculars the lieutenant watched clusters of troops in mustard-colored uniforms racing down a ravine on the north side of Hill 698, heading toward the railroad tracks, looking for a withdrawal route.

"Sergeant Sua," called Stemple over his shoulder, "bring your guns over here." Sergeant Malaya Sua and his crew set up two machine guns overlooking the scene. "Whenever you're ready," said Stemple, and Sua opened his guns on the swarming troops across the river.

Corporal Roy Pearl saw it from a different angle. Someone shouted, "Will you look at that!" Pearl, standing with Colonel Davis near the road, turned to look at where the man was pointing and saw a column of Chinese marching in route step, two abreast, heading north along the railroad tracks in broad daylight. Pearl: "These people were only a hundred yards away from us but none of them seemed to care. It was unreal. All of a sudden our machine guns opened up and others joined in. That included me, and I was just getting warmed up when I felt a hand on my shoulder. 'You've had your fun, Pearl,' said the colonel. 'Get back to your radio.' "

Lt. Joseph Owen: "When I heard about the Chinese massing on the tracks, I grabbed a phone and headed for a vantage point, and it wasn't long before our baby atom bombs were raining down on them. We call the 60-mm mortar a weapon of opportunity, and man, was this ever an opportunity. Those rounds followed them into ditches, craters, behind knobs, all over the riverbed. There's no such thing as defilade from a 60-mm mortar." The Marines watched the last few Chinese crawling over their comrades in a frantic effort to get away, and picked off the survivors as casually as if they were snapping-in at the rifle range.

Lt. Col. Frederick Dowsett, Litzenberg's executive officer, summed up the action at Sudong this way: "The Chinese launched a well-coordinated attack with their battalions, but at company level and below there was no originality of thought and no small-unit leadership. I saw our machine guns take out half a company on the railroad tracks. Sheer slaughter. I saw an officer blow his whistle, and the survivors re-form and start marching again. Our guns cut into them until, finally, the ten or fifteen survivors broke and ran like mad. The Chinese had no regard for life, not even for manpower per se. We should have had a special manual for fighting the Oriental."

After the battle wound down, Lt. Yancey allowed himself to relax a bit. Stretched out on the ground, he lit a smoke and looked around. PFC James Gallagher started to pass by, and Yancey joshed him about his to-the-rescue performance with the machine gun: "What makes you act that way, Gallagher?" Gallagher blushed and answered the pokerfaced lieutenant with this earnest explanation: "My mama didn't raise us boys to be no cowards."

Stemple recalls that when Able Company came down the hill, Litzenberg was standing at the bottom, canteen cup of coffee in hand, slapping each man on the back as he passed by. The Great White Father, as he was called—not always with affection—was clearly pleased with the performance of his riflemen, mortarmen, and machine gunners. Recognizing Stemple as a former member of his staff, he insisted the lieutenant stop long enough for a sip of coffee. "Should we drop surrender leaflets on them, Stemple?" he asked jocularly.

"I don't think we've seen the last of them, Colonel."

"Well, they're not going to bother us for a while."

"No sir, I expect not."

Sgt. Robert B. Gault's job was necessary but rarely discussed: he and his helpers disposed of the regiment's dead. Colonel Litzenberg, always on the lookout for good men, noticed the black Marine's "intense commitment to thoroughness" in his regular duties and asked him one day if he would take charge of the Graves Registration section. Gault, a quiet, steady man from Indiana, said that would be fine.

"The job had no hours," he recalls. "We just drove up and down that road. There were five of us in all, with a truck. We would park it and walk up to a line company and the riflemen would point to where their dead lay. You would take the dog tags from the chain around the Marine's neck, put one around the ankle with wire and the other around the wrist. You had to go real slow and careful because his friends were watching and wanted him treated with respect. You would write down his name, rank, and serial number in the little book. You would go through his pack and pockets looking for letters and other personal items. Sometimes the tags had been blown away in the explosion that killed him, and maybe there were no letters, and maybe there was nobody around who knew him because he was a replacement. So you'd have to take the fingerprints, and back at headquarters they would match them up with the record book so they could look up the address and figure out who to break the news to."

At the battalion aid station Staff Sergeant Van Winkle's friends kept popping in to wish him well before he was evacuated to the hospital in Hamhung. Though grateful for the visits, he was not in a conversational mood because of the pain. Van Winkle had been shot in the elbow while leading a counterattack, losing so much blood that when Lt. Harrol Kiser stopped by to visit, he thought at first he was looking at a corpse. "I couldn't believe anyone could be that white and still be alive."

Lt. Chew-Een Lee was waiting impatiently in the same tent to see the battalion surgeon, who, he was confident, would check his wound and send him back to Baker Company, his natural home. In the corner a strapping young Marine private sat weeping, his face buried in his hands. The sight and sound of it offended Lee greatly. "What the hell are you blubbering about?" he demanded. "Where's your wound?"

The young man raised his head and sobbed, "I seen my buddies killed!"

Lee rose and strode over to him, cradling his throbbing right arm with his left hand. "Let me see the wound."

The private had nothing to show him, for his wound was in his heart and head. Like General George Patton in an infamous incident during World War II, Lee found it impossible to tolerate, let alone sympathize with, a demoralized infantryman. Standing in front of the cringing private, he gestured broadly with his good arm.

"Look around you. Here are men with legitimate wounds. That man over there, for instance, has a fragment wound in his stomach. This one here was shot in the shoulder. Do you hear *them* sniveling or blubbering?"

Lee did not slap him, as General Patton might have done; instead he called the dumbstruck private a big phony and said he was a disgrace to the Corps.

"From now on," said Lee, "you will keep silent out of respect for these brave Marines. Is that understood?"

The young man nodded, his eyes glazed.

A few minutes later the battalion surgeon insisted that Lee needed to be evacuated to Hamhung to have his wounds properly tended to. Lee protested vigorously but to no avail. Lt. Joseph Owen recalls the angry look on his colleague's face as he climbed, wincing, into the southbound ambulance. Lee refused to say good-bye, certain he would be back shortly.

10.

NIGHTFALL, NOVEMBER 3RD, marked the end of the first confrontation between the Marines and their Chinese adversaries. The remnants of two regiments of the 124th Chinese Communist Division had withdrawn three miles to the north and were now digging in on two hills overlooking the road as it ascended toward Funchilin Pass. Marine engineers would widen it later, but at the moment the road was impassable to tanks; this meant that the T-34s of the 344th North Korean Tank Regiment had to remain at the foot of the pass. The tank crews tried to hide themselves and their vehicles as the 7th Marines began to inch forward on the morning of the fourth. (Americans would refer to the crewmen as fanatics for remaining with their tanks, but today their names are engraved on the Scroll of Heroes in Pyongyang.)

Marine Recon scouts now slipped through the railhead hamlet of Chinhung-ni, two miles further up the narrowing defile, passing Samgo Station at the north end. It was here that the narrow-gauge railroad from Hamhung ended and the steep cableway took over, leading to the forlorn village of Koto-ri on the plateau high above. Rounding the bend, Corporal Joseph McDermott, at the very point of the regimental column, noticed what he later described as "a lone and incongruous stack of brush and hay." Accompanied by PFC Walter Cole, he moved off the road to investigate. By the time they were halfway across the rock-strewn field they knew it was a T-34. McDermott moved to the vehicle's rear, yanked away some of the brush, and climbed up on the stern. After attempting to open the main hatch, he knocked over the periscope with the butt of his rifle, forcing its glass cover inward. Proceeding from daring to foolhardy, he peered into the aperture—and just missed being hit by the burst of automatic fire that swept past his face. Pulling the pin from a grenade, he let the spoon fly off, then dropped it into the opening.

The muffled explosion sent a blast of hot air through the pipe. A moment later the tank's engine came to life and the vehicle charged forward like an enraged elephant. Hanging onto the turret with one hand while trying to unclip another grenade from his belt proved impossible, and McDermott jumped off and scurried on hands and knees to where Cole was waiting behind a boulder. The tank circled around and stopped near them. It was now PFC Cole's turn to flirt with peril. Leaping aboard the idling tank, he stuffed a grenade down the aperture and ducked his head before flame and smoke belched from the gun ports and the base of the bent periscope. The engine groaned, the tank juddered ahead a few feet, then died for good.

Back down the road, 1st Lt. Donald Sharon saw a thatched hut disintegrate as another tank emerged, its 85-mm cannon swinging menacingly toward the Marine column. The troops quickly dispersed to both sides of the road and formal countermeasures were called into play. Between rocket-launcher crews, recoil-less rifle crews, air strikes, and Recon Company, all four tanks were destroyed, and that was the end of the 344th North Korean Tank Regiment.

While all this was going on, a more intimate drama was taking place still farther down the road. Lieutenant Colonel Davis had not forgotten the lone-tank foray that had so boggled his men the evening before. Wanting to be prepared for another such intrusion, Davis had obtained several mines from the Antitank Company and kept them in his jeep, sacked in sandbags. On the morning of the fourth, hearing reports of the tank action up ahead, he summoned his runner, PFC Watson. "I told him to position himself beside a certain culvert where the roadbed was constricted. I gave him one of the mines and said, 'If a tank comes down the road, I want you to put this in a spot where the treads will run over it. Got that?' "

A few minutes later, Davis showed up at the culvert to see if Watson was ready. "He was obviously upset over something. I figured he was confused about his assignment, so I went over it in detail. He listened very intensely. I thought I noticed sweat on his forehead. When I mentioned something or other about his best escape route, he said, 'God, Colonel!'

" 'What is it, Watson?' "

The young man was trembling. In a breaking voice he explained that he had thought the colonel wanted him to hold the mine under the oncoming tank's treads. "In other words," says Davis, "the poor kid thought he was supposed to perform some sort of kamikaze mission and get blown up with the tank. I told him that wouldn't be necessary. His name was Robert R. Watson. I don't recall his hometown of record. He was a good Marine."

After dark, November 6, the 11th Marines fired off a series of artillery barrages that devastated what was a left of the 124th Division. Colonel Litzenberg summed it all up in a businesslike manner in a later interview. "On the destruction of the reserve regiment of the 124th Division, this constituted the conclusion of the defeat of that division."

General Smith's comment was equally bland. "Quite a fight," he said.

Mortarman Joseph Owen put it more pungently. "We kicked the shit out of those bastards, and proved we were as tough as the 5th Marines in their southern campaign."

It had taken the 7th Marines five days and nights to drive the enemy from the hilltops, gorges, and draws around Sudong. Litzenberg lost about fifty men killed in action and 200 wounded out of a force of three thousand. As for the Chinese, reports indicate that some 1,500 had died on the battlefield.

The carpets of corpses were a curiosity to the younger Marines (but not to the veterans who had often seen the like during the Pacific campaigns), many of whom wandered over to stare at the dense clusters before resuming the northward march toward the pass. The Chinese soldiers wore mustard-colored coats and pants of quilted cotton, and fur-lined caps with earflaps. A few wore fur-lined boots, but most of the corpses were shod in canvas shoes with crepe soles which the Marines usually called tennis shoes. Examining the contents of their knapsacks, intelligence staffers discovered that each man carried a four- or five-day supply of food— rice, corn, beans—already cooked so as to avoid the telltale smoke of the campfire. Each soldier had been issued from eighty to one hundred rounds of ammunition and a few stick grenades.

General Almond lost a few more points with the Marines when, on a battlefield inspection, he noticed the barrels of the Marines' eighteen howitzers pointed skyward—the high angle directing shells onto reverse slopes—and remarked to Litzenberg, "I didn't know you had antiaircraft guns up here." That was amusing enough, but the Marines would have been appalled had they known the X Corps commander did not consider the battle of Sudong worthy of mention in his command diary. On the day of heaviest fighting in the gorge, this was his sole entry: "Inspected the Pullman and coach car which are to be prepared for the use of the X Corps staff."

In Tokyo, MacArthur's intelligence chief, Willoughby, still confident the Chinese intervention consisted of a few volunteers, had announced on November 3 that there were only 16,500 to 34,000 Chinese soldiers in country. These figures were far off the mark. By now the Ninth Army Group's twelve divisions were pouring across the Yalu bridges to confront X Corps, while Lin Piao's Thirteenth Army Group of eighteen divisions was already deployed in front of General Walton Walker's Eighth Army. There were at that moment some 300,000 Chinese soldiers in North Korea.

11.

PFC AL BRADSHAW, DOG COM-
pany/7, Reservist: "One day I'm working in the *Post-Dispatch*
mailroom and the next day I'm in a place called Chinhung-ni reporting to the 7th Marines personnel section. They sent me up a
hill on the west side of the road so Easy Company could look me
over. I was nothing but sweat and heavy breathing and they
weren't impressed with my potential. They told me to report to
Dog Company, which meant go back down the hill, cross the road,
and climb an even bigger hill on the other side. They don't have
hills like that in St. Louis, believe me.

"At the bottom I had an adventure. Someone yelled, 'Look out,'
and here's this gook standing there with a rifle slung over his shoulder. He just stood there like he wasn't planning anything, like he
was standing guard duty; but this was an *armed gook,* after all,
the first I ever laid eyes on, so I raised my M-1 to my shoulder just
as another Marine shot him down. Poor guy just wanted to surrender, but how can you be sure?

"Up at Dog Company they put me in Lieutenant Sota's platoon,
and when I got settled in, what do I discover but the guy in the next
hole is none other than Irl Dement from St. Louis, of all places,
who is a real character. One thing about Irl Dement, he was quick
on the trigger. I found that out the first night when the wind blew
a piece of paper across the ground and Irl Dement blasted it with
his .45. Next morning here comes Captain Milton Hull: 'I want to
know who did the shooting and where's the body.'

" 'Sir, it was only a piece of paper.'

" 'Fine, I want to see it. Now.'

"Irl Dement and me went searching while the captain waited
with his arms folded. We found it about thirty feet down the slope
and brought it to him.

" 'Fine,' he says. 'Where's the hole?' The captain didn't appreciate it that one of his men had opened up on a piece of paper, but the worst thing was, Irl Dement didn't even *hit* it.

"That night I stood up in my hole, fixing to drain my radiator over the side, when I hear a safety click off over to my left. Believe me, I dropped down real quick, because pissing in a C-ration can may not be the best way to relieve yourself, but it's better than getting drilled by Irl Dement. First thing next morning, who do I see grinning at me from the next hole but Irl Dement.

" 'So I guess you saw that gook last night.'

" 'Irl, you crazy bastard, that was no gook; that was me trying to take a leak.'

" 'Oh.'

"Old Irl. Him and me were friends from St. Louis."

That night the sound of bugles echoed down Funchilin Pass, strident notes bouncing off canyon walls two or three miles to the north, growing weaker and finally fading out. On the night of November 7–8, the Chinese simply disappeared.

There were several theories as to why the 124th Division made a stand at Sudong. It might have been an attempt to protect the security of the hydroelectric grid in northeast Korea, which generated power to Manchurian towns across the Yalu; or it might have been an early defense of their border. General Smith speculated that the 124th had been stationed at the foot of the pass for the purpose of delaying the Americans while "something stronger" was being prepared up north. Though the Marines had won a brilliant local victory at Sudong, Smith could not help wondering where the other two divisions of the Forty-second Chinese Communist Army were at the moment.

North of Samgo Station and the smoldering hulks of the T-34s, the road ascended sharply. 1st Lt. Nicholas Trapnell recalls the road as "leading us into a mysterious Oriental kingdom. I always expected to see a giant ogre lurking on those sawtooth horizons."

For much of the eight-mile length of the pass, the road was a one-way shelf with a cliff on the right, a chasm on the left, and a series of hairpin turns so tight that trucks with trailers sometimes had to unhitch to negotiate the passage. It was a slow, steady climb to the high country. Off to the west, grass fires blazed in the cooling wind, and the smell was pleasant.

12.

OLIVER PRINCE SMITH, FIFTY-five, was not a typical Marine general, assuming there is such a thing. A quiet, contemplative pipe-smoker, he was a somewhat shy gentleman whom no one would ever think to call colorful. Born in Texas but raised in northern California, he worked his way through the University at Berkeley doing odd jobs ("mostly gardening"), received his commission as a Marine lieutenant in 1917, studied at the École Supérieure de Guerre in France, and participated in the World War II battles of New Britain, Peleliu, and Okinawa.

Shy he was, but not timid. In a conference with General Almond on November 7 he presented his objections to the dispersed condition of his regiments. "I pointed out that in the 1st Marine Division, Almond had a powerful instrument, but that it could not help but be weakened by the dispersion to which it was being subjected." Portions of the division were as far as 170 miles apart that day: Puller's 1st Marines near Wonsan, Murray's 5th Marines in the Sinhung Valley, Litzenberg's 7th Marines just north of Sudong.

"I again urged that in view of the approach of winter, consideration should be given to halting the advance in view of the difficulty of supplying units in the mountains. Almond seemed agreeable to concentrating the division." The Marine general's sense of relief was short-lived, however, for Almond added that he wanted the Marines to advance through Funchilin Pass and beyond Koto-ri all the way to Hagaru, a junction village at the foot of the giant Chosin Reservoir.

Smith now began to worry about his left flank, which was wide open. Almond had assured him it would be covered by patrols sent out by the X Corps Special Operations Company. Smith did not find this information reassuring, for he had already heard negative reports about their performance. On November 2 a Special Operations sergeant had flagged down a Marine trucker to report that his company was under attack by some 300 Chinese soldiers and needed help. Elements of the 1st Marine Tank Battalion happened to be in the neighborhood, and a three-tank patrol was soon on its way. The Marines encountered a small number of enemy soldiers a mile west of Munchon "and drove them into the hills without delay," said Smith later. "The performance of the Special Operations Company was not very creditable in this engagement." It would not be the last time during the Chosin Reservoir campaign that the Marines would deal with an underperforming U.S. Army outfit.

Colonel Alpha L. Bowser, chief of operations: "Our Marine division was the spearhead of X Corps. General Almond had already begun to notice that the spearhead was hardly moving at all. We were in fact just poking along—deliberately so. We pulled every trick in the book to slow down our advance, hoping the enemy would show his hand before we got even more widely dispersed than we already were. At the same time, we were building up our levels of supply at selected dumps along the road."

Lt. Chew-Een Lee was not a docile patient at the 121st Army Evacuation Hospital in Hamhung; nor did the Army medics there look upon him with affection. Crankier than usual because of the throbbing pain in his right arm, Lee regarded his sojourn among the rear-echelon pogues as "absolutely disgusting. These people expected me to do nothing. I had no duties, no responsibilities, no purpose."

Frustrated, Lee muttered darkly, "I *must* get away from this place."

Staff Sergeant William Keller, an 81-mm mortar section leader who had been wounded in the thigh, was almost as restless as Lee.

"I'm going for a walk, Lieutenant. Care to come along?"

Outside, the two of them strolled aimlessly about the compound—Keller limping, Lee cradling his sore arm—and found themselves at the edge of the hospital's motor pool.

Keller spotted a jeep with the key in the ignition. The two men looked at each other, their faces brightening. In the far corner of the lot, several Army drivers stood warming themselves around a fifty-five-gallon oil drum containing a booming fire. Lee eased onto the passenger's seat, while Keller got behind the wheel and started the motor. The drivers' heads turned in unison, and one of them yelled, but before they could take action the jeep was burning rubber through the city streets, heading north. Near the edge of town, Lt. Lee twisted around to assure himself there were no military police on their tail—and was astonished to see three Army ambulances close behind.

"We're being followed, Keller. Go faster."

Neither of them could figure out how three drivers could have gotten into action so quickly, but that didn't matter at the moment; the race was on, and in a few minutes they were out in the boondocks, zipping along the top of a levee with paddies on either side. Lee kept turning around in his seat, keeping watch on the pursuers. The ambulances were gaining on them.

"Faster!" said Lee.

"Sir, if I go any faster—"

Now the road veered abruptly to the left, and Keller, reluctant to turn the wheel too far lest the jeep roll over, failed to make the last part of the turn.

"We sailed off the road like an airplane," recalls Lee, "and landed on all four wheels in a dry paddy." The jeep rolled to a bumpy stop as the ambulances made the turn behind them and disappeared up the road to Sudong. "That's when we realized they weren't following us at all." In relating the anecdote, Lee says he and Keller sat groaning in pain from the rough jostling for a minute or two but then burst into laughter.

Lee pretended to ignore Joseph Owen's raucous greeting when Owen spotted the diminutive lieutenant trudging up the hill. The officers and men of Baker Company made it plain they were glad to see Lee's stern, disapproving face. As they gathered around him, he nodded curtly to each in turn. Captain Myron Wilcox removed his glasses and massaged the bridge of his nose. "So! Did the hospital turn you loose, Lee, or is this just a visit?"

"I'm reporting for duty, sir. I understand that Lt. Graeber has been evacuated with a concussion."

Captain Wilcox nodded.

"I desire to take over his platoon."

"It's yours."

The Marines of the Second Platoon were somewhat daunted by

the news, knowing that life under Lt. Chew-Een Lee was going to be different than life under Lt. William Graeber. Joseph Owen: "Lee did everything by the manual. Foxholes had to be so many feet deep, so many feet wide, with shelves for grenades. He would inspect everything carefully until you did it by the book."

Lee set about re-equipping himself at the quartermaster's tent, methodically preparing himself for the next battle.

"I wasn't yet convinced I had earned any glory," he says.

13.

FRETTING OVER HIS UNPRO-
tected flank, Colonel Litzenberg decided to reconnoiter the badlands to the northwest before sending his regiment into the most
constricted, ambush-inviting stretch of Funchilin Pass. Accordingly,
he sent out a call for volunteers to take part in a possibly hazardous
twenty-five-mile-long patrol.

PFC Ralph Boelk, Weapons Company, 1/7: "When the colonel
asked for volunteers, about two hundred of us showed up. Some
wanted to strike back at the enemy, others were restless and
wanted action, a few just needed exercise. I was one of those who
wanted to strike back." Litzenberg asked each of his three infantry
battalion commanders to nominate a lieutenant to lead the mission.
1st Lt. William Goggin, a platoon leader in Dog Company, was
chosen. "He was picked over the two others," explained Litzenberg
later, "because of his reputation for being careful. An officer can
be aggressive and at the same time carefully husband the lives of
his men." Lt. Col. Raymond Davis, briefing the patrol, had a last-
minute tip for Goggin. "If you get lost up there, just head east until
you come to the gorge, then climb down to the road." There were
eight checkpoints. The patrol's radio code name was Driftwood
Item.

November 8 was a cool, misty day. The fifteen-man column
shoved off around noon, heading west. The first leg was a three-
mile hike along a rocky stream bed between two peaks. Because of
the mountains, Lt. Goggin was unable to make radio contact with
the battalion at Checkpoint 1 or Checkpoint 2. At mid-afternoon
the column turned north and began ascending a steep slope that
continued for miles, leading to the high plateau. No enemy in sight.

In the early darkness Goggin decided to stop and rest for a few
hours. Corporal Robert Mandich was standing watch around midnight when he heard the scrape of shoe leather on the downhill

slope. Several people were approaching. When he challenged the intruders in the Stateside manner—"Halt! Who goes there?"—they turned and fled noisily. Some of the Marines, including Boelk, thought it an innocent party of civilians, but Goggin decided it would be wise to assume it was a column of Chinese infantrymen. He was leading a recon patrol, not a combat patrol, and so the better part of valor was to pick up quickly and move on.

By the time they reached Checkpoint 3 and the top of the mountain, the sky in the east was beginning to lighten. Emerging from the treeline, the Marines found themselves gazing down on a narrow east-west valley where the Changjin River flows west past the village of Koto-ri. Ralph Boelk: "I remember there was a late moon, just setting, and the landscape was covered with the first frost of the season. It was a strange and beautiful sight. Down below were some gook shacks with smoke coming from the chimneys, and some of the shacks had horses tethered outside them."

Across the river, several civilians were sluice-mining for gold. This was no surprise to the Marines, for the Japanese maps the division was using showed the presence of many gold mines in the region. Boelk: "A Chinese soldier came outside one of the shacks to take his early morning piss and we all hit the deck. After he went back inside, we started moving again. Then a dog began barking at us and we hit the deck again. Then several gooks came out and one of them spotted us. They all ran inside, shouting and yelling, and came out with rifles. I'd guess there were thirty or forty of them. We started moving east pretty fast, wanting to get the hell out of sight."

There was a brief exchange of shots, and Lt. Goggin was struck in the hand. Corpsman James Walsh crawled over with his B-1 bag, cleaned the officer's wound, and applied a bandage. The Chinese ended the firefight abruptly, loaded saddlebags on the horses, and led them down the road toward Koto-ri. The patrol remained atop Hill 1413, which was Checkpoint 4, and watched the road for an hour and a half, as instructed. There was no further traffic. After the ninety minutes were up, the Marines moved over to Hill 1328, overlooking the village. Koto-ri appeared deserted. Boelk: "As we were pulling off that position, we spooked three or four deer out of the brush nearby, which gave us quite a scare."

Corporal Donald Hamilton, manning the radio, was able to

make contact with Colonel Davis at last as they were nearing the rim of the gorge. The time was 2:47 P.M., November 9. Boelk: "I heard Manning ask Colonel Davis to wait while he called Lieutenant Goggin over. I heard the lieutenant say, 'Sir, we're near the top of the gorge right now. We're going to show ourselves on the skyline. We're going to stand up and wave our arms.' He was worried we'd be mistaken for gooks and draw fire; but the Marines below returned our waves, and we were home free."

Goggin's volunteers had covered twenty-five miles in twenty-six hours, over the most tortuous terrain imaginable, and had learned that the east-west road from Koto was probably not being used for the transport of troops or supplies.

During the rest of the climb up the stiff grade, the only opposition encountered by Litzenberg's regiment was an unfriendly bear that, on the night of November 9–10, paid a growling visit to George Company's First Platoon, frightening several Marines in their bags before lumbering up the cable-car right of way, which angled off to the northeast. Early on the tenth, Lt. Col. Davis's First Battalion, 7th Marines (1/7), with Chew-Een Lee's platoon leading the way, emerged from Funchilin Pass onto the open plateau, and Colonel Litzenberg sent this curt message to General Smith: "Have occupied Koto-ri this date."

Davis's staff chose an obvious location for 1/7's command post: the railroad station where the cable-car system ended and the narrow-gauge tracks recommenced; but when Davis saw what they had done; he frowned at the choice. "It was central, but it was too vulnerable. We beefed up the security posts around the building and held a practice evacuation with all hands moving to a ravine a couple of hundred yards east of the village." After taking care of that matter, Davis had a sponge bath in the Changjin, which here turns north and flows ten miles to Hagaru, where it empties into the south end of the sprawling reservoir. Davis washed himself in the cool water, unaware that this was the last day of autumn.

November 10, 1950, was the 175th anniversary of "our grand and glorious Corps," as Davis called it. The moment was celebrated with due solemnity under conditions less than ideal. The usual birthday message from the Commandant was read to all hands, and in the evening there was a modest ceremony in General Smith's mess in Hamhung. Up on the high plateau, Lt. Col. Davis read aloud the prescribed passages from the Marine Corps manual, then cut into a large cake with a captured North Korean officer's sword, the first piece going to the oldest Marine present, the second piece to the youngest.

Davis: "That evening they brought in a Chinese straggler, a tiny fellow who smiled continuously. He was very hungry and wolfed down the C-rations we heated for him, and a chunk of birthday cake. We stuffed him into a sleeping bag and he fell asleep immediately, right there in the battalion command post. When he woke up he told the interpreter he wanted to go back into the mountains and collect some comrades who were ready to desert. I figured, why not? So we loaded him up with rations and cigarettes and heat tablets and sent a fire team to escort him to the edge of the perimeter, and he took off up the incline. He stopped at the top and gave us a big wave and disappeared. Never saw him again."

A word about Lt. Col. Raymond G. Davis, a native of Georgia. When the Korean War broke out in June 1950, Davis was serving as Inspector-Instructor of a reserve battalion in Chicago. He had been a lieutenant colonel for eleven years. Such longevity of rank was not unusual in the Corps, which trained its officers with painstaking care and promoted them only after the individual in question had proven himself worthy of the honor.

Davis's Ninth Infantry Battalion arrived at Camp Pendleton on the train at five o'clock in the morning. The troops were lined up along the tracks as an occasional car flashed by on Highway 101; they were then counted off in groups of seventy-five and marched away in the dark, never to be seen again by the officers who trained them. "Frankly, I still resent the abrupt and disorderly manner in which our reserve battalion was disbanded in the darkness that morning. We were something approximating a family, and suddenly we were all separated from one another. In the Corps things are usually done in an orderly fashion. This was, I grant you, an unusual situation. The Republic of Korea was being overrun by the Communist North Koreans, and if we were going to save the South Koreans, things had to be done fast. I know all that. Still . . .

" 'Where the hell have you been?' was Colonel Litzenberg's greeting when I reported in. 'You have five days to form the First

Battalion of this regiment and get it aboard ship.' He assigned me three officers, all majors, and we got to work raising a battalion. We shanghaied some of the trucks bringing supplies in from the depot at Barstow, and each of us drove around the base, stopping every time we saw a group of Marines—a work party or a training class or just off-duty men hanging around—to ask for volunteers. Going overseas to fight a war is what the Marine Corps is all about, and we didn't have any trouble filling the trucks.

"In the next four days we only had time to run one command post exercise in those Pendleton hills, but we stayed out there until we got the system working. The hardest part was the way Colonel Litzenberg kept showing up in a helicopter, hovering directly overhead, asking one question after another by radio. My solution, of which I'm not proud, was to post sentinels to listen for the chopper and sound the alarm; then everyone would turn to, looking frantically busy while the colonel was hovering.

"One evening, shortly before Taps, I made them a speech. 'We're going to war,' I said. 'This outfit is going to be the finest in the division. When we work, we'll work harder than anyone else in the regiment. When we fight, we'll go all out. There will be no slackers in this battalion. The burdens are heavy enough without having to carry deadwood too. We need to be ready to ship out at a moment's notice. If you have family nearby, you will have time for one farewell visit.' "

By now the temperature in the mountains had dipped again, with a promise of even colder weather to come.

General Smith: "I ordered the cold-weather gear to be issued from the beach dumps at Hungnam. This was difficult because the gear, which amounted to half a shipload, was scattered throughout the ammunition and ration dumps. We outfitted the 7th Marines first because they were already in the high elevations. The gear consisted of mountain sleeping bags, alpaca-lined parkas, windproof trousers, heavy woolen socks, and shoe-pacs. The parkas were long Navy types, more suitable for standing watch aboard ship than long marches in the mountains. As to the shoe-pacs, they were really duckhunter's boots—an invitation to frostbite in subzero temperatures."

Colonel Litzenberg, knowing how clever the Chinese were at concealing themselves from aerial observation, was still not convinced they had left the area. Before the confrontation at Sudong, after all, Marine Air had discerned neither hide nor hair of the 7,500–man 124th Division. Mortarman Joseph Owen: "Most of us suspected that somewhere out there was a shitload of gooks waiting for us."

14.

GENERAL MACARTHUR HAD EVidently shrugged off the Chinese attacks in early November. Walker's Eighth Army in the west and Almond's X Corps in the east were to press on independently toward the Yalu. Once they reached that river—the border between Korea and China—the short little war would be concluded, after only five months of fighting. Such was MacArthur's expectation.

The Chinese had different plans. If tactical matters unfolded as General Sung Shih-lun expected, the Marines would soon be stretched thinly between Chinhung-ni, Koto-ri, Hagaru-ri, and Yudam-ni. General Sung could then order his units to surround the separate components of the Division, blow up the bridge in Funchilin Pass, and destroy the Americans piecemeal. Such was Sung's expectation.

The typical Chinese Communist division fielded anywhere from 6,500 to 8,500 men. There were three divisions to an army—called a *corps* in the west—with three regiments and an artillery battalion in each division. (Because of the mountainous terrain, lack of motor transport, and vulnerability to American air strikes, Sung had left most of his artillery behind.) The individual Chinese soldier in North Korea wore a two-piece reversible uniform of quilted cotton, white on one side, mustard-yellow on the other, and a cotton cap with fur-lined earflaps. Chinese soldiers encountered at Sudong, as we have seen, wore canvas shoes with crepe soles; later arrivals wore a half-leather shoe, and some a full-leather boot. Their communications system was primitive, the radio net rarely extending below regiment; telephones were almost never found below battalion. At company level, communication depended on runners or signaling devices such as bugles, horns, whistles, cymbals, flares, or flashlights. Company officers were granted little or no tactical leeway, and a unit was likely to stick stubbornly with the same plan

until its ammunition ran out, even if the unit was beating its
head against the strongest part of the enemy's line. The Chinese
preferred to wage war after dark, maximizing their strengths—
stamina, stealth, superior numbers—and minimizing their weak-
nesses—vulnerability to air strike, lack of motor transport, and
limited artillery support. There was no provision in the Chinese
army for honorable discharge; once a Chinese peasant became part
of that endless moving column, he was expected to march in lockstep until he was killed, captured, or wounded too badly to be
useful any longer.

Some of the older officers and enlisted men were veterans of the
legendary Long March. In October 1934, breaking out of encirclement by Chiang Kai-shek's Nationalist forces, Mao's ragged army
had fought its way more than 6,000 miles, crossed eighteen mountain ranges and twenty-four rivers, averaging twenty-four miles a
day for 235 days. Of the 100,000 who began the epic journey in
Kiangsi Province, only 20,000 reached the new base at Yenan.
(General Sung, forty-two, had commanded a regiment in the Long
March.) In 1950 the Chinese Communist infantryman was probably the toughest and hardiest in the world. In the fall of that year
Sung's Ninth Army Group was tasked with the twofold mission of
providing flank protection for the Thirteenth Army Group in
northwest Korea (the forces facing Walker), and of destroying the
1st Marine Division and any other troops under General Almond
in the vicinity of the Chosin Reservoir. In his treatise *On Protracted
War*, Mao Tse-tung had written, "The reason we have always ad-
vocated a policy of luring the enemy to penetrate deeply is because
it is the most effective tactic against a strong opponent." Luring X
Corps deeply into the unforgiving mountains was the key to Sung's
strategy in northeast Korea.

Almond had assured General Smith that his GIs would guard his
supply dumps, but the Marine general was doubtful of the Army's
follow-through in the matter. Having left a garrison at Chinhungni,
Smith now detached another to remain at Koto-ri as the 7th Marines resumed their northward crawl. Reluctant to commit his
troops to a winter campaign he was logistically unprepared to fight,
and faced with unrealistic demands from X Corps, Smith had
slowed the Marine advance to the point of insubordination.

The Chinese may or may not have momentarily quit the scene;
but now another enemy, equally dreadful, was about to appear.

General Winter, having won many a campaign down through the centuries, was about to reap a heavier harvest of casualties at the reservoir than the armies themselves with their bombs and bullets. In early November there had been a brief period of weather akin to America's Indian summer, but now the evenings were chilly once again, the mornings misty, the skies no longer blue. During the night of November 9–10, the first snowfall of the season whitened the bleak narrows of the pass. The following day, shockingly, the temperature plummeted forty degrees in a few hours. By nightfall it was eight degrees below zero, made much worse by a twenty-to-thirty-knot Siberian wind.

Lt.(jg) Henry Litvin, U.S. Navy, battalion surgeon: "I was so preoccupied I didn't notice how cold it got until I started eating my breakfast that morning. There was no mess tent, so I stood there in the wind shoveling these supposedly scrambled eggs into my mouth as fast as I could. The taste was so awful I wanted to get it over with. I had set my canteen cup of coffee on a fence post, planning to enjoy it after I got rid of the eggs; but when I picked it up—Holy mackerel!—the tin was so cold my fingers stuck to the metal and there was a film of ice on the coffee itself. For the first time in the campaign I wondered if the weather might turn out to be a medical problem. The effect on the line Marines was drastic. There were numerous cases of what appeared to be shock—but it was the shock of a terrific cold spell they weren't ready for. We broke out the warming tents, set them up, got the stoves perking, while the galley provided steaming water you could heat your C-rations in."

Lt. Col. Davis: "It was bad. My staff and I moved around among the troops, looking for the characteristic candle-white splotches that signaled frostbite; and when we spotted it coming on, we would hustle the man to the nearest fire."

Sergeant Carl Winslow, Fox/7: "I woke up nearly paralyzed from cold and hurried to light a fire for coffee. The night before I had collected twigs for tinder. Now I took off a mitten and lit a match—and watched it snuff out in the wind despite the screen of my poncho. The poncho was whipping and fluttering so hard you could hardly hear anything else."

Corporal Roy Pearl: "I grew up in Minnesota, so I was used to temperatures like that, but the thing that shocked me was the suddenness of it. I saw several guys, some of them from the South, in tears. We dragged over some boards from a bombed-out house and, with the help of a splash of gasoline, got a fire going. Our C-rations turned out to be frozen solid. It wasn't easy to heat them up, even in a roaring fire like that, because of the wind."

Almond established a new command post in Hamhung on November 11 and asked General Smith to send over a company of Marines to guard it. Smith regarded this as a gross misuse of a rifle company, since there were at least 2,000 support troops at Hamhung-Hungnam; but he sent Charlie Company, 5th Marines, anyway, under Captain Jack Jones. This seemingly minor incident demonstrated anew to the Marines that the X Corps commander did not understand the principle of husbanding one's resources and was too ready to expend his men carelessly. On that same day, Almond peremptorily ordered the Division to resume its march to the Yalu. Smith measured the distance on his map and found it to be roughly 150 miles from Funchilin Pass to the border.

On the thirteenth, under gray skies, Smith helicoptered to Chinhung-ni; there he borrowed a jeep from Robert Taplett's Third Battalion, 5th Marines, which was guarding the railhead supply depot, and headed up the pass. "The road," Smith recalled, "was cut out of the side of the mountain. For the most part it was one-way and had numerous hairpin turns, with turnouts every few hundred yards. The drop-off was anywhere from four hundred to a thousand feet to the bottom of the gorge."

About two-thirds of the way through the pass, on the uphill side, stood a hydroelectric substation with four giant pipes descending to a power plant in the valley below. Along the downhill side of the building was a one-way concrete bridge over a sheer drop. "On the day of my visit," said Smith, "the temperature was below zero, and the road was icy in spots where spring water had overflowed and frozen. We found the temperature in the mountains to be almost twenty degrees lower than down at Hungnam." In a postcampaign interview with historian S. L. A. Marshall, Smith observed: "The country around Chosin was never intended for military operations. Even Genghis Khan wouldn't tackle it."

15.
LT. CHEW-EEN LEE'S POINT FIRE
team was picking its way cautiously across the long concrete bridge
over the Changjin River. The temperature was five degrees below
zero. The 7th Marines had finally arrived at Hagaru, at the southern tip of the enormous man-made lake called Chosin Reservoir,
visible now as a sprawling sheet of blue ice already thick enough
to support a jeep. The road forked at the village—the left fork
heading northwesterly toward Yudam-ni, fourteen miles away, the
right running northerly along the east side of the reservoir and,
according to the vague Japanese map, going nowhere in particular
and petering out in the mountains.

PFC Al Bradshaw: "There was some junk and stuff on the bridge
and I was worried about booby traps. I had goose bumps until I
reached the end and started walking down the street. Our orders
were to leave the very young and very old alone but to take into
custody any young men we found. My fire team started working
the center of town, taking turns who would enter a building first.
When we came to this big schoolhouse it was my turn. There were
several classrooms inside, and an auditorium—something you
don't expect in a village like Hagaru. There was a stage, and on
the back wall a portrait of Mao and another of Stalin. I looked
around in the dim light and saw a door at the edge of the stage,
and right away had this uneasy feeling in the stomach.

"The door was slightly ajar. What I did, I banged through real
fast and felt something big on the other side: I had knocked this
civilian against the wall. He held a pistol in his right hand. I stuck
the point of my bayonet up against his ribs, snatched the pistol out
of his hand, and hustled him outside. I was about to turn him over
at the collection point when the son of a bitch took off and dodged
around the nearest street corner. I stepped to the corner and drew
a bead on him just as he glanced over his shoulder; and when he

saw he was about to have a hole blown in him, he dropped to the ground like a smart fella. I ran up to him, gave him the boot, and dragged him by the collar to the collection point. 'Let the bastard go,' says Irl Dement, 'and see if he runs again.'

" 'What the hell for?'

" 'So's I can test-fire my weapon.'

" 'Don't be a jerk.' "

Far back down the road, the Second Battalion, 7th Marines (2/7), was advancing toward Hagaru under steel-gray skies. Lt. Col. Randolph Lockwood, the new battalion commander, was trying out his binoculars. "Superb magnification of long-range objects," he said later. One of the objects magnified was an iron-doored portal to a mine shaft a quarter mile west of the road. Lockwood sent a fire team to check it out; on returning, the corporal in charge reported finding unwashed rice bowls and chopsticks and the smell of garlic-eating men. Lockwood: "We continued up the road, and I recall that the wind increased in velocity. It got so bad we shielded our faces with our gloved hands and even walked with our backs to it."

Colonel Homer Litzenberg was widely respected as a regimental commander, but he was also known to be difficult at times. Alpha Bowser remembers him as "a very stubborn Dutchman. Argumentative. Couldn't take criticism. Always convinced he was right. He demanded performance from his officers, which was fine, but he was known as a bit of a bully, a breaker of lieutenant colonels." One lieutenant colonel who came up against him—but remained unbroken—was Randolph Scott Dewey Lockwood, Harvard cum laude, graduate of the Naval Academy at Annapolis. Lockwood had reported to Litzenberg on November 9 at Koto-ri. The colonel stared balefully at the somewhat pudgy, pink-cheeked officer, recognizing that Lockwood, with two pairs of binoculars and a camera hanging from his neck, was probably not the single-mindedly aggressive type of officer he preferred to have in the 7th Marines, even though Lockwood was well-trained, highly motivated, and intelligent.

"I see you're overweight," said the colonel.

Lockwood retorted jovially that the campaign in the mountains would probably pare the excess poundage.

"I'm giving you the Second Battalion," said Litzenberg, who had no choice in the matter: Lockwood outranked Webb Sawyer, a major. "I'm a hard taskmaster," he warned.

"That's what I've heard, Colonel," said Lockwood.

After setting up his command post in the railroad roundhouse where the cable-car line ended, Lockwood began taking photographs with his Leica, a recreational activity that did not further endear him to the regimental commander.

PFC George Crotts: "Our squad found shelter in a boxcar on a siding, and I was sent off to collect kindling. Hagaru was one dismal joint. The poverty! Stacked up in a warehouse beside the tracks, ready for shipment God knows where, were sacks of broken glass and worn-out shoes. I found a bag of chopsticks, perfect for kindling, and on the way back I spotted a can of strawberry jam behind the company chow wagon which I scooped up in passing, and when I got back to the boxcar they treated me like a hero. We got a fire going with the chopsticks and added some bigger stuff. There was nothing we could do about the smoke; it was either freeze to death or die of smoke inhalation. We didn't stop long in Hagaru. That's the thing about Marines: here today, gone tomorrow."

Randolph Lockwood: "Regiment had actually set up a post-exchange in that miserable bombed-out village. All they had to sell was shoe polish—can you imagine?—cigars, and candy bars. I went up to the counter. 'I hear you have cigars. What brand?'

" 'Sir, we have Red Dot. Two for a nickel.'

" 'I'll take two packs.'

" 'Sorry, sir, they're restricted to one cigar per Marine per day.'

" 'How can you sell one cigar when you charge two for a nickel?'

" 'Easy, sir. You just buy two cigars every other day.' "

George Crotts also recalls the Hagaru PX. "It was a tent beside the railroad track. All they sold was cigars, shoe polish, and candy. I bought a couple of cigars. I had never smoked a cigar, but there I was, a fuzz-faced private of eighteen strutting around like a fuzz-faced private of eighteen, this ugly stogie planted in my mug. When I got back to the boxcar, the squad was saddling up and everyone was all disgruntled because the new colonel had decreed that everyone had to occupy positions outside and be on the lookout for hostiles. And word was making the rounds that the colonel was going to arrange that none of us ever saw the underside of a roof again."

Interaction between Marines and civilians was rare. Graydon Davis of Fox Company and two men in his squad had a brief encounter with the natives. "We stopped off at this gook hootch to get out of the cold and heat some rations. The Mama-san was doing some cooking and her runny-nosed kids were playing in the corner. The chimney was ducted under the floor, we discovered, so the room was comfortably warm, something we hadn't experienced in a long time. While we were eating, one of the guys whistled a bar or two of an old hymn and this caught the Mama-san's attention. She sent one of the kids outside and a few minutes later in comes Papa-san. The whole family was smiling at us. We didn't know what was going on. Papa-san stuck his arm in a sack of potatoes and pulled out an old tattered hymnal. Then they lined up and sang a hymn for us, and I recognized the tune." (North Korea was the most fruitful Christian missionary territory in all of Asia until the Communists took over.)

By the afternoon of the fifteenth the 7th Marine Regiment was consolidated at the southern tip of the reservoir and the bulldozers of the 1st Engineer Battalion were already at work constructing an airstrip. That night the temperature dropped to fifteen below zero. Lockwood recalls a strange meteorological phenomenon: "The wind, which had been blowing down from the north carrying fine dust with it, now subsided as the mercury plunged, and all the following day a great column of steam rose from the surface of the lake. By midnight the black ice was thick enough to support a loaded truck."

During the brief interlude at Hagaru the members of Lt. John Yancey's platoon had a chance to take a closer look at Private Stanley Robinson. "He was a hard case," recalls Corpsman James Claypool. "The first time I ever laid eyes on him was at dockside, San Diego, as we were about to sail. He was with a group of prisoners brought down from the brig. We watched the MPs march them in lockstep up the gangway. I don't know how Robinson managed to avoid permanent residency at Portsmouth Naval Prison; he had gone Absent Without Leave [AWOL] repeatedly and was considered incorrigible. The division was badly understrength when the Korean War broke out and needed every man it could scrape up, so Robinson was offered the classic choice: the brig or the infantry. He was a tall kid, but scrawny; he looked about four-teen. Everyone knew he had taken over Cagliotti's squad on Hill 698, broke up a Chinese assault with grenades, destroyed a machine-gun crew with a white-phosphorous grenade, and held the crest by himself for a few minutes."

Claypool, a veteran of World War II, exerted himself to become acquainted with Robinson. "Talking with him at Hagaru, I learned he went AWOL because he had this kid wife and they had a baby and there were problems. His first piece of good luck was getting assigned to Yancey's platoon. Yancey was about the toughest Ma-rine you could find anywhere, but he was kindhearted to people who needed a bit of kindness. He talked with Robinson for about five minutes and got to know him better than all the Navy psy-chiatrists who had been trying to figure him out for months. Rob-inson was made to understand that he was now responsible to Yancey and Lieutenant Ray Ball, the exec, and Captain Walter Phillips, the company commander; and it seemed that overnight he turned into a first-class fighting Marine. It was the case of a lost soul finding something he was good at in a life that hadn't had much purpose up to then; because the truth is, he wasn't much good at anything else. I heard in later years he was killed in a shoot-out with Colorado state troopers.

"The Marine Corps motto, which in better days every school-child in America knew—now nobody gives a damn about such things—was *Semper Fidelis,* which means 'Always faithful.' Marines took the concept seriously. And the Corps, you see, gave a youngster like Robinson something worth being faithful to.

"He and I had one moment of direct communication during our brief stay in Hagaru. A bunch of us were hunkered around a fire at the edge of town, trying to thaw our hands, when up comes this Korean man and a girl of about eight. Despite the language barrier, there was no hiding the delight these young Marines felt in having a kid around. Unlike most of her elders, she was completely una-fraid of them. The man stood by the fire, smiling and nodding, and don't ask me why but I got the impression he was something other than a farmer; maybe it was because he was under forty and acting nervous. Anyway, my eyes met Robinson's across the fire and, funny thing, we stood up at the same moment, grabbed this guy, searched him thoroughly, and ran him over to the bridge where the MPs were holding civilians suspected of being spies or sympathizers. When we got back we found the guys were feeding the girl C-rations and trying to make her smile.

"Later that afternoon a jeep pulled up and there was Colonel Litzenberg himself in the passenger seat. Down at platoon level you rarely saw your battalion commander, let alone anyone from regiment; so it was like being visited by a celebrity, and we all stood up and stared at him. It turned out he had heard about Robinson's performance on 698 and wanted him for a bodyguard. He called Robbie over, looked him up and down, and told him to collect his gear and climb in the backseat."

Yancey and his troops thought they had seen the last of Robinson and were sorry to see him go; but it turned out that Stanley Robinson would go AWOL one more time.

16.

DURING A PRESS CONFERENCE on November 15, President Truman reassured Peking before the world that the United States had no intention of carrying the war into China. "I wish to state unequivocally that because of our deep devotion to the cause of peace and our long-standing friendship for the people of China, we will take every honorable step to prevent any extension of hostilities in the Far East."

That same day, General MacArthur sent a signal to Almond that changed X Corps' line of march. The 1st Marine Division was now to advance to Yudam-ni at the western extremity of the Chosin Reservoir, turn west, cross the formidable Taebek Range, and occupy the road-junction town of Mupyong, fifty-five miles away. General Oliver P. Smith's anxiety over the separation of his regiments now became acute because of one component of the plan: As Litzenberg's 7th Marines swung west from the reservoir, Murray's 5th, after ascending Funchilin Pass, was to march up the east side of the lake, ostensibly to guard Litzenberg's right flank but really too far distant to provide any protection. Puller's 1st Marines were still fifty miles to the rear.

Brigadier General Edward Craig, assistant division commander: "Before he left our command post, General Almond stressed the need for speed. We had reached Hagaru at the south end of the reservoir and now he wanted Litzenberg to head northwest to Yudam-ni, fourteen miles away, while Murray was to take the 5th Marines up the east shore. 'We've got to go barreling up that road,' he said. General Smith's involuntary response was *No!* but Almond pretended not to hear it. After he departed, General Smith said, 'We're not going anywhere until I get this division together and the airfield built.' "

So fretful had Smith become over the scattering of his units that he took the extraordinary step of writing a personal letter to Commandant General Clifton Cates, complaining about the situation in detail.

> Although the Chinese have withdrawn to the north, I have not pressed Litzenberg to make any rapid advance. Our left flank is wide open. There is no unit of the Eighth Army nearer than 80 miles to the southwest of Litzenberg. . . . I do not like the prospect of stringing out a Marine Division along a single mountain road for 120 miles from Hamhung to the Manchurian border. . . . There is a considerable difference in temperature where we are and where Litzenberg is. Yesterday at 0900 it was 18 degrees Fahrenheit here and 0 degrees Fahrenheit in Hagaru. . . . Even though the men who are up front are young and are equipped with parkas, shoe-pacs, and mountain sleeping bags, they are taking a beating. . . . I have little confidence in the tactical judgement of X Corps or in the realism of their planning. There is a continual splitting up of units and assignment of missions which puts them out on a limb. Time and time again I have tried to tell the Corps Commander that in a Marine Division he has a powerful instrument, and that it cannot help but lose its effectiveness when dispersed. My mission is still to advance to the border. The 8th Army, 80 miles to the southwest, will not attack until the 20th. Manifestly we should not push on without regard to the 8th Army; we would simply get farther out on a limb. I believe a winter campaign in the mountains of Korea is too much to ask of the American soldier or Marine, and I doubt the feasibility of supplying troops in this area during the winter or providing for the evacuation of sick and wounded.

The following day, Smith departed his Hungnam headquarters in a heated station wagon and headed north. Halfway between Koto and Hagaru he overtook an open jeep on the road, and, recognizing Major General Field Harris in the passenger seat ("blue with cold"), he pulled over and stopped. "Care to join me, General?"

Harris hobbled over on numb feet and climbed in. "Goddamn, this is more like it. Got a second station wagon, O.P.?"

"Why, yes, I do."

"How about letting me have it?"

As Smith told historian Robert Leckie later, it turned out to be a small favor indeed for a man whose 1st Marine Air Wing would contribute as much to saving the Division from annihilation as any other factor.

Field Harris's son, William, had been appointed commanding officer of the Third Battalion, 7th Marines, six days earlier; the proud father was on his way to Hagaru to congratulate him. After he had done so, Harris rejoined Smith and the two of them went to find—as Smith later put it—"enough flat real estate in the vicinity to build a five-thousand-foot airstrip." They found it at the southwest edge of the village, and the engineers set to work at once. Company D of the 1st Engineer Battalion, working with five large caterpillar tractors, began hacking out a runway from ground that was already frozen hard as concrete. The work became increasingly difficult as the temperature continued to drop, and it was necessary to weld steel teeth onto the bulldozer blades so that they could cut into the ground.

The best news of the day was that Murray's 5th Marines had closed up behind Litzenberg, Lt. Col. Harold Roise's Second Battalion having led the way through the pass.

With Chew-Een Lee's platoon in front, Baker Company, 7th Marines, now pushed slowly across the mountains toward the hamlet of Yudam-ni at the western end of the reservoir. Lieutenant Lee's arm, cradled in the sling, was still sore; and he was having trouble with his knee. "It wouldn't lock. It kept buckling. I told no one, of course." All this made him more irascible than usual. Halfway to Yudam-ni, Lee saw a sight that appalled him: Baker Company Marines on the skyline, nakedly exposed to enemy snipers. This was one of the worst of infantry sins, as bad as "bunching up." Lee wasn't surprised to hear the characteristic *thunk* of an 82-mm round being launched from its mortar tube several hundred yards away. The Marines on the skyline froze in place, waiting to see where the round would land. It landed exactly where they had hoped it wouldn't, wounding several Marines. Adjusting the lay of the tube, the unseen mortar crew pumped out five more rounds, and as they were arcing across the sky one of Owen's mortarmen, Corporal Frank Bifulk, involuntarily snapped a warning to the small officer standing nearby: "Lee—get down!" After the second flurry of rounds exploded harmlessly, the lieutenant turned ominously toward him. "What was that you said?"

"Sir, I—"

Lee jabbed a forefinger toward the ground at his feet. "Come over here. Now."

Bifulk slid down the slope, stones and pebbles preceding him, as another 82-mm round impacted nearby. Bifulk ended up in a heap near the furious officer's shoe-pacs.

"Get up!"

Bifulk scrambled erect and assumed the rigid position of Attention as another round landed, spraying shards of hot steel in all directions.

"Are you listening to me?"

"I am definitely listening to you, sir."

"You will never, *ever* refer to me as 'Lee' again. Do you understand?"

"I definitely understand, sir."

Still another round landed. Bifulk said later he was sure he was about to die.

"My name is Lieutenant Lee or Mister Lee. Is that clear?"

"Yes it is, sir."

Soon the story was circulating about the by-the-book lieutenant chewing out the stunned enlisted man—as shrapnel flew—for failing to observe the rules of military courtesy. Joseph Owen, who saw it all, thought it a hilarious moment in the campaign. Lee himself did not regard it as an occasion of humor and told an interviewer in later years: "I realize the poor fellow was only thinking of my safety, and so forth. Even so!"

When the dust cleared, Lee sat down to enjoy his pipe. ("I kept the pipe and tobacco pouch in my map case and only smoked it after an action. I started smoking a pipe when I was eighteen because I wanted to develop some dignity.")

Though there was hardly any enemy opposition, the 7th Regiment continued to advance at a snail's pace. (Between November 10 and 26, the average progress was one mile per day.) Colonel Alpha Bowser: "We devoted a good deal of attention to building up the supply dumps. The ultimate goal was to accumulate ten units of fire and to bring up the tanks. Able Company, 1st Engineers, was setting up a small sawmill north of Hagaru for the production of timbers to be used in bridge repair. Mind you, all these preparations, and many others—all the result of General Smith's foresight—were ultimately to save the lives of thousands of fighting men and may well have saved the Marine division as a whole."

*   *   *

Corporal Darrell Burt, 11th Marines, recalls the dawning of the twenty-fourth. "When the sun came up, the sky was clear, but the moisture in the air was frozen and everywhere you looked it was like seeing a billion diamonds refracting. In the middle of all that ugly landscape was this beautiful spectacle." By mid-morning the skies were dark again, snow was blowing, and the wind was beginning to howl. 2nd Lt. Patrick Roe: "Around noon that day an excited civilian appeared with the news that a Chinese patrol had entered the settlement of Sinha-ri, an insignificant scattering of huts eight miles west of Hagaru, and ordered all civilians to evacuate their houses because ten thousand Chinese soldiers needed shelter. That seemed a ludicrous figure at the time. We hadn't yet learned about the enemy's amazing ability to cram great clots of men into the tiny houses of a Korean hamlet."

In the afternoon the traditional Thanksgiving menu was distributed. Given the weather and the setting, it seemed an incongruous piece of paper. The menu included shrimp cocktail, turkey, gravy, cranberry sauce, candied sweet potatoes, fruit salad, minced pie, fruitcake, mixed nuts, stuffed olives, and hot coffee. Corpsman William Davis: "The gravy froze first. Then the potatoes."

First Battalion, 7th Marines, was still four miles south of Yudam-ni. Lt. Col. Raymond Davis: "We were out on the very end of the limb tactically. When the turkeys caught up with us they were frozen solid and the cooks couldn't figure out how to thaw them. What we finally did was make a mountain of birds around two fired-up field kitchen stoves, then covered the whole affair with two pyramidal tents sealed tight with snow. By morning the birds were thawed enough for the cooks to cut up and cook, which took several hours. We rotated the platoons down from the slopes throughout the day. Lieutenant Lee's platoon, at the point, didn't get the word, however; each man had to settle for a cup of reconstituted milk and two slices of fresh bread. I felt bad about that."

Lt. Lee: "It was quite delicious." (One of his admirers, who prefers to remain anonymous, recently observed that Lee would have liked it even better if it had been a cup of cold water and a crust of stale bread.)

Lt. Col. Davis remembers, "This was to be our last hot meal for seventeen days, though we didn't know it at the time."

It was a day for homesickness, and there wasn't much you could

do about it except write a letter home. Lt. Lawrence Schmitt, Fox
Company/7, wrote to his wife.

> We sang the "Star Spangled Banner," "America," "My Country Tis of
> Thee." The Chaplain said a prayer, and the Colonel gave a talk. Me, I
> have a lot to be thankful for: my wonderful wife and boy, our house,
> our health, and our faith. May the good Lord continue to be generous
> to us.
>   All my love.
>   Larry

There were twenty-eight guests at General Almond's Thanksgiving table, including Marine Generals Smith and Harris and Colonels Puller and Bowser. "It was a plush state of affairs," Bowser recalls. "The meal itself included all the appointments one would expect in, say, a formal function in Washington: a cocktail bar, white tablecloths and napkins, china, silverware, place cards." It has been said about Marines that they aren't happy unless they're miserable. The four Marine officers were distinctly uncomfortable eating the stately meal in such luxurious surroundings, but they had much to be thankful for nonetheless: all three infantry regiments would soon be together again, and in the past ten days there had been hardly any casualties.

The following day, the twenty-fifth, the 7th Marines entered the hamlet of Yudam-ni. 1st Lt. Joseph Owen: "Yudam-ni. That's where the shit hit the fan."

17. MacArthur had flown over

from Tokyo in his C-54, *Bataan,* to witness the jump-off of the Eighth Army offensive. "If this operation is successful," he told the journalists, "I hope to get the boys home by Christmas."

The day before, he had ordered the following communiqué distributed to all troops under his command:

> The United Nations massive compression envelopment in North Korea against the new Red Armies operating there is now approaching its decisive effort. The isolating component of the pincer, our air forces of all types, have for the past three weeks, in a sustained effort of model coordination and effectiveness, successfully interdicted enemy lines of support from the north so that further reinforcement therefrom has been sharply curtailed and essential supplies markedly limited. The eastern sector of the pincer, with noteworthy and effective naval support, has now reached commanding enveloping position, cutting in two the northern reaches of the enemy's geographical potential. This morning the western sector of the pincer moves forward in general assault in an effort to complete the compression and close the vice. If successful, this should for all practical purposes end the war, restore peace and unity to Korea, enable the prompt withdrawal of United Nations military forces, and permit the complete assumption by the Korean people and nation of full sovereignty and international equality. It is that for which we fight.

The day's military operations were anticlimactic; there was no opposition. After watching the jump-off, MacArthur ordered his pilot to head north, then east. The general desired to "interpret with [his] own long experience what was going on behind the enemy's lines." There was, however, no sign of the enemy. "All that spread before our eyes," MacArthur wrote later, "was an endless

expanse of utterly barren countryside, jagged hills, yawning cre-
vasses, and the black waters of the Yalu locked in a silent death
grip of snow and ice. It was a merciless wasteland."

General Smith's laconic reaction to MacArthur's pronuncia-
mento is found in the November 24 entry of his command diary.
"The Eighth Army attack jumped off. General MacArthur issued
the usual flowery communiqué on the grand pincers movement
which was to be effected. We now find that the 1st Marine Division
is the northern arm of the pincer."

The X Corps order to swing west into the Taebeks had chilled
Smith's operations chief. "This goofy order," said Bowser later,
"came as quite a shock to General Smith." Almond's own chief of
staff, Major General Clark Ruffner, had a harsher word for it. In
a letter to historian Eric Hammel in 1979, Ruffner called MacArthur's decision to attack westward from the reservoir "an insane
plan."

Lt. Chew-Een Lee's platoon, up front as usual, pressed on. (Explaining why the Second Platoon so often led the way, Lee told an
interviewer years later, "Captain Wilcox considered my platoon
the most reliable, with the best leadership.") Following at a distance of fifty yards or so, Lee rotated three-man point teams, with
the rest of the platoon strung out behind him. "I was never relieved, because relief was never needed. I was always in complete
control of the situation and so forth."

Being a Marine platoon leader did not mean acting the role of
surrogate father or elder brother; it meant being a leader, and in
order to lead it was sometimes necessary to be harsh. PFC Calvin
Gunn, a member of one of the point teams, tended to lag behind
the others. Lee sidled up to him one day. "Gunn, I notice you're
not keeping up with the others. Why is that?"

"My foot hurts, sir."

"Does it?" Lee moved in close and brandished his carbine in
Gunn's face. "See this? Your suffering is going to increase sub-
stantially when I shove this up your ass!" Gunn never lagged behind again.

It was at about this time in the campaign that Lee noticed another private had taken a special interest in him. Lee: "His name
was Attilio Lupacchini. A BAR man. He was an immigrant who
hoped by serving honorably in the Corps to become an American

citizen. In any case, it was during the march to Yudam-ni that I noticed how he always tried to stay close and keep an eye on me. I was on the point of speaking to him about it when I realized he was being protective. He had actually appointed himself my personal bodyguard."

By late afternoon, November 25, two of the 7th Marines' battalion commanders, Davis and Harris, had maneuvered their units to the high ground overlooking the forlorn hamlet of Yudam-ni, nestled in a mountain-ringed valley. The westernmost tip of the reservoir lapped close to the village. Much of the valley floor was sectioned into wheat fields instead of the paddies the Marines were accustomed to seeing; the fields had been recently plowed, but a few shocks of wheat were still standing. Combing slowly and methodically through the scattered buildings and huts, the Marines found the place deserted.

Late in the day Davis's operations officer, Major Thomas Tighe, noted signs of human activity in one of the huts on the valley floor and decided to check it out personally. Taking an interpreter with him, he walked to a covered spot within shouting distance and, through the interpreter, demanded that anyone inside the hut was to come outside. There was no response. Tighe then warned that the hut would be set on fire in one minute. Tentatively, a Chinese soldier emerged, hands over his head, followed by two others. Tighe turned them over to Captain Donald France, Litzenberg's intelligence chief. The prisoners were remarkably forthcoming, answering France's questions in detail. They asserted that the 58th, 59th, and 60th Divisions of the Twentieth Chinese Communist Army had been in the Yudam-ni area for six days. All three identified themselves as riflemen belonging to the 60th Division.

Lt. Col. Frederick Dowsett, executive officer, 7th Marines: "The prisoners said that one division was going to attack the Marines at Yudam-ni from the north and another from the west. A third division, they said, would cut the road between Yudam-ni and Hagaru. A fourth would attack Hagaru and cut the road to Koto. And a fifth would cut the road between Koto and Chinhung-ni. The general assault would be launched, they agreed, soon after the two forward Marine regiments had passed to the north of Toktong Pass, which was located halfway between Hagaru and Yudam-ni. The assault would be launched after dark, they said, out of respect for Marine close air support. . . .All this was certainly very interesting, but we doubted that ordinary private soldiers could be privy to such high-level information, so we didn't put much faith in what they told us; in fact, we were so skeptical that we wondered if the three men had been *planted* in that hut as bait, charged with delivering misleading information to the enemy."

That night a civilian was stopped as he blithely trudged into Harris's lines, and taken to Captain France. Under questioning he revealed that he was on his way home after guiding an apparently endless number of Chinese troops in a southwesterly direction. When asked how many troops he was talking about, the man said the column was three hours' long. He said it included horse-drawn artillery and that some of the officers were mounted. Other civilian reports placed heavy Chinese concentrations west and south of the road to Hagaru.

General Smith: "Civilians who had been victims of Chinese demands for food supplies, civilians who had been forced to serve as guides, and line-crossing agents all contributed to a picture indicating the enemy's strong capability and probable intention to cut our supply route and stage counterattacks against us."

Lin Piao's Thirteenth Army Group of eighteen divisions would unleash its primary attack against Walker's Eighth Army on the evening of the twenty-fifth. Sung's Ninth Army Group of twelve divisions would at the same time envelop and attempt to destroy the 1st Marine Division at Yudam-ni, Hagaru-ri, and Koto-ri, as well as elements of the Army's 7th Infantry Division, which had reached the eastern shore of the reservoir by this time. Chinese forces would then destroy the 3rd Infantry Division, the rest of the 7th Division, and the two Republic of Korea divisions then advancing along the coastline. Chinese operations against X Corps were to begin on the evening of November 27.

Judging from their experience against the Eighth Cavalry in early November, the Chinese had no reason to fear the American divisions. On November 20 a *Military Lessons* bulletin, published by Sixty-sixth Army Headquarters, was distributed to all hands. The anonymous author noted that the American army relied heavily on tanks and artillery, but that "their infantry is weak. These men are afraid to die, and will neither press home a bold attack nor defend to the death. . . . Their habit is to be active only during daylight hours. They are very weak at approaching the enemy at night. . . .

If their source of supply is cut, their fighting spirit suffers, and if you interdict their rear, they will withdraw."

A pamphlet by one of General Sung's political commissars was distributed to the troops of the Ninth Army Group. It contained the following lines: "Soon we will meet the American Marines in battle. We will destroy them. When they are defeated, the enemy will collapse and our country will be free from the threat of aggression. Kill these Marines as you would snakes in your homes!"

18.

GENERAL SMITH: "WHAT I WAS trying to do all along was stall until we could bring up the 5th Marines and then the 1st Marines. I was unable to accomplish that until the twenty-sixth. By that date I was able to put one of Puller's battalions at Hagaru, another at Koto-ri, and the third at Chinhung-ni at the bottom of [Funchilin] Pass. They were there to guard our main supply route." Thus on November 26, Smith accomplished what he had been striving to do ever since the Wonsan landing a month earlier: concentrate the 1st Marine Division. This concentration was, as Smith said later, "very opportune" in view of what was about to happen. With two regiments at Yudam-ni, a battalion at Hagaru, a battalion at Koto, and a battalion at Chinhung-ni, the division had been pulled together into a tactical zone that could be traversed from end to end by jeep in one hour.

Colonel Alpha Bowser: "Even so, we were now at the end of a long, cold, snow-covered limb. The limb was sixty-five to seventy-five miles long, depending on where you started to measure."

The assistant division commander, Brigadier General Edward Craig, was fretful over the distance separating the 5th and 7th Marines. Though closer than they had been for weeks, the two regiments were still separated by an arm of the reservoir. Once again, X Corps seemed perversely intent on arranging it so that the two forwardmost Marine regiments could not support each other in case of trouble; and Craig expected trouble. "I was very jittery about the situation up there. When I spoke with General Smith about it, all he said was, 'It's what the Army wants.' The whole setup looked bad to me."

The first of the U.S. Army units to arrive on the east shore of the reservoir—relieving the 5th Marines of tactical responsibilities there—was Lt. Col. Don Faith's First Battalion, 32nd Infantry, 7th

Infantry Division. General David Barr's division as a whole was in shaky condition. The opening of the war had caught the unit so understrength that it was deemed necessary to impress 8,000 Korean civilians to fill out the ranks. (In addition, the division was stripped of 1,000 corporals and sergeants to strengthen two other Army divisions.) These shanghaied Koreans, Barr wrote later, were essentially young men who were forced to take part in combat operations without any training or preparation. He described them as "stunned, confused, and exhausted." General Barr himself was considered inept; it was widely believed that the assistant division commander, Brigadier General Henry Hodes, did much of the outfit's generaling.

Just before noon on the twenty-sixth, Hodes visited Lt. Col. Faith's command post, bringing some good news: the Third Battalion of the regiment, under Lt. Col. William Reilly, and most of the Fifty-seventh Field Artillery Battalion under Lt. Col. Ray Embree, were on their way up the mountain and would soon join forces with him. Colonel Allan D. MacLean, the regimental commander, would take charge of the composite force.

Attached to Faith's battalion was a Marine officer, Captain Edward Stamford, commanding a three-man team trained to call down naval gunfire and air strikes, using techniques the Marines had developed in the Pacific and had brought to a fine art in Korea. Their presence with the Army unit would prove a blessing.

Stamford: "There wasn't much going on at the time. After I got my three enlisted men settled in, east of the reservoir, Father Brunert and I—he was the Catholic chaplain—drove back to Hagaru and attended mass, and afterward we looked up a friend, Father Otto Sporrer, the 11th Marines chaplain. I remember how Father Sporrer resented it that the Marines had been ordered to go so far inland. He called it 'a misuse of a trained amphibious force.' "

After conferring with Faith, Lt. Col. Raymond Murray, commanding the 5th Marines, drove back to Hagaru and then headed northwest in the direction of Yudam-ni, the ultimate destination of his regiment. Murray: "It didn't take on meaning until later, but I had an interesting sighting on that ride. At the top of Toktong Pass, halfway between Hagaru and Yudam-ni, I spotted an Asian man sitting among an outcropping of rocks high above, watching the road. He was like a statue up there—didn't move a muscle, even though it was bitterly cold. He couldn't have been there for any reason but to gather intelligence for the enemy."

General Smith: "By the twenty-sixth all elements of the 5th Marines had been relieved east of the reservoir by troops of the Army's 31st Infantry Regiment. These units had been moved north piecemeal and in great haste. In their hurried movement they had brought little tentage and few stoves with them. Moreover, many of the men were not properly outfitted with cold-weather clothing and equipment." Smith recorded in his aide-mémoire that the Army commanders asked him for winter gear. "These poor devils from the 31st and 32nd Infantry came to me to get liners for their parkas and other gear. 'Look,' I said, 'we only have one parka per man ourselves.' "

On Saturday morning, November 25, the temperature at Chinhung-ni, at the bottom of the mountain, had reached eight degrees below zero. At Yudam-ni, thirty-five miles uproad, it was several degrees colder.

Over on the western front, Eighth Army was advancing ahead of schedule, putting miles of conquered territory behind it. So confident were General Walton Walker and his lieutenants that his Army divisions were sent down the roads without flankers and many of the forward-echelon units were allowed to move beyond the range of their artillery.

The Chinese made their move around sundown, unleashing a sudden attack that virtually destroyed the Republic of Korea II Corps and uncovered the central core of Walker's army. The Chinese then struck Major General Laurence Keiser's 2nd Infantry Division, which lost over 4,000 men and most of its artillery before the day was over. MacArthur's grand offensive was thus shut down before the Marines' attack westward from Yudam-ni had been launched.

The Marine division's mission, it will be recalled, was to act as an arm of the giant pincers that was expected to trap large numbers of enemy troops. From the X Corps viewpoint it was considered imperative that the Marines cross the Taebeks rapidly to relieve the pressure on Walker's right flank by drawing Chinese units into battle; but those elements of Walker's army that would have benefited by the Marines' presence were even now fleeing southward in disorder. As General Smith explained later in his pokerfaced way, "In an envelopment, the holding force is required to hold until the enveloping force can carry home its attack. In this case the holding force [Eighth Army] began its withdrawal on November 25, and by the time the enveloping force [1st Marine Division] attacked on November 27, the Eighth Army was in full retreat. Therefore the attack by the 1st Marine Division on November 27 could have no effect on the fortunes of the Eighth Army, and the division itself was to become involved in a fight for its life against a Chinese army group separate and distinct from the Chinese Communist Forces following up the retreat of Eighth Army."

It wasn't until Sunday evening, the twenty-sixth, that Almond himself received the shocking news that the left wing of MacArthur's grand offensive had been shattered and that Eighth Army's retreat was threatening to turn into a rout. Neither Almond nor any member of the X Corps staff bothered to pass word of the disaster to the Marines.

19.

GENERAL SMITH ARRIVED AT Yudam-ni by helicopter early on the morning of the twenty-sixth. Lt. Col. Raymond Davis happened to be near the landing spot and experienced a moment of severe apprehension when he saw the aircraft "drop like a stone the last ten feet." Neither Smith nor the pilot were injured, just shaken up. Smith nodded to Davis and asked, in his courteous way, for directions to Colonel Litzenberg's command post.

"Right over there, General. Are you all right?"

Smith said "Fine" and strode off toward the windblown tents.

All we know about Smith's conference with Litzenberg is that he told the regimental commander that Murray's 5th Marines would be taking over the lead in the march to the west, a development the aggressive Litzenberg probably wasn't happy to hear.

The weather was clear and cold when Smith headed back to Hungnam. From his airborne vantage he scanned the terrain below but saw no sign of enemy activity on the snow-clad slopes.

In response to a growing number of civilian reports, Litzenberg decided to send a strong patrol southwest of Yudam-ni. On the morning of the twenty-sixth, 1st Lt. Eugenous Hovatter's Able Company, 7th, set forth, its mission to determine the strength, disposition, and attitude of the enemy. The plan was to head southwest along the ridge for three or four thousand yards, then drop down the slope and return to Yudam-ni by the valley route.

It had snowed the night before, and movement along the ridge was hard going. The Marines sensed that they were under constant observation. Late in the afternoon Lt. Frank Mitchell started moving ahead too fast, forcing the rest of the company to scramble to catch up. All this made too much noise, so Hovatter took off on his own to tell the platoon leader to slow down. Dusk was coming on by the time he arrived. Mitchell and his point fire team had just reached the end of a terrain finger leading down from the ridge, overlooking a cluster of houses noted on the map as Hangsan-ni. A moment later the point man sent word that several strangers— that was the word he used—were moving in and out of the huts, talking with each other and showing no inclination to fight. He thought they might be Chinese. Accompanied by the interpreter, Hovatter climbed down the slope with the intention of conversing with the "strangers," who appeared to be unarmed.

Hovatter asked the interpreter if they were Chinese.

"Yes, Chinese soldier."

Lt. Hovatter: "I told him to tell them I wanted to climb all the way down to converse with them but I needed assurance they would hold their fire. There was an interchange in Chinese and Kim said they understood my request and would hold their fire. We then continued downslope, covered by the weapons of the point fire team. Before we got to the bottom, all hell broke loose— heavy automatic and rifle fire. Kim and I hit the deck and saw rounds shearing off the branches of the trees around us. Then Kim was hit. Under covering fire I was able to drag him a few yards up the slope." Corporal Jewel Coquat, the fire team leader, went down, and so did his BAR man.

In the confusion and growing darkness Corporal Walter O'Day got separated from his squad. Pulling back, the Marines left these three down the slope—temporarily, they assumed. It had turned into a hot fight, with muzzle flashes winking in the dusk in all directions. Hovatter saw Lt. Mitchell spring forward, scoop up the fallen BAR man's weapon and grenades, and launch a one-man rescue attempt. Staff Sergeant Jesse Swafford: "Mitch was a human dynamo. He fired the BAR until he was out of ammo, then tossed a couple of grenades before he got cut down by a burst of burp-gun fire. The son of a bitch was magnificent."

PFC Timmy Killeen heard someone say, "What the hell's wrong with Mitch?"

No one wanted to admit that Lt. Frank Mitchell was dead. Lt. William Davis, Able Company mortarman, was perhaps the only one not surprised to learn about Mitchell's death. The two had shared a compartment aboard an LST between Inchon and Won-san, and during the voyage Mitchell had confided in Davis his pre-monition of death in North Korea.

Though his platoon leaders wanted to remain in the area and recover the bodies early the next morning, Hovatter feared that his wounded would not survive the night. Killeen: "It was a clear, starlit night, like a Christmas-card scene with the mountains and the evergreens and the snow. But that wind was a killer."

Hovatter: "Marines have always prided themselves on their extreme efforts to retrieve their dead and wounded, so it was agonizing to have to leave Mitch and Coquat and O'Day out there under the stars; but to have gotten them out would have resulted in additional casualties and loss of life, and I decided it would be just plain dumb. Of course we intended to come back for them the following day. There was no question of that."

As night fell on the twenty-sixth, the temperature once again dropped below zero degrees Fahrenheit. The north wind howled across the frozen lake, lashing Marines and soldiers alike on the shore. Just west of Yudam-ni, Lt. Col. Harold Roise, commanding the Second Battalion, 5th Marines, met with his three company commanders inside the flapping walls of the blackout tent to work out the plan for tomorrow's march to the west. Captains Samuel Smith, Uel Peters, and Samuel Jaskilka learned that the move would begin at 0800, 2/5 moving through Litzenberg's lines to take over the division point. 1st Lt. Wayne Richards's platoon of engineers would support the advance, along with a light spotter plane from the Air Wing.

Dr. Henry Litvin, battalion surgeon, was unaware that 2/5 was about to become the vanguard of the division. "I was profoundly bewildered. Hadn't a clue where we were or where we were going. All I knew was that this place was a lot bleaker-looking than the place we had come from. I was so preoccupied that I didn't even notice this huge flat expanse of ice off to the east. Reservoir? What reservoir? My military ignorance was profound. It wasn't because I was dumb or even naive. It was because I had had no military training at all!

"On our way to the landing at Inchon a supply sergeant had handed me a carbine, a bayonet, and a couple of loaded magazines. I stared at these metallic, plastic, wooden objects for a few seconds and then handed them back, making a little joke about how I wouldn't know which end to point at the enemy. He made me take a .45-caliber pistol and a holster and showed me which end to shoot with. The Marines were very patient with me. Early the next morning I happened to notice a good deal of unpleasant noise going on outside. When I climbed the ladder and took a look, what greeted my eyes was the Inchon landing.

" 'Doc, you're in the eighth wave.'

" 'Holy cow!'

"I tried to keep that in mind, but I didn't know what to do about it except to shuffle slowly along the passageway with the heavily laden Marine infantrymen. I knew I was attached to Lt. Col. Roise's battalion, but so far the only human being who had come into focus was Lt. Karle Seydel, whom I had become acquainted with on the voyage across the Pacific. He was a machine-gun officer in Dog Company, a big guy with a mustache. He recognized how bewildered I was and sort of took me under his wing. He was a well-educated and cultured young man, and his concern over my welfare meant a good deal to me.

"So there I was, staggering along the passageway under this heavy pack that Karle Seydel had rolled for me, when I realized I was expected to climb down the net over the ship's side into a landing craft that was bobbing in the water far below. I was terribly soft, you understand. I had received no physical training at all.

" 'Over the side, Doc.'

"Over I went. Lt. Seydel climbed down the net beside me, coaching me all the way. I found myself clutching one rung with both hands, my feet on the next rung, the rest of me hanging down like a sack of potatoes.

" 'Hang on tight with both hands,' he said.

" 'I *am*, I *am*.'

" 'Now pull your right foot straight back about six inches. . . . That's good, Doc. Now straighten out your right leg slowly. . . . Fine. Now put your right foot on one of the horizontal ropes.'

"My very first medical case ashore was a horrifying gaping wound in the upper thigh. In the heat of battle someone had tied on a tourniquet *below* the wound. As nervous and upset as I was, that upset me even more, but at least I was able to function. I learned fast by watching the corpsmen, especially Chief Corpsman Nunn, who was a World War II veteran. The noises of the battle tended to undo me. The first time the battleship opened up behind us I thought it was a freight train in the sky and found myself clawing the ground, trying to get under it. Corpsman Nunn said, 'Don't worry, Doc—that's outgoing.'

" 'Whew!'

"You can't imagine the difference between the aid station at Inchon and that gorgeous operating room at Philadelphia General where I did my internship. Corpsmen holding flashlights. Wounded men sprawled in the dirt. Nothing remotely sterile except the dressings and morphine. At least there was a rear I could send the wounded to. At the reservoir, after the Chinese surrounded us, there was no rear at all. The shocks were continual, it seemed. So many corpsmen were killed on the road to Seoul that the Navy had to fill in the slots with ships' corpsmen.

"There were many things about the Korean War I never got over, and one of them is this: Two very young men with blond hair reported for duty one night outside Uijongbu. They had come directly from one of the ships in the harbor. They asked me where I wanted them. I sent them to Fox Company, which was having heavy casualties at the time. The two of them—they were friends— headed straight up the road to Captain Uel Peters's command post, and they were dead before dawn.

"What a horrible thing . . . The two of them coming ashore like that to lend a hand and both snuffed out before they even got to see what Korea's mountains and villages and rice paddies looked like. I asked Corpsman Nunn to write down their names on a piece of paper. He handed it to me and I put it in my wallet. I still grieve for those two very young men with blond hair."

20.

20. UP AT YUDAM-NI THAT FIRST night, Lt. Col. Harold Roise's executive officer, Major John Hopkins, mentioned that it was his birthday. Doc Litvin impulsively reached into his bag and pulled out a two-ounce bottle of medicinal brandy and handed it over. The major, surprised and pleased, offered to split it with him, but Litvin declined the offer. Hopkins walked over to where Roise was standing, the colonel puffing as usual on a Camel. (Doc Litvin: "I admired Colonel Roise because he was calm and masterful. He never displayed anxiety, unless you count the chain-smoking; but he smoked even when there was nothing going on.") Hopkins poured half the brandy into a canteen cup and handed it over.

"What's this?"

"It's my birthday. Doc contributed some booze."

Roise took the cup and raised it. "To your health."

Hopkins raised the little glass bottle, gazed toward the forbidding mountain range to the west, and, referring to the next day's move toward Mupyong-ni, said, "To the longest fifty-five miles we'll ever march."

After dark on November 26, only one small and relatively powerless Marine outfit remained on the east side of the reservoir: Captain George King's A Company, 1st Engineer Battalion, was bivouacked at an abandoned sawmill settlement identified on the Japanese map as Sasu-ri. It was located two miles north of Hagaru, just in from the shoreline, in a relatively isolated position.

Fox Company, 7th Marines, was still at Hagaru. Lt. Larry Schmitt, the company's machine-gun officer, had set up a makeshift firing range west of the village to determine how well or ill the company's small arms functioned in subzero temperatures. "The M-1s worked fine, but the carbines failed to feed. We tried to fix this by stretching the operating-slide spring to give more force to the forward motion of the bolt. The machine guns, they were okay. The BARs, though, gave us some trouble, mostly failure to feed, which we attributed to crud in the magazines."

Things were quiet in Hagaru. Captain Benjamin Read's 105-mm artillery unit, How Battery, was bivouacked at the northern edge of town, waiting for its next assignment. At 1:45 A.M. the battery's gunnery sergeant, Elmer Walling, awakened Captain Read and suggested that he listen in on the line linking the gun crews. Sipping his rapidly cooling coffee, Captain Read listened in as PFC Stanley Lockowitz began: "This is broadcasting station H-O-W, deep in the wilds of Cold Korea. The *Mystery Voice* program is now on the air, sponsored by Lieutenant Wilbur Herndon's Tennessee Twist Chewing Tobacco. . . . But before we hear the Mystery Voice, PFC Bergman is going to favor us with a Christmas carol." Siert Bergman, a twenty-year-old Swede from Michigan, waited for the polite applause to subside, then sang "Silent Night." "And now," said Lockowitz, "the Mystery Voice." Changing timbre, he declared in a solemn drone that it was not a fit night out for man nor beast. The men in the gun pits were supposed to guess whose voice he was imitating.

"Harry Truman?" ventured someone from Number 3 section.

"That is incorrect."

Other guesses were made, all wrong, and Lockowitz offered a hint: "You shall all return, as *I shall return,* by Christmas." The hint was heavy and everyone knew it was General MacArthur, but the prize went to the man who said so first. "You have just won the grand prize," Lockowitz told him, "which is a one-hundred-five-mm howitzer with two rounds of white phosphorous and the opportunity to fire both rounds at the target of your choice. Good-bye and good luck." Relating the anecdote later, Read said it demonstrated how high the Marines' morale was just before the stuff hit the fan, despite the temperature and the wind and the growing menace of the Chinese presence. By now, at Yudam-ni, the premonition of a Chinese onfall was general.

After a brief snowfall, the temperature began to plunge. It would bottom out after midnight at twenty-five degrees below. The men on watch began to suffer greatly, and a rotation system was established, aimed at giving each Marine a few minutes warm-up time in a tent with a glowing stove. It was obvious by now that the weather was seriously affecting the performance of the troops, if not yet their morale. (Homer Litzenberg later estimated that a man lost two percent of his efficiency for every degree below zero. Thus when the thermometer reached twenty-five below, the troops were operating at roughly half power. In practical terms this meant it took twice as many men to perform routine tasks such as setting up warming tents.)

At dawn on November 27 the bottomland and slopes at Yudam-ni came alive with parka-clad Marines stamping their boots and clapping mittened hands to get the circulation going. Soon there were knots of men standing around small fires trying to thaw out their rations and their weapons. Despite the paralyzing cold, the built-in organizational energy of the Division began to uncoil. ("A Marine unit abhors stasis," Marine General Victor Krulak once observed.)

Roise's Second Battalion shoved off westward into the badlands at 0730. The terrain became more difficult a mile outside the village; the mountains were considerably higher than the Marines had encountered in any previous campaign. The spotter plane came tilting in, dropping a message tube onto the road. The container was brought to Captain Uel Peters, whose Fox Company had the lead.

Several roadblocks ahead. Appear unmanned.

The roadblocks, nine in number, were made of logs and boulders. Fox Company, slipping to the right, bypassed them easily, flowing across the low shoulder of Hill 1403, leaving the engineers to shove the piles aside with the bulldozer. With Peters now on the right, Roise sent Captain Samuel Smith's Dog Company to the left, keeping Jaskilka's Easy Company in reserve.

Fox Company was now approaching the foot of Sakkat Mountain, the highest prominence in the neighborhood. Visible along its eastern face, in tiers, was an arrangement of bunkered gun emplacements. Enemy fire was desultory at first, but soon there were signs that the Chinese were present in large numbers. The volume of fire increased steadily, and by noon it was apparent the Chinese were no longer interested in merely delaying the Americans but intended to halt their movement entirely. For the Chinese there would be no more falling back. Roise: "The situation overall didn't look good. I talked it over with Colonel Murray and he said, 'Okay, hold up for now. We'll make a new start in the morning.' "

It was 2:30 in the afternoon. 2/5 had advanced about a mile.

Once again, General Almond was going to be displeased with the Marines' progress on the road.

Roise: "As far as I'm concerned it was divine intervention that kept us from going very far that day. Just imagine what would have happened if we had gone another mile or two into those mountains."

A PFC named Robert Johnson was at the very point of the division when the march was called off. He had led the column between two hills that were under Marine control: Hill 1426 on the left, Hill 1403 on the right, each manned by one of Lt. Col. William Harris's companies. In front of Johnson now was a frozen stream and a stone bridge, with Sakkat looming in the background. No one realized it yet, but for the 1st Marine Division the stone bridge and frozen stream represented the end of the line.

Lt. Chew-Een Lee was nearing exhaustion as he led Baker/7 onto Hill 1276, overlooking Yudam-ni from the south. His arm hurt, his knee was giving him trouble, he had a bad cold; all in all he was feeling rotten. Lee: "I don't usually acknowledge sickness of any kind, but Captain Wilcox could see the condition I was in and he ordered me to take the day off." Thus he missed out on the Baker Company patrol sent out to locate and bring back Able Company's three corpses.

About three miles down the road, southeast of Yudam-ni, the patrol turned into a small side valley and moved west for an hour. Lt. Joseph Owen was relying as usual on the extraordinary eyesight of his runner, Corporal Robert Kelly. Sure enough, Kelly spotted the Chinese on the skyline before anyone else.

"Where?"

Kelly pointed. "Man, there's a mess of 'em," he said. They were all in white, standing on a ridgeline about five hundred yards away. "See 'em?"

"I see 'em. Go tell the captain, Kelly."

When Kelly pointed them out to the company commander, all Wilcox said was, "Go back and tell Owen to keep moving."

In their white uniforms they blended with the snow. As the patrol moved, the angle changed, and other groups came into focus. One group, halfway up the slope, was having a meal, working their chopsticks as the Marines filed by.

PFC James Keegan: "It was obvious there was going to be big

trouble. Captain Wilcox took us to high ground, where we could defend ourselves better. On the way up I saw two officers with white capes standing on the next ridgeline, and it was just after that that the Chinese opened up. I can remember the sound of it to this day, the way the bullets twanged off the rocks all around us."

Sergeant Sherman Richter: "Once a firefight begins, you stop thinking and just do. Your mind sort of goes berserk. What other explanation is there for the way I kept pumping round after round into people I knew were dead as a doornail?"

Lt. Joseph Owen: "The gooks came in close, and we began to take hits. In a situation like this, when you're far from base, casualties are a compound problem: you lose manpower over and above the wounded man himself because it takes four people to carry a loaded stretcher in mountain country. By this time we were seriously pinned down and I was getting tense. I never went into a firefight without feeling these stabs of terror flashing around my gut."

Owen's mortar crew had one of the tubes set up by then and got a round off at a maneuvering element coming across a sloping field off to the south. Owen watched the tail-finned round climb slowly into the sky and come plummeting down into the enemy's midst. A perfect shot—except that it was a dud. Owen: "Sometimes you could spot duds beforehand by the green crud on the metal, which indicated they had been improperly stored by the Army supply pogues. Fuckin' doggies again! Couldn't even take care of their gear in Japan, which is where most of our ammo came from. After a while we realized that the gooks had done a complete encirclement on us. Lt. Hank Kiser and me happened to be side by side at this point, and we took vows of perpetual goodness. The gooks kept coming in closer, then veering away, and finally it just annoyed the hell out of me. By this time I had taken an intense dislike to the platoon commander who was leading the assault. Instead of shooting him, I decided to chase the bastard."

Owen, six and a half feet tall, sprouting several days' growth of beard, reared up out of the snow and advanced menacingly, brandishing his bayonet-tipped carbine. Owen's men shot the Chinese officer first. (Owen: "It was a dumb move on my part, but I didn't care.")

Captain Wilcox was struck down by a bullet in the jaw. In considerable pain, able to walk but not talk, he turned over command of Baker Company to his executive officer, Lt. Joseph Kurcaba.

"We gotta get the hell outta here," said Kurcaba.

First he set up a tight perimeter on the ridge, then informed his men that they were going to break out as soon as it got dark. Teams of four were organized to carry the wounded. Able Company's left-behind dead—Lt. Frank Mitchell, Corporal Jewel Coquat, Corporal Walter O'Day—had not been seen during the action; the situation was so dire that a search was never really undertaken.

PFC James Veeder: "We did a lot of praying."

PFC Joseph Hedrick, Lt. Kurcaba's radio operator, spotted a couple of Corsairs and used his ground-to-air radio to call them in. "Any aircraft," he called. "Any aircraft."

One of the pilots came on. "This is Lovelace." They were returning from a mission up around Yudam-ni and had some fifty-caliber ammo left. PFC Veeder: "Next thing you know, the snow and dirt off to our left was being churned up as the lead Corsair zeroed in on us. It was growing dark by now and the muzzle flashes were like a string of flashbulbs. I realized with a sickening feeling that the two pilots thought *we* were the gooks. They went around for a second pass, and that's when I witnessed the bravest act I saw during the campaign: PFC Sam Rice stood up and waved an air panel, signaling to the pilots that we were fellow Marines. There was just enough light left in the sky for them to see him, and that saved our ass."

Baker Company made a break for it as soon as it was dark, but the Chinese expected the move and opened up anew. Owen: "It was like having a big swarm of hornets following you whichever direction you turned. After we had moved east for an hour, we saw lights straight ahead. We were still three miles south of Yudam-ni, and at first we couldn't figure out what was going on; but they turned out to be headlights."

It was Lt. Col. Davis with some jeep ambulances. He had asked the drivers to turn on their lights to guide Baker Company down to the road. Davis had brought Captain John Morris's Charlie Company with him, in case a rescue force was needed.

Owen: "We didn't need rescuing. It turned out that it was Hard-luck Charlie Company that needed the rescuing—but that comes later in the story."

A convoy of trucks now rounded the bend up ahead, rolling south from Yudam-ni. The hollow booming sound they made on the rutted road identified them as empties. Colonel Davis stood in the middle of the road and flagged down the lead vehicle, bringing the convoy to a halt. The wounded Marines were loaded aboard and the convoy resumed its fourteen-mile journey to Hagaru. It was the last convoy out of Yudam-ni, before the stuff hit the fan.

Lt. Kurcaba's bedraggled Baker/7 returned to its perch on Hill 1276, while Morris's Charlie Company settled into its new position three miles south of Yudam-ni, assigned by Litzenberg to guard a lonely stretch of the main supply route. (The position, Hill 1419, was dubbed Turkey Hill because of the vast litter of turkey bones deposited there on Thanksgiving Day.) What no one understood yet was that the Chinese had followed Baker/7 most of the way back to the road and were now poised to fall on Morris's under-strength company. The fragmentation and isolation of the Marine division was about to begin.

21.

TWO OF RANDOLPH LOCK-
wood's three rifle companies—Easy/7 and Dog/7—had reached
Yudam-ni without incident. Colonel Litzenberg was not happy to
learn that the battalion commander himself was still in Hagaru
with Fox/7 as well as his Weapons and Headquarters Companies.
Summoning the two newly arrived company commanders, he told
them they would be operating under Lt. Col. Davis's command
until Lockwood showed up. Davis, now responsible for five rifle
companies, immediately sent Captain Walter Phillips's Easy/7 and
Captain Milton Hull's Dog/7 to occupy two adjoining hills that
overlooked the village from the north and northeast: Hill 1282 and
Hill 1240.

PFC George Crotts, Dog/7: "They strung us out on top of a
prominence where we could see the reservoir off to the right front,
looking like a gigantic skating pond. On the lakeshore you could
see the blackened ruins of a hamlet. Word was passed at sundown
that a combat patrol was going to investigate those ruins tomorrow
because of some kind of furtive activity down there. November 27
was a day of major fuckups as far as I was concerned. First off,
the guy who was supposed to wake me up didn't do a very good
job of it, and by the time the patrol was saddled up and moving I
was still half-asleep, all garbage-mouthed and needing a cup of
coffee. Worse, Captain Hull saw me jogging to catch up with the
tail of the patrol and yelled at me to get my ass in gear."

After the eighty-five-man patrol had descended the hill, word
came to the command post on 1240 that one of the platoon commanders, Lt. Paul Mullaney, was to be relieved and sent to division
headquarters for Stateside processing. (The personnel section in
Hungnam had just discovered that the lieutenant had two Purple
Hearts; division policy was that a second Heart exempted you from

front-line duty.) The trouble was, Mullaney's platoon was leading the patrol and was already approaching the ruins of the hamlet at the edge of the reservoir. Captain Hull decided to withhold the order from division for the moment.

PFC Alfred Bradshaw, Dog Company: "This was some gorgeous country, with the steep hills and snow and all. I was enjoying the scenery when all of a sudden several Chinese soldiers in white appeared on my right about twenty yards away. Their rifles were slung and they looked like they were ready to call it quits. It was as if we had run into each other by mistake and they didn't care to fight it out. I gestured the one nearest me to hand over his rifle, but each time I took a step in his direction he would back up. We stared into each other's eyes, not wanting to break eye contact, and after a few seconds I figured out what was going on: he was trying to get me to follow him. So I stopped. Suddenly shooting broke out nearby and I automatically joined in, and one of the gooks I shot was this fellow who had been trying to lure me away from the column. After that, the shooting got bigger, and next there were Chinese aiming at us from the ridgeline. I saw a six-man party creeping along our flank, none of them noticing me, and so I held my fire until they were out in the open. Me and two other Marines cut loose at the same second and down they went."

PFC Crotts: "After the firing ceased, the odor of ozone and sulfur hung heavy in the air. It was as if both sides were taking a break. . . . There are times when the only thing you want is a smoke. I hadn't had my breakfast and I hadn't had my morning smoke. Never mind that the company was about to be wiped out; a cigarette was more important. I dug the crumpled pack out of my inner clothing—a major task in that weather with all those layers—but I couldn't find the book of matches. I yelled over to the nearest Marine and he threw me his, but it landed short by about three yards. I crawled over, snatched them out of the snow, and jumped back. There was the crack of a distant rifle and this other Marine—his name was Neal—cried out, 'Oh, my God, I'm hit.' I don't know if that round was intended for me or him, but I felt relief and guilt at the same time. I couldn't help wondering if Neal got hit because I needed a light. He was hit through both calves, no bones involved. But his fighting days were over.

"A bit later the volume of fire drove me and two others to seek shelter behind a cluster of charred farm buildings. Captain Hull was storming around, rallying the troops, and naturally he had to find us skulking in the lee of this little shack.

" 'Who the hell do *you* belong to?'

" 'We're attached to Lieutenant Thompson's platoon, sir.'

" 'Well, what the hell are you doing down *here,* then?'

"Me and the other two guys had considered ourselves officially pinned down up until then, so none of us could think of a reasonable way to answer his question. *He* wasn't pinned down. He was stalking back and forth like Stonewall Jackson at Bull Run; so how could *we* be pinned down?

" 'Get your sorry asses up that hill,' he shouted above the din. '*That's* where Third Platoon is.'

"So we jumped up. I grabbed my rifle and two boxes of ammo and headed out with the other two; but the fire was even heavier than before, and there was no question that we would've been killed if we hadn't turned around and sprinted back behind the barn again. Captain Hull had stomped away all pissed off at us; and now, so help me, the three of us came under his terrible gaze yet again. The man definitely had eyes in the back of his head. Even though forty-five years have gone by, I still cringe when I recall what happened next. He yanked the .45 out of his holster and showed us the muzzle. 'You have a simple choice,' he shouted. 'Either you get your asses shot off on the slope, or your company commander is going to blow your heads off right here and now.' He was one mean and glorious bastard, that Captain Hull.

"We raced up that slope, heading for a line of trees at the top, and set the gun up, and began hosing down gooks. The hardest part was seeing Lieutenant Thomas Thompson sprawled on his back only a few feet away. It shocked me to see him like that, and I had trouble taking it in; I kept looking over at him. He was a real neat guy, easygoing but firm. You've probably heard about the average life span of a Marine lieutenant in combat. I forget what it is, but it's short. They come and they go, these lieutenants. It's part of the deal when you get your commission.

"We had a ringside seat to Lieutenant Mullaney's charge. He stepped up to the crest, waved his carbine over his head, and shouted, 'Let's go, Marines.' Those of us lucky enough to stay behind poured covering fire into the Chinese positions, keeping some of their heads down. I saw Lieutenant Mullaney get hit and drop. This was his third hit in sixty days, but once again he survived to tell the tale. I saw a photo of him later in a Stateside hospital."

PFC Al Bradshaw: "I spotted a gook machine gunner about a hundred and fifty yards away. The gun was a British Lewis type, with the drum mounted horizontal on top. When Sergeant Lane crawled up I told him, 'I can see this guy but he hasn't seen me yet.'

" 'What guy?'

" 'The fuckin' gook gunner!'

"Sergeant Lane couldn't see him from where he was. 'Okay, Bradshaw, can you still see him?'

"The gook wasn't firing in our general direction, so I stuck my head up and there he was. 'Yeah, I can still see him.'

" 'Okay,' says Lane. 'Then *shoot* the son of a bitch.'

"So like they taught us at the rifle range, I took a deep breath and held it, sighted in, froze, and squeezed the trigger slowly. It was an easy shot. The result was spectacular: the gook toppled over, thrashing, knocking over the gun, and did a big end-over-end down the slope. It was very satisfying, especially with my squad leader watching. I puckered up my chapped lips and whistled 'The Marines' Hymn,' which got a big smile out of Sergeant Lane."

Captain Hull leapfrogged his platoons back to Hill 1240, the Chinese following them part of the way. Hull had sixteen casualties, and it was difficult carrying them with the enemy on their tail. The sun had set behind Sakkat-san by the time the Marines had staggered back to their holes atop 1240. Everyone was tired and hungry—and shocked at the fight the Chinese had put up at the abandoned hamlet.

PFC Crotts: "As it was getting dark there was a mail call, which made the day a little less terrible. I was still pumping adrenaline because of all the excitement and couldn't stop babbling. PFC Bill Russell was trying to read a letter from home in the twilight and I kept interrupting, reliving the harrowing events of the patrol. Finally he turned and said, 'Stop being an asshole, will ya?'

" 'Huh?'

" 'Shut the fuck up, Crotts. Can't you see I'm trying to read my letter?'

"Pretty soon we had a fire going. We learned later that the order had been passed to douse all fires and go on the alert, but once again we didn't get the word. After we ate, we straightened up our gear for the night and arranged our ammo where we could grab it fast. I took off my shoe-pacs and yanked out my frozen socks and tried to shake out the ice-clusters but ended up stuffing them under my armpits, which was a good way to thaw them but also a good way to make yourself colder than you already were.

"The schedule called for two-hour watches. I was the only one in the team with a wristwatch. The guy in the first slot asked to borrow it and I handed it over. Then I crawled into the bag and lay on my back and gazed at the stars. I can't say I *knew* we were going to have hostile company that evening, but the way those Chinese followed us was pretty scary, and I had dreams about it."

Half a mile west of 1240, Captain Walter Phillips's Easy Company, 7th Marines, was settling down atop Hill 1282. Lt. John Yancey: "We had the village of Yudam-ni to our back and a series of ridges ahead of us. Nobody saw any shambos during the day but we all knew they were out there."

At nightfall a machine gunner on the right detected movement in front of his position, threw a grenade, and heard moaning. After the moans died out, the gunner investigated with a flashlight and found the still-warm body of a Chinese officer equipped with a surveying instrument called an alidade, a plotting board, and a large tape measure. In his clothing the Marines found papers identifying him as a member of the 79th Chinese Communist Division. Yancey: "One of my runners, Rick Marron, asked me what it all meant. I told him it meant the enemy didn't yet know we were on that hill and they were trying to plot it for mortar concentrations."

Lockwood's third rifle company, Fox/7, was seven miles down the road, occupying a strong position in Toktong Pass. Captain William Barber had taken command of the unit only a few days earlier. A former enlisted man from Kentucky, he was a veteran of the World War II battle of Iwo Jima, where he commanded a platoon and was twice wounded.

Lt. Lawrence Schmitt: "He showed up fresh from Japan in starched and pressed dungarees. The rest of us, we all looked like shit from being on the move for the past few weeks." Barber won few admirers with his coming-on-board speech. One statement in particular annoyed the men: "I may not know much about strategy, but I know a lot about tactics, and frankly I'm a hell of a good infantry officer."

Lt. Col. Lockwood and Captain Barber drove north in the early afternoon of the twenty-seventh, with orders from Litzenberg to find a suitable location for guarding the main supply route as it wound through Toktong Pass. The men of Fox Company stood waiting in the wind beside the half-completed airstrip in Hagaru as the two officers negotiated the narrow road in the battalion commander's jeep. It was Barber who recognized the good defensive position on the shoulder of Toktong-san, the towering mountain that dominated the pass.

"Right here looks pretty good to me, Colonel."

Lockwood, deferring to the combat veteran, pulled over. (Lockwood himself had been stationed at Pearl Harbor on December 7, 1941, but had experienced no infantry combat.) Leaving the idling jeep, the two officers climbed the slope and looked around. Barber noticed a terrain saddle that stretched about nine hundred yards toward Toktong-san, its slopes falling away sharply on both sides.

"If they come," he said, "they'll come that way."

Lockwood agreed that it was the most likely approach.

According to the map, the position was a mile closer to Hagaru than to Yudam-ni. Lockwood recalls: "This was very much to Fox Company's advantage, for it allowed artillery support from Hagaru." If the position had been a quarter mile further north, Fox would have been out of range of How Battery, 11th Marines, whose guns were sited on flat ground east of the Changjin River, about twelve hundred yards north of the long concrete bridge leading into town.

"Let's go," said Lockwood. It was mid-afternoon and Fox Company was still seven miles away.

"Sir, I'd like to stay here and study the terrain and think about where to put my rifle platoons and supporting units."

Reluctantly, Lockwood agreed to leave Captain Barber alone on the hill. Lockwood: "When I climbed back down to the road, a warrant officer I knew came along and pulled over for a chat. We discussed the Korean civilians and how they had been behaving differently toward the Marines in the past day or two. Before, they had asked for food, and the children didn't hesitate to beg for candy. But now the children had disappeared and the rare civilian we saw did his best to avoid contact with us. We discussed another phenomenon with the same theme: the abundant game in the region, particularly the deer, were spooked and could be seen bounding down from the heights as though driven. We agreed these were ominous signs."

After Lockwood headed south, Captain Barber walked back and forth over the position, planning his defense. It is likely that he was observed at this by Chinese soldiers; the hills were alive with them by now. For the moment Barber was safe, since the road below was close and heavy with traffic. Back in Hagaru, Lockwood was having little success rounding up transportation for Fox Company. 1st Lt. Robert McCarthy: "The prospect of a seven-mile uphill march, departing Hagaru after 1500, caused some concern within the company. Finally, 2nd Lt. Donald Campbell, an artillery forward observer attached to Fox, brought the welcome news that Captain Benjamin Read, commanding How Battery, was sending his nine trucks over. The convoy pulled out shortly, twenty-five to twenty-seven Marines in each truck with weapons, packs, sleeping bags, rations, and ammunition." Captain Read was to prove himself a staunch friend of Fox Company. His generosity with the battery's trucks was not the last of his services to Barber and his men.

PFC Richard Grogan: "It was a miserable trip. It was already growing dusky when we reached our destination, and all I could see was a couple of abandoned shacks beside the road and a small spring that was still flowing despite the below-zero temperature."

Captain William Barber: "One thing I mulled over a long time: whether or not to give the order to dig in. Digging in would be a tough job. The ground was frozen and the men were tired. I told myself, To hell with it; we're not going to get any action tonight; but at the last minute I changed my mind. Did those people ever bitch!"

The troops hacked and chipped away with their entrenching tools, certain it was a waste of time and effort. Today Barber doesn't hesitate to say that Fox Company, 7th Marines, would have been annihilated that night if he had not given the order to dig in. "By any rationale, we couldn't have survived."

The company was settled in by 9 P.M., half the men asleep in their heavy down bags. The landscape was aglow in the silvery light of the moon. The wind whipped the small bushes and short pines on the slope, masking the sound of stealthy movement as Chinese formations drew nearer.

The last convoy came rattling down the road an hour later, headlights ablaze; then silence descended on Toktong Pass.

22.

THE MARINES HAD managed to achieve a significant degree of concentration, the Army troops of David Barr's 7th Infantry Division were still scattered, many of the units out of touch with one another. As evening fell on the twenty-seventh, elements of the 31st Regimental Combat Team were strewn along the road from Hagaru northward on the east shore of the Chosin Reservoir.

PFC Edward R. Arney, G Company, 31st Regiment, 7th Infantry Division: "Everything was a mess. I don't think anyone knew where they were going. All I know is I followed the asshole in front of me but I didn't know where it was leading me. I only knew that this countryside was like the end of the world."

The regimental commander, Colonel Allan Maclean, had no idea where his Second Battalion was. This was the second unit over which he had lost control that day. One of the enduring mysteries of the Chosin Reservoir campaign revolves around the 31st Infantry's Intelligence and Reconnaissance Platoon. Led by Lt. Richard Coke, this small unit, riding in jeeps with mounted fifty-calibre machine guns, was sent by Maclean in a northeasterly direction to establish an outpost near the Pungnyuri River, which flowed into the reservoir from the east. Maclean received not a single report from Coke, neither by radio nor runner. To say that the I & R Platoon was "wiped out" would not be strictly accurate, since two of its members, Sergeant James Arie and PFC Roy Shiraga, turned up a few days later in Hagaru; but as a military entity the unit was obliterated. The attack must have been sudden and overwhelming, because neither Coke nor his radio operator had time to contact anyone and ask for help. From Maclean's point of view the I & R Platoon had simply vanished.

Eight Chinese divisions, totaling 60,000 men, had by now left their places of concealment—forests, mine shafts, tunnels, villages—

to converge on the bleak, snow-covered hills that rise above the reservoir. Unseen and unheard, the endless columns wound through valleys and over mountain trails, heading toward Yudam-ni and Hagaru. According to historian Roy Appleman, the march discipline of the Chinese soldier in this campaign equaled that of any other army in history. The day's move ordinarily began at 8 P.M. and ended at 3 A.M. Security measures against air attack were completed by dawn, with every soldier concealed. During daylight hours the only movement was that of small patrols ranging ahead to select the bivouac for the following night.

Tactically the Chinese had several advantages, including surprise. (It was true that every Marine at Yudam-ni knew there were Chinese about, but no one suspected that they numbered in the thousands or that the two Marine regiments were being surrounded.) Unencumbered with tanks, trucks, heavy artillery, or bulldozers, the Chinese also held the advantage of mobility. Their greatest advantage was, of course, their sheer numbers.

"To offset these odds," wrote General Smith later, "the outnumbered Marines would have to rely on superior firepower, command of the air, and another weapon called esprit."

While three of the eight Chinese divisions were making eleventh-hour preparations for the attack on the Marines at Yudam-ni, another division, the Eightieth, was preparing to seize Hagaru after moving down the eastern shore of the reservoir. In order to complete that march it would be necessary, however, to brush aside MacLean's unorganized force.

The morale of the Army troops was drastically below that of the Marines. One reason for that was the presence of the all but useless Korean augmentation troops, referred to as KATUSAs (Koreans Assigned to the U.S. Army). Lt. James Mortrude, a platoon leader in the Third Battalion, 31st Infantry, making his rounds soon after dark, recalls that the KATUSAS "were in their usual ostrich posture." He ordered them out of their holes and made them walk around with him to restore circulation and bring them, he hoped, to some degree of alertness. The GIs were all aware that their South Korean allies were sadly unprepared for battle and could not be relied on for support.

General Almond had shown up in Hagaru that afternoon and got an impromptu briefing from Litzenberg's executive officer, Lt. Col. Frederick Dowsett. The briefing consisted largely of an overview of the Marine positions and an account of how Roise's 2/5 had been stopped cold after a short westward advance.

"I already know all this," Almond interrupted. "Where's your intelligence officer?

"He's right here, sir." Dowsett introduced Captain Donald France.

"What's the latest information?"

Caught off guard, the young officer answered bluntly. "General, there's a shitload of Chinamen in those mountains."

That evening, back at his comfortable headquarters in Ham-hung, Almond scribbled a perfunctory entry in his diary: "November 27. The weather was bitterly cold throughout the day, particularly in the mountains and on the plateau surrounding the Chosin Lake." That was all.

Though the 5th and 7th Marines were operating side by side at Yudam-ni, there was no central authority over them on site, for Brigade General Edward Craig, assistant division commander, had departed Korea that afternoon, summoned to the bedside of his dying father in Texas. In his absence the regimental commanders applied common sense to the deployment of their battalions. Major Henry Woessner, operations officer, 7th Marines: "We would have preferred to hold hands in one tight perimeter, but that was impossible because of the lay of the land. Our two regiments were covering one hell of a big piece of real estate. Too broad to be defended in a continuous line, the valley was 'screened' by means of an intermittent perimeter. That was the best we could do."

During a late-afternoon conference with his officers, Captain Samuel Jaskilka was taking some good-natured joshing because he had just received orders transferring him to the States.

"Who in hell do *you* know?" asked Lt. Edwin Deptula.

"The Commandant and me are pals," said the Easy Company commander. "You didn't know that? Sure, he needs me at Headquarters."

The meeting broke up and the platoon leaders turned to rejoin their units. After taking a couple of steps, Lt. Deptula fell to the ground.

"Hey, Skipper."

"Yeah?"

"Guess what? I'm hit."

"Knock off the grab-ass," Jaskilka barked. "Don't pull a phony stunt like that."

"No, I'm really hit! Take a look."

Sure enough, a bullet had passed through Deptula's left calf. As he was being loaded, grinning, aboard a stretcher, he said, "See ya Stateside, Captain."

"You and me," Jaskilka complained, "we're going to miss all the fun."

PFC Chester Bair, U.S. Army, was a truck driver/mechanic assigned to the 32nd Heavy Tank Company. On the twenty-seventh he was sent to one of the Army positions east of the reservoir, where a work party of GIs began unloading ammunition from his truck. Bair noticed how tense the men were. "And that made *me* tense," he recalls. "I just wanted to get empty and bug outta there. In my eagerness I made a terrible mistake. I happened to see Colonel Faith's motor officer, Lieutenant Hugh May, and asked if it was okay to take off. He said no. . . . There would be a convoy leaving in the morning. 'I'll let you know when it makes up.' And that's how I got trapped in the trap by being too conscientious. I could have just driven down the mountain if I had kept my big flap shut!"

For the rest of the afternoon Bair pitched in, helping to get stalled trucks running. The vehicles had long since been winterized, but that didn't mean they would always start. "Ice in the fuel pumps caused lots of problems," Bair recalls. "We removed fuel-pump bowls from several vehicles, cleaned them, and replaced them. It was so cold your skin sometimes got stuck to the metal parts." Drivers had to run their engines periodically to prevent their freezing up; this increased the consumption of gasoline at a time when gasoline—and most everything else—was in short supply.

Like many Marines in the reservoir sector, Lt. Col. Olin Beall observed the Army contingents with a baleful eye. In his travels between Hungnam to Yudam-ni, the commander of the 1st Motor Transport Battalion had plenty of opportunity to observe the ways of the "doggies." According to his driver, PFC Ralph Milton, Colonel Beall was offended by the lack of organization, discipline, and overall sloppiness that prevailed. Ironically, the "doggies"—those who survived the campaign, that is—would soon regard the frowning Marine officer as their savior.

23.

LT. COL. HAROLD ROISE'S three rifle companies, along with Captain Leroy Cooke's How Company, 7th Marines, were settling down along the northwest quadrant of the intermittent perimeter at Yudam-ni, while Lt. Col. Robert Taplett's Third Battalion, 5th Marines, stood by in reserve between them and the village. Taplett expected to be ordered to commit his 900-man unit to the renewed westward attack in the morning; in the meantime his instructions were to bivouac where he was for the night. The hill to the immediate north of his position, he was told, was occupied by Captain Walter Phillips's Easy Company, 7th. Taplett doubted this; he could neither see nor hear any sign of life up there. At nightfall he climbed partway up the slope and shouted through cupped hands: "Hey! Are there any Marines up there? . . . Hello, up there! Anyone on the hill?"

Back in the communications tent a few minutes later, Taplett was talking by phone with a staff officer at the regimental command post. "They're up there," he was told. "Quit worrying."

The battalion commander then asked to speak with Colonel Murray.

"What is it, Tap?"

"I've got a bad feeling about this. My flank is wide open."

"Walt Phillips is holding the hill just north of you."

"I don't think so."

"All right, hold on a sec."

The regimental commander came back on the line two minutes later. "We're certain Easy Company is up there."

Taplett, an infantry officer of considerable experience and self-confidence, decided to honor his gut reaction by establishing an outpost partway up the slope. The outpost included a couple of heavy machine guns manned by an attached South Korean military police unit—a disciplined, dependable, Marine-trained outfit. Taplett's phone rang just before 10 P.M. Regiment was calling. Taplett was right; a mistake had been made. Phillips's Easy Company occupied 1282, which was half a mile to the east. The hill overlooking Taplett's Third Battalion was unoccupied, as he had said all along.

It was a night colder than any of them had ever experienced. Lt. John Yancey, Easy Company, 7th: "Yassir, it was frozen Chosin in the freezin' season. I had to growl at those kids to get themselves dug in. They were shivering with the cold, and they were footsore and bonetired and probably suffering from dietary deficiency, what with the C-ration diet. Tactically they were in good positions, because I had climbed down the forward slope a hundred feet or so and studied the crest of 1282 from down there, getting the shambo viewpoint on things. It was a good way to figure out where our automatic weapons ought to be, too. There was this one dead shambo on the slope, the officer with the alidade. I remember him now because of the way the slope looked later, when there were so many bodies you could hardly see the snow on the ground.

"After I assigned all the positions, I made myself a little campfire. I could make a fire real fast because I always carried kindling strapped to my pack, usually a busted-up ammo crate. Some of the kids wandered over after I got it blazing."

Corpsman Claypool: "The 'kids,' as he called them, enjoyed his light banter. He could be very funny, and he enjoyed making you laugh. He knew how to break up Captain Phillips with his farfetched silliness. I recall one time he expounded on the character, dimension, and location of hell, which he said was located in New Jersey, just across the river from Manhattan. Evidently he had passed through Jersey once and never got over it. Yancey was essentially a country fella from the Ozarks. His banter was always upbeat, and that last night around the fire he made those youngsters forget they needed a hot meal, that they were cold and scared and homesick."

Someone asked Yancey to recount the legendary tale about how he blew up the bank in Uijongbu—"I used too much C-3 and blew the front door out the back!"—and someone else asked him to tell the story of the nail factory at Yongdong-po. That was the time the platoon bivouacked in an abandoned factory and Yancey went out on a long beer-foraging patrol, and when he returned everything was different. "My God, there was bacon and eggs sizzling in a big frying pan," he said. "There was a whole pig roasting over a spit and several chickens on trays. Native ladies were washing laundry in tubs while others hung shirts and pants and socks and underwear on lines to dry. There were Marines walking around naked except for towels. And, worst of all, from the office upstairs came girlish laughter and squeals of delight.

" 'Staff Sergeant O'Toole, front and center!'

"Well, I accused my platoon sergeant of letting things go completely to hell in my absence. Didn't he understand that fraternizing with indigenous personnel was strictly forbidden? Didn't he know that requisitioning livestock and fowl was a no-no? Didn't he know it was bad public relations to force the locals to do our laundry? Not to mention—

" 'Sir,' says O'Toole, 'that ain't the way it happened.'

" 'What?'

" 'The men have paid for everything.'

" 'How? We haven't had a payday since—'

" 'We paid for it with the dough you stole—uh, confiscated—from the bank in Uijongbu.'

"Just then a naked Marine came over and held out a morsel of savory-smelling meat. 'Care for a drumstick, Mr. Yancey?'

" 'What could I say? What could I do? Command authority went down the drain at that moment. I grabbed the drumstick and chomped down on it, even though I was sick with worry that Captain Phillips was going to pick this moment to drop by for an inspection."

Only two of Easy Company's three rifle platoons had been deployed so far. The third, led by 1st Lt. Robert Bey, was waiting on the reverse slope for orders. The company executive officer, 1st Lt. Raymond Ball, came over to Yancey's campfire to confer with him. "Ray wanted my thoughts on where to put Bey and his gang. I recommended putting them out on the right flank, strung out in the direction of the adjoining hill, 1240, which was a few hundred yards to the east. Within half an hour the platoon was deployed along part of this broad saddle that connected us with 1240. (There was still a big gap between the two hills, though.) I think now I made a mistake in that recommendation. We should have kept Bey in reserve on the back slope instead of stringing his people out in that long thin line. We should have gone for depth instead of range. . . . Well, I don't want to talk about that any more, I feel so bad."

The last convoy had pulled out of Yudam-ni at about ten o'clock. A few minutes later the Marines of Captain Barber's Fox Company at the top of the pass heard the booming reverberation of the empties and the laborious shifting of gears as the trucks negotiated the steep grades and sharp turns, then watched the headlights flash by the bottom of the hill. Finally the sound of the motors faded away as the convoy disappeared down the road to Hagaru. Fox Company was "in the rear," and it did not occur to Barber or any of his men that they were entirely cut off by enemy units even now stealing down from the heights to sever what had been the sole main supply route and was now nothing more than a wide path for Chinese infantry.

Captain Benjamin Read had driven his jeep to Yudam-ni to pick out tomorrow's site for How Battery. "The trip was punishingly cold," he later recalled. "I had to hold my mittened hand in front of my face to keep my cheeks from freezing. After I picked out my spot I said hello to Lieutenant Robert Messman of King battery. He said he would follow me back to Hagaru. I've always believed I was the last man to travel from Yudam-ni to Hagaru that last night. Messman didn't make it."

This much is known: Soon after ten o'clock, Robert Messman told a staff officer of the 11th Marines that he was about to scoot down to Hagaru in his jeep to be in position to expedite the delivery of 155-mm ammunition early the following morning. The officer watched him climb into his jeep and head down the moonlit mountain road. The jeep was found later three miles south of Yudam-ni. There were no bullet holes or blood smears on the vehicle. Though it was likely that Messman had been stopped and captured, the only witnesses to the event were the Chinese soldiers who took him prisoner. Messman would make a brief appearance— or at least make himself heard—a little later in the campaign.

Here is a rough overview of the deployment of the Marines and Army troops at this time, the night of November 27–28: East of the Chosin Reservoir, two U.S. Army infantry battalions and one artillery battalion—nearly 3,000 GIs; west of the reservoir, Litzenberg's 7th Marines and Murray's 5th Marines occupying selected hills around Yudam-ni—approximately 8,200 Marines with attached Navy corpsmen; three miles down the road, Charlie Company, 7th Marines, guarding the road where it began its ascent to the top of Toktong Pass—190 Marines with corpsmen; two miles further on, Captain Barber's reinforced Fox Company, 7th Marines, dug in at the top of the pass—218 Marines with corpsmen; at Hagaru, 3,000 Marines with corpsmen, plus 600 U.S. Army troops; at Koto-ri, 1,500 Marines with corpsmen, plus 1,000 U.S. Army troops; at Chinhung-ni, 1,600 Marines with corpsmen. Rough total: 13,500 Marines with corpsmen; 4,500 U.S. Army troops. Estimated Chinese troops in the sector: 60,000.

24.

LT. MINARD NEWTON'S PLA-
toon of Captain Leroy Cooke's How Company, 7th Marines, was
resting in reserve at the bottom of Hill 1403, a prominence that
marked the northwest corner of the Yudam-ni perimeter. Newton
and his men felt safe; after all, Roise's 2/5 was dug in a short
distance to the left, and Taplett's 3/5 was bivouacked a few hundred yards to the right. The feeling of safety was deceptive. Because
of the steep loftiness of Hill 1403, the other two platoons of Captain Cooke's company were relatively isolated on the crest, entirely
out of touch with Taplett and Roise.

PFC Robert P. Cameron, How/7: "Like most China Marines, I
could get along okay in the bars, cathouses, and bazaars in Tient-
sin, but when it came to getting information from prisoners my
language skills weren't worth a damn. But they gave me a desk in
the intelligence shop in Hamhung anyway and put me to work
interviewing POWs from the fight at Sudong. I faked it as long as
I could, hoping the officers wouldn't notice the prisoners thought
my Chinese was hilarious; but before long my section chief sent
over a Chinese-American Marine to test me. His verdict was that
PFC Cameron speaks very good Chinese for a three-year-old.
'Cameron,' says the captain, 'you're going north.' That's how I
ended up in How Company on top of 1403 the night the shit hit
the fan."

Around ten o'clock, phone communications between the platoons and Captain Cooke's command post blinked out, and a few
minutes later the Baltimore Reservist saw figures plunging down
the reverse slope to his right—Marines, whose positions were
about to be overrun. There had been no firing as of yet. At this
point the telephone line between 1403 and Lt. Col. William Harris's command post a mile away was cut.

PFC Robert P. Cameron: "So there I was on 1403, right in the path of the Siberian Express, which is what we called that wind, manning the last machine gun on the left and trying not to turn into a block of ice. I had the cover of the gun unlatched and up. Every couple of minutes I would grasp the handle and work the action back and forth to keep it from seizing up."

Cameron liked to handle the gun, and he liked thinking about the gun. In his spare time he had been working on a letter to the *Marine Corps Gazette,* proposing a design for an adjustable foreleg on the tripod. "I kept putting off sending it because I suspected they never published letters from enlisted swine. . . . Anyway, that's what I was thinking about when I heard this racket down the slope. It was like the sound of a Chinese birthday party, wedding, and funeral all rolled into one: people chanting, blowing horns, ringing bells, clashing cymbals, beating drums. When the illuminating rounds popped overhead, I saw a whole lot of people heading our way. Memory tends to exaggerate, but I'm telling you there were a thousand individuals down there in massed infantry formation. It reminded me of the parade ground at Parris Island on a Saturday morning. As far as I was concerned, they had a single destination: the machine-gun position of PFC Robert P. Cameron, USMC."

Cameron slapped the hatch shut, double-primed the gun, and began squeezing off short bursts. The enemy came in ranks and fell in ranks. Those who got through fanned out about a hundred yards downslope. Each skirmish line was about equal in manpower to a Marine platoon—thirty to forty men. The artificial lights kept popping and squeaking in the sky overhead, making weird shadows, giving the scene a nightmarish effect. The ranks kept coming. Cameron tried to limit his bursts to four rounds. The ammo cans held 250 rounds each; it wasn't long before he was working on his fourth can and worrying about running dry.

Over on the right, Corporal Leif Hegg, another machine gunner, had unlocked his gun from the traverse bar and was spraying the slope as a man might water his lawn. Bodies were piling up, the dead and wounded creating temporary cover for those still functioning. There were so many people in the enemy's pool of manpower that the attacking force inched closer and closer even though the Marines were slaughtering them freely; and now How Company was dealing with grenades in their midst.

PFC Leroy Martin, How/7, was awakened by the sound of grenades going off, but the sounds were muffled and he assumed there was fighting on some other hill. He rolled over and went back to sleep. The next thing he knew, his fire team leader was shaking him violently. "Get the fuck outta here, man!"

PFC Martin poked his head out of the bag and saw white figures and burp-gun muzzle blasts. Out of the bag in a flash, he grabbed his rifle and a bandolier of clips and raced down the slope to where Sergeant Garth, the platoon guide, was waiting. Garth, it turned out, was the rear guard for the general pullback of the platoon; he was ready to fight but was having trouble with his frozen carbine. The two Marines, side by side, started firing at the skyline to keep the enemy from coming over on them. Garth could only fire single shots; every time a silhouette appeared he would fire and then say, "Shit." When he ran out of ammunition he said, "Come with me," and the two of them crawled backwards in the snow. PFC Martin was surprised to find the remnants of the platoon close by. They had been pushed out so fast that they left a machine gun up on the crest, and now Lieutenant Kreig was trying to find volunteers to go back with him and retrieve it."

At this point Captain Cooke appeared and said, "We have to take that ground back."

Platoon Sergeant Walton Watson led the counterattack. Reaching the crest, the Marines found Chinese soldiers searching through dead Marines' packs and ration boxes left behind. Watson was killed, the counterattack fizzled out, and the survivors came crawling back down the slope. Lt. Kreig was reported as missing in action.

2nd Lt. George Caradakis was calling down fires from the 81-mm mortars at the bottom of the hill. The men of Newton's reserve platoon, still relatively clueless, found this bothersome. They were close to the roadblock and the 81s were making a great deal of noise, and there was a shower of powder-increment sparks every time a round was fired. The battery of tubes was thus very conspicuous in the darkness, and Newton feared they would attract the attention of the Chinese, who so far had left the reserve platoon alone.

During a lull, PFC Cameron and two others raced over to the dump for more boxes of ammo and a burlap bag full of grenades. When they returned to their position, the section leader told Cameron to pick out a secondary position for the gun in case a fallback was necessary. Cameron found a spot about fifty feet to the rear, but when he got back to the gun he saw that the situation had changed drastically: the Chinese had broken through on the right and Captain Cooke was dead. Everyone was falling back. PFC Cameron and Corporal Leif Hegg, on two separate guns, kept pumping out rounds. Cameron: "I figure I burned off a good ten boxes of ammo that night. . . . The Chinese were so close now, coming from different directions, that I began to worry about hand-to-hand combat. That was something we had all been trained for, but we trained in T-shirts and shorts; now we were dressed in these constricting layers of clothing.

"I watched a corpsman drag a wounded Marine to the rear, leaving his rifle with bayonet behind. As a machine gunner, all I had for a personal weapon was a sidearm, so I scrambled over and grabbed the M-1 just as a squad of gooks appeared on my left, moving at an oblique angle. We had been taught the classic Biddle bayonet offense system at Camp Lejeune, but in the heat of the moment I reverted to primitive basics: stick the gook before the gook sticks you. The gooks hadn't spotted me yet, and when this one on the end started walking past, I stood up and gave him the long thrust in the side. His eyes opened real wide and down he went, all curled up. I jabbed him a second time to put him out. At that moment Bill Sports went by with Leif Hegg's gun on his shoulder, and here comes Hegg carrying the tripod, holding his forty-five in his right hand. It was time to go."

Taplett's field phone was jangling. It was the battalion surgeon, Lt.(jg) John H. Moon: "Can you come over, Colonel?"

"What's up?"

"I've got casualties here that don't make sense."

"Huh?"

"They're 7th Marines."

Taplett and his executive officer, Major John Canney, headed for the nearby aid station. There they found stragglers from How Company/7, many of them dazed, shivering, barefoot, wanting to talk about the onslaught of Chinese soldiers on Hill 1403. Their condition made it clear that they had been caught by surprise and quickly overrun.

Lt. Minard Newton's platoon was sacked out along with Sergeant Vick's 75-mm recoilless rifle crew at the bottom of the hill. When the shooting started atop 1403, the lieutenant woke everyone up and shifted them to a defensive position in a dry streambed nearby. They moved so fast that they left their campfires burning and abandoned their sleeping bags and shelter-half tents. After a heroic effort by a team of wiremen, the landline from the Third Battalion, 7th, command post was restored. Lt. Patrick Roe: "I heard Colonel Harris say, 'Let me speak to Six,' and that's when they told him Captain Cooke was dead and every one of his lieutenants except Newton was wounded or missing. He was visibly shaken by all this."

The battalion commander's immediate reaction was to send 1st Lt. Howard H. Harris to take charge of the situation on 1403. On his way to the foot of the hill, Lt. Harris noticed for the first time the crazy network of blue, red, and green tracers in the sky and on the slopes; he realized with a shock that the fight for 1403 was part of a greater battle involving other hills on the Yudam-ni perimeter. Reaching the foot of 1403, Harris scooped up Newton's platoon and led it up the slope.

Corporal John Gallagher, How/7: "It was about three A.M. and I was wondering if we had been forgotten. Corporal Herbert Knight, reliable Marine that he was, said he was going to stay right there—where Lieutenant Denny had originally placed him and his gun—until hell froze over. I saw a gook rear up on the skyline and lob a grenade. Knight gave him a short burst, then made like a pancake in the snow as the grenade landed, rolled, and exploded. Then I heard a voice close behind me—it made me jump. 'You hear me, Marine?' It was Lieutenant Howie Harris. 'I'm talking to *you*.'

" 'Sir, I hear you.'

" 'Get your folks in hand. We're moving off the hill.' "

PFC Robert P. Cameron: "There was substantial fireworks going on nearby, but not on 1403. I heard a gabble of voices over to my left and started crawling in that direction, looking for friends, and I came across a gun tripod with no gun. The voices turned out to be Chinese, so I stopped. I had enough presence of mind—or pessimism, one—to begin rehearsing certain phrases in Chinese that would, I hoped, instantly convert the enemy soldiers into pals—little colloquial expressions which I've long since forgotten, the equivalent of 'How ya doin'? or 'What's new?' One thing I haven't forgotten, though, is the psychic pain I felt over having to quit that hill. I had come to Korea three weeks earlier convinced that we were invincible and that I was immortal; now my outfit was dis-integrating before my eyes and I wasn't sure I'd live to see another dawn. I picked up the tripod and collapsed its legs and, moving on my knees, made my way over to a rock where I pulled myself erect. I couldn't stop shivering, and I was afraid the gooks were going to hear my bones rattling.

"Then I saw a sight straight out of a nightmare. Right smack in front of me was a gook facing the other way, kneeling. There was just enough light in the east now to see that he was trying to take the parka off a dead Marine, trying to work the corpse's arms out of the sleeves. The scariest thing of all was that he had heard my approach a second before I saw him. He turned his head to say something, obviously thinking I was a fellow gook. My response was to scramble up behind him, haul off with the nine-pound tri-pod, and swing it full force against his head. I hit him in the right temple and I only had to hit him once; his skull cracked like an eggshell.

"I couldn't bring myself to look at the Marine. To me a dead Marine was a shocking and hideous sight. For one thing, I was afraid I might recognize him, might know his name. So I turned away and started down the path and—Jesus!—when I came around the bend I saw several gooks hunched around a fire. It was a blessing that their attention was on the flames and that the wind and the fire were so noisy. They didn't see me; they didn't hear me. It was like a miracle.

"I have only one thing more to tell you, Mr. Russ: I was re-sponsible for snuffing out many lives with my machine gun that night, but the only killing that haunts me was that last one. I slaughtered that man as would a common thug. Sneaking up be-hind this poor fellow who was trying to acquire a warm garment for himself! Bludgeoning him to death! When I had time to think about it later I was overwhelmed with shame. Up to this moment I've never mentioned it to a soul, nor have I told anyone about the dead Marine I left up there on 1403. I can still feel it in my stomach whenever I read about how proud the Marines were about bringing out most of their dead—and here I couldn't even bear to look at one dead Marine's face."

From all reports, Lt. Col. William Harris was severely disturbed by the turn of events on 1403, and by a report that Chinese troops had slipped around the east side of the hill. (As a lieutenant at the start of World War II, Harris had been taken prisoner by the Japanese in the Philippines. He and another Marine managed to escape on the first night of captivity and spent several weeks trying to find a way to reach Australia. Though the other Marine eventually succeeded, Harris was recaptured. It was common knowledge that he was a different man after the experience.) On that night in late November 1950, Lt. Col. Harris was showing signs of coming apart at the seams: issuing contradictory orders, giving away personal items—his leather toilet kit, his K-bar knife, his binoculars. He began fretting openly about the security of the command post, and this led to the premature order for the remnants and reinforcements on 1403 to abandon the heights.

The loss of 1403 gravely imperiled Roise and his battalion, for the enemy was now able to look down on the road to his rear, the lifeline that connected 2/5 with the rest of the regiment at Yudamni.

Some of the How/7 survivors remain prickly to this day about the company's performance that night. Former corporal Joseph F. Finn speaks for many when he says, "We did the best we could with what we had. We were out there on that steep hill by ourselves, not tied in with any other unit. We only had two of our rifle platoons up there. We held out as long as we could, but because our flanks were open, we were soon up to our asses in gooks. Some say we broke and ran. We didn't break, but some of us ran, which was exactly the right thing to do at the time, because if we had stayed there any longer we would have been wiped out, and what good would that have done, I ask you. In the end we were ordered off the hill by Colonel Harris himself. In no sense were we driven off. To suggest that we failed to do our best, or failed to uphold the honor of the Corps—that is an insult to our dead brothers of How Company, 7th Marines."

25.

AT DUSK A GHOSTLY FOG CREPT up the valley. The moon, four days past the full, broke loose from the hazy skyline a little after six. In Lt. Col. Harold Roise's sector its light remained dim for an hour or so, until the mist began to dissolve in the rising wind. Masses of Chinese infantry silently maneuvered toward the line held by Captain Uel Peters's Fox Company, 5th Marines, and Captain Samuel Jaskilka's Easy Company, 5th Marines.

At ten o'clock, 2nd Lt. Jack Nolan reported to Jaskilka that he could hear people talking a short distance in front of his platoon's position.

Corporal Howard Baxter, machine gunner attached to Easy/5, was ordered to open up, which made no sense to him. "Okay, but where's the target?"

"Open fire!"

Reluctantly Baxter cranked off a short burst, convinced he was wasting rounds; but the streaking tracers illuminated a knot of Chinese soldiers moving across his front. They were only yards away, close enough for Baxter to see the expression on their faces as bullets punched holes in their flesh.

PFC Jack Stefanski, Dog/5: "First we heard a Chinese officer giving his men a pep talk. Then it was quiet for a minute. Then they started up with the horns and cymbals. We didn't want to give away our positions, so instead of firing our rifles we pulled pins and threw grenades as far as we could in the direction of the commotion. After the explosions the Chinese just faded away. It was only a probe, you see. They just wanted to find out where our automatic weapons were, but we wouldn't play their game."

The main attack materialized ten minutes later.

"Here they come!"

Three hundred tightly-bunched Chinese now attempted to drive a wedge between Peters's and Jaskilka's companies. Two machine-gun positions were quickly overrun. The path to Roise's command post lay straight ahead. PFCs John Meade and Donald Kjellman, accompanied by Navy corpsman Leland Arntz, rushed over to fill the breach. Others joined them without waiting for orders. Ammunition began to run low and Meade ran back for more. He made three such trips to the ammo dump, distributing to the men on the firing line and adding his accurate fire to their volleys. On his fourth trip he was knocked down by a bullet in the leg and kept trying to get up to deliver a sack of grenades to the Marines on the line. Corpsman Arntz ran over to him, held him down by force, dressed his wound, and dragged him to the rear. His comrades later estimated that Meade alone had downed at least twenty-five enemy soldiers, many of whom now lay writhing or sprawled dead on the ice of the frozen stream.

When the illumination rounds finally popped overhead, the shadows of trees and jogging Chinese infantrymen lanced across the slopes. Even under the glare of the flares it was hard to see them against the snow in their white uniforms; the Marines were nevertheless surprised at the vast number that were visible.

Dr. Henry Litvin had just glanced at his wristwatch—it was 10:05 P.M.—and when he looked up his eye fell on a corpsman taking a spoonful of something from a can of Campbell's soup. It was an odd shade of green. "What *is* that?"

"Celery soup," he said.

Then a young Marine came bursting into the tent. He was shoeless, without parka or gloves, and blue with cold. Litvin: "Keep in mind that the temperature was well below zero; when those tent flaps parted, the air cut through us like a knife. This youngster was not only half-frozen, he was in a daze, his eyes all wild. 'Where's the colonel's tent?'

" 'What's the trouble?'

" 'The gooks have broken through our lines.'

"Holy cow!"

Corporal Arthur Koch, a squad leader in Easy Company, was dug in on the right flank. Around nine o'clock he heard bugles in the near distance, their ragged blatting echoing off the slopes as they drew nearer. Koch: "It was enough to make your hair stand on end if you had any hair, which we did at that time. When the bugles died away we heard a voice through a megaphone and then the blast of a police whistle. I was plenty scared, but who wasn't? I couldn't believe my eyes when I saw them in the moonlight. It was like the snow come to life, and they were shouting and shaking their fists—just raising hell. At the same time, there was some big rumpus going on on the hill to our right [Hill 1403]. The Chinese didn't come at us by fire-and-maneuver, the way Marines do; they came in a rush like a pack of mad dogs. Even though I was ready it was a terrible shock."

Corporal Patrick Stingley, machine gunner attached to Easy/5: "I enjoyed being part of a machine-gun crew, even though I had a permanent dent in my shoulder from lugging the thirty-pound gun; and my knuckles tended to drag on the ground from carrying those ammo boxes." Stingley was asleep in the root cellar of an abandoned house when Platoon Sergeant Jackson called through the entrance: "Machine gunners still down there?"

"Yeah."

"Get your asses out here on the double. We're about to be overrun."

When he stumbled out into the moonlight, the first thing Stingley saw was Gunnery Sergeant R. W. Barnett. "If you ever needed someone to climb the Empire State Building and swat airplanes out of the sky, here was your man. He had this strange habit. He would pick you up and hold you at arm's length above him whenever he wanted to emphasize a particular point. This was great fun to watch when he did it to someone else, but this time it was happening to me.

" 'What I want you to do, Stingley, is shoot any gooks who try to come up that draw.' He indicated the spot with his big jaw. 'Got that?'

"We set up the gun at the top of the draw and found plenty of targets, but it didn't take long before our ammo ran low. Back at the dump I saw some leaderless Marines obviously spooked out by the sudden onslaught. I told them to grab two boxes each and come along.

" 'Who the fuck are *you*?' this one character wants to know.

"I told him I was Corporal Patrick Stingley, United States Marine Corps, and he better do as I said because it was going to be Gook City in about one minute. That got 'em hopping!"

At 10:15 Roise ordered his Headquarters and Service Company to deploy in defense of the command post.

Doc Litvin: "A lieutenant whose name I won't mention came bursting through the tent flaps and announced in a loud voice: 'Doctors, corpsmen, chaplains, clerks, cooks, bakers—*every*one—I want you all outside, right now!' After we piled outside he said, 'I want you to aim your weapons down that draw.' And he pointed. 'When I give the word, you *will* fire.'

"I can't speak for anyone else, but I was looking for a place to hide and couldn't find one. All around us were the sounds of bugles and whistles and shouting. I kept wondering when my .45 was going to discharge itself and shoot me in the foot or worse. I still didn't understand how the safety worked, mind you, and I was too darned embarrassed to ask someone to show me. I finally found a spot beside the Catholic chaplain, who was clutching a carbine. 'Say, Father,' I asked him, 'are you actually going to shoot that thing when he gives the order?'

" 'I don't think so, but I'm not sure.'

" 'Fire!' shouted the lieutenant."

Doc Litvin emptied his clip at the shadows moving up the draw, learning incidentally that his safety had been in the off position all along. The priest did not fire. (Litvin's comment forty-five years later: "So the doctor pulls the trigger and the priest doesn't; I'm still trying to sort *that* out.")

A few minutes later Litvin was back in the aid tent, working by the glaring white light of a Coleman lantern. The first priority, with most of the wounded, was to stop the bleeding and immobilize the fractures, then cleanse the wound with antiseptic solution and apply a tight pressure dressing.

"A little later, in comes the same young lieutenant who had ordered the headquarters people outside. Ordinarily a happy-go-lucky gent, he now appeared quite shook, as the Marines would say. 'Lie down,' I told him, pointing to my bag in the corner. I outranked him, so he did it. I brought him a couple of two-ounce bottles of cognac. 'Drink them both down and go to sleep.' "

In his own way, Litvin was as shook as the young lieutenant. "I did feel like going to pieces more than once," he admitted, "and might have done so if there hadn't been so many patients lined up. . . . To see so many of these young Marines die without being able to help them, it was the most heartbreaking experience of my life. If you took a bullet in the lung and were taken to a base hospital, you'd have a chance of surviving; but out there on a litter, in weather so cold your spit would freeze before it hit the ground, there was no way to get you out."

Lt. Col. Roise wanted to know what was happening in the battalion's rear. He sent Captain Franklin Mayer, his headquarters commandant, to find out. How Company stragglers were beginning to cross paths with small groups of enemy infantry as they made their way either to Roise's lines or Lt. Col. Robert Taplett's. If the Chinese could manage to get their breakthrough forces organized, they would be in an ideal position to strike Roise's rear and sever him from the rest of the Marines at Yudam-ni.

Mayer: "I started down the road by myself in the dark. Not a smart move, but I was still under the illusion that 'the rear' was relatively safe. Then I began to worry about being mistaken for an infiltrator. Just then I ran into a group who turned out to be the last stragglers from Hill 1403. They said the Chinese were right behind them. I peered over their shoulders into the gloom and got off the dumbest remark of the evening: 'I don't see any Chinamen.'

"One of the stragglers said, 'Just walk down that road and you'll see all the Chinamen you ever want to see.' That's when I decided I had gone far enough.

" 'What did you find out?' asked the colonel.

" 'The Chinese are behind us.'

" 'What else?'

" 'What else? Sir, that's pretty big news by itself!'

"Colonel Roise always had a cigarette going. He took a puff, let out the smoke, and said, 'We'll take care of them.' "

The battle in Roise's sector reached a turning point when one of Jaskilka's gunners fired a burst at several Chinese running into a mud-and-straw structure about two hundred yards in front of the line. The tracer rounds, chasing them, set the hut's straw on fire and backlit the enemy into perfect targets. As Jaskilka was to put it in the language of an official report, "The enemy could be seen clearly and was shot down at will in large numbers. He was seen making feverish efforts to remove his wounded but was forced to abandon these efforts."

At 6 A.M. the few remaining able-bodied Chinese soldiers in

the attacking force could be seen hustling away into the forest, stumbling over a grisly carpet of their own dead. Patrick Stingley: "My God, there were bodies everywhere. None of us really understood what had happened until it got light. Then we saw there were so many corpses they actually changed the contour of the terrain."

Jaskilka: "I realized I wouldn't be leaving the Division anytime soon, even though my orders had already relieved me of duty. There was a campaign to be fought and no able-bodied Marine was leaving until we got ourselves out of this mess."

Estimates of enemy dead varied from three hundred to four hundred. The Chinese tactic of isolating a segment of the enemy, then using all available manpower to chew it up, wasn't working so well because of Marine firepower. Roise's battalion had suffered seven killed and twenty-five wounded during the night, plus sixty cases of frostbite.

Stingley: "Someone came up and said, 'Stingley, there's a phone call for you' and jerked his thumb in the direction of the lieutenant's field phone. A phone call for you—that's civilian talk, so I assumed it was some kind of joke and said I wouldn't take the call because it might be collect. 'Better get a move on,' he says, and I says, 'Okay, I'll take it in the bedroom.' Then the guy got urgent: 'Better hustle, man—it's Barkin' Barney!' Gunny Barnett, in other words. When I got on the phone, this menacing voice says I should stop by the command post 'at your convenience.' Well, I practically ran over there.

" 'What's up, Gunny?'

" 'Not much,' he says. 'Just thought you might like a cup of coffee.'

"You can imagine my surprise. It turned out that during the battle some idiot reported me as missing in action and the Gunny spent half the night thinking I was one of those Marines he saw lying stiff in the snow; and when he found out I was still going, he decided to say 'Glad you're still with us' by making me a cup of coffee, which he did, which might suggest the man was human even though I knew better."

The Marines were beginning to huddle around campfires that had sprung up in the dawn all across Roise's sector. PFC Jack Stefanski: "While I was trying to get my fire going, a sniper took a shot at me and I had a very foolish reaction that shows the shape

I was in. I thought, Man, if the gooks didn't get me last night, they sure as hell aren't going to get me now. Well, less than a second later I realized what a stupid idea that was and scrambled behind some cover and did the whole fire-starting deal from scratch. As I was breaking up some kindling, along comes Mr. Mac—1st Lt. George McNaughton.

" 'How's things going?'

"That's when I learned how shook I was: I couldn't find my voice. Mr. Mac just stood there, waiting. When I finally found it, the sound came out in a croak.

" 'Mr. Mac?'

" 'Yeah?'

" 'There was a whole lotta gooks last night.'

"Mr. Mac laughed and gave me a big clap on the back and moved on down the line to the next man. A few minutes later the fire was going good and there were several of us sitting around it. We started singing songs. 'On a Chinese Honeymoon' was one. That was a Mills Brothers hit. 'I'll Be Home for Christmas' was another. Mr. Mac tried to discourage us from singing that one because he said he didn't want us to get overhopeful. We were all dreaming about getting down off that plateau and back aboard those troop ships with their hot chow and hot showers, leaving this godforsaken Korea behind us. Not one of us was overhopeful, not after the night we had just been through. It just shattered all our hopes and dreams."

Dr. Litvin informed Colonel Roise that there were four wounded men in particular who were sure to die unless they were taken to the rear at once.

"Send them down the road as soon as you can, then, Doc."

Litvin had them loaded aboard a truck, and the driver took off; but he only got as far as the south end of the perimeter. The Marines at Yudam-ni had still not grasped that they were completely surrounded, that the Chinese had cut the road behind them.

At 1:45 A.M. on November 28, Roise was handed a message from Regiment that summed up the general ignorance of the situation. Roise was directed by Operations Order 41-50 to "continue the attack and to seize Regimental Objective One." This meant, basically, that 2/5 was to resume its westward march into the wilderness of the Taebek Range. The unflappable Roise read the order, nodded his head, and went back to the business of saving his battalion from annihilation. It had not even occurred to the ever-dutiful officer that the new dawn would bring anything other than a resumption of the march.

26. THE MARINES OF LT. COL. ROB-
ert Taplett's battalion were having trouble distinguishing between
How/7 stragglers and groups of Chinese grenadiers. As the stragglers approached singly or in groups, Captain Harold Williamson's
men aggressively challenged them and engaged them in profane
banter, making certain they were Marines before allowing them to
pass. Taplett was skeptical of the stragglers' claims that they had
been overrun by overwhelming numbers of Chinese; he assumed
they had panicked under the same kind of minor probing his own
troops were even then enduring. Part of this skepticism—which
was general among Taplett's troops—had to do with the extraordinary acoustics at play that night. Because of the topographical
relationship of slope, gully, and wind, the battle for 1403 was in-
audible to Taplett and his men. It was so quiet that Major Thomas
Durham, the battalion operations officer, noticed as he made his
rounds that the snow squeaked under his boots "the way it does
when it's very cold." Durham recalls that the moon was high and
nearly full, the valley eerily bright. He ducked into the command
post just before Taplett arrived from a visit to the aid tent. The
battalion commander was not happy to find the CP crowded with
clerks and drivers trying to warm themselves by the stove. "All you
people clear out of here," he snapped. "Get back to your units."

Durham: "I was somewhat extraneous myself, since the colonel
acted as his own operations officer, seldom consulting anyone
about anything. Colonel Taplett was tall, lean, and very impatient
and had little tolerance of human frailties such as the occasional
desire to eat, sleep, and get thawed out."

Sending that handful of Marines back into the cold was one of
many just-in-time moments of the campaign, for the battle in Taplett's sector broke out almost immediately. Durham was alone in
the staff tent when a babble of Chinese voices revealed that the

enemy was on the other side of the canvas. He slid his automatic out of the holster and tried to pull back the slide to chamber a round but found it frozen as though welded. The best thing to do, he decided, was to sit there at the desk, weapon in hand, ready to beat a Chinese over the head with it if one tried to enter. He turned down the valve on the Coleman lantern and stoked the stove with wood. (It was an oil-burning stove, but the feed line had frozen and they were burning pieces of ammo crates.)

"Having done everything I could think of, I sat there beside the phone waiting for whatever was going to happen next. Stray rounds and grenade fragments cut through the canvas occasionally like through-and-through wounds, and the wind came whistling through the holes. There was nowhere to hide. I felt that I was fulfilling a useful role just sitting by the phone, heeding the spirit of dear old General Order Number Five, which is one of the first things you learn in the Corps: "I will not quit my post until properly relieved." Oddly enough, the phone never rang. I realize now that the line had probably been severed."

Grenade shrapnel had knocked out the switchboard in the communications tent. 1st Lt. Hercules Kelly, the communications officer, was trying to restore it to service, while PFC Louis Swinson, acting as his bodyguard, accounted for several Chinese who were roaming freely among the headquarters tents.

Hercules Kelly: "We really had ourselves a mess. The worst moment was when I had to go to the staff tent and ran into the big muzzle of the .45 in Major Durham's right fist. He recognized me and lowered the weapon with a smile. Made my old heart leap, I'll tell ya."

The first call Durham received after the switchboard was repaired came from Captain Williamson, reporting that the situation on his company lines was "exciting but not critical." Williamson wanted to know what was happening around the battalion command post. Durham, preferring to downplay the action in the rear, replied, "Oh, nothing much." (It was a statement often quoted with laughter after the dust had cleared.) Captain Harold Schrier reported, "Item Company's action's been fairly heavy but doesn't appear critical right now."

The tactical situation around the command post was definitely critical. Major Canney, the battalion executive officer, had just informed Taplett that his Headquarters Company had pulled back across the road. "John," said the colonel, "you tell those bastards to get their sorry asses back over here." Taplett then poked his head through the tent flaps and, ignoring the momentarily raised muzzle of the .45, told Durham to tell Captain Hermanson to get George Company saddled up and ready to counterattack. "Attack and counterattack," said Taplett later. "That's what Marines are all about."

PFC Fred Davidson of Oklahoma, a member of George/5, was the classic bitching Marine infantryman. "It was always cold," he recalls, "and there was always one more mountain to climb. It was cold when it snowed and it was cold when the sun was shining. And I was dog tired; I had been on the march since the August campaign down south, not to mention the Inchon landing and the capture of Seoul. My nose was all the time running. I kept wiping it with my wrist—they don't issue hankies in the Corps—to keep the mucous off my upper lip. Finally I just let it run, and then I had this frozen buildup on my mustache that was disgusting, but at least I had lots of company. And my knees were bloody from slipping and falling on the icy slopes. Also, my hands had no feeling in them. Not to mention the foot situation, which I don't even want to go into. Tell you one thing, I much preferred the muggy hundred-and-six-degree heat in the Pusan perimeter to that damn wind at the reservoir. I was nearing that point where I didn't give a shit one way or the other. I had even stopped hitting the deck when the Chinese opened up. 'To hell with ya,' I'd say."

George/5 was assembling on the road for the counterattack when white-phosphorous shells came dropping in, and that's when Davidson experienced a drastic change in attitude: he turned and ran like hell—because the shells seemed to be walking in on him, personally. Sure enough, the third round exploded in a large puff of orange-white sparks not far behind him and the wind of it slammed him facedown in the snow. He was so cold it took him a second or two to realize he was burning. Davidson hollered for help and soon two Marines were ripping through his clothing with K-Bars and packing the burns with snow. That didn't help much, so they took him down to the aid station, where the Navy corpsman said the burns were more painful than serious. He was handed a dead man's sleeping bag, and, with no room left inside the tent, he settled down under the stars with other wounded Marines, all of them covered up to the chin with tarpaulin. He lay there on his side listening to the burgeoning sound of the battle of Yudam-ni. At about 0300 one of the corpsmen came out to tell them that as soon as the Chinese roadblocks were cleared between Yudam and Hagaru they would be evacuated by truck.

Davidson: "That gave me a start. The gooks had closed the road! I let that sink in a while and then hauled myself out of the bag and climbed onto my feet. Better to stay with George Company, I figured, than hang out with the casualties. The burns on my back were painful, but they were going to keep hurting no matter what I did. So I rolled up the bag and made a sling out of commo wire to carry it, picked out an M-1 from a pile of discarded weapons, and went back to the outfit."

As two of George Company's platoons were forming up on the road, flares began popping overhead, making the usual squeaking noises as they descended under their small parachutes. PFC Davidson did not return to the company in time to participate in one of the great counterattacks of the campaign, as Lts. John Cahill's and Dana Cashion's platoons advanced swiftly across the road and, taking advantage of the element of surprise, swept the Chinese out of the headquarters area. Carried along by their own momentum, the seventy-five Marines continued on up the same slope Taplett had climbed a few hours earlier.

"It was one of the finest sights I ever saw," says Taplett, who watched the movement from his tent. "They attacked abreast with marching fire, sweeping across the low ground where the tents were, howling like wild Indians the whole time. Blackie Cahill passed so close I could see him grinning and chomping on a wad of tobacco. 'Keep going,' I shouted."

In the middle of all this, Taplett was called to the phone and a staff officer at regimental headquarters passed along a routine order about the resumption of the march westward at dawn. "For Christ's sake," Taplett exploded, "don't bother me with an idiotic message like that at a time like this—we're counterattacking!"

Lt. John Cahill: "Dana and I wanted to keep going, up over the crest and down the other side, but the colonel called us back. We were really disappointed because we had the enemy on the run and the troops were all hot to trot."

Taplett: "They would have gone all the way to the Yalu if I hadn't ordered them back. That counterattack saved the day for us."

Before the two lieutenants pulled their troops back, they paused long enough to build a fire and toss in some ammo, the notion being that some of the rounds would go off and keep Chinese heads down while the Marines withdrew. Cahill says today he thinks the ruse worked; in any case, some of the ammo did cook off, and the two platoons made it back down the hill without being fired on.

Taplett's exhilaration was dampened considerably when PFC Swinson slipped into his tent to inform him that Major John Canney, his indispensable executive officer, had been killed by a bullet through the head. Swinson had just discovered the body in the snow behind the communications tent. The two Marines observed a moment of stunned silence, then continued with their duties. Mourning would come later.

27.

BACK IN SEPTEMBER THERE HAD been some resentment in Easy Company over the sudden influx of Reservists, and when the veterans of the First Platoon learned that their new officer was a "weekend warrior," they expected the worst. Lt. Yancey, getting wind of this, gathered his thirty-five men on the grass of a soccer field outside Uijongbu and delivered a short address. "I know what's on your mind, you Regulars. Yes, I'm a Reserve officer, but I earned this commission the hard way, and I'm not going to stand for any foolishness about Regulars versus Reservists. When the fighting begins you won't be able to tell one from the other. We're all United States Marines."

Yancey let them find out for themselves that he had won a battlefield commission by leading a squad against a crowd of Japanese, accounting for thirty dead himself, including the commanding officer "who attempted with great vigor to decapitate me with a samurai sword." Yancey had joined the Reserves after the war, got married, and opened a business called Yancey's Liquors in Little Rock.

Corpsman James Claypool: "Yancey and I were wondering how Private Stanley Robinson was doing back at Regiment as Litzenberg's bodyguard. I was worried that outside the umbrella of Yancey's supervision this youngster might be unable to restrain the wild streak in him. This was the kid who was considered such a badass he had to be brought aboard ship under guard. . . . Well, guess who came toiling up the hill late that afternoon? We were glad to see him and his BAR; but I noticed he was limping and got him to sit down and take off his boots even before he reported to Mr. Yancey.

"I was always fanatical about foot care. During the march to Yudam-ni, whenever we took a break I was all over those kids: 'I want those shoe-pacs off and I want those felt liners out and I want those socks changed.' I made them dry their feet and rub them. I made them keep their wet socks inside their clothing to dry out. I wouldn't let anybody keep their shoe-pacs on when they crawled into their bags. I wouldn't let them wear dirty socks because the dirt in the cloth was like fine sandpaper and led to abrasions. As soon as we occupied 1282 I went right to work on their feet, making them clean them with snow, applying boric-acid ointment after they were dry.

"Robinson of course tried to give me a hard time. I looked him in the eye and said, 'Are you going to argue with me?' He thought it over and finally unlaced his boot. I was shocked by what I saw. The skin between his toes was raw, and the skin on his ankles too. There was infection. He had the equivalent of second- and third-degree burns. He was virtually crippled with frostbite. 'You're going back down the hill,' I told him.

" 'The hell I am.'

" 'Robinson . . .'

" 'Don't fuck with me, swabbie.'

"In the end I had to go tell Yancey; it was like a teacher reporting a defiant student to the principal. I told Yancey that Robinson's feet were beyond my resources to treat, that he would probably have to be evacuated. He didn't ask to look at Robinson's feet; he just accepted my word for it. 'Robbie, I'm glad to see you,' he told him, 'but you're going to have to go back down the hill and turn yourself in to Battalion Aid.' Robinson was so angry he didn't even say good-bye. We watched him limp down the back trail. We were *all* disappointed.

"After Robinson departed, Yancey got into a tense discussion with PFC James Gallagher. Gallagher was a blatant racist from Philadelphia. You might think the jarheads of that day were racist in general, so many of them hailing from the poor white South, but that wasn't the case; a fellow like Gallagher really stood out. His Irish father and Italian mother lived in a neighborhood that black folks were beginning to move into and Gallagher didn't like it. Yancey, though a Southerner, wouldn't tolerate racism in his platoon.

"He was a daring young man, that Gallagher. Short, powerful, tough. Face like an Italian leprechaun. At Sudong he was as much a hero as Robinson, running half a mile up 698 with a machine gun and two boxes of ammo to keep Robinson company on the crest. Frankly, I didn't like the kid much, but I was glad he was on our side. Anyway, Yancey was trying to set him straight when someone on watch interrupted to call our attention to a man in white on the skyline a few hundred yards to the left front. He had a pair of binoculars trained on us. We let him look. We didn't have anything to hide."

Captain Walter Phillips had placed Yancey's and 1st Lt. Leonard Clements's platoons in a semicircle on the crest. The usual fifty percent watch was in effect. Phillips and Captain Milton Hull on Hill 1240 had arranged to send out a patrol from each company every half hour, to meet halfway along the saddle connecting the two hills. The night's password: *Lua lua lei.* The countersign: *Hawaii.* Shortly before dusk, Yancey sent Corporal Lee Phillips and his squad about three hundred yards out and told him to dig in. This was to be Easy Company's listening post for the night. Phillips had barely reached the spot when two F4U Corsairs came roaring in over 1282; both cut loose with a burst that plowed long furrows in the snow, barely missing Phillips and his men. 1st Lt. Neal E. Heffernan, the forward air controller, got on the radio and called them off: "Secure the mission, Blueberry!"

Yancey: "I brought Phillips in after that because I didn't trust those airdales."

("When the Chosin Few get together at these reunions, you know," says Yancey, "they always pay tribute to the Corsair pilots and their close air support; but some of us recall the times when the pilots were too eager or got their signals crossed and instead of threatening the shambos they threatened the Marines. That's the reality of it.")

The moon came up over the southern skyline at a little past six. Yancey: "It rose behind us, and that worried me, because we were silhouetted on the skyline. In front of us was this desolate landscape with the lake off to the right, with open spaces of black ice where wind had blown away the snow."

Some of the Marines thought they heard music in the distance; when the wind changed, they realized it was the sound of Chinese bugles, faint and eerie.

At 9:45 P.M. Easy Company's radio operator picked up an odd warning from Dog Company on 1240: "Heads up, over there! One of our guys just got bayoneted in his bag." While the radio operator was trying to confirm this, word was quietly passed along the crest of 1282 that "Mr. Yancey wants to see bayonets on the end of those rifles and carbines."

Corporal Earl Pickens, machine gunner: "Sergeant Cruz was the first to detect movement out front. As he was reaching for the sound-power phone, a Chinese soldier jumped up about ten feet in front of us and charged. I saw Cruz thrust out his .45 and shoot him in the face before I realized what was going on. When Gallagher opened up with the machine gun, it was music to my ears, because I had been worried about the gun freezing up. Because of their white uniforms, all you could see were their shadows and the muzzle blasts of their burp guns. There were only a handful of them, though. It was another probe, aimed at drawing our fire so they could tell where our automatic weapons were."

After the Chinese were driven off, Captains Phillips and Hull, conferring by radio, decided to cancel the hourly patrols along the connecting saddle. It remained quiet on 1282 and 1240 for two hours.

"Something you gotta see, Lieutenant."

"Later, I'm busy."

But Gallagher persisted and Yancey went over. Yancey: "You get to see some strange sights in war. Here's Gallagher with this grin on his face, and what he's grinning about is this string of bodies stretching right up to the gun, with the elbow of the last one actually touching the forward leg of the tripod. 'Pretty good, huh, Lieutenant?' I told him to drag in two or three of the bodies and use them like sandbags in front of his position. He thought that was a great idea."

Yancey went back to making his rounds. Some of the young Marines needed calming down. "Sure, they'll be back," he told them, "but we're ready for them, understand? Just do what I tell you."

A shot rang out at long range and the spent bullet grazed Yancey's right cheek and lodged in his nose. Calmly he removed one glove and plucked it out. Yancey: "Blood was oozing down my cheek into my mouth, but then it froze up. I didn't say anything about this to anyone."

Knots of Chinese had now slipped across the saddle between the two hills and were beginning to fire directly down on the 5th Marines headquarters in the valley below.

2nd Lt. Thomas Gibson, a 4.2–inch mortar officer on phone watch, began getting inquiries about green tracers flying across the sky. The roar of the Coleman lantern masked the start of the battle; Gibson hadn't heard any gunfire at all. After the third inquiry he stepped outside for a look, and there they were. Gibson: "Americans don't use green tracers. I went back inside and woke up the operations officer and told him about it. He wasn't impressed; he went back to sleep. After making the appropriate notations in the logbook, I started checking around by phone. I couldn't find anyone who was stirred up about it. When the tempo of the firing began to pick up, I shook the ops officer awake again. Squinting one eye open, he cocked an ear and was just telling me there was nothing to worry about when a long burst of automatic fire came ripping through the tent, rattling the tin spark-arrestor on top. I think the ops officer was shod and armed and outside before the burst ended."

Everybody was flying out of their tents now, taking up defensive positions in the roadside ditch. Lt. Col. Raymond Murray: "We had been subjected to night attacks throughout our operations in Korea, so at first I considered this just another local action. But all of a sudden the command post came under fire and that's when I began to pay attention. I turned to my exec and said, 'We better get our asses out of here.' I recalled a mound of earth next to the road and thought that if we could get a phone line put in over there we could operate with a bit of cover. I was able to stay in touch with all three battalions without any of them knowing I had opened shop in the middle of an empty field. When I called Taplett and asked what was happening in his neighborhood, he said the enemy was attacking his command post at that very moment and could he call me back later. We heard lots of gunfire over in his sector and a good deal of shouting. At first I assumed it was the Chinese doing the shouting and thought he was being overrun. I was on the point of bringing Jack Stevens's battalion [1/5] into counterattacking position, but then Tap called back to say that two of his platoons were counterattacking and I realized it was our guys who were doing all the yelling."

Murray, on learning that Roise's flanks were in the air, decided it was time to pull 2/5 back and have Roise tie in with William Harris's 3/7 on the left and Taplett's 3/5 on the right.

At 5:45 A.M. on the twenty-eighth the regimental commander

alerted Roise to the probability that his battalion would be retracted. Rearward was not a direction Marines liked to go; Roise's immediate reaction, when he found the coordinates Murray had given him on the map, was that there had been a map-reading error at regiment. He asked for confirmation of the coordinates and was surprised when they were confirmed.

Thus Lt. Col. Harold Roise learned that the forward momentum of the 1st Marine Division had been brought to a halt, perhaps permanently as far as this particular campaign was concerned. Years later he told an interviewer, "I had a hard time accepting it. When an entire battalion is geared up for a sustained attack, it's hard to cancel out. I felt frustrated, frankly. I think we all did."

28.

YANCEY: "It had been quiet for an hour or two, then we began hearing these odd noises down at the bottom of the slope, like hundreds of feet walking slowly across a big carpet of cornflakes." Yancey cranked the handle on the field phone. The response was a whisper from the company exec, 1st Lt. Raymond Ball.

"That you, Ray?"

"Go ahead, John."

"They're coming up the hill."

"You sure?"

"I can hear the fuckers crunching through the snow. How about some illumination?"

"Hold on."

1st Lt. William Schreier, mortar officer: "The cold weather affected the burning rate of the fuses. The first rounds hit the ground before they flashed. We increased the charges to maximum and finally got them to illuminate overhead. We only had about thirty rounds of illum and less than a hundred of high explosive. This wasn't nearby enough, as we were soon to discover."

By then the crunching noise had stopped and the Marines of the First Platoon heard the shrill voice of an officer shouting in English: "Thank God nobody lives forever!"

Yancey: "I don't need to tell you that's not the kind of thing you expect to hear on an Asian battlefield; but it's what the man said and we all heard it. I had a violent reaction: I decided he must have learned his English at a Christian missionary school. The son of a bitch had been fed and sheltered and given a good education by Americans—and here he was leading Red troops against us. That annoyed me."

The first flare popped overhead, and Yancey spotted the officer in front of the first rank of troops, holding a machine-pistol in one hand. The Marines were shocked to see several ranks of Chinese arrayed behind him, spaced ten or fifteen yards apart, the whole formation ascending the slope. The battle of 1282 began in earnest when Yancey yelled, "You're damn right nobody lives forever, you renegade bastard!" and brought him down with a burst from his carbine. The ranks continued to ascend, the soldiers now wailing in a minor key: 'Son of a bitch Marine we kill. Son of a bitch Marine you die.'

Yancey: "It was altogether most eerie."

Corpsman Claypool: "Gallagher, firing short bursts with his machine gun, was taking incoming in return; but he never flinched. The company mortars were in pits just behind us, and every time they fired there were sparks and fireworks as a round left the tube. I heard someone yelling for a corpsman and that meant I had to leave the protection of my hole. Then a star round burst overhead and everything in that wilderness of snow below us was brilliantly illuminated. I saw men in white writhing on the ground while others stepped over or around them. The Marines fired methodically, spanged empty, reloaded, fired again. Sergeant Allen Madden, Yancey's platoon sergeant, saw me and beckoned and pointed to two downed Marines. Together we carried the first one out of the line of fire, and when I came back for the second I had a shelter half to use as a sled; but there were more wounded Marines now and I didn't have time to lay the cloth down and load each man aboard, so I began dragging them backward by their parka hoods."

Captain Walter Phillips, already wounded in the arm and leg, was hobbling about offering encouragement. "You're doing fine," he told his troops.

The Chinese were hurling their grenades in clusters. ("They looked like flights of blackbirds," said Yancey.) Some of the survivors said they saw Chinese carrying *baskets* of grenades. Yancey was moving from hole to hole, passing out bandoliers of M-1 ammunition, when an explosion blew him off his feet, a piece of shrapnel piercing the roof of his mouth. "After that, blood kept trickling down my throat and I kept spitting it out."

Captain Phillips's voice broke through the din again and again: "You're doing well, Marines. . . . Stay loose, Marines. . . . You're doing fine, Marines."

Corporal Earl Pickens: "The Chinese were charging us continually, wave after wave. They wanted that hill."

Staff Sergeant Robert Kennemore, a machine-gun section leader, was making himself useful by crawling among the wounded and dead, collecting ammunition and distributing it to those who needed it. The Chinese were so close that he could hear them tapping the handles of their potato-masher grenades on the frozen ground to arm them. In the gloom below, Kennemore thought he saw a group of Chinese dragging a machine gunner from a foxhole by the legs, clubbing him, bayoneting him. Kennemore maneuvered down the slope, looking for a shooting position.

"Where are you going?" It was Captain Phillips, white-faced and wobbly.

"One of my gunners, sir—"

"Don't go down there, you damn fool." The officer resumed his painful progress along the lines while Kennemore dragged a load of ammo to the other gun in his section, still in action with a crew of three despite the hail of fire. A Chinese grenade plopped in the snow beside the assistant gunner; Kennemore scooped it up and sidearmed it down the slope before it exploded. Another landed nearby and there was only time for Kennemore to put his foot on it, driving it into the snow, as a third grenade landed beside it. Kennemore, willing to die to save his fellow Marines, dropped his knee on it and absorbed the force of both explosions. The three crewmen were temporarily deafened but otherwise unhurt.

Yancey: "Sometime during the night I caught a glimpse of Ray Ball firing his carbine from a sitting position. The Chinese were coming over the ridge on the right flank and he was calmly picking them off, one by one. He continued to do this until a burp gunner blindsided him, catching him in the side with a burst. I thought he was dead but he wasn't."

Easy Company's machine gun platoon leader, a second lieutenant, had been sent down the reverse slope earlier to report to the battalion command post, where he was to link up with ammo-bearers and reinforcements and guide them back to 1282. Yancey: "I heard Ray Ball talking with him on the radio, telling him to get his ass back to 1282. The lieutenant said he would try, and Ray said, 'Try? That's not good enough.' " The lieutenant, for reasons of his own, could not bring himself to return to that hilltop scene of concentrated, deadly chaos, where it seemed a company of United States Marines was in the process of being wiped out.

*   *   *

Private Stanley Robinson lay disgruntled and foot-sore on a stretcher in the battalion aid station, listening to the sound of distant firefights, wondering how Easy Company was doing. An ambulance jeep pulled up outside; litter-bearers brought in a stretcher and put a wounded man down beside him.

"What outfit you with?"

"Easy Company, 7th."

"They got hit pretty good?"

"Clobbered. The captain and Mr. Ball are down. Mr. Yancey's been hit but he's still going."

Robinson sat up. In the darkness of the tent he began to pull on his boots, grunting with pain as he stuffed his swollen feet into the stiff shoe-pacs. It took several minutes to do the job. At last he stood up, pulled on his dirty parka, and went stumbling through the tent flaps. Outside he snatched up a rifle and cartridge belt from the pile of discards. A corpsman appeared. "Where do you think you're going, Robinson?"

"What does it look like, Doc?"

"Go back inside."

"Get the fuck outta my way."

The scrawny youngster slung the rifle and tottered toward the big hill like a crippled old man. An hour later, having been forced to crawl up the steeper portions of the path, he was asking directions to the First Platoon.

"Top of the hill, straight over."

"Seen Mr. Yancey?"

"He's been hit twice, but he's still at it."

Yancey was hunched beside a machine gunner, directing his fire, when he felt a sharp slap on the bottom of his boot. "I looked down and there he was, with his off-kilter grin, looking sloppier and dirtier than ever. 'What the hell are *you* doing here?'

" 'I heard you candyassed pogues needed help.'

" 'I'll be damned.'

" 'So,' said Robinson, 'you got any work for a BAR man?'

"I pointed over to the right. 'See those kids over there? Go over and get 'em squared away. They need a little encouragement.' Robbie was younger than any of them, but I knew he would get results."

Claypool: "Robinson had returned to his true home."

Yancey's platoon was running out of men. He went over to talk to 1st Lt. Leonard Clements about it. "Clem, can you spare a squad? I got to get these shambos off my flank." As we were talking, a bullet caught him dead center in the forehead and down he went. He had just called the squad leader over. 'The lieutenant's dead,' I told him. 'Get your kids in hand and follow me.' I scooped up some other Marines and ended up with about twenty altogether, including Robbie and his four or five."

PFC Wilmer Swett: "He shouted, 'Here we go,' and him and Robinson took off, but when he looked back there was nobody following him. This pissed him off royally. 'Gung ho, you miserable cowardly bastards! I said *Follow me*.' He stood there waiting, and one by one the rest of us moved up, and pretty soon we had something like a skirmish line in motion."

Yancey: "Once we got going, two or three of the kids actually moved ahead of me. I recognize how hard it is to get your ass in gear in a situation like that, where chances are you're going to get killed or at least hurt pretty bad; but that's what Marines are supposed to do. Marines don't get any slack."

The battle atop 1282 began tapering off around 2 A.M., as the Chinese, responding to the signal from a bugle, began to pull back down the slope. Soon it was quiet except for the moans of the wounded and dying.

29.
THE NEXT ASSAULT BEGAN
around 3 A.M. Yancey turned to his runner, PFC Marshall Mc-
Cann. "I don't need you right now, McCann. Get up there in the
hole with Rick, and make every shot count." Soon after the attack
began, Yancey heard a Marine yell, "I'm hit."

"Where're you hit?"

"In the balls."

Yancey crawled across open ground and took a look. "You ain't
shot in the balls, you're grazed in the hams. Pick up that rifle and
earn your pay!"

Corpsman Claypool: "When you get hit, your first thought is
that you're dying. This one Marine was knocked down by a burst
from a burp gun, but I found that his skin wasn't even broken. His
parka and field jacket and wool sweater and vest and wool shirt
and utility jacket and long johns had saved him. He was convinced
he was dying of multiple wounds.

" 'I tell ya, I'm on the way out, Doc.'

" 'Uh-huh.'

" 'Doc, listen to me—I been hit all over!'

" 'Son, you're not even wounded.'

"That really offended him. He called me an old bastard."

(Dr. Henry Litvin: "Somewhere in your book I hope you'll tell
the reader about the role of the Navy corpsman. He was the guy
who stopped the bleeding and made it possible for a wounded
Marine either to stay in action or at least stay alive until he could
be sent back to the surgical team. The up-front Navy corpsman
was the most important link in the whole chain of evacuation.")

Claypool: "Whenever a Marine would die on me I would just
move over to the next man. At the start of the battle I would write
'KIA' [killed in action] on each tag along with the approximate
time of death and attach it to the top button of his jacket. But soon

we had so many casualties I didn't have time to tag them. Several times that night the thought crossed my mind that I wasn't going to get off that hill alive. With so many dead and dying Marines around me, it was obvious my chances were slender. There were so many grenades going off that I stopped paying attention to them. I spent a lot of time bent over, and sometimes when I stood up, the tail of my parka wouldn't drop down because it was pinned against my pants by slivers of shrapnel; every so often I'd reach back and yank the tail down and pull the slivers out of the cloth."

Claypool kept seeing Yancey stalk back and forth, yelling and spitting blood, shouting through a blood-clogged throat: "Gung ho, Marines!" By the light of the flares he made a perfect target.

"Gung ho," said Gallagher.

"Gung ho," said Robinson."

Yancey: "It was as close to Custer's Last Stand as you can get outside of the movies. I kept asking myself, 'Where did all these shambos come from?' "

Claypool: "A couple of times I tried to stop him and treat his wounds but he was too busy moving 'the kids' to the best spots to keep the Chinese from overwhelming us. No one wanted to argue with Yancey, and none of us wanted to stay on that damn hill without him being there too."

The Marine line was faltering, about to break. Captain Phillips appeared behind them holding an M-1 rifle tipped with a bayonet. Turning it upside down, he rammed it into the hard earth with all his diminishing strength. "This is Easy Company," he shouted hoarsely, "and this is where we stand!"

Shortly afterward, a burst of fire cut him down. Lt. Ball, nearly immobilized with multiple wounds, took command, yelling instructions and occasionally firing his carbine from a sitting position.

Claypool: "The other company corpsman was a guy named George Fisher. He was a good-natured fellow much younger than me—I was twenty-six at the time—and much smaller. George was sort of insignificant looking, peering out at the world through a pair of government-issue glasses. We worked pretty well together. Because I was so much bigger, I was the one who dragged the wounded Marines off the line if they couldn't negotiate under their own power, while George stayed busy at the aid tent."

Yancey: "Yes, I remember George Fisher very well—for two reasons. First of all, he cried a lot. The suffering of the Marines really tore him up, and he couldn't hide it. Second, he had no aptitude for the work at all: he was not only physically clumsy, he was sort of delicate, and he seemed to have to force himself to keep going. But he did his duty. Marines have a lot of respect for their Navy corpsmen, as you know."

Claypool: "We put as many of the wounded as we could in sleeping bags to keep them warm so that shock wouldn't kill them. We tried to save our morphine for Marines hit in the chest or gut. (You had to hold the syrettes in your mouth to keep them thawed out.) Often we had to inject a wounded man on the little-finger side of the wrist. Not a very sterile situation: everyone's wrist was black with dirt and soot from the campfires. We had too little morphine, too few bandages, too little time, and we had to make decisions that were extremely unpleasant. On the spot we had to decide which Marines were worth working on and which to ignore since they were going to die shortly, and sometimes you didn't even have time to stop and hold a kid's hand. Most of them asked for their mother. I was accustomed to all that from World War Two. George wasn't."

A Chinese soldier about twenty yards away fired a burst in Yancey's direction, and one of the rounds hit him under the right eye, jarring the eyeball loose from its socket and knocking him over. With his left eye Yancey saw the soldier crouch down and jam another magazine into his weapon. Yancey groped around for the carbine and, not finding it, took the .45 from under his armpit and pumped two rounds into the soldier. Then, as carefully as he could, Yancey removed his gloves and pushed the eye back where it belonged. "It was like pushing a hard-boiled egg into a knothole, but it went in and stayed there."

It was clear by now that unless the companies on 1282 and 1240 were reinforced, the northern defense line was going to fold. Phillips's Easy Company was barely hanging on; Hull's Dog Company had been shoved off 1240 but was presently fighting its way back to the top. During the lull after midnight, Phillips called Lt. Col. Davis and, in the understated Marine style of the day, asked for assistance. "We've taken too many casualties. We're holding, but we can use some help."

With the luckless Randolph Lockwood stuck in Hagaru, Raymond Davis, as we have seen, was burdened with five rifle companies, at least two of which were now in serious trouble. After Davis discussed the situation with Murray at the combined regimental headquarters, reinforcements from First Battalion, 5th Marines, were placed on full alert. A platoon of Captain Jack Jones's Charlie Company/5 was assigned to support Hull's counterattack on 1240; the other two were sent to rescue Phillips's remnant on 1282.

Lt. Col. John W. Stevens, 1/5's commanding officer, recalls that the confusion of the moment was compounded by a frantic call from the C.O. of the Third Battalion, 7th, Lt. Col. William Harris, begging Stevens to send his entire battalion to extricate him from entrapment. "I more or less put him on hold—told him I'd call back. After that I went out to brief the troops [elements of Jones's and Heater's companies] who were about to climb the back of the two northern hills in the dark. The briefing didn't have a great deal of substance. All I could tell them was that when they got to the top of their respective hills they could expect a terrific fight."

Captain Jack Jones recalls the resentment he felt at having his company split up; it was against doctrine. On the other hand, he recognized it was an emergency and what was needed on the hilltop were warm bodies, armed.

PFC Ray Walker, Able Company, 5th: "We were bedded down close to the village and feeling pretty secure. I had just stretched out on a pile of straw and saw a stream of green tracers come scooting over the crest of a hill north of us. It was quite a show: The tracers raced like comets, bouncing off slopes, zooming straight up toward the stars—and every once in awhile you could see the yellowish light from Chinese flares. My enjoyment of the show was interrupted by the appearance of Gunnery Sergeant Stanley Millar.

" 'All right, drop your cocks and grab your socks! We're going up that hill.'

" 'What's going on, Gunny?'

" 'The 7th Marines need help, as usual. Saddle up!'

"Right away we started bitching about the pitiful Reservists who couldn't handle a few stragglers and were now whining for the Regulars to come get them out of a fix." About half of the 7th Regiment was made up of Reservists.

2nd Lt. Nicholas Trapnell, Able/5, recalls that things got quiet when the reinforcements began climbing the slope, and that the point man kept calling out: "Easy Company . . . Where you at, Easy Company? . . . Hey, Easy Company!"

Lt. John Yancey: "We didn't know reinforcements were on the way, because our phone lines were cut and the radio had been smashed in the fight. During this second lull, one of things we found time for was wrapping the dead Marines in ponchos and carrying them to the top of the back trail so the ammo carriers could drag them off the hill."

When the moon went down behind the mountain, Yancey had a reaction to the sudden darkness: he thought he saw "all sorts of boogymen." The Chinese corpses down below came to life: wriggling, rolling over, crawling, sitting up, getting to their feet—turning into nightmare monsters.

Corpsman Claypool: "There were bodies everywhere, especially in front of Gallagher's and Robinson's positions. I watched Robinson search through a dead soldier's pack and pockets. He found a lump of rice mixed with some other grain cooked into a ball about the size of a grapefruit, wrapped in a brown handkerchief. He showed it to me: 'Look at this, Doc!' "

Lt. Robert Bey and his men were watching the Chinese on the crest as Staff Sergeant Daniel Murphy approached him. Bey: "The only thing I could hear up there was the Chinese language being spoken. There was no question they had the top of the hill."

"If you let me counterattack," said Murphy, "I think we can push them back from the command post."

Bey turned his Third Squad over to Murphy. Corpsman Claypool volunteered to go along. He was warmly welcomed. Claypool: " 'Volunteer' might not be the right word. I was coming down from Yancey's command post when I spotted several Chinese soldiers. They didn't see me, and I hugged the ground until they passed by. When Sergeant Murphy was getting his group together, I figured that maybe being with them was the safest place on the hill, so I tagged along. In terms of numbers we didn't amount to much: Murphy and Sergeant Keith's squad plus five stragglers from Lieutenant Clements's platoon; but we clawed our way upslope and chased the Chinese off the crest. I saw a Chinese officer up close: he was wearing a dark sweater under his coat and the coat was open. What I remember best about him, though, is that he didn't shoot me with the revolver he was carrying."

As he started tending to the wounded, Claypool could hear Murphy asking questions. "Where's everybody?"

"The Skipper's dead. Mr. Ball's dying."

"How about Lieutenant Clements?"

"Dead."

A voice sounded out of the darkness. "The hell I am!" Lt. Leonard Clements had been struck in the forehead by a burp gun bullet and lived to tell about it. Clements: "It felt like someone had hauled off with a sledgehammer. I didn't dare touch the spot with my hand because I was afraid part of my head was gone. When I asked after Lieutenant Yancey, someone said he had been shot several times and had bled to death. Funny, John thought I was dead and I thought John was dead."

Clements then spotted what he later called "this squared-away gent" climbing toward him, followed by a column of fresh-looking Marines. "I'm Jack Jones," said the squared-away gent. "I've got part of a company with me."

"Let me show you where my people are," said Clements.

By the light of a flare, the dying Lt. Ball greeted Captain Jones with a smile and a feeble wave.

Lt. William Schreier: "We were all wounded." Schreier himself was having difficulty walking, surprised that a simple wound in the wrist could affect him so strongly. What he didn't know was that a piece of shrapnel was lodged in his chest, that one of his lungs had collapsed and the other was filling with fluid. Try as he might, he couldn't function, and he was soon headed downhill on a stretcher. Schreier: "I felt bad because there was lots of fighting left to be done and I wanted to do my share. But I just couldn't hack it."

The lull in the battle came to an end with a bugle call, followed by "the most amazing pyrotechnical display I've ever seen," according to Lieutenant Trapnell. "Roman candles, Vesuvius fountains, pinwheels, skyrockets, and an infinite number of firecrackers. When that was over, the enemy started to climb toward us once again. The slopes of the saddle were quite steep, and the enemy got close before the shooting started up again. We smelled them before we saw them. Some folks are skeptical about this business of the garlic. It wasn't only garlic on the breath, it was in the clothing too. When you eat garlic over a period of time, it exudes from your pores and, believe me, it carries.

"Soon we were engaged across our entire front and hard pressed to keep them from spilling over into the draw behind us. When it got light enough, you could see that the whole top of the hill had been ground to pumice by grenades, mortars, and artillery shells."

PFC Ray Walker's BAR had stopped working; he couldn't get the bolt to slide forward. A group of enemy soldiers went by on his left; they saw the young Marine but didn't do anything about it. Walker was busy dismantling his weapon: he removed the trigger group, threw it one way, took out the firing pin, threw that another way. There were weapons all around, and he picked up an M-1 and fired one round with it before it malfunctioned too. Down the hill he saw a Chinese soldier walk up behind a Marine gunner ("very casually, as if he were a barber about to give a customer a haircut"), put a pistol to his head, pull the trigger, and walk on down the slope. Walker: "By this time I was frantically trying to find a weapon that worked and feeling nakeder and nakeder. Then a small Marine with curly black hair appeared and said, 'I know where we can get some grenades.' We dragged a whole case back to the spot, opened it with a K-Bar, and began tossing grenades down the slope. There was so much lead flying that there was no sense trying to find a safe place to throw from. By this time it looked like the whole hill was crawling with big white worms."

Walker never understood how it happened, but when he reached for the next grenade it was already sputtering, the spoon gone. He threw up his right arm and was backing away when it went off. Shrapnel from the explosion broke his right ulna, penetrated his left chest, and cut his lip, forehead, and fingers. A corpsman named Parker took an ampule of morphine out of his mouth and gave Walker a shot. A few minutes later, just at daybreak, he was heading down the backside of the hill with a group of wounded Marines that included John Yancey.

Corpsman Claypool was stepping around some brush and rocks looking for wounded Marines when he saw a Chinese soldier sitting with his body facing the corpsman but with his head twisted around and his weapon aimed toward a line of wounded descending the reverse slope. When Claypool shot him—from about ten yards away—his head hit his knees and the quilted hat with earflaps flew off. "He didn't know what hit him, didn't have time to experience the dread of death."

It was light enough now for air strikes, and the first one of the day was so close that the Marines on 1282 saw the upended wing of a Corsair flash by on the other side of the ridge, going from left to right—so close it seemed as though the pilot was scraping off his payload only a few yards in front of them.

Lt. Yancey's jaw was dislocated—he was never sure how it happened—and he had bound it up with a strip of blanket. Spotting Captain Jones, he went up to him and tried to give him an informal briefing on the situation on 1282. His face was covered with crusted blood, one eye was closed, and he was groggy from all the concussion grenades. Captain Jones took one look and told him to join the walking wounded being escorted down the hill.

Yancey: "A sergeant yelled at me, 'This way down!' and reached toward me with a long stick. I grabbed hold of it and he led me down the trail. By the time we got to Battalion Aid, I was bleeding again, so one of the corpsmen tied me sitting up to a tent pole to keep me from choking in my own blood."

Claypool: "None of us would have survived the night if Yancey hadn't been there. No one else could have bullied his troops into standing and facing almost certain death the way he did. Sometimes I wonder if maybe Yancey single-handedly saved the Marines at Yudam-ni, not just the Marines on 1282; because if the Chinese had taken 1282, they would have poured through the breach and overrun the 5th and 7th Marines command posts. All I know for sure is that the Chinese would have overrun 1282 if Yancey hadn't been there.

"I have one more thing to say about him. If a son or grandson of mine had to serve in combat, I wouldn't want him to serve in John Yancey's platoon. His troops took twice as much ground and killed twice as many Chinese, but he also lost twice as many men. Then again, that's the way Marines do business. . . . But not with *my* kids."

The official history sums up the action on 1282 as follows: "[It was] basically the story of the suicide of the 1st Battalion, 235th CCF [Chinese Communist Forces] Regiment." There is no official tally of Chinese dead in the battle for 1282, but there were hundreds of corpses piled up on the forward slope and on the crest. As for the Marines, Easy/7 suffered 120 dead and wounded, out of the original 176. (Stanley Robinson and James Gallagher walked off the hill unscathed.) Jones's Charlie/5 had ten dead, thirty wounded. Heater's Able/5: five dead, thirty-seven wounded.

The second lieutenant who was sent down the hill for ammunition never did return. Such military cowards are in a peculiar way immortalized along with the heroes; they are often mentioned in discussions, the veterans still shaking their heads over a former comrade's moment of weakness on the field of battle. His privacy is always protected; the name is never mentioned in the presence of outsiders. Contempt or disgust are hardly ever expressed toward him. If any emotion is manifest it is likely to be pity, for everyone understands that the coward has to live with his shame for the rest of his life. In the case of this particular officer, his transgression was major: he could not bring himself to return at a moment when his unit desperately needed the ammunition and reinforcements he had been sent for.

Ignoring his own wounds, PFC Ray Walker spent part of that morning helping men who couldn't stand up to urinate into cans, "so they wouldn't wet themselves." He came across his assistant BAR man, PFC Middlekauf, on a stretcher; Middlekauf's jaw was badly swollen from a shrapnel wound. "I made some hot cocoa and helped him sit up and drink it." (Thirty-four years later, a portly, bald gentleman introduced himself at a Chosin Few reunion and thanked Walker for the companionship and comfort he had provided at a lonely moment.)

A Marine he didn't recognize came through the tent flaps.

"Hey, Walker—aren't you a friend of Reuben Fields? I got him outside in the truck."

"What's wrong with him?"

"He's had the course."

"You mean he's dead?"

"Not quite."

Walker: "Reuben Fields was a moonshiner's boy from Harlan County, Kentucky. I helped carry him in, busted ulna notwithstanding. He was unconscious and moaning. The doctors wouldn't treat him. I was indignant, then outraged—until someone explained that he was brain-injured and beyond help. We carried him back outside and put him down on some hay. He died in my arms. I cried. At least he wasn't alone."

*   *   *

Claypool: "Later that morning I found Mr. Ball down in the battalion aid station. He was just conscious enough to recognize me. 'What about the company?' he asked.

" 'Still holding on, sir.'

"He was gray from lack of blood. What plasma we had was frozen and unusable. The sun hadn't hit the valley floor yet and it was awfully cold in that tent. I took the sleeping bags off two dead Marines—not an easy job, what with rigor mortis—and put them around the lieutenant, stuffing the edges under the stretcher, tucking him in for the long journey. I was holding his hand when he passed. It was around 0830.

"I was going to miss Lieutenant Ball, and Captain Phillips too. They were close friends, by the way, and they complemented each other. Lieutenant Ball was quiet and studious and thorough. Captain Phillips was outgoing and dashing, a natural troop commander. Both of them had dedicated their adult lives to the Marine Corps, and they made being a Marine something special. I admired them. But then I admired the whole damn outfit. Easy Company, 7th Marines—they were the most exceptional group of people I've ever encountered."

30. THE SITUATION WAS EVEN
worse on Hill 1240, a mile to the southeast. One of Captain Hull's
platoons had been overrun and the other two had withdrawn to
avoid envelopment. Dog Company as a whole had evacuated the
hill by 2 A.M., leaving many dead behind.

PFC Al Bradshaw: "The probing started around nine, and by
eleven we were in the thick of a hell of a fight. Funny, the things
you remember. John Demer turned to me in the middle of it and
asked me to light him a cigarette. He had never smoked a cigarette
in his life. We got so busy right after that I didn't get a chance to
see if it made him sick, which it probably did. What happened was,
a machine gun began cranking off rounds in our direction from
behind us. Demer and me saw bullet holes appear in the canvas
shelter-half we had put up as a windbreak. Between bursts we
yelled like crazy for them to cut it out, but they wouldn't, so we
decided the gooks had captured one of our guns and were putting
it into action against us. When the kill zone moved elsewhere, I
popped up and emptied a clip of eight at them and that was the
end of it—no more action from *that* gun. To this day I'm not
absolutely certain it was gooks and not fellow Marines, but what're
ya gonna do?

"Then Sergeant Lane showed up and said they needed a BAR
man on the reverse slope to help protect the command post. So
Demer went off with Sergeant Lane—'Watch your ass,' I told
him—and that was the last time I ever saw John Demer."

PFC Franco LaCentra: "I was out on a listening post with my
fire team when the first illumination round went off and we saw
lots of Chinese. I said, 'Guys, we're leaving,' and the four of us
just ran back to the main line; but when we got there all we found
was dead Marines. I ran down to the command post tent and it

was empty and riddled with holes. That's when I realized Dog Company had been driven off the hill. It was a terrific shock.

"Then a gook with a burp gun stepped around the side of the tent. We both raised our weapons and pulled the triggers, and both our weapons failed to fire. Then a couple of other gooks jumped on me and down I went. This one gook gestured that I should unzip my parka and the two others crouched down and removed the grenades clipped to my cartridge belt. What surprised me most was how lackadaisical they were, as if they didn't have a care in the world. One of them removed my wristwatch. Then they stood up and stepped back, and the gook with the burp gun shot me, the bullet hitting me in the thigh. After they left, I crawled to a bunker that was open at both ends. Later I heard people talking Chinese close by and realized the gooks had set up a machine gun on top of the bunker. I could see their feet hanging down as they sat there.

"Looking back, it seems to me I was deliberately spared. That gook who shot me; why didn't he fire at my head, or give me a burst in the chest? He must have aimed at my thigh just to keep me out of the action. Those gooks on top of the bunker, they would ordinarily have chucked a grenade into any bunker before approaching it, but they didn't this time. Why was I spared and so many others weren't?"

Corporal Roy Pearl: "It looked like the enemy was breaking through between the two hills to the north and the battalion command post was in danger. Colonel Davis ordered all the clerks and drivers and messmen and communications people into a makeshift defense line around the headquarters tents. That included me, so I started to go outside, but the colonel said, 'Pearl, you stay.'

"He was very busy assessing the overall situation as reports came in by radio, phone, and runner. The only time he raised his voice in all the weeks I served with him was when Captain Hull reported by radio that Dog Company was no longer on the hill. The colonel's voice got loud: he told Captain Hull to get his people together and retake that hill and stay up there."

Lt. Col. Raymond Davis: "I suffered frustration and then guilt that night over not being able to do enough for the five companies. I don't hesitate to say I was tormented for hours by the situation: Easy Company barely holding onto 1282, Dog Company driven off 1240, and, later on, the mess Fox and Charlie Companies got into. Only one of my companies—Baker/7—was in anything other than an emergency situation." (Lt. Chew-Een Lee: "All the stuff that hit the fan that night did not hit the fan in our particular sector because of our aggressive patrolling.")

PFC George Crotts: "For me, the battle of 1240 started when someone woke me up by jabbing the toe of his boot into my side. I just exploded out of that bag, blinking myself awake, trying to get alert. There was a small man standing between me and the glowing embers of the campfire. I grabbed the M-1 and tried to shoot him, but the trigger was frozen. The only thing I could think to do was breathe hard on the action, and though it was fifteen below zero, it must have had some effect, because I was then able to fire off a clip. The muzzle flashes blinded me temporarily, but when vision returned he was gone. Unsolved mystery! There was no way I could have missed. You tell me.

"Anyway, the big shooting had commenced, and I spent part of the night with Chesterfield and Bob Martin tossing grenades to keep the gooks away. Later I saw a figure approaching and was about to open up when this voice calls out, 'Hold your fire! It's me, Bartels. The gooks are coming this way.'

"After Bartels joined us, Marty turned the gun around and got off a couple of bursts at an oncoming skirmish line. The last few rounds in the belt were inching toward the breech. When it was time, I loaded a fresh belt, closed the cover, and Marty got off one more burst before the gun jammed up. He tried frantically to clear it but couldn't. What do you say at a time like that? I'll tell you. You say, *'Oh, shit.'*

"The rest of the guys were pulling back, scrambling down the rear slope. Marty, Chesterfield, and me picked up the gun, the tripod, the ammo boxes—with the long belt trailing after us—and raced down to where Captain Hull was reorganizing troops for a counterattack.

" 'Bill Russell's dead,' Marty tells me. Bill was the one who had my wristwatch. Actually it was my *dad's* watch. On the day my Reserve unit was activated, he insisted we switch watches, because his was everything-proof and mine was nothing-proof. Have I explained that I loaned my watch to the other guys that night to stand watch with? Anyway, I considered looking for Bill's body so I could retrieve the watch, but then I imagined how it would look if someone saw me stripping the watch off a dead Marine. I was

close to Bill Russell, and the loss of the watch was a small matter
compared with his death; besides, I knew my dad would understand. But when I mentioned all this to Marty, he said Bill had
passed the watch to Jean Bartels the night before. But guess what?
Bartels had just been wounded and was already being stretchered
down the hill.

"Jesus, what a night *that* was."

"Okay," said Captain Hull, "let's go get the bastards."

The Chinese, unprepared for counteraction, recoiled in surprise,
and Hull's men regained a foothold on 1240. At dawn, sixteen
Marines held a hasty perimeter near the crest, so small that Hull's
runner, Corporal Walter Menard, was able to toss grenades from
its center to any Marine on the line who needed one.

PFC Al Bradshaw, one of the sixteen, was later assigned to carry
wounded Marines down the backslope. Bradshaw: "This one Marine was too big for me, so PFC Ernest Caldwell got him in a
fireman's carry and lugged him all the way down, with me carrying
their rifles. I had to walk backward because the Chinese were following us at a distance. Platoon Sergeant Arthur Wills picked a
very good time to join us, and he helped me hold off the Chinese
until we got to the bottom. That was the last time I saw PFC Ernest
Caldwell alive.

"When I got back to the perimeter, things were hot and heavy.
Eight-round clips get used up real fast. I was jamming in my last
one when I took a round in the right calf. The Chinese were so
close I could have hit them with a stone. Then I got hit in the right
thigh. I saw another Marine get hit and roll down the slope like a
log. Then I ran into Staff Sergeant Wills. Grenades started coming
in, and Sergeant Wills and me was blasted into the air. When he
came down, his head was bleeding, so I says, 'Well, there's your
Purple Heart,' and he smiled. That was the last time I saw Staff
Sergeant Wills alive.

"The thigh wound was pretty bad. You could tell it was an ar-
tery because it pumped out a spout of blood with every heartbeat.
The only way I could stop the bleeding was to stick my finger into
the hole and press off to one side. Try doing that sometime with
a finger that's dirty and a hole in your flesh that's nothing but raw
meat. PFC Grover Boaz showed up and handed me a bandage from
his first-aid kit, and while I was tearing it open he dumped some

sulfa powder into the two holes. Grover Boaz, by the way, had been wounded himself, wounded in the head, but he was doing a good job ignoring it. Only after he said 'So long' did I realize he had used his own first-aid kit on me. And you probably know what I'm going to say next. That was the last time I saw Grover Boaz alive.

"At daybreak an explosion blew my helmet off and tossed me in the air again. I was sure I had been blown in half. When I landed a few yards downhill, all I could see was white. After a minute or two my eyesight cleared and I started crawling around looking for something to shoot with. I found a wounded gook holding a Thompson and snatched it out of his hands. He just lay there looking at me, and I went ahead and yanked the magazine belt from around his waist.

"Things weren't looking too good at this time. It seemed like every Marine on the slope was dead or wounded and the next charge by the gooks was going to take us all and we would be nothing but memories. There was no wind that morning, and gun smoke from all the shooting and grenades hung in the air above us, like an overcast of cloud. And here's my last memory of the fight on 1240. Over to my right and downhill a ways I saw two gooks dragging a Marine by his heels while a third walked alongside sticking him with a bayonet. The Marine was either dead or on the way, so I aimed the Thompson and gave them the whole magazine, Marine and all."

Soon after daybreak, a platoon from Captain Jack Jones's Charlie Company, 5th Marines, appeared, under the command of 2nd Lt. Harold Dawe. The PFC who was leading the way took a look at the squad-size perimeter, grinned, and said, "Looks like y'all been having your troubles."

Franco LaCentra: "I heard American voices and the occasional explosion of a grenade, and I realized it was Marines driving the gooks back, preceding each movement with grenades. When they approached the bunker I was hiding in, I called out to them, but my voice was weak. Then I heard a Marine say, 'There's someone in that one.'

" 'It's a gook.'

" 'Hey, you stupid assholes! I'm a fuckin' United States fuckin'

Marine! Quit throwing those fuckin' grenades, you stupid fuckin' idiots!'

"When they pulled me out of the bunker, I saw the three gooks were dead and their machine gun was all dented and twisted. I took a bayonet off one of them as a souvenir."

PFC Al Bradshaw: "By daylight I was weak from loss of blood and my brain wasn't working too good, so maybe it was my imagination, but I don't think there was a single live Marine in sight. Nothing around me but live Chinese. But then I heard a voice, 'There's another one over there.'

" 'No, he's dead.'

"They started to pass me by, and I scared hell out of them when I spoke: 'You guys better haul ass, because there's nothing around here but gooks and dead Marines.'

"A sergeant with a red mustache thought that was funny.

" 'Where's the rest of your company?'

" 'This here's it.'

" 'Huh?'

" 'This here's Dog Company, 7th Marines.' "

At the aid station later that morning, Bradshaw was trying to get some food down his throat when he heard someone calling his name. He looked around. There were wounded Marines on stretchers on all sides, but none were paying any attention to him. A few minutes later a Marine from Dog Company stopped by.

"He was asking for you."

"Who was?"

"John Demer."

"Oh, yeah? Where's he at?"

The guy nodded over toward the corner. "He just died."

". . . Shit."

Bradshaw says he can still hear John Demer calling out his name.

31.

LT. COL. RAYMOND MURRAY, commanding 5th Marines: "Upon receipt of information that the enemy had cut the roads to our rear, I realized we were in a serious predicament." This cool, affectless remark, almost comical in its understatement, was made to historian S. L. A. Marshall a month after the campaign. It conceals the wave of gloom Murray had experienced, as he admitted in a letter to a writer years later. "I felt that first night that we had had the course. Once I learned we were being hit from virtually all sides in considerable strength, and knowing we were out there all by ourselves, I figured we were finished. Frankly I thought that Yudam-ni, North Korea, was where I was going to die." Trained by his command experiences on Guadalcanal, Tarawa, and Saipan to ignore the emotions of war, Murray took the time to compose and send a simple, straightforward message to his units.

> From: C.O. 5th Marines
> To: 1/5; 2/5; 3/5; 1/11; H & S Co; 4.2 Mortar Co
> *All hands make sure every shot counts*

Radio communication between General Smith and the regimental commanders was poor to begin with, because of the intervening mountains. The 5th Marines, most of the 7th, and three battalions from the artillery regiment had been surrounded for several hours, but the Marine command was just becoming aware of it. That General Smith was as yet uninformed as to the scale and severity of the Chinese attack is clearly indicated by an entry in his diary that evening: "Late in the day reports were received that both the 5th and the 7th Marines were hit by the CCF. . . . No details are available yet."

Ordinarily this was a situation in which the assistant division commander would have been sent to Yudam-ni to assume command of both regiments; but Brigadier General Edward Craig, as we have seen, was at that moment heading eastward across the Pacific in a transport plane. On the twenty-sixth he had been handed a message that began, "Father not expected to live . . ." Craig talked it over with General Smith, who later made this comment: "General Craig was very close to his father and wished to be with him in his last hours. . . . Thus I was without an assistant division commander during the Chosin Reservoir operation."

Lt. Col. Murray: "Colonel Litzenberg called me on the morning on the twenty-eighth and said, 'We'll have to coordinate our movements closely from now on. Our staffs should be within easy reach of each other.' His command post was in a small stone house with glass windows and a wooden floor. He now invited me to move in with him. As the senior officer present at Yudam-ni, he had every right to determine what should be done and to issue the requisite orders. I'll always be grateful that he chose instead to treat me as an equal in the venture. I was, after all, a thirty-seven-year-old lieutenant colonel at the time. Officers of that rank normally command battalions, not regiments. Litzenberg was ten years older and a full colonel."

The first thing the two officers determined was that the 5th Marines would *not* resume their westward march. Then they went to work with the combined staffs, consolidating and reorganizing. Basically what they were doing was figuring out how to strengthen the perimeter by reducing it.

On a personal level the thing that impressed Murray most about the situation was what he called "the sheer unreality of it. We just went about our daily business, as though we were on maneuvers. Vehicles moved freely up and down the roads on the valley floor. Men who were not actually on the line sat down and wrote letters to their wives and sweethearts. Men lined up with their tin mess gear outside the mess tents. The routine of signing reports continued in the usual fashion. But at the same time you could look up at the slopes and see Marines and Chinese throwing grenades at each other. I watched through binoculars as a platoon of Marines retook some terrain they had lost a few minutes earlier. I saw one Marine stand up, fire a couple of rounds, then drop. Two of his mates approached to help him, but the fire became so intense they had to fall back. I then saw a Chinese squad come across the skyline, and two soldiers stopped by the fallen Marine to divest him of his parka and boots. It was like watching a play."

As the daylight lull set in, Marines standing watch stamped their feet or wiggled their toes inside ice-clogged shoe-pacs and worried about frostbite. Doc Litvin: "Everyone knew by now how important it was to avoid sweating—which was not always possible in the heat of a firefight—because the sweat would freeze into a film of ice between your foot and the innersole of the rubberized shoe-pac; and if you didn't remove the shoe-pac occasionally, rub your feet, and change your socks, you were a good bet to become a cold-weather casualty."

The aid stations were overwhelmed, and many of the wounded had to be laid out on the ground outside, the corpsmen spreading tarpaulins over them, stopping by now and then to brush fresh snow off the faces of the helpless. It was easy to tell who was alive and who was dead; the faces of the dead were masked with snow.

Lt. Comdr. Chester Lessenden, regimental surgeon, 5th Marines: "We couldn't use plasma because it wouldn't go into solution and the feed tubes would clog up with particles. We couldn't change dressings because you needed to take off your gloves, and if you did, your hands would get frostbitten. We couldn't cut a man's clothes off to get at a wound because he would freeze. Often a wounded man was better off if we left him alone. About the only positive aspect was that the cold slowed down a wounded man's bleeding. Otherwise it was all negative. Have you ever tried stuffing a wounded man into a sleeping bag?"

Navy Lt.(jg) Robert Wedemeyer was examining the legless Sergeant Robert Kennemore, who had miraculously survived after smothering two grenades on Hill 1282. Kennemore, in a morphine haze, inquired about the state of his genitals. Dr. Wedemeyer found a graceful way to respond. "What the hell," he said, "you wouldn't worry about half a tank of gas, would you?" Kennemore eventually fathered seven children.

In the 2/5 aid tent Doc Litvin attended to a never-ending stream of wounded Marines and struggled to remain calm. By now everyone knew the road south was blocked, and there was a rumor that Litzenberg and Murray were going to split their forces and attempt independently to make their way to the sea. Litvin: "This frightened me, and I understood for the first time how bad our situation really was. Every so often one of those fragile helicopters—they looked like big dragonflies—would land nearby to pick up a critical case, and I could barely restrain myself from slipping over to the landing pad and climbing aboard. I want you to understand that I could stick my head through the flaps and see vast numbers of armed Chinese on the hills around us. . . .

"I kept wondering when that famous objectivity doctors are supposed to protect themselves with would kick in. Up until Chosin I had felt omnipotent, as all young doctors do; but up there at Yudam-ni I felt pretty darned useless whenever one of those youngsters gave up the ghost. The boys wounded in the chest or belly were the hardest to deal with. And what about the poor devils who were dying from internal bleeding? You can't put a pressure dressing around a liver or a spleen or a lung."

In whatever shelter they could find to get out of the rock-glazing wind that morning, Marines with numb fingers were disassembling M-1s, carbines, Browning automatic rifles, and machine guns, wiping off lubricating oil made gummy by the cold. The carbine had been recognized by now as the weak sister in the family of small arms, the gasses of its small cartridge too feeble in the cold to carry out the reloading action. The Garand M-1s had proven more reliable, and prudent Marines were trading their carbines for rifles plucked from the stacks outside the aid stations.

All weapons were in fact adversely affected by the cold. Grenades failed to explode. The barrel jackets of the heavy machine guns had to be filled with antifreeze solution, while the light machine guns were fired every few minutes, with or without target, to keep them from freezing up. The mortars worked satisfactorily, except when the base plates cracked from the pounding of the recoil. The volume of artillery fire was well below normal because of the cold; after each shot, a howitzer barrel could take as long as half a minute to creep back into position for the next round.

In the warming tents snow was melted and water brought to a boil atop oil-burning stoves. C-ration cans were plopped into the water to thaw out. Too often it was only the outer layer that thawed, and many Marines who ate the icy core later experienced the gnawing pains of enteritis and the stabs of diarrhea.

PFC Robert P. Cameron, one of the survivors of 1403, was standing in line waiting to have his wounds tended to. Cameron: "The Marine at the head of the line was slowly twirling in place to help the corpsman apply a long bandage to his head, mummy fashion. A guy I recognized named Bobbie Jean Callison came in through the tent flaps. We had served together in China. I called out to him. He didn't recognize me at first because my right eye was swollen shut, the eyelid the color of a Pacific sunset, and I had a compound fracture of the upper jaw with four teeth partially broken off in front, leaving spikes hanging down like stalactites when I smiled. Bobbie Jean Callison was a funny guy. When he finally recognized me, he came over, took a long look, and said, 'Cameron, you get better looking every time I see you.' He shook his head. 'Yes, sir,' he said, 'you seem bound and determined to become the handsomest jarhead in the Fleet Marine Force.' I would have busted out laughing if my jaw hadn't hurt so much; but the others in the line did the laughing for me and I just let my one eye sort of gleam."

Like the medical staff in the aid tents, Sergeant Robert Gault and his Graves Registration team had more work than they could handle. Gault: "What's the use of rushing when you're surrounded by dead Marines and the dead Marines are surrounded by live Chinese? It was hard to get used to the situation. They were on every skyline. They reminded me of a bunch of Indians doing a war dance.

"Once in awhile a Marine would ask if he could have a dead man's parka, because he got to sweating while climbing some slope and took it off and dropped it. We would remove the parka for him—if we could—while he stood there, not wanting to touch the body. Sometimes, though, you'd find a big bloody hole in the parka when we turned the man over, and the fellow wouldn't want it any more." Gault told the interviewer that since the corpses were frozen it meant there was no smell to bother you. "Down in the Pusan Perimeter it was different, what with the temperature going above a hundred every day."

The rumor about the 5th and 7th Regiments trying to make their way independently to the sea was baseless; Litzenberg and Murray had every intention of staying together. Right now they were trying to figure out how to break through the enemy cordon without merely blasting their way through successive roadblocks. One of their first joint actions was to send the 7th Marines logistics chief, Major Maurice Roach, over to the edge of the reservoir itself to determine whether the ice was thick enough to support a convoy of trucks. If it was, everything could be moved to Hagaru over the ice, under air cover. With an armed escort Roach walked out onto the surface of the manmade lake, brushed off the coating of powdery snow with his gloved hands, did a test boring with an awl borrowed from the Engineers, and decided that three inches of black ice wasn't enough to support a string of heavily laden trucks.

At one point during the afternoon of the twenty-eighth, Lt. Col. Murray expressed frustration at the casual attitude of the Division staff at Hagaru toward the predicament of the 5th and 7th at Yudam-ni. Murray: "They didn't seem to understand how much trouble we were in. I finally spoke to Litz about it. 'Let's send a message with the word 'grave' in it. Let's tell 'em the situation up here is 'grave.' That'll shake 'em up."

"No," said Litz. "We're not going to do that."

The Division staff was, in fact, just beginning to grasp how bad the situation was; but for now there wasn't much they could do about it. Interrogation of Chinese prisoners had revealed that the Marines at Yudam-ni were confronted with three Communist divisions: the 79th to the north, the 89th to the northwest, and the 59th to the southwest. Other divisions would soon join them. The Chinese had achieved two major objectives in their overall plan of annihilation: They had broken the 1st Marine Division into three major fragments, isolating them from one another: the first at Yudam-ni, the second at Hagaru, the third at Koto-ri. And they had blocked the road connecting them. (There were two minor fragmentations as well: Charlie Company/7, three miles down the road at Turkey Hill, and Fox Company/7 at Toktong Pass, seven miles down the road.)

The cloud cover began breaking up by noon, allowing the rays of the pale, heatless sun to shine through. An intermittent stream of Marine and Navy fighter-bombers from carriers offshore and Wonpo Airfield outside Hungnam provided some protection to the ground forces throughout the remainder of the day. That, more than anything, forced most of the Chinese to lay low during daylight hours on the twenty-eighth.

32.

AT 4:27 P.M. LITZENBERG RE-
ceived a message from Division ordering him to open the road
between Yudam-ni and Hagaru. Summoning the artillery commanders, he directed them to organize one-third of their firing batteries and a quarter of their Headquarters personnel into
provisional infantry platoons of thirty-five men each; these were to
be funneled into the depleted line companies. The adage "Every
Marine a rifleman" was about to be tested.

Meanwhile, the officers of Lt. Col. William Harris's 3/7 were
reluctant to admit that their battalion commander was showing
signs of emotional breakdown and collapse. Lt. Patrick Roe: "One
of his more bizarre acts was to appoint several officers in a row as
his Headquarters and Service chief. Every time an officer came
through the flaps he would say, 'You're our H and S commander.'
At first we thought it was his idea of a joke. I finally realized how
shook he was when I heard him instructing his driver to burn all
his gear and belongings except for his sleeping bag, his backpack,
and his .45. He was obviously getting ready to take to the hills.
You can understand that his behavior had a chilling effect on us."

PFC Leroy Martin, How/7: "I could see that the other survivors
from Hill 1403 were feeling as low as I was. There was little conversation between us, and no joking around. We must have looked
beaten. All at once the lieutenant [2nd Lt. Minard P. Newton]
ordered us to assemble outside. Out of the original seven company
officers, he was the only one left, so he was company commander
by default—if you can call what we had a company. A normal
wartime company, full strength, has maybe two hundred Marines;
there were about forty of us now. Anyway, the lieutenant got us
organized into fire teams and squads, saw to our weapons and
ammo, and before we knew it we were a functioning unit once

again. A good Marine lieutenant is worth his weight in gold. The only trouble is, they don't last very long."

PFC Robert P. Cameron, How/7: "When I found the chaplain and saw how busy he was comforting the wounded and dying, I said to hell with it; but as I turned away I spotted Sergeant Matthew Caruso, the chaplain's assistant. He said Chaplain [Cornelius] Griffin would be busy for a while but maybe there was something he could help me with. I told him my heart was heavy over the way I clubbed that Chinese soldier to death on 1403 and because of the way I left that dead Marine up there. Sergeant Caruso's words made me feel better: 'The tripod was the only weapon you had, right? He would have killed you if you hadn't killed him first. As far as the dead Marine goes, the correct thing was for you to get off that hill, since everyone else had already pulled out. It wasn't your responsibility to carry him down with you.'

" 'I couldn't even look at his face!'

" 'What difference does that make?'

" 'I didn't even check his dog tags!'

" 'So?'

"I told him the reason I didn't look at his face was I was afraid I might recognize him; and even if I didn't recognize him, I knew I'd have to remember his face for the rest of my life."

The narrow Hansang Valley was like an open invitation to the Chinese to attack the southwest portion of the Yudam-ni perimeter. Litzenberg was worried enough about it to direct Major Francis Parry to position his 105-mm howitzers in the direction of the tactical funnel it presented. By noon the Marines of Able Company, 7th, realized that they were not going to be allowed to return to Hansang to retrieve Lt. Frank Mitchell's body and the bodies of the other two Marines who died in action on the twenty-sixth; such a nontactical mission would weaken a perimeter that already had too many holes in it. PFC Timmy Killeen, Able/7: "There was a lot of soul-searching and self-reproach over leaving those three men out there, and even a feeling of betrayal. All that was misguided. During the combat patrol on the twenty-sixth, our first loyalty was to our wounded, and we were lucky to get them back safely."

Litzenberg had worked out a plan for extricating Fox and Charlie Companies from their dangerous predicament. He would order

Captain William Barber's Fox/7 to fight its way up the road to where Charlie Company was holding on—barely—at Turkey Hill, a distance of three miles, while Able and Baker Companies fought their way down the road from the perimeter. The three companies, converging on Charlie/7, would, he assumed, be strong enough to drive off the surrounding Chinese. But when he attempted to set the plan in motion, Litzenberg ran into an unexpected reality. Captain Barber informed him by radio that because of the position and strength of the enemy and the number of Fox Company casualties, he deemed it physically impossible to carry out an order to fight his way three miles uproad to relieve Charlie Company. "Request permission to remain in present location," he said.

The colonel thought it over for a moment, then said, "Permission granted."

Litzenberg's next move was another long shot. In a brief radio contact with Lt. Col. Randolph Lockwood—the only one of his battalion commanders not to reach Yudam-ni—he directed him to clear the road north of Hagaru and join Fox Company at the pass. At this time the only troops remaining with Lockwood were his Weapons Company, minus detachments of heavy machine guns and 81-mm mortars loaned to Barber, and his Headquarters and Service Company. Lockwood set off up the snowy road, still unaware that two of his infantry companies had been shattered the night before on Hills 1240 and 1282, and that his third company was surrounded at Toktong Pass. After proceeding as far as the abandoned gold-mine shafts a mile north of Hagaru, he called a temporary halt to sweep the horizon through his Zeiss binoculars.

Lockwood: "What I saw was a long line of evenly spaced dots that turned out to be Chinese soldiers. Long-range small-arms fire began plunging into the snow nearby. I deployed my men, but every tactical move I made was mirrored by the enemy. Without heavy machine guns, without mortars, with a recalcitrant radio that wouldn't let us call in artillery fires or air strikes, I had to content myself with holding in place, smoking my pipe, and awaiting further orders. Colonel Litzenberg, when he was finally able to contact me, ordered me back to Hagaru."

Lt. Col. Raymond Davis, at the wheel of his jeep, was checking ammunition stockpiles in the Yudam-ni perimeter. Corporal Roy Pearl was as usual riding in the backseat with the battalion radio.

Pearl: "I kept picking up this faint transmission, just like the other day when Baker Company was in trouble. I thought I could hear gunfire in the background and someone shouting.

" 'Sir? Could you stop the jeep for a minute?' The colonel pulled over and I hunched over the handset. I could hear gunfire and shouting in the background. 'Could you turn off the motor, Colonel? The signal's very weak.'

" 'What is it, Pearl?'

"I finally determined that the signal was from the Charlie Company radio operator. He said Charlie was surrounded and needed help. I held out the handset and the colonel took it." Lieutenant Colonel Davis: "I could hear the relief in the man's voice when he realized he was talking to his battalion commander."

The situation at Turkey Hill was dire. Captain John Morris's truncated company (one of his platoons had remained within the perimeter to guard the Litzenberg-Murray command post) was threatened with extinction. Davis: "I went directly to Litz and asked permission to take Able and Baker Companies out of the perimeter and down the road to try and extricate Charlie Company. It was a tough choice for Litzenberg. If he said no, Morris was probably finished. If he said yes, it meant the southern side of the perimeter would be even more exposed to an attack from the Hansang Valley than it already was.

" 'Take the guard-duty platoon with you,' he said after a while. I was turning to leave when he added, 'I'm giving you the option of moving on after you relieve Morris. In other words, you may continue south and relieve Barber in the pass, as long as you and Morris and Barber are back here by nightfall.'"

33.

CHARLIE COMPANY'S POSITIONS lay astride the lower slope of Turkey Hill (Hill 1419), their weapons oriented toward the crest overlooking the road from the east. Like certain other units on the night of the great Chinese onfall, Captain John Morris's Marines were not as alert as they might have been. The presumption had been made that C/7 was safely tucked between two regiments three miles up the road at Yudam-ni and a reinforced company three miles down the road in Toktong Pass.

The Chinese descended on Turkey Hill at 2:30 A.M., November 28, overrunning Lt. Jack Chabek's platoon on the right, inflicting many casualties, then swinging to the left against Staff Sergeant Earl J. Payne's platoon. (The latter was short a squad, for Payne had sent Corporal Leland Brown and his men upslope earlier to establish an outpost.) Captain Morris reinforced his two platoons at the critical moment by sending every available man from his Headquarters and Mortar Sections to the line. Enemy fire had rendered the radio inoperative, and Morris was unable to obtain help from the Corsairs on station overhead or any of the artillery batteries at Yudam-ni.

There had been no word from the outpost since the start of the action. When the fire slackened momentarily at daybreak, Captain Morris cupped his hands and shouted uphill: "Corporal Brown! Corporal Leland Brown!" There was no response.

Corporal Curtis Kiesling volunteered to climb the slope and make contact with the outpost. Grateful for the offer, Morris watched the young Marine work his way through the boulders on the steep slope until he was lost from sight. After a tense ten-minute wait, Kiesling reappeared and called down, "No sign of them, skipper."

Kiesling then moved to his left, resuming the search. As he was working his way around an outcropping of rock, a machine gun opened up and Kiesling's body came sliding down the slope in a rush of pebbles and stones.

Because of the number of casualties, Captain Morris decided that further attempts to find the outposted squad would be foolhardy. Charlie Company was surrounded; ammunition was critically low; more than ten Marines were dead, some fifty wounded. It looked as though the only thing that could save Charlie Company from annihilation was a working radio. Corporal Leonard Delenski was struggling with numb hands to repair it, as the rest of the company watched the Chinese methodically close the ring around their small tactical island.

PFC Richard M. Dunlap: "A machine gunner out in front of my position got hit, and Staff Sergeant Earl Payne told me to crawl out there and bring the gun back. You can't imagine the abject terror I felt as I crawled across this piece of open ground that was being torn up by enemy bullets—I could see them drilling holes in the crusted snow all around. I remembered something my mom told me before I left home: 'Try not to hate your enemies,' she said. Well, I never hated the Chinese, not even when I was crossing that field of bullets. Anyway, when I reached the gun I found the gunner still alive, so I got right up next to him and asked if he could climb on my back. Well, he did, and I crawled back to the ditch with him riding piggyback. Later some of the guys expressed amazement that I hadn't been hit; but I guess I was just meant to continue."

Around noon the radio suddenly buzzed to life in Corporal Delensky's hands, and he let out a jubilant shout. Lieutenant Colonel Davis: "I don't recall exactly how the conversation went when Charlie Company made contact with us, but I got across the basic message: Hang on! We're on the way."

Using the resurrected radio, the battalion air liaison, Lt. Robert Wilson, called in a napalm strike on a large group of Chinese near Morris's position; few of them survived the sticky flames which sucked oxygen from lungs and vaporized cotton-padded uniforms in an instant.

Lt. Col. Davis: "It didn't take us long to get saddled up. I told the two company commanders, Hovatter and Kurcaba, that we were going to strike off down the road very fast and see how far we could get before moving into the hills. About two miles later I sent Able Company up the slope, keeping Baker Company down below. Lieutenant Hovatter soon radioed that he had found a path by which Able Company could outflank the enemy."

Major Thomas Tighe, 1/7 operations officer: "From the ditch beside the road I suggested that the colonel take cover. A dead or wounded battalion commander, I told him, was not what we needed right now. Davis smiled and explained that he could better coordinate the tactical moves from the road, where he could see the situation as it unfolded. It may have been foolhardy of him, but the men of 1/7 were glad to have the battalion commander up front like that, sharing the danger and risk."

Lt. Chew-Een Lee: "I had thrown away my arm-sling. This was one of my very rare mistakes. The wound became bothersome after that: due to my liveliness and constant movement, I kept breaking the scab, causing renewed bleeding, and the wound remained raw. None of this slowed me down, of course; my men needed leadership and I was obligated to provide it."

The final assault was simple and straightforward. Able Company, moving behind a barrage of 81-mm mortar rounds, drove the enemy over the top of the crest toward the road, allowing Baker Company to cut them down in a crossfire. Corporal Pearl: "The Chinese broke up into small bands, running every which way."

During the slaughter, as Davis talked on the tactical radio with Hovatter, long-range machine-gun fire began peppering the road around him. Davis: "A jeep driver ran up to me and said, 'Colonel, won't you at least get down behind the jeep?' It was bothering him so much that I decided to do as he requested, and I continued my radio conversation crouched next to one of the rear wheels."

A light snow began to fall as the battle wound down. The hours had dragged by, and it was obvious to Davis that he would not be able to continue on to Toktong Pass and rescue Fox Company. 1st Lt. George Klieforth's platoon of Morris's company—the one that had been guarding the combined command post—now arrowed directly into Charlie Company's position, where the men began loading casualties onto stretchers and carrying them down to the road. Lt. Joseph Owen: "There wasn't much fight left in Charlie Company."

Lt. Col. Davis: "I've always thought a better job could have been done supporting those Marines out there." (This was his respectful-of-authority way of criticizing Colonel Litzenberg for having left C/7 in such a vulnerable and tactically dubious position.)

Back inside the perimeter, all buttoned up for the night, the Marines at Yudam-ni felt a little less vulnerable with all three companies of 1/7 once again in the fold.

Captain William Barber's Fox Company was still on its own, out in the cold.

34.
THE HILL BARBER HAD CHOSEN
to occupy rose sharply behind two abandoned huts on the road; he had set up his command post in one of the huts. There was a stand of tall pines halfway up, but mostly the hill was bare. On the north side a narrow saddle formed a bridge to a boulder-strewn ridge, and behind the ridge loomed Toktong-san, the highest mountain in the immediate neighborhood. Barber knew that if the Chinese should decide to dispute the presence of Fox Company, this land bridge was the most likely approach.

At the base of the hill, near the huts, was an eight-foot embankment built in 1932 when the Japanese cut the road through the mountains. A crude, bird's-eye sketch would show Fox Company's lines in the form of a horseshoe, the legs anchored near the road, the arc curving across the top of the hill. Lt. Robert C. McCarthy's platoon occupied the center, with Lt. Elmo G. Peterson's platoon on the left and Lt. John M. Dunn's on the right.

Lt. Lawrence Schmitt: "We were too damn satisfied with our tight cozy perimeter, right there beside northeast Korea's own Lincoln Highway. Personally I thought our position was impregnable, so strong the gooks wouldn't dream of bothering us. The only gooks in the neighborhood, I figured, were maybe a lookout or two assigned to keep an eye on us. Captain Barber didn't share the general complacency. He took every precaution, did everything by the book: assigning platoon defense sectors and fields of fire, supervising everything closely, shifting the heavies around until he got the angles we wanted. He behaved as though he expected an attack that very night. God bless this tremendous captain of Marines for all his fussing! He saved our collective ass."

Lt. Donald Campbell, the artillery forward observer, informed Barber that it was impossible to register Captain Benjamin Read's battery because the 105-mm howitzers, seven miles away, were at extreme range. Fire missions could be called on an individual basis, he said, though accuracy was not guaranteed. Master Sergeant Charles C. Dana: "We had built some fires before dusk. The captain allowed us to keep them stoked for a while after dark, but they were doused by 2100. We had a twenty-five percent watch from that point on."

The last truck convoy came rumbling down the pass, gears grinding on the steep grades, audible for a mile in the still night before their headlights swept into view. After they roared past Fox Company's outpost and disappeared around the bend, silence descended on Toktong Pass. The night was clear, bright, and bitterly cold.

From the viewpoint of Fox Company, the last formal event before the Chinese onfall was a routine mission carried out by a battalion wire team that came all the way out from Yudam-ni. PFC James Windham: "Sergeant Casey Nix showed up with orders to get a phone line down to Fox Company as soon as possible. It was very late, sometime around midnight. I remember the moon was out and there were lots of stars. There were five of us, including the jeep driver. The jeep was rigged to dispense wire from a reel off the back. I had the feeling something big was about to happen and was very tense as we pulled away from the command post. I learned later that the others felt the same way, but nobody said anything about it at the time. Wiremen are always worried about getting ambushed because they often have to lay wire out to isolated spots off the road. The sound the reel made seemed noisy as hell, and since we had the feeling we were being watched, it only made the whole thing scarier than it already was. To this day I wonder why the Chinese let us pass. They could have taken us so easy. The thing that haunts me is that just after we got back inside the Yudam-ni perimeter the road behind us was flooded with Chinese heading toward Fox Company. What if we had started out five minutes later!"

On Fox Hill, Lt. Donald Campbell was watching the distant flares in the sky over Yudam-ni and listening to the faint echoes of heavy fighting that wafted up the pass. Campbell was another of those who, with no hard evidence, sensed that the enemy was coiling to strike. Acting on impulse, he contacted Read's How Battery in Hagaru and requested a few rounds of what he later called precautionary fire. Captain Read responded to the request personally, conveying to Campbell the unhappy news that How's six-gun battery had been ordered to respond only in an emergency. There was more bad news: Campbell's radio signal was growing weaker, even though the battery had been newly installed, and he wasn't sure how many more chances he would have to raise Hagaru during the night.

Around one o'clock in the morning Lt. McCarthy noticed that things were unnaturally quiet and decided it would be a good time to inspect the lines. In the moonlight he hiked from hole to hole, becoming increasingly annoyed at the dopey behavior of men supposedly on watch, men who were not only sleepy but stunned by the cold. McCarthy summoned his platoon sergeant, his three squad leaders, and his section chiefs. Huddling in the lee of a boulder he warned that their collective rear ends would soon be slung unless they kept their troops in a full state of alertness. An hour later he carried out another round of inspection and was pleased to hear the proper challenges ring out from each position. McCarthy returned to his own shallow hole, pulled off his ice-encrusted footgear, and eased into his bag.

Along with a surprising number of his comrades, Lt. Lawrence Schmitt experienced a premonition of peril during the hours leading up to the Chinese assault.

Nov 27
Dear Evelyn
I enjoy writing to you darling because when I write I feel as though we are spending time together. If you shouldn't hear from me for a couple of days you'll know I am busy.

Schmitt, in the roadside command post, had been assigned the first watch, nine to eleven. Worried about drifting off to sleep, he upended an ammunition box and sat uncomfortably on it, ready to receive the routine all-clear reports every half hour from the sentinels. The hours crawled by, and then it was time to turn the watch over to the next man in line. He nudged Staff Sergeant Groenwald awake.

"Take over, buddy. It's 2300." As the platoon sergeant settled himself beside the phone, Schmitt pulled off his shoe-pacs and wormed gratefully into his bag. "I was asleep by the time I pulled the zipper all the way up."

*   *   *

"Captain! Captain Barber!"

Groenwald was poking the company commander, calling him out of a deep slumber.

"Yeah, what is it?" mumbled Barber.

"Second Platoon reports a whole bunch of natives coming down the road."

"Natives . . . . What time is it, Groenwald?"

"Almost 0400, sir."

Barber sat up and rubbed his face. "Okay. Tell Second Platoon to hold them there until we can question them. Mr. Chung?"

"Sir?"

"Get down there and check those people out."

PFC Jack Page, machine gunner, was on watch behind a heavy Browning near the bottom of the hill when he heard the shuffle of feet in the road. He could see no one. Page reached over and fully loaded the big weapon by yanking back the bolt, then sat listening as the sound grew louder. Around a curve a hundred yards up the road he saw, by the light of the setting moon, a long column of men, four abreast. Page: "Every time you see the enemy it's hard to believe he's real, hard to believe you're seeing what you're seeing. Me and my assistant gunner talked it over in whispers, trying to decide if these troops were friendly or not." All doubt dissolved when the column approached close enough for Page and the others to see the ear-flapped headgear and the stubby burp guns slung from their necks. The section chief had already reported the sighting to the command post, and Mr. Chung, the interpreter, was on his way down; but Sergeant Page could wait no longer. The legendary Battle of Toktong Pass was about to begin.

"Here they come!" shouted Corporal Thomas Ashdale, one of McCarthy's squad leaders.

Lt. Larry Schmitt: "The temperature at this moment—so we learned later—was around fifteen degrees below zero."

Some of the Chinese who had scattered after Sergeant Page's opening burst found temporary shelter against the eight-foot-high embankment, protected from Page's bursts but not from the Marines at the downhill end of Peterson's line who rolled grenades over the top of the cut and then shot those who tried to flee up the road.

The Marines in the roadside shack were jolted awake when a burp gun cut loose, sending a spray of slugs through the walls. Every man was out of his bag in an instant, grabbing for his boots. Lt. Schmitt, who had been using his for a pillow, now jammed them on without lacing them up.

"Where the hell are my boots?" yelled Captain Barber. "Wright, you got my boots?"

Lt. Clark Wright, the exec, replied, "No, sir."

The captain was frantic. In the dim light of the lantern Schmitt could see him tossing around bedding and gear in a desperate search.

"Goddamn it, Wright, I found your boots! You must have mine on!"

"Oh, *shit!*"

"Never mind," said Barber, pulling on Wright's frozen shoe-pacs. "Schmitt!"

"Sir?"

"You stay here on the phone and relay orders."

A moment later Schmitt and the radio operator were alone in the shack, the latter trying to contact Yudam-ni: "Bilgewater, this is Bilgewater Fox. Do you read me? Over." Then the phone went dead. The logical conclusion was that the enemy had cut the line, which meant there were Chinese between the command post and the platoons up the hill. The first thing Schmitt discovered when he went outside was that the 81-mm mortar crew wasn't manning the tubes. Then he saw them hiding behind the other shack.

"What's going on here?"

"Sir, Jonesy said to get out of there and we did."

Schmitt was able to convince them that the company needed the tubes and ammo and got them to carry the gear up the slope. They had a problem at first because one of the base plates had frozen to the ground, but a few raps with an entrenching tool jarred it loose.

Lt. McCarthy had deployed his platoon in the classic two-squads-up, one-squad-back arrangement, with a machine-gun crew on both flanks. It was a strong position, yet the Chinese onslaught was so heavy that within minutes the forward squads began to waver. McCarthy barely had enough time to pull the survivors back to the reserve position, leaving the crest of the hill to the enemy. Of the thirty-five Marines in the up-front squads, fifteen were dead, with nine wounded. Three of his men were missing. Platoon Sergeant John Audas: "We learned later that each of these three had been picked up, bag and all, and dragged off when the gooks realized they were trapped in their bags. In the below-freezing temperature your breath could make the bag's zipper-track freeze up with ice, and that's probably what happened."

PFC Harrison Pomers and two other Marines occupied a hole on McCarthy's line. Pomers: "We heard someone down the line yell 'Here they come,' then all hell broke loose: bugles, whistles, burp guns. I took all eight clips out of my cartridge belt and lined them up on the edge of the hole. We waited until the gooks came close. You could see their silhouettes against the flares over Yudam-ni, and whenever our machine guns fired off a blast, the tracer rounds would illuminate their faces in red. There was so much noise you couldn't hardly think, and the gooks came on in waves. I aimed for anywhere between the neck and waist. I was too busy to be scared but not too busy to pray, and I said this prayer over and over: 'God, if I have to die, please don't let me shit in my scivvies.' I had a case of diarrhea, and the water was gurgling in my lower belly at the time."

PFC Peter Holgrun: "We spent the night shooting gooks as they approached, one bugle-blowing wave after the next. It was pure battle. You had no idea who was winning and who was losing."

Long before the action started, Private Hector Cafferata and PFC Kenneth Benson and two others had been sent out about twenty-five yards in front of McCarthy's line.

Cafferata: "I didn't want to come fully awake, but the shooting got so heavy I had to, and when I opened my eyes I saw all these gooks coming at us across the snow. They were so close you didn't have to think about aiming."

As soon as the Chinese moved past them and were swallowed up in the terrain, Benson and Cafferata grabbed all the ammunition they could carry and ran back to where the remainder of the platoon was barely holding on. Cafferata: "Benson pointed out that I had forgotten my boots. Well, I wasn't about to turn back for them. There were gooks everywhere."

PFCs Harrison Pomers and Gerald Smith occupied the hole Benson and Cafferata tumbled into; it was located at the very point in Fox Company's line that was under the severest pressure, as the Chinese tried to separate McCarthy and Peterson's platoons. Pomers. "At this time the officers were shifting men around, filling in positions where Marines had been killed or wounded, and it was a very good thing that Cafferata and Benson showed up when they did, because there were too few of us, or too many of them, depending on how you look at it. Grenades were coming in on us like hail. One landed in our hole and I went for it. *Bam.* It blew me against the other side of the hole. Another went off just after bouncing off my helmet. *Bam.*

" 'Pomers? Hey, Pomers.'

"I couldn't even open my mouth to answer, but I was able to move one arm, so I wiped my head with my hand, saw some blood, and put my helmet back on. I was numb all over, and both ears were ringing, and someone was calling my name over and over. A Navy corpsman was crouching over me, wiping my head with snow.

" 'You're okay,' he said.

"I was still in Palookaville but I managed to pick up my rifle and crawl over to Cafferata.

" 'We thought you got hit real bad,' he said.

" 'That's what I thought too.' Thank God it was concussion grenades and not frags.

" '*Whoa,*' Cafferata says, 'here come the son of a bitches again.'

"Every time he fired he exposed the upper half of his body. I saw this guy perform miracles. Did I mention that Hector was not only the biggest guy in the platoon but also our biggest fuckup? Anyway, Benson and me watched him catching live grenades and tossing them back at the gooks who threw them. One of them landed on the lip of the hole and Hector had to lean way back to scoop it up and sidearm it—but he wasn't fast enough and lost part of his hand in the explosion. He began spitting and cursing, then reloaded his rifle and fired off another clip. After he ran out we saw him swing the rifle like a baseball bat and knock a live grenade out of the park, *thwok!*"

Another grenade landed beside Benson and exploded, the blast blowing off his glasses, temporarily blinding him. Unable to fire his BAR, Benson began feeling around for rifle clips and handing them up to Cafferata whenever he heard the *spang* of an empty clip being ejected from the M-1.

"Can you see yet?"

"Nope."

The official Marine history states that the failure of the Chinese to penetrate the Marine line at that point was largely due to the efforts of Hector Cafferata, Kenneth Benson, and a PFC named Gerald Smith, and that the three of them are "credited with annihilating two enemy platoons."

35.

HAGARU, SEVEN MILES DOWN the line from Fox Hill, had not yet been molested. The only Hagaru-based unit to engage the enemy that night was Captain Benjamin Read's How Battery, firing in support of the distant outpost at Toktong Pass. Only a handful of officers at Hagaru knew anything about the desperate fighting to the north. At Koto, eleven miles south of Hagaru, the troops had enjoyed a quiet night.

At General Smith's direction Colonel Alpha Bowser, division operations chief, made the trip from Hamhung to Hagaru in a helicopter. Flying low, Bowser and the pilot counted no less than nine roadblocks and took some small arms fire from the ridges as they passed overhead. Bowser: "These people were here to stay, and they were feeling cocky about it. Because they were so sure they could take us, they were no longer as concerned about staying out of sight. It was apparent—though no one had officially said so— that the Marines at Hagaru and Koto were in the process of being surrounded. I wanted to continue on to Yudam-ni and talk with Litzenberg and Murray—get a firsthand report on what was going on and see how bad it really was up there—but General Smith said no. 'There's fourteen miles of bad weather between Hagaru and Yudam-ni, and I'm not happy about you traveling in a helicopter to begin with.' He traveled by the same means, of course, but he was never worried about his own safety." (Lt. Col. Joseph Winecoff, assistant division operations officer, volunteered to make the trip later that day, and Bowser commented that Winecoff's report from Yudam-ni "was instrumental in our decision to begin thinking about planning a withdrawal, whether an order came down from X Corps to that effect or not.")

At a much higher level of command, Vice Admiral C. Turner Joy, commanding U.S. naval forces in the Far East, foresaw as early as November 28 that if the Eighth Army continued to retreat, X

Corps would have to chose between falling back or being out-flanked. On that basis he warned Rear Admiral James H. Doyle, the amphibious forces commander, that a large-scale evacuation might become necessary. At that point Admiral Doyle began planning for the evacuation of X Corps from Hungnam.

During his short stay in Hagaru, Bowser was approached by Lt. Col. Thomas Ridge, commanding the Third Battalion of Colonel Lewis Puller's 1st Marine regiment. (Ridge's 3/1 was the only one of Puller's three infantry battalions to reach Hagaru.) Ridge recommended to Bowser that an overall defense coordinator be appointed with operational control over the piecemeal outfits, Marine and Army, on site. He reminded Bowser that only two of 3/1's infantry companies had reached Hagaru, and that the third—Captain Carl Sitter's George Company, plus the 300 men of the British 41 Commando—were still at Koto and should be sent north as fast as possible. Bowser agreed.

Ridge had called a meeting earlier that day with the two company commanders who had reached Hagaru—Captain Clarence Corley and 1st Lt. Joseph Fisher—to inform them of the massive enemy onfall at Yudam-ni and direct them to send patrols out to verify refugee claims that large enemy formations were gathering to the west and southwest of the village.

General Smith arrived at Hagaru by helicopter late in the morning and opened his new command post in an inconspicuous two-room house just north of the village, near the long concrete bridge that brought the road across the Changjin River and into town. "All it was," says Bowser, "was a place for him to lie down. He spent most of his time in the staff tent." On a wall in the modest bungalow hung a portrait of Soviet dictator Josef Stalin. When a staff officer reached up to take it down, the general said, "Leave it there. It might inspire us."

Oliver Prince Smith was something rare: a colorless Marine general. One of his former staff officers, asked to recall an anecdote about him, any anecdote, could only come up with the following: "Later in the campaign, when they started serving hot pancakes in the galley, why, the general was right there in line—and he went back for seconds!" Smith was as spare as the Marine Corps itself. Tall, gaunt, and gentlemanly, he was known for his steadiness and common sense. Working his way very slowly up the ranks, he had been a captain for seventeen years; in those days that was not unusual in the Corps, where officers were rigorously tested before being promoted.

During World War II Smith had commanded the 5th Marines at New Britain, served as assistant division commander at Peleliu, and was deputy chief of staff for the Tenth U.S. Army on Okinawa. In 1948 he was appointed assistant commandant of the Corps. Close to retirement when the Korean War broke out in June 1950, the white-haired general was sent to Camp Pendleton to take command of the 1st Marine Division. A soft-spoken, undemonstrative leader, Smith preferred to set policy, issuing carefully considered general orders, and trust his hand-picked subordinates to carry them out in detail. Ironically, he is best remembered today for a colorful remark he is supposed to have made later in the campaign. "Retreat, hell! We're attacking in another direction."

In those days, as journalist George Hildebrand points out, "Marine generals tended to come in two varieties. First, there were the ones like Field Harris: stocky, pugnacious men who operated by means of growls and barks. Second, there were the ones who looked like bankers. Homer Litzenberg, soon to be promoted to brigadier general, was one of the latter." Oliver Smith did not fit into either category. He would have been appropriately cast in an amateur play as a small-town druggist, a man whom older ladies would call nice looking if only he would put on a little weight.

Bowser: "You can't say it too often when speaking of the Chosin Reservoir campaign: It was due to General Smith's foresight that the Division survived. If the three infantry regiments had been as far apart as General Almond desired, the Division would have been destroyed piecemeal. It was also due to General Smith's foresight that we had heavy stockpiles of ammunition and essential supplies at Hagaru—not to mention the construction of the airfield, which was entirely his idea."

According to Bowser, one of the first things the general wanted to know when he climbed out of the helicopter at Hagaru was how soon the airfield would be finished. When Generals Smith and Harris had inspected the site on November 16, the black loam was dusty and friable. By the twenty-eighth it was frozen to a depth of eighteen inches, and the engineers reported that the strip was only forty percent completed, even though they had been working through the night, every night. It would not be ready for three days, the general was informed.

The battered village at the south end of the reservoir was a dreary panorama of huts, tents, and supply dumps, reminiscent of photographs of Klondike gold-mining camps. Dreary the site may have been, but its stockpiles, hospital facilities, and partly finished airstrip turned out to be of supreme importance in the Marine scheme of things. Hagaru was, as the official history has it, "the one base offering the 1st Marine Division a reasonable hope of uniting its separate elements."

Bowser: "I appointed Tom Ridge as Hagaru defense commander and the general seconded the motion. We knew the Chinese were going to descend on Hagaru soon, probably that very night. If Hagaru were to be taken by the Chinese, the two regiments up at Yudam-ni would be finished."

Colonel Ridge turned to, as Marines say, and began preparing to defend Hagaru with his understrength battalion and Read's six-gun battery as the core contingents, plus a few U.S. Army troops presently milling around inside the perimeter. Sorely needing more infantry to augment Corley's and Fisher's infantry companies, Ridge urged that Sitter's George/1 and the British commandos be rushed forward from Koto-ri. Ridge told Bowser about the four-mile circuit of the natural amphitheater two of his officers had made a few days earlier, and their conclusion that it would take a couple of *regiments* to adequately defend the basin. Like Yudam-ni, Hagaru was surrounded by mountains; but these were set much farther back than they were at Yudam-ni—except for one prominent landmass jutting above the east side of the village. The terrain offered the enemy two major covered avenues of approach. One was the close-in "East Hill," the other a draw leading toward the southwest arc of the perimeter, near the airfield construction site. Ridge was thus confronted with the choice of trying to defend everywhere and being weak everywhere, or of being strong in one or two places and hoping these were the places where the enemy would strike. It was apparent that major segments of the perimeter would have to be defended with his sparse artillery alone.

Before sunset that day, Captain Benjamin Read made a crucial decision to keep How Battery where it was, even though Ridge was then in the process of contracting the northeast arc of the perimeter. The contraction left his six tubes in an exposed position though backed at a distance by troops of the 1st Marine Service Battalion. The reason for Read's decision: he wanted to remain within firing range of Fox Company at Toktong Pass, extreme though it was, in case Captain Barber and his troops needed support. He knew that withdrawing into the relative safety of the perimeter would require re-laying the tubes and possibly losing the tenuous registration on Fox/7's position.

Read and his artillerymen could now hear the boom of heavy fieldpieces three miles up the east shore of the reservoir, where one artillery and two infantry battalions of the U.S. Army's 7th Division were already in contact with the enemy.

36.

36. THE 1ST MARINE DIVISION
wasn't the only unit depending on the narrow mountain road for
its survival. Elements of the U.S. Army's 7th Infantry Division were
pushing northward along the same road at the same time. The
Marine and Army units, having separate missions, were in no way
coordinated. While the Marines had expected to march west from
Yudam-ni, the 7th Division was planning to advance north of Hagaru and pass along the eastern shore of the reservoir. So far three
battalions of the Army division had ventured into that wasteland,
and a temporary command post had been set up at Hudong, an
abandoned hamlet three miles north of Hagaru.

Four miles farther on, at the southern edge of Pungnyuri Inlet,
Lt. Col. William Reilly's Third Battalion, 31st Regiment, and Lt.
Col. Ray Embree's 57th Field Artillery Battalion had stopped for
the night. Lt. Col. Don Faith's First Battalion, 32nd Regiment, was
encamped three miles north of the inlet. The bivouacs of these three
groups were desultory affairs, ill thought out, for none of the commanding officers expected to remain in position longer than overnight, and none expected to be attacked in place. The units of Task
Force MacLean—as the three separate groups came to be called—
had no stockpiles of ammunition, fuel, or rations. Nor had any
effort been made by X Corps to issue winter clothing to the Army
troops; MacLean's soldiers were outfitted in field jackets with pile
liners, and thin cotton pants. The item most sorely lacking was the
long hooded parka.

Lack of preparation was also evident in the nonexistent elec-
tronic communication between the three groups. At the time of the
Chinese onfall, the two senior officers east of the reservoir—Colonel MacLean and Brigadier General Henry Hodes—found themselves out of touch with one another, each at the extreme end of
the three encampments. Hodes, the assistant 7th Division com-

mander, remained at the Hudong command post; MacLean was with Faith at the forward perimeter. Thus the battles fought on the eastern shore of the reservoir were fought as separate actions, with none of the three Army groups able to support one another.

The Chinese announced their presence with bugle calls, whistles, and shepherd's horns, launching their assault on Faith's perimeter shortly before eleven on the night of November 27. After penetrating the American line between A Company, west of the road, and C Company, east of it, the Chinese then turned against the center of A Company. PFC James Ransone, assistant BAR man, A Company: "This is something I've been trying to put out of my mind for over forty years. It was the horns that woke me up. Flares were lighting up the landscape and I heard hollering and moaning and all kinds of weird noises that made my hair stand on end. We were being overrun, and the Chinese were already mixed up with the KATUSAs. There were people running back and forth and the GIs were firing at everything that moved. Lots of folks on both sides got shot by their own men. Those ROK troops were worse than useless—they got in the way."

Task Force MacLean's 3,000 men included 700 Republic of Korea troops. The 7th Division commander, Major General David Barr, said later that the South Koreans could not "by the wildest stretch of imagination" be considered combat-worthy; they were civilians who had been shanghaied out of the alleys and rice paddies of South Korea without warning and dumped into the 7th Division. Barr described them as being stunned, confused, and exhausted. Under the emergency conditions of the war's early weeks there had been no opportunity to train them. They were unpaid, cut off from their families, poorly equipped, and indifferently supplied. Almost one-fourth of the 7th Division was composed of these worthless "augmentation troops" who tended to behave more like prisoners of war than soldiers.

A small group of Marine engineers was at work a mile below Hudong. Supervised by Captain George W. King, they were busy stripping the sawmill of its lumber for use in Hagaru. Other than King, the only Marine officer to be found on the dismal eastern shore of the reservoir was Captain Edward Stamford, Faith's forward air controller. A brawny barrel-chested man, Stamford had been a dive-bomber pilot in the Pacific War. (Stamford: "In Korea I was one of several Marine pilots on temporary duty with the infantry—in this case the Army infantry—but basically I was a pilot waiting to get back into a Marine squadron.") Faith had asked Stamford to move his Tactical Air Control Party (TACP) to a position behind A Company's line, ready to provide air support for the battalion in the morning. The TACP was comprised of Stamford and three enlisted Marines: Corporal Myron Smith, PFC Wendell Shaffer, and PFC Billy Johnson. The four of them occupied a bunker not far from Army PFC Ransone's foxhole. Stamford had seen to it that his men were warmly dressed, having made a special jeep-run to Hagaru to obtain a full complement of winter clothing: shoe-pacs, heavy wool socks, long johns, alpaca vests, fur-lined gloves, and hooded parkas.

It was close to eleven, the night of the twenty-seventh, when Stamford was jolted awake by gunfire and voices chattering in Chinese nearby. He was reaching for his .45 when the poncho that served as a door was yanked aside and Stamford saw a fur-rimmed Oriental face in the moonlight. The Marine snap-fired, but not before the intruder had underhanded a sputtering grenade; it landed at the foot of Stamford's sleeping bag and exploded, wounding one of the enlisted men. Small-arms fire now began to strike the bunker, and rounds were coming through the cracks in the log roof. All four Marines went scrambling through the exit and found cover in a slit trench. An A Company lieutenant appeared and informed Stamford that Captain Edward Scullion, the company commander, was dead, and that the Marine officer, the most senior in the vicinity, would have to take command.

Stamford: "For an aviator to take over an infantry company was something like putting a baseball player in as quarterback for a football team." His Marine training stood him in good stead at this point, however, especially the thirteen-week course he had taken at the Marine Air/Infantry School at Quantico in 1944. "I believe it gave me a pretty good understanding of basic infantry tactics." Stamford at once began to assemble the scattered GIs into defensive patterns and direct small counterattacks that eventually drove infiltrators out of the company sector.

As gray dawn approached, the air turned even colder and snow began to fall. By now Stamford had reestablished A Company's position but had to give orders to cease fire because jumpy GIs were still shooting at each other. Stamford had lived with these poorly trained, poorly motivated soldiers for many weeks; he knew them, understood their problems, and was aware that they were doing the best they could. Unlike most of his fellow Marines in the reservoir sector, Captain Edward Stamford, USMC, was tolerant of the *doggies* (a word invariably used by Marines to signify soldiers of the U.S. Army) and never ridiculed them for their woeful ineptitude.

PFC James Ransone: "At daybreak the word was passed that every man was to check the foxholes nearby for Chinese. The nearest hole was only about ten yards off and I was sure it was empty; but when I walked over and took a look I got the shock of my life: there was a Chinese soldier with a burp gun crouched in the bottom of it. As soon as he saw me he threw up his hands. He was wearing a green quilted jacket and baggy quilted pants and he was shivering with the chills. On his head was a fur-lined cap with the earflaps down. The poor man was wearing tennis shoes! I couldn't understand that. Still can't. Then his right hand moved, and I jerked the rifle at him; but he kept trying to slip his hand into his jacket as if he was reaching for a pistol. I don't know why I didn't shoot him. What he brought out, though, wasn't a pistol but a small plastic wallet, which he opened and held up for me to see. There was a photograph of his young family—his wife and two small children. I prodded him out of the hole and herded him over to the place where the prisoners were being collected. I was hard in those days—the picture didn't move me at all; but it does now, to think of it."

With daylight coming on, the moment was fast approaching when Stamford and his TACP would demonstrate what they were trained for. Stamford sent PFC Johnson to fetch the air-ground radio from the jeep, for the planes were on their way.

"Boyhood One Four, this is Fireball One. Acknowledge. Over."

A minute later, four dark gull-winged Corsairs from VMF-312 appeared as specks in the sky to the south. Harnessing his "flying artillery" by voice from the ground, Stamford directed the pilots toward the first target of the day: a crowded Chinese position to the east of B Company. These troops, soldiers of the 80th Division, had become so foolishly bold that they were standing up and gawking at the Americans. In the dreary, almost treeless wasteland of the east shore, there was nowhere to hide as the Corsairs swooped down with their five-inch rockets and 20-mm rounds.

MacLean was expecting Lt. Col. William Reidy's Second Battalion, 31st Infantry, to show up momentarily. With this reinforcement, plus the tank company at Hudong, he was sure the task force could prevail. Though MacLean didn't yet know it, word had been received at the Hudong command post that Reidy's men were still many miles to the south, and that enemy action had stopped all traffic between Chinhung and Koto-ri.

The perimeter at Pungnyuri Inlet, held by the Third Battalion, 31st Infantry, and the 57th Field Artillery, had suffered greatly during the night. Lt. Col. William Reilly had been wounded along with the artillery commander, Colonel Embree. Embree's executive officer was dead. The surviving troops, compressed into hasty perimeters around the artillery pieces, had managed to keep the enemy at arms' length until daybreak when, apparently fearing air attack, they withdrew.

The Chinese, wary of the twenty-two tanks parked at Hudong, had not bothered the tankers, engineers, service troops, or regimental staffers bivouacked there. Brigadier General Hodes slept through the night, unaware of the assaults on the two Army positions to the north. On waking and hearing distant gunfire at the inlet position, Hodes tried but was unable to contact Reilly or MacLean by radio. He then ordered Captain Robert Drake's 31st Tank Company to go forward and provide whatever tactical support was needed.

Leaving six tanks behind for the defense of the shoreline command post, Drake took off at 10 A.M. with sixteen tanks, Hodes and Drake following in a jeep. There was trouble from the start, as some of the tanks began to slip, slide, and skid out of control, one becoming mired in icy mud. After thirty minutes of this, Chinese troops attacked the stalled column with captured American 3.5–inch rocket-launchers, getting close enough to climb atop several tanks and attempt to lift the engine-compartment doors in order to drop grenades. The enemy knocked two tanks out of action before machine-gun fire from the rear cleared them off the turrets. Hodes and Drake decided to cancel the mission after discussing the situation. Drake and company backtracked to Hudong, having lost two tanks to enemy action, with two more mired in the ditch beside the road.

The temperature at that time was fourteen degrees below zero and the wind was blowing up a gale. On the way back the Americans saw a strange and unnerving sight: long lines of horse-mounted Chinese, several hundred of them, moving toward the Hagaru perimeter. A mile to the south, Marine Captain King and his engineers at the sawmill saw them too and kept working.

Hodes and Drake made it safely back to the schoolhouse, with its glowing potbellied stove, by noon. Drake told General Hodes that if he had some infantry support he could probably do better the following morning. But there was no infantry at Hudong, and in the U.S. Army of that day, every GI was *not* a rifleman.

At this point Hodes borrowed one of Drake's tanks and headed down the road to Hagaru, to seek assistance from the Marines. He never returned.

37.

GENERAL EDWARD ALMOND preferred to believe that the reports of vast numbers of Chinese were grossly exaggerated, and that the distress signals from the reservoir represented little more than a loss of nerve on the part of Army and Marine commanders. Accordingly, he decided to fly north and personally stiffen the collective backbone.

Around noon on November 28 a helicopter dropped out of the leaden sky, depositing the X Corps commander on the frozen turf beside General Smith's newly opened command post at Hagaru. Smith had already seized the initiative by ordering consolidation of the perimeter at Yudam-ni as well as preparations for an attack by Litzenberg's regiment to reopen the road back to Hagaru. In a notation in his diary that evening—an astonishingly uninformative entry considering the circumstances—Almond wrote: "Had conference with Maj Gen Smith on the local situation." The substance of that conference is not known.

Almond departed Hagaru at 12:55 P.M. and flew to Colonel MacLean's command post several miles up the east shore of the reservoir. During his walk from the helicopter to MacLean's tent, Almond managed to win the disfavor of the GIs on the scene, perhaps unfairly, for being so well turned out: clean-shaven, perfectly groomed, dressed in starched cold-weather pants and a new parka. The GIs who saw him striding confidently across the field could tell, as Oliver Smith had, that the aggressive, bumptious corps commander did not yet grasp the dreadful seriousness of "the local situation."

Task Force MacLean was weak and vulnerable, barely able to defend itself against the enemy, let alone mount an offensive. Common sense dictated an immediate withdrawal to Hagaru; instead, the corps commander ordered a renewal of the offensive. Almond unfolded a large map on the hood of a nearby jeep, as Lt. Col.

Faith tried to inform him in detail of the previous night's assault by elements of two Chinese divisions.

"That's impossible," said Almond. "There aren't two Chinese divisions in the whole of North Korea! The enemy who is delaying you for the moment is nothing more than the remnant of units fleeing north. We're still attacking, and we're going all the way to the Yalu. Don't let a bunch of goddamn Chinese laundrymen stop you!" With a grand sweep of his arm, he gave Faith a direct order: "I want you to retake the high ground you lost during the night. When Reidy arrives you are to resume the attack northward."

As Almond was delivering his back-stiffening speech to the doomed battalion commander, organized units of "laundrymen" were either closing in on or bypassing the spot where they stood. None of the Chinese troops were fleeing north; they were in fact marching south in good order, segments of them preparing to attack Task Force MacLean, others getting into position to launch the first major assault on the Hagaru perimeter.

Finished with the briefing, Almond told Faith that he had three Silver Stars in his pocket and wanted to award them—one going to Faith himself, the other two to whomever Faith cared to designate. Lt. Col. Don Carlos Faith, a general's son and a West Pointer, was offended by Almond's cavalier attitude and the casualness with which he was prepared to pin medals on people. Barely concealing his disgust, Faith glanced around and spotted a wounded lieutenant named Everett Smalley sitting on a water can.

"Smalley, can you come over here and stand at attention?"

"Yes, sir."

Just then the Headquarters Company mess sergeant, George Stanley, happened to walk past.

"Stanley, step over here for a minute."

Faith rounded up a dozen clerks, drivers, and walking wounded to act as witnesses to the ceremony. The bewildered lieutenant and mess sergeant stood at attention and, along with Faith, received their undeserved decorations. (Overgenerous awarding of battle decorations has long been a characteristic of the U.S. Army. Recent example: More than 8,600 medals were awarded after the 1983 invasion of Grenada, even though less than 7,000 GIs set foot on that island.) According to several who were present, Faith angrily ripped the medal from his jacket as soon as Almond turned toward the idling helicopter. Lt. Hugh May, Faith's motor officer, later said he heard him mutter, "What a damned travesty." Major Wesley Curtis, Faith's operations officer, walked back to the tent with him.

"What did the general say?"

"You heard him. Remnants fleeing north."

Lt. Smalley went back to his water can. ("I got me a Silver Star, but I don't know what for.") He unpinned the medal and slipped it into his pocket.

Brigadier General Henry Hodes arrived in Hagaru in the borrowed tank early that afternoon and went directly to Smith's command post to inform him of the critical situation east of the reservoir. Smith listened carefully to the report, then told Hodes that immediate assistance was out of the question. Sending a Marine unit to reinforce Task Force MacLean would weaken the already-stretched-to-the-limit Hagaru perimeter, which was nothing less than the kingpin of the overall American deployment in northeast Korea.

Smith was by no means convinced that Task Force MacLean was as helpless as Hodes's report suggested: his gloomy account was based largely on the failure of Drake's northward move from the schoolhouse and the sound of heavy fighting at the inlet, three miles further on. Though he did not say so, Smith knew there were about as many combat troops with MacLean as there were in Thomas Ridge's defense force at Hagaru; presumably Task Force MacLean could fight its way back to the perimeter, if the situation became serious enough.

On his return to Hungnam, Almond was handed a message from General MacArthur's headquarters, summoning him to a conference in Tokyo, 700 miles across the Sea of Japan. Lieutenant General Walton Walker received the same message; for him it would be an 800-mile journey. In battle dress, both generals flew separately to the council of war.

Back in September, MacArthur had ignored the advice of experts in launching the Inchon invasion, an operation that was brilliantly successful. Had his forces then succeeded in reaching the Yalu before the Chinese intervened, he would surely have been hailed as one of the great captains; but it was now clear that MacArthur had blundered badly in crossing the Thirty-eighth Parallel, outsmarted by a peasant army without air support or tanks and hardly any artillery, whose communication and supply systems could only be called primitive. Shortly before the war council convened, Mac-Arthur had sent a coded cable to the Joint Chiefs in Washington containing the much-quoted sentence "We face an entirely new war." The message continued,

> It is quite evident that our present state of force is not sufficient to meet this undeclared war by the Chinese. . . . This command has done everything humanly possible within its capabilities but is now faced with conditions beyond its control and its strength.

The cable was delivered to General Omar Bradley in the early morning hours at his quarters at Fort Myer. Bradley telephoned President Truman at 6:15 A.M., read the message to him, and commented that the Chinese had entered the war "with both feet." At his morning staff meeting two hours later, the president announced, "We've got a terrific situation on our hands."

MacArthur's cable had struck the leadership in Washington like a thunderbolt; it disclosed a complete about-face in the general's strategic view and suggested for the first time the possibility that UN forces might be forced to pull out of Korea entirely.

In Tokyo the council of war convened at 9:30 P.M., November 28, at the supreme commander's residence in the American embassy. No record of the conference has been found, but it is known that MacArthur solicited the opinions of his two field commanders as to the immediate course of action. Walker, a realist, replied that he could hold the North Korean capital of Pyongyang at the narrow waist of the Korean peninsula, and stated his intention of establishing a defensive line northeast of the city. Almond, a dreamer, aware that Eighth Army was in full retreat toward Pyongyang after heavy losses, euphorically stated his intention to resume the offense nonetheless. That X Corps had reached the end of the road was inconceivable, apparently; it was still his intention to send the Marines across the Taebeks to cut the enemy line of communication at Mupyong-ni.

When the meeting broke up at 12:40 A.M., both field commanders had new orders. Walker was to hold Pyongyang if he could but pull back if the enemy threatened to move around his flank. Almond was directed to withdraw his forces from the reservoir and concentrate on the coast in the Hamhung-Hungnam area.

A message from the Pentagon arrived a little later, expressing approval of MacArthur's decision to pass from the offensive to the defensive but asking, "What are your plans re: the coordination of operations of the Eighth Army and X Corps and the positioning of X Corps, the units of which appear to us to be exposed?"

By the time of the generals' conference in Tokyo, Oliver Smith had taken matters into his own hands. Having ordered the 5th Marines at Yudam-ni to hold in place while the 7th Marines prepared to open the road back to Hagaru, he now arranged for a parachute-drop of ammunition and supplies (and replacements, as soon as the airstrip was ready) and ordered Colonel Puller to open the road from Koto-ri up to Hagaru. These independent moves by the Marine general were to save his division from destruction.

Colonel Alpha Bowser: "We had the right general commanding the 1st Marine Division during the Chosin Reservoir campaign."

38.

BY NOW ALL HANDS AT HAGARU had heard that the 5th and 7th Marines, fourteen miles up the road, were struggling to survive. Around the cook fires and inside the warming tents they talked about little else, knowing that their turn was coming soon, perhaps that very night.

The short plain at Hagaru was crammed with tents, supply dumps, and troops representing fifteen to twenty different units that had arrived too quickly to be digested administratively. Toward the southern end of the plain, five caterpillar tractors chugged back and forth, carving an airstrip out of frozen turf.

Hagaru straddled the sole escape route leading south; if the Chinese were to overrun Hagaru, the destruction of the Marines at Yudam-ni and Toktong Pass would likely follow. Hagaru was therefore to be held to the last man; and with the thickening of Chinese formations in the mountains nearby, it looked more and more as though it might come down to that.

Throughout the morning and past noon, Lt. Col. Ridge kept stepping outside for a look at East Hill, which dominated the northeast end of the valley floor. Ridge had been counting on the arrival of Captain Carl Sitter's George Company, 1st Marines, to meet the threat from that quarter; but at mid-afternoon he received the unhappy word that efforts to open the road from Koto-ri northward were meeting stiff resistance. Sitter's 200 men had been stopped by the enemy halfway between Koto and Hagaru. Ridge now realized that any Chinese effort to occupy East Hill would have to be met in large part by supporting arms and whatever service troops he could scrape together.

The largest Army unit at Hagaru—D Company, Tenth Engineer Battalion, under Captain Philip Kulbes—had gone into bivouac just outside the perimeter, beside the road leading southward to Koto-ri. At mid-afternoon a jeep came flying down the road from town and slid to a standstill at Kulbes's bivouac. PFC Franklin Kestner was walking guard duty at the time, the only man outside the tents. The Marine major at the wheel called out, "Soldier, where's your commanding officer?" Just then Captain Kulbes came outside, approached the jeep, and saluted. The major's instructions were starkly simple: Leave the tents behind, bring your weapons and ammunition, and report to the Marine in charge of the road-block at the foot of East Hill.

There was no question that the Chinese were gathering to attack the perimeter; the problem now was to learn when, where, and in what strength the attack would come. Back at Majon-ni, Ridge had recruited twelve Korean civilians to serve as counterintelligence agents, assigning 2nd Lt. Richard E. Carey to run them. Carey now instructed the agents to collect information from refugees at the roadblocks. The refugees, it turned out, all had the same story to tell: they had been evicted from their houses by Chinese soldiers—of whom there were many. Though civilian estimates of numbers were still regarded as exaggerated, it was clear that major units were gathering nearby.

Carey decided to risk sending a pair of agents on a walking circuit outside the perimeter, with orders to make direct contact with any soldiers they encountered. The mission was a success. Reporting back later in the afternoon, the two men said they had talked freely with Chinese soldiers, including an officer who boasted that his troops would occupy Hagaru before midnight. How close to the perimeter were the enemy units? About five miles.

Late in the afternoon Ridge sent out Corley's entire company, accompanied by three tanks, to see how far it could safely proceed along the road to Koto-ri. The Chinese brought them to a standstill half a mile south of the perimeter with a heavy volume of fire, and a Marine observation plane swooped low to drop a message: "Large numbers Chinese moving your flanks."

Corley's force returned to the perimeter. The sky began to darken at 4:30. Lieutenant Carey, figuring the enemy formations would start moving soon after nightfall, calculated that it would take three and a half hours to reach the line of departure. In his formal report to Ridge the young intelligence officer predicted a Chinese attack in division strength as early as 9:30 P.M. On the basis of Carey's report, Ridge decided to concentrate his main strength against an attack from the southwest; accordingly, he lined up his two infantry companies side by side with their backs to the airstrip. Captain Clarence Corley's How Company and 1st Lt. Joseph Fisher's Item Company, both of the First Regiment, would defend the southern third of the perimeter's circumference, but it would be necessary to stretch the two companies to the limit, with individual riflemen dangerously far apart. (The platoon fronts, it was estimated, averaged 380 yards each.) Supporting arms—tanks, mortars, heavy machine guns—would presumably take up the slack.

Captain Benjamin Read's How Battery, as we have seen, remained in its gun pits outside the northernmost angle of the perimeter—trapped there, so to speak, by its obligation to support the besieged Fox Company at Toktong Pass. The only other artillery battery at Hagaru, Captain Andrew Strohmenger's Dog Battery, also occupied a relatively isolated position. Without infantry support, his six guns were sited on the edge of a frozen marsh east of town. Strohmenger had already enjoyed some success with counterbattery fire. Four enemy mountain-gun positions had been spotted by alert observers as they were being set up, preparing to deliver fire into the crowded perimeter. (The main ammunition dump, at the foot of East Hill, was a most inviting target.) One of these guns had already opened up, the shell exploding beside Ridge's command post, killing his personnel officer and wounding a supply sergeant. Strohmenger responded by initiating a simple but risky ruse. He moved one of his howitzers a hundred yards out from its pit, exposing it openly as a decoy. Its crew then loaded and fired repeatedly, hoping to draw fire from atop East Hill; and when that happened, the other five guns, silent until then, fired back at the muzzle flashes. There was no more trouble from Chinese artillery.

Ridge organized the remainder of his defenses as quickly as possible, sending junior officers out among the crowded tents as census-takers to determine what units were available and what weapons they had at their disposal. These officers told anyone in command of a unit, regardless of its size, to meet at the flagpole in front of the two-story mayor's office at 1600.

PFC Charles Grainger: "They needed warm bodies. I can still hear this one lieutenant yelling, 'Let's have the corporals! Corporals raise your hands!' In those days a Marine corporal had lots of clout, partly because promotion came so slow in the Crotch that anyone wearing two stripes had really earned them and knew his stuff."

Ridge's defensive force—two-thirds of an infantry battalion, with artillery and rear echelon troops—were as ready as they would ever be: roughly 3,300 Marines with attached Navy corpsmen, and 500 GIs—a relatively tiny band of 3,800 Americans. Now it was a matter of waiting. A strange hush fell over the perimeter as the shadows of dusk stretched into nightfall. The air was slightly damp and smelled of snow.

Major Edwin Simmons, Ridge's Weapons Company commander, was standing at a roadblock in the shadow of East Hill when an Army lieutenant, followed by several GIs, approached him in a tentative manner. The young officer explained that he was in charge of a small X Corps signals detachment, had just been assigned a portion of East Hill to defend, and had no idea how to do whatever it was he was supposed to do. Could the major give him some general guidelines? Simmons, a seasoned veteran of Pacific campaigns, was touched by the lieutenant's frank request for help.

"Would you be willing to operate under a Marine enlisted man?" The officer said he would be grateful for any and all assistance. Simmons turned and called out, "Gunny, step over here."

"Sir?"

"I want you to go with this officer and see that his outfit gets set up on that knob there." Led by the Marine gunnery sergeant, the eleven-man group climbed the steep slope and settled down in a position overlooking the roadblock.

A short time later a long-in-the-tooth Army captain showed up with much the same problem as the young lieutenant. Captain Kulbes's D Company, Tenth Engineer Battalion, X Corps, was a much larger group: over seventy GIs and nearly a hundred South Koreans. Like the bemused lieutenant before him, Kulbes had been ordered to defend a portion of the hill. Simmons could only shake his head over the Army's unpreparedness: not a single radio was to be found among the 170 men, nor even one machine gun. Ready to help out once again, Simmons sent his executive officer, Captain John Shelnutt, and a radio operator, PFC Bruno Podolak, with them to lend some Marine tactical expertise and provide liaison with supporting arms. Kulbes, Shelnutt, and the rest disappeared in the growing darkness, passing across the knob held by the young lieutenant's group under its Marine honcho.

An hour later Simmons received a call from Captain Shelnutt reporting that he was unable to locate the Marine service troops supposedly occupying the northern half of the ridgeline.

"Hold on," said Simmons. Contacting Lt. Col. Charles Banks's command post, he was told that his service battalion troops were definitely on the hill.

"John," he relayed to Shelnutt, "they're up there. Keep looking."

The defense of East Hill was not shaping up well at all. Ridge, Simmons, Banks, and others could only hope that the Chinese had not resolved to occupy the crest in strength that night.

The Marine engineers were working on the airstrip around the clock. Despite the risk of sniper fire from still-undefended portions of East Hill, floodlights had been set up on the edge of the strip and turned on, full blaze. The engineers' task was made especially hard by the low temperature. As the official history puts it, "So difficult did it prove to get a bite of the frozen earth that steel teeth were welded to the blades of the motor graders and scrapers. When the pans were filled, however, the earth froze to the cutting edges and could be removed only with a jackhammer." Other Marines from the engineer battalion were busy making use of lumber sent down from the sawmill, much of it going into frames for the twelve-man pyramidal tents to be used on a rotating basis to thaw out the troops.

The Marines of the two infantry companies—Corley's How/1 and Fisher's Item/1—tried to ignore the cold as they prepared their positions for an assault everyone knew was coming; but the cold was a dominating factor. Automatic weapons—if they worked at all—worked sluggishly. Grenades refused to explode; propelling charges in mortar rounds and artillery shells were rendered feeble by the cold, resulting in occasional short rounds that endangered friendly troops. Behind the lines, fuel oil for the stoves tended to freeze into a solid block unless the cans were kept close to the blazing stove itself.

Historian Lynn Montross has pointed out that the company commander is the highest ranking officer who can hope to know every private in the outfit personally. 1st Lt. Joseph Fisher served at one time or another as referee, banker, marriage counselor, psychologist, and father confessor to the young Marines of Item Company. Edwin Simmons recalls: "Joe Fisher was a platoon sergeant at Iwo Jima, stayed in the corps and got a commission, and was given Item Company of the 1st Marines by direct order of Chesty Puller. He was a great Marine and also quite an actor. He wore a BAR belt instead of a pack, where he kept his toilet articles and anything else he needed. He carried an M-1 rifle." Fisher believed that keeping the troops busy on the eve of battle was the best way to build up confidence. Montross: "If a man works hard to prepare a hot reception for the enemy, he won't have time to worry about himself and he's going to be almost disappointed if the enemy doesn't show up to take his medicine."

With a continuous frontage of more than a mile and a quarter to defend, both Fisher and Corley each put all three of their infantry platoons on line. Supporting arms would have to do a job ordinarily done by troops in reserve: three tanks positioned between How and Item, covering a wide draw through which the enemy was expected to come. How and Item were well dug in, even though the ground was frozen in depth, which made digging with ordinary entrenching tools impossible. Fisher had talked the engineers out of a thousand sandbags and a quantity of C-3; using this explosive to blast holes in the earth, it then became a matter of enlarging them and stuffing the dirt into sandbags. The sandbags were used to build protective parapets. By mid-afternoon both company fronts bristled with concertina wire, trip flares, and thermite bombs. The troops strung barbed wire through piles of bricks and poured water on them, freezing the metal in place.

Beginning at 5 P.M., hot food was served in rotation to the tired but exhilarated Marines. A fifty percent alert went into effect as soon as night fell. At ten minutes to eight a feather-light snow began drifting out of the sky, muffling the clank and growl of the floodlit bulldozers at work behind them.

Fifteen minutes before the expected attack, both company commanders ordered a one hundred percent watch. Nine-thirty came and went. The enemy was nowhere to be seen or heard, but he was close at hand.

39.
IT WAS STILL SNOWING AN HOUR later when PFC Aubrey Gentle, an artilleryman with Dog Battery, heard the sharp blare of bugles several hundred yards away, followed by a clanging of cymbals and the shrill blast of a police whistle. "Then three flares lit up the sky and I saw what appeared to be a sea of humanity moving slowly along. They weren't headed in our direction, thank God." Lt. Col. Thomas Ridge saw it from another angle. "It was as though a whole field got up on its feet and walked forward. I never saw anything like it."

Fisher's and Corley's men watched as trip flares and exploding mines revealed the approach of probing patrols comprised of five to ten men. Then white-phosphorous mortar rounds began to scorch the Marine lines. The main Chinese assault followed immediately afterward, with both company sectors hit by assault waves closing to within grenade-throwing distance. Marines on the left flank watched as a jeep hauling 60-mm mortar rounds overshot the front line, its badly shaken driver abandoning it in enemy territory. 2nd Lt. Edward Snelling, How Company's mortar officer, ran through the "sea of humanity" to recover the vehicle and its trailerful of precious ammunition. (Snelling's 60-mm mortar crews would fire over twelve hundred rounds during the engagement.)

Item Company was barely hanging on. Fisher strode from hole to hole, shouting encouragement over the din of battle. Historian Lynn Montross: "This was a time when combat effectiveness depended on something more than discipline, something beyond mere weapons proficiency. It is difficult to describe. It is the feeling a man has when he knows he can count to the end on the men on either side of him and they can count on him. War has its brutal side, but there is nothing finer on earth than the unselfishness so often found on the firing line. Pettiness seems to vanish in those moments."

Corporal Alan Herrington, a veteran of Guadalcanal, was one of Fisher's machine gun section leaders. "Before it all began I noticed that the new guy—a kid name of Darr—was looking panicky. The kid had just been assigned to my squad and he had never been in any kind of fight. I was planning to talk to him, to try and settle him down—if there was time before the Chinese showed up—when suddenly here he is telling me he's scared shitless and didn't think he could cut it. I told him we were all afraid of what was to come, without exception; some of us handled it better than others is all. It's like an actor waiting in the wings: he's got stage fright, butterflies in his stomach, all that; but as soon as he hears his cue and steps onstage he's okay, because he's too busy acting out the part he rehearsed for. You've been trained for this, I told him. It was for this moment that that drill instructor at Parris Island acted like such a bastard. If you were going to break, why, you'd have broken in boot camp and not out here in the field with your brothers depending on you. He just nodded and went back to his hole."

The show started right after that. The guns of Herrington's section eventually became so hot that the barrels glowed in the dark and the assistant gunners had to keep packing snow on them to cool them down.

PFC Foster Weidenheft was a BAR man in Fisher's company. He was sipping from a canteen cup of rapidly cooling coffee when his squad leader yanked aside the tent flap, stuck his face in, and said, "Get back to your holes, on the double—they're coming." After everybody was back on line, Lt. Fisher appeared and reminded them they were under no circumstances to quit their positions. "Stay right where you're at," he said, "or you'll have to deal with me."

The Marines on line rotated to the warming tents on a regular basis, even as the attack developed, and smoked cigarettes. Weidenheft: "If we heard a gunner leaning too heavily on the trigger, we took it as a kind of S.O.S. and everyone would pile outside into the freezing air and run as fast as they could to the holes and resume firing, sometimes opening up just as another wave of gooks was coming on. It was like a job, where you get regular cigarette breaks."

Dead Chinese soldiers began piling up, with succeeding waves climbing unhesitatingly over them. Marine casualties, so far, were light.

During the first lull in the action, the Catholic chaplain appeared, moving from hole to hole in a crouch, looking for his boys.

"And you are? . . ."

"Foster Weidenheft, Father."

"Ah, Foster. And how are you? Would you like me to hear your confession?"

"Later, Father, if you don't mind."

"Certainly, Foster."

PFC Charles McCarren's hole was directly in front of Lt. Fisher's command post, and he could hear the company commander working the phones: "Hold your fire. . . . And don't fire again till I give the word." The terrain out front was relatively flat, but there was a dip in one spot and it was there that McCarren first saw the Chinese. "By the light of a burning house I saw their hats first, then their shoulders, and finally their arms and hands and weapons. You could hear them chattering to each other, keeping up their spirits. Behind us, Lieutenant Fisher yelled 'Open fire!' and that's how it began. A hell of a lot of Chinese went down, but a hell of a lot more kept coming. You got the impression the waves were endless, like surf lapping on a beach. . . .

"Then my M-1 jammed, and the guy I was sharing the hole with, Fillmore Farin from Pittsburgh—his carbine jammed. We reached around and grabbed some grenades and pulled the pins and threw them out front as fast as we could, and that bought us a few seconds of time. I went back to trying to fix my rifle. I had the notion that if I stretched the recoil spring it would do a better job of stripping the top round off the clip. So I took the weapon apart right there in my lap with the snow coming down and the gooks coming on. After I got it disassembled Farin says, 'They're here, Mac.' It was the worst moment of my life; but as you can see, I'm still here. Farin made it out too."

Captain Orin Turner's Dog Company, 1st Marine Engineers, were still hard at work carving out the airstrip under the floodlights, the scrapers and graders moving back and forth behind Corley's and Fisher's lines even as stray rounds whizzed past the operators and their machines. Other strays plunged into the hospital that had been set up in a schoolhouse near the southwest corner of the village, some passing all the way through the walls where surgeons were operating on the wounded. The division command post also took some hits, one round penetrating General Smith's quarters, producing what Smith mildly recalled as "unusual sound effects when it ricocheted off pots and pans in the galley."

Captain Corley had just finished inspecting his center platoon when a hailstorm of hand grenades arched across the snow-laden sky and bounced, exploding, among the Marines on line. It was shocking to discover, so abruptly, how close the enemy had been able to crawl without being detected. The third platoon leader, 2nd Lt. Wendell Endsley, was among those killed in the flurry. At about this time all communications blinked out between Corley and his three platoons. Two wiremen were killed trying to locate the cuts in the wire. The Chinese continued to arrive in steady waves. Shortly after midnight they broke through the center platoon, penetrating as far as Corley's command post, reducing the empty tent to tatters with their burp guns.

Corley and a handful of enlisted men held their ground nearby, acting as a base of supporting fire as 1st Lt. Harrison Betts, the machine-gun officer, tried with a handful of Marines to plug the gap through which Chinese troops were beginning to pour. Severely outnumbered, Betts and his men were swept aside as another wave of Chinese carried the assault still further to the rear, again threatening the engineers at work under the lights. Lt. Robert McFarland, Dog Company's equipment officer, organized a group of engineers and led a counterattack that cleared the far end of the airstrip.

Lt. Roscoe Barrett: "I spotted five or six figures heading my way from the airstrip. I didn't identify them as Chinese until the nearest one, the one on the end, paused to toss a grenade into a tent. He was carrying a Thompson submachine gun. I froze up as he turned and started to walk toward me. When he was about fifteen feet away I got my wits about me and fired my carbine at him on full automatic, but it jammed after one round. I had fired at exactly the moment he fired at me, and fortunately he was a lousy shot. He bent over, either from pain or to clear his weapon, I couldn't tell which. I walked over and put a bullet through his head with my .45."

The Chinese who had penetrated Corley's lines seemed to congregate around the galley and the supply tents, demonstrating—as the official history has it—"that they knew better how to create a penetration than to exploit one." Warm clothing was what seemed to interest the looters most as they milled around the abandoned headquarters.

Lt. Grady Mitchell, Colonel Ridge's assistant operations officer, arrived with twenty-five Marines, sent over by Ridge as scratch reinforcements. Mitchell was killed and several others were shot down, but by 3 A.M. the breach in the line had been plugged, the Chinese behind the lines were dead, and order was restored in the How/1 sector.

Corporal Alan Herrington: "After the battle petered out, this kid, Darr, came over to my hole, reached into his parka, and pulled out a pipe. 'I want you to have this,' he said. 'A friend sent it from home, but I don't smoke.' I told him, 'Maybe you don't smoke now, but you will if you stay in this game.' He insisted I take the pipe as a memento. I still have it."

40.

DAWN REVEALED A SPECTACLE that the Marines of Corley's and Fisher's companies would not soon forget. Snow had drawn a white shroud over the Chinese corpses; the ground in front of the two units was dotted with hundreds of these mounds. (General Smith later reported that "an estimated one thousand CCF [Chinese Communist Forces] were killed in the attack." Fisher's Item/1 sustained twenty-four casualties: two dead, twenty-two wounded. Corley's How/1 reported thirty-seven casualties: ten dead, twenty-seven wounded.)

The battle was over but the killing continued. PFC Charles McCarren: "We saw a Chinese soldier setting up a machine-gun tripod about four hundred yards away, on the other side of all those bodies. Mr. Fisher, right behind us, was watching too. Steam from his breath had frozen on his mustache and the mucous from his nostrils had turned into icicles. He was like some Ice Age monster. We watched as a second gook appeared and put the gun down on the tripod and locked it. A third gook appeared with a couple of ammo boxes and began to feed the end of a belt into the gun. Mr. Fisher stood there, his hands on his hips, patiently waiting to see if any more gooks were going to appear. None did, so he said, 'Fire!' and the trio was practically vaporized by our volley. I couldn't help admiring the cool way Lieutenant Fisher waited so patiently for the whole crew to assemble before lowering the boom on the poor bastards."

It turned out that not all of the snow-covered mounds represented dead bodies. McCarren: "The quilted cloth some of the gooks were wearing was still smoldering from our tracer rounds. This one gook sat up suddenly and started fumbling with his clothing. At first I thought he was trying to put out the fire in the cotton, but he was just getting out his cigarettes. We watched him extract one from the pack with his numb fingers and light up. He kept looking around as if he couldn't figure out where he was. Somebody finally put the poor son of a bitch out of his misery with a round through the chest. After that Mr. Fisher had us go out there and drag the nearest corpses farther away from our lines, so there'd be no danger of them coming alive and throwing grenades. Occasionally you'd hear a shot ring out as a Marine made sure the body he was approaching was really a body."

It was a good time to collect souvenirs, and many of the Marines returned to their holes carrying Thompson submachine guns, Mauser machine pistols, and Japanese Nambus. Others brought in burp guns and ammo belts—six connected pouches holding two magazines each. Lt. Fisher didn't object when a man decided to ditch his carbine for a souvenired weapon. The carbine had proved a great disappointment; not only did it freeze up too easily, but its stopping power was weak.

2nd Lt. Roscoe Barrett was still tense and keyed up, as though the battle were still raging. Barrett: "I was walking up and down the line in a daze. Fifteen of my men had been wounded. Half of them had a bad case of frostbite. What shocked me most were the dead Marines. Captain Corley and the exec, Mr. Johnson, showed up and took a look at me. I must have looked pretty bad because—to my everlasting astonishment—they both moved up close and wrapped an arm around me. I was speechless." After the two officers released him and moved on, Barrett found a private spot in the little Buddhist shrine nearby, wept hard, vomited, and wept some more. A few minutes later, after washing his face with snow and sprucing up a bit, he walked over to Captain Corley and told him, "I'm not sure I can do this every night." Corley smiled and reassured him that such nights were rare.

Lieutenant Colonel Ridge found time that morning to banter with his intelligence officer, Lt. Richard Carey. "You were right about the enemy's strength and the date of the attack—but how come you were an hour off?"

"That's easy, Colonel. The Chinese are night-fighters."

"So?"

"So they're not on daylight-savings time."

From prisoner interviews Carey had determined that the attacking force was the 58th Chinese Communist Division, and that two of its regiments, the 172nd and the 173rd, had been committed, while the third, the 174th, remained in reserve. In subsequent years there has been speculation that the Chinese failed to understand that Hagaru was the key to victory, and that if Hagaru had fallen on the night of November 27, the 5th and 7th Marines at Yudamni could not have survived.

There were at least six Chinese divisions in the Chosin sector. The question is: Why was only one of them sent against so important a target? The answer is simple. The Chinese assumed that two regiments of infantry were more than enough to overwhelm Ridge's two-thirds of a battalion; in addition, the 80th Division was scheduled to add its weight to the attack but had to deal unexpectedly with Task Force MacLean on the east shore of the reservoir. A coordinated attack at Yudam-ni and Hagaru had been the original plan for that night, but weather, terrain, and circumstance dictated otherwise, and the 58th Division showed up a day late.

Lt. Col. Ridge was still counting on the arrival of Sitter's George Company and the Royal Marines to shore up his defenses. Reinforcement was essential if the perimeter was to be held for another night. George/1 and 41 Commando had departed Koto that morning in a strong convoy that included an Army infantry company, a few Marine tanks, and half the Division's headquarters personnel. All Ridge knew was that the column was somewhere between Koto-ri and Hagaru, fighting its way north.

At about 1:30 on the morning of the twenty-ninth, Ridge heard the rattle of gunfire atop East Hill and rushed outside to see the twinkle and flash of automatic weapons and grenades along the looming skyline to the northeast. The Chinese had lapped over the crest, overrunning some of the X Corps troops, and were now threatening to descend into the valley. On the left the GIs were fleeing for their lives down the icy slopes. Near the center Lt. John Shelnutt tried to close the gap by extending his troops, but enemy fire prevented that and Shelnutt was killed. Deprived of the Marine officer's leadership, the GIs had given in to demoralization, and another spontaneous withdrawal began. Later, at the bottom of the hill, a rough count was made and it was found that ten GIs in the group had been killed and twenty-five wounded, with nine missing in action. Most of the South Koreans were missing as well, many having sought refuge in empty houses in the village.

PFC Bruno Podolak, wounded, had remained on the hill with his SCR-300 radio. Throughout the rest of the night this brave, steady Marine kept Colonel Ridge informed of enemy movements, as the Chinese sought to strengthen their foothold on East Hill. At one point the defense commander asked Podolak if he could estimate the number of Chinese on the crest. "Maybe a battalion," was the whispered reply.

"You're saying a few hundred?"

"Two, three hundred, maybe."

By 4 A.M. only Marine artillery could prevent the enemy from making a complete breakthrough on East Hill, capturing the supply dump, and attacking the division command post. (The latter was guarded by the well-armed and -trained 1st Marine Division Band.) Three of Read's How Battery guns were now turned to bear directly on the steep slopes. Read and Strohmenger's batteries fired more than 1,200 rounds that night, and POW interrogations later disclosed that enemy concentrations were broken up repeatedly. Podolak was given credit for observing and adjusting several of these effective barrages.

As the assaults against Fisher and Corley died away, Ridge asked his executive officer, Major Reginald Myers, to collect as many service troops and stragglers as he could find and lead them in a counterattack up the East Hill slopes. Within the hour Myers had brought together a few odds and ends in a ditch paralleling the railroad tracks, the only spot that offered protection against the plunging fire from the heights. Myers made radio contact with Podolak. "What's the situation up there?"

Podolak said there were Chinese all over the place and that he would appreciate it if the major could hurry.

"We're on our way."

PFC Robert Greene, a member of a Tactical Air Control Party attached to Ridge's battalion: "It was about three A.M. on the twenty-ninth when Major Myers informed me I would be among those about to storm that ugly-looking hill on the other side of the tracks. The arctic wind was blowing like crazy. It was so cold that some of us tied sandbags around our boots to keep our feet from freezing."

Major Myers: "In a situation like this there could be no subtlety of attack—it had to be a straight frontal assault. It was the only tactic I dared employ with so disorganized a force of men mostly unknown to each other, half Marine, half Army. I had to cajole and bully them to keep them all climbing. I knew we would sustain casualties if the ascent continued into daylight, so I pressed them as hard as I could. All the while Podolak was urging me to hurry."

PFC Greene recalls that the steep six-hundred-foot ascent took over an hour. Fresh snow on the icy crust made footing treacherous, and heavily laden men took painful falls. Frightened but resolute, Greene gasped for breath as he climbed, lugging his M-1 and a box of machine-gun ammo entrusted to his care. During the tortuous ascent, his helmet tipped off and rolled out of reach.

PFC Greene: "As I look back on it now, the thing that bothered me most was that during the last hundred feet I got the impression I was alone. This was totally unlike any other combat experience I ever had, where there was always a member of my team nearby and we all looked out for each other, which is the Marine way. Having Marines around you has a calming and reassuring effect, even if you're in the middle of a firefight. During those last few yards, the only comfort I could find was thinking about the booklet my mom had sent, which I carried in my parka pocket. All it had between the covers was the Twenty-third Psalm: 'Yea, though I walk through the valley of the shadow of death I will fear no evil.'

"We were under direct fire when I crouched down and took the helmet off a GI whose face had been shot off. There was frozen blood in the helmet but that didn't bother me because I had been worried about my unprotected head with these grenades going off all around. I can recall the peculiar stench of Chinese gunpowder. When we got to the top finally, we waited in holes for a few minutes, expecting a counterattack."

About fifty Marines and fifteen GIs remained with Myers at this point. As daylight came on and their positions became more evident to the enemy, they began taking machine-gun fire from the high ground to their left. Myers: "We had four or five killed at this time and maybe ten more wounded. The trouble was, every time a man would get hit it would take four men to carry him down to the bottom of the hill. And very few of those bearers ever showed up again."

Marine air arrived on station at 9:30 A.M., the Corsairs peeling off to lay a load of napalm, rockets, and fragmentation bombs across the back of the hill. Enemy gunfire struck one of the planes, crippling it; the gull-winged fighter-bomber was trailing smoke as it emerged from its run. The pilot, Lt. Harry Colmery, made a rough but safe landing in front of Captain Corley's lines. The

How/1 Marines cheered as he shoved the canopy back, jumped to the ground, and sprinted through all the snow-covered corpses into the Marine lines.

Myers: "After that, we went forward at a bound and took the crest. I caught sight of a lone Marine up ahead, waving at us. It was Podolak, and I can still recall the grin on his face. Though wounded, he climbed out of the hole and joined our skirmish line as we moved along the crest. As soon as I had the opportunity, I reported to Colonel Ridge: 'We found your radio operator. He's wounded but still full of fight.' "

Myers ordered the survivors to take cover, if they could find any, and draw up a defensive line while awaiting a supporting attack from the north. This was to be carried out by elements of Captain George King's Able Company of the 1st Marine Engineer Battalion, the unit that had been operating at the sawmill two miles north of Hagaru. King's outfit reached East Hill without incident at noon and proceeded immediately to the assault.

Myers: "I recognized the platoon leader, Lieutenant Canzona, and for the first time that day I had a group of people to whom I could assign definite tasks and know they would get done."

The details of how King's engineers came to the support of the troops on East Hill are interesting. Warrant Officer Willard Downs, 1st Marine Engineers, recalls that the sawmill was isolated, a stone's throw from the lake shore. There was a wooden skidway which in thaw season ran from water's edge to the mill so that logs brought over by barge could be dragged ashore. Next to the mill were piles of high-quality lumber stacked in rows. There was a one-room office, which Captain King used as his command post. "The whole place was kind of an engineer's paradise because of the fine lumber, and we were enjoying our work. Our sole complaint was the weather. On the night of November 27–28, out of sheer laziness we allowed the fire in our stove to burn out, and in the morning the inside skin of our tent had crystallized into a solid sheet of ice."

That the sawmill was isolated had no particular significance until the following night, when the engineers heard the massive outburst of fire two miles to the south. Lt. Nicholas Canzona gazed toward the Hagaru perimeter and, as the official history has it, "the awesome spectacle of a night battle made him think of a volcano in eruption. Gun flashes stabbing the darkness were fused into a great ring of living flame, and the thousands of explosions blended into a steady, low-pitched roar." (Lt. Col. Randolph Lockwood: "In spite of the carnage of combat, it really was a beautiful show—the red, blue, yellow, green, orange, white fireworks in the sky, flashing across the hills, the snow reflecting it all.")

Gunner Downs, watching the awesome spectacle from the sawmill, noticed something odd: high-arcing streaks of fire rising from positions halfway between the mill and Hagaru. "It took me a moment to understand that these were muzzle flashes from Chinese mortar tubes. I realized with a shock that there were *several* mortar crews and probably lots of infantry between us and the Marine lines at Hagaru. At the moment they had their backs to us. I went directly to Captain King and pointed out the mortar positions. His immediate response was to get in touch with the artillery at Hagaru and call in fire missions, the captain acting as a forward observer behind enemy lines—a very unusual situation."

Toward daylight, November 29, the action had died down and King was directed by Lt. Col. Ridge to send a reconnaissance patrol to the east of the sawmill to determine enemy strength in that quarter. At a time when most Marine units were buttoning up, this was a dangerous order, but Ridge needed to know if fresh enemy formations were heading toward East Hill from the north. Gunner Downs was to lead the patrol. As they were preparing to depart, Downs walked to a spot on higher ground and looked through binoculars at the terrain they would be moving into—and found the ridge teeming with Chinese. He trotted back down the slope and told the captain what he had seen.

"The patrol is canceled."

This made Downs and the others very happy. Soon after that, King received a message from Hagaru to move—lock, stock, and barrel—into the perimeter. To evade enemy observation, the engineers moved the vehicles between the two stacks of lumber, struck the tents, and loaded everything as quickly as they could. Downs: "You never saw men move so fast; it was like one of those speeded-up movie sequences. The Chinese could have swatted us like a fly if they'd had a mind to. Looking back now, my guess is that they knew we were there but didn't want to bother with such a small support outfit when they had the whole Hagaru perimeter to deal with."

The convoy consisted of nineteen units: trucks and trailers, bulldozers, a road grader, plus miscellaneous equipment such as air compressors, welding equipment, and whatnot. The vehicles started down the lakeshore road, heading directly into the Chinese lines from the rear. The engineers could see them watching the convoy from the ridges but their guns remained silent.

Having sustained no casualties, King and company reached the perimeter around noon on the twenty-ninth. Lt. Canzona was directed to form his men into an infantry platoon and, as soon as darkness fell, ascend East Hill and try to link up with one of the scratch units below the crest. When the engineers reached the crest they were pinned down by enemy fire as they started to advance along a narrow trail. A quarter mile further on, Major Reginald Myers was still holding his precarious position with stragglers and service personnel. None of the Marine/Army attacks on East Hill had been impressive, yet these mixed troops had accomplished something of tactical importance: they had kept the Chinese on East Hill busy, distracting them from the vulnerable targets in the valley below.

Hagaru remained surrounded, and by now everyone knew it had to be held if the division was to survive. Colonel Alpha Bowser, the division's operations chief, later admitted that he and other staff officers weren't all that confident that Hagaru *could* be held. An interviewer later asked if he thought the 5th and 7th Marines might find it impossible to break through the encirclement and reach Hagaru in time to save it.

"We considered that a definite possibility," he said.

The pallid winter sun was sinking behind the skyline when a disturbing piece of news reached the Hagaru operations center. Captain Carl Sitter, whose George Company was presently under heavy assault on the road between Koto-ri and Hagaru, had just requested permission to turn back.

41. THE SURVIVORS OF FOX COMpany, 7th Marines, listened impassively to the cries of the fallen Chinese out front—pitiful sounds that faded away as one by one the soldiers froze to death or died of wounds. When gray dawn lightened the sky over Toktong Pass, the platoon leaders began to count the corpses that were strewn over the slopes. The aggregate number eventually reported by Captain Barber was "about 450." Fox/7 had lost twenty Marines during the night, with fifty-four wounded and three missing. Fifteen of the dead belonged to Mc-Carthy's platoon.

Sergeant Charles Dana: "When Lieutenant McCarthy stopped by our hole, we told him we needed ammo. 'We're all low,' he said. 'You have to take it off the dead.' So we went crawling from hole to hole, taking off cartridge belts and bandoliers, which was tough if you happened to know the guy. Word was then passed to take a close look at the Chinese bodies and shoot any we thought might be playing possum. Because of their white uniforms they were hard to find in the snow. Sometimes you could see the steam of their breath. Then you'd hear a shot."

The characteristic light-brown color of frozen flesh reminded PFC Ernest Gonzales of wax dummies. "I remember this one Chinese soldier curled up in the snow, lying facedown, still breathing. He had a head wound shaped like a perfect pie-cut, exposing part of his brain. When I fired a shot into his midriff, he turned slowly onto his back and looked at me as if to say, 'Why must you make me suffer more?' before he died. Though it was common practice on both sides, I never again killed a wounded Chinese soldier." Gonzales searched through the man's pockets and pack and found a container of special cold-weather weapon lubrication, a booklet with color-tinted pictures of China's political and military leaders, and a folder of snapshots of the dead man and his family on an outing in a city park.

The battle was not quite over for Private Hector Cafferata. Gazing around in wonder, he nudged PFC Kenneth Benson—who was still blind—and tried to describe what he saw in the stark light of dawn.

"Everywhere around us, Benson—nothing but dead gooks!"

Having watched several Marines bringing back burp guns, Thompsons, and Springfield '03s, he decided to crawl downslope to collect some souvenirs too. "I'll be right back," he said.

"I can't see to cover you, Hector."

"Don't worry. They're all dead."

A few seconds later, the flat report of a rifle shot sounded sharply in Benson's ears.

"Oh, shit."

"What's up, Hector?"

"Son of a bitch of a sniper." The round had struck Cafferata in the right shoulder, knocking him down. Benson climbed to his feet, preparing to grope his way down to where his comrade lay.

"No! I can make it back on my own. Stay in the hole."

PFC Harmony Geer: "It was funny, really. Hector lay there bitching up a storm, royally insulted—outraged, even—that some gook had put him out of action."

The Marines who carried him back discovered a startling fact: the huge private was wearing nothing on his feet but ice-encrusted socks. Unable to locate his shoe-pacs in the early moments of the attack, Cafferata had given up trying when he discovered how close the Chinese were; he fought through the night in his stocking feet.

Geer: "This was one champion field Marine, this guy."

Benson: "After they took care of Hector they came back and led me over to a cook fire. I could smell the coffee from way off, and when they put a canteen cup in my hands—man, it tasted like a million bucks. After I got thawed out I asked somebody to lead me over to the aid tent so I could visit Hector. He was in a lot of pain from the wound and his frostbitten feet." (Cafferata did not lose his feet; Benson regained his sight.)

The two aid tents had been set up in a stand of pines. The three Navy corpsmen—James Morrissey, Mervyn Maurath, James French—had worked throughout the night by candlelight. The dead were laid out between the tents in two rows.

At about mid-morning the survivors of Fox Company heard the drone of an approaching flight and cheered lustily when Corsairs came into view above the peaks. Though they continued on toward Yudam-ni, the mere sight of them gave the Marines at Toktong Pass a boost in morale. When the wind was right, they could hear the reverberation of bombing and the distant racket of diving cannon fire at Yudam-ni. A little later Fox Company got a flight of its own: P-51 Mustangs from the Australian squadron. Their strike was directed mostly at the boulder-covered ridge across the way, which was where most of the sniper fire was coming from.

The reader will recall that it was during daylight hours of November 28—the record isn't clear as to the specific time—that Barber had received the jolting message from Colonel Litzenberg ordering Fox Company to break contact with the enemy and fight its way to Charlie Company's precarious position three miles up the road. Once joined, the two companies were then to fight their way to Yudam-ni. Without mentioning his seventy-seven casualties, lest the enemy overhear, Barber had explained to the regimental commander that Fox/7 was too heavily engaged to make such a move.

Throughout the remainder of the day the Chinese were kept at a respectful distance by Marine sharpshooters, air strikes, and the meager artillery fire delivered by the battery at Hagaru. Captain Read's guns were so low on ammunition that when Lt. Donald Campbell called for a fire mission to break up a Chinese concentration near Toktong-san, Read could only send three 105-mm rounds. "It nearly broke my heart," he said later. "I wasn't able to explain to Don over the net why we were being so stingy. I finally said, 'Praise the Lord and pass the ammunition,' and added this: 'About the only thing we can do now is praise the Lord.' "

Later that afternoon Barber received another message from 7th Marines headquarters, giving him the option of moving Fox Company down to Hagaru. Lt. Lawrence Schmitt: "Colonel Litzenberg still didn't understand that we were up Shit Creek. I heard the captain trying to explain, without revealing the fix we were in, why the order was impractical."

It was an attractive suggestion nonetheless. Barber knew by now that he was holding a key position. If Fox Company pulled off the pass now it would mean severing contact with the 8,000 Marines at Yudam-ni who were counting on his small band to hold the rear door open so that they could join the 3,000 at Hagaru.

A Marine C-47 was making a slow pass over the outpost. The side hatch was open and the Marines on the ground exchanged vigorous waves with the flight crew. On the second pass they began shoving out big bundles. The plane was flying so low the chutes barely had time to open before the packages hit the ground. It was a perfect drop, everything landing neatly at the base of the hill: medical supplies, ammunition, blankets, stretchers. 1st Lt. Joseph Brady, the 60-mm mortar officer, wounded in the hand, went down to retrieve some mortar rounds, cradling two of them under his good arm and zigzagging his way back up the hill. Brady had been a halfback on his college football team. When he got back inside the perimeter, Captain Barber pulled him aside. "I bet you never made a run like that at Dartmouth." Brady laughed.

After the packages had been retrieved, the company supply sergeant, realizing parachutes could be used as bedding, climbed down the slope to gather them. Lt. Schmitt heard a single shot and saw Sergeant Smith roll into a ditch beside the road. The bullet had gone through his left calf-bone. Schmitt grabbed a litter and, with four volunteers, ran downhill and loaded him onto it. On the way back he heard another shot and felt his right leg snap like a dry branch. Schmitt: "It turned out I got almost the same medicine as Smitty: my right shinbone was shattered. Two guys grabbed me under the arms and dragged me up to the aid tent, where Joe Brady gave me a precious shot of Scotch he had been hoarding. I'll never forget the unselfishness of that act, because he was hurting too. The corpsmen set my leg with two sticks."

Barber sent a fire team out to flush the sniper from his lair while Lt. Clarke Wright, the exec, organized more volunteers to haul the rest of the air-dropped supplies up the hill.

PFC Clifford Gamble: "Just as it was starting to get dark, Lieutenant Peterson came around to check the foxholes on the western side of the hill. He had been wounded twice but was staying on the job. He sat down with us and together we watched formations of Chinese moving about, five or six hundred yards away. You could see them when they went through clearings in the woods. They looked like company parade formations: roughly five men across, twenty-five deep. Four of these units ran through the clearing."

It began to snow as the Marines settled down for their second night on the hill. There was an air of expectancy and dread as the light faded in the sky. No one doubted that the enemy would launch another series of assaults and try to finish off the survivors of the first night's confrontation. Most of the Marines now had extra weapons in their holes, taken from dead Chinese, to supplement their M-1s, carbines, and Browning automatic rifles.

PFC Donald Childs: "Their basic rifle was the 1918 Mauser design in 7.92 mm, manufactured in China. Many of these were new and showed exceptional workmanship and finish. It was a very effective weapon at long range in trained hands." Childs and his BAR man, PFC Norman Jackson, kept five of these reliable rifles in the rear of their hole as backups.

Captain Barber, after monitoring the radio all day, had summoned his officers for a brief meeting before dark. "Here's the latest dope from division," he told them. "The 5th and the 7th are heavily engaged at Yudam-ni and they've taken a hell of a lot of casualties. Last night the perimeter at Hagaru got hit hard. Down at Koto they're surrounded and cut off. Because of all this, there's no possible way we can be relieved right now." Their only chance for survival, he explained, was if the Marines at Yudam-ni were to join the Marines at Hagaru, and that of course hinged on Toktong Pass remaining in Marine control. "We can expect heavy attacks tonight, but we have nothing to worry about as long as we fight like Marines."

The briefing had a sobering effect; but in general the officers and men of Fox Company shared a feeling of confidence in their ability to hold, even though their ranks had been considerably thinned. Sergeant Patrick Scully: "We really didn't give a lot of thought to being relieved. The basic attitude was, Hey—the Marine Corps takes care of its own. When the time comes we'll get to you."

It was still snowing at 2:15 A.M. when whistles shrilled and groups of Chinese began probing the Marine lines. The whistles were replaced by bugles and then the human-wave attacks began, striking with great force against Peterson and McCarthy's platoons. Barber: "We had done a good job of neutralizing the battalion that hit us the first night. On the second night they came at us with the remains of that battalion, plus a fresh one."

McCarthy's platoon, down twenty casualties, was already stretched to the breaking point. Gaps now opened in the flanks, and, while McCarthy was moving fire teams around, forty to fifty Chinese broke through. The din of battle died down momentarily as white-clad figures, chattering excitedly, milled around in the patch of small trees behind the lines. Lt. Peterson, turning one of the machine guns around, was quick to take advantage of their confusion. PFC Richard Bonelli carried another gun from position to position, pausing to fire short bursts. Between Bonelli and the lieutenant, few of the Chinese survived.

PFC Childs: "The line to our right was breached after a machine gun jammed. A figure approached us on hands and knees and I almost shot him before he identified himself as a Marine. We reached out and jerked him into the hole. He was without boots and his rifle had been destroyed in the fight. He immediately began loading magazines for Norman's BAR and putting together clips of eight for my M-1. With his feet in Norman's bag he did a great job helping us, whoever the hell he was. All through this, grenades were going off around our hole, but by the grace of God we didn't get a scratch. We had no idea how many positions had fallen, but when there was a lull, I saw over my right shoulder lots of Chinese moving through the trees. Norman and I, with the other guy's help, began to deliver the heaviest fire a BAR and an M-1 can produce, and we saw a lot of these white figures turning and running the other way, some of them falling."

Captain Barber was helping Lieutenant McCarthy pull his platoon back when both officers were sent sprawling by the same bullet. Barber: "It was an unusual shot. First it went through Bob McCarthy's arm and then through the stock of his rifle. It was rather well spent by this time, but it had enough drive left to lodge deeply in my hip. I was too involved in the battle to pay much attention to it just then."

At 3 A.M. the temperature sank to twenty-four degrees below zero. Many of the Marines were forced to operate their half-frozen automatic weapons one round at a time, and they often had to pry the ice-covered spoons from their grenades before throwing them.

Harrison Pomers: "We were about fifty feet below the crest, laying on the snow, waiting to counterattack. When we got the word from Sergeant Audas we jumped up and did it. I shot all eight rounds right away but didn't take time to reload because there were so many Chinese soldiers around, so I charged the nearest one with my bayonet—and he shot me." Pomers says it felt as though a train hit him head-on. He couldn't move and he couldn't hear a sound. Even though the temperature was far below zero, he didn't feel cold. He lay there in the snow, looking up at the sky, and then he began to say his prayers. "Dear God, forgive me all my sins and please take me quick. I have no fear. Thank you."

Then he heard someone calling his name. Two Marines dragged him to their hole and one of them washed his face with snow. The pain in his forearm and one hand was bad, and a corpsman appeared to give him a shot of morphine. Pomers was unable to move his right arm or his right leg. They carried him over to one of the aid tents, which was already jammed with casualties. The tent was on the side of a slope so steep that when they put him down he was half sitting up. A stove was blasting away inside the tent, but at the same time the wind was whistling through the bullet holes in the canvas. Pomers: "They ran out of morphine, so I never got a second shot. The pain got so bad at one point that I asked one of the corpsmen if he would apply still more pressure to my hand. He had been holding my hand whenever the pain got really bad.

" 'If I squeeze any harder I'll break your fingers.'

" 'My arm and hand are useless anyway, Doc. Go ahead and break them.'

"Well, he wouldn't go along with that."

Captain Barber had seen enough of the enemy at Toktong Pass to form a solid opinion of their leadership. Barber: "Their tactics were extremely poor; in fact, they were stupid. We were attacked in the same places at almost the same time every night, and they always made lots of noise before they charged—the blowing of bugles, the whistles, the yelling. They made no attempt at all to surprise us."

At first light Sergeant John Audas led a ragged skirmish line in a counterattack that killed many Chinese and drove the others down the slope. By six o'clock the position was restored and there were an additional 200 bodies out front.

42.

PFC JAMES RANSONE: "COLOnel Faith should have told him: 'General! We're in deep trouble out here and need help real fast or we're going down the drain. If you can't send any help, General, then for God's sake please pull us out of here.' "

Why Almond ordered an advance at this late hour instead of a withdrawal will forever remain a mystery, unless one is willing to ascribe the decision to sheer stupidity. ("When it paid to be aggressive, Ned was aggressive," said one of his staff officers afterward, "and when it paid to be cautious, Ned was aggressive.")

But why did Colonel MacLean fail to question this mad order? Captain Michael Capraro, Marine public information officer: "It's hard for an officer of any rank, even a full colonel, to question a general's desire to remain on the offensive. To do so exposes the officer to charges of timidity, which is not a good way to get promoted. My theory is that Almond and MacLean simply underestimated Chinese strength and overestimated their own."

Shortly before midnight, November 28–29, elements of the Chinese 80th Division launched another attack against the two forward perimeters of the U.S. Army task force. Two hours later, as the battle raged, MacLean decided to pull Faith's First Battalion, 32nd Infantry, back to where the Third Battalion, 31st Infantry, was holding out—barely—at Pungnyuri Inlet. (The inlet, it will be recalled, was located four miles north of the Hudong schoolhouse, where Drake's tanks were uselessly parked.) MacLean was still expecting, momentarily, the arrival of Lt. Col. William Reidy's Second Battalion, 31st Infantry. With his force thus consolidated, MacLean would then be ready to mount the Almond-ordered offensive the following day, jumping off from the inlet. What he didn't know was this: Reidy's battalion was still at Hamhung, far out of reach.

The withdrawal began two and a half hours later. First Sergeant Luna of B Company was ordered to leave everything behind, including supplies and bedding, to make room on the trucks for the wounded. Many of the vehicles would not start and were abandoned in the helter-skelter rush to pull out. The four-mile move, in sixty roadworthy vehicles, was made without difficulty; the Chinese, perhaps diverted by the prospect of rich plunder among the stockpiles left behind, did not pursue the convoy.

It was early afternoon when the tail of the column began to cross the concrete bridge spanning Pungnyuri Inlet. Major Wesley Curtis, Faith's operations officer, found the situation at the shrunken position grim indeed. "The perimeter of the 3/31 and the 57th Field Artillery was a scene of destruction. It had been effectively 'reduced' and was offering no organized resistance. There was smoke and fog and very little visibility."

Colonel MacLean was riding in the cab of one of the last vehicles in the convoy, moving along the northern side of the inlet, when he spotted a column of troops half a mile away approaching the perimeter from the south. So intensely was he anticipating the arrival of 2/31 that he shouted with joy, certain he was gazing at last upon the vanguard of Reidy's battalion. His joy turned to chagrin, however, when the GIs on the perimeter began to take random shots at the oncoming troops.

"Cease fire! Those are my boys! Cease fire!"

MacLean jumped out of the truck, climbed down a short slope onto the ice, and strode toward the far shore of the inlet, intent on putting a stop to the shooting. It was a quarter mile to the other side; as the colonel was charging across the ice, his men saw him fall. Faith and Curtis saw him then climb to his feet and continue on a few steps, only to fall again. Everyone was slow to realize— because it was so fantastic—that the column MacLean was trying to protect was a Chinese formation, and that some of the enemy soldiers were now beginning to shoot at the frantically gesticulating figure on the ice. Witnesses say that MacLean fell four times and climbed back on his feet each time; but it was impossible to say whether he was repeatedly struck by bullets or whether he was slipping on the ice in his haste to reach the other side.

Chinese soldiers broke away from the column and intercepted MacLean as he reached the shore, taking him by his arms and pulling him up the bank and out of sight. It was a moment of severe shock for the Americans who witnessed the capture of their commanding officer. (Colonel Allan MacLean died on the march to a prisoner-of-war camp during his fourth day of captivity. He was buried in the snow beside the road at an unknown location.)

By default, Lt. Col. Don Faith was now in command of the three Army battalions at the inlet.

At 8:27 P.M. all troops in the Chosin Reservoir sector, including the three Army battalions, were placed under the operational control of General Oliver P. Smith. Brigadier General Henry Hodes had by now informed Smith that the Army units at the inlet had suffered about five hundred casualties and were unable to fight their way to safety. Smith directed him to send a dispatch to the effect that Faith should make every effort to reach Hagaru. It was an awkward fact, as already mentioned, that the 31st Regimental Combat Team had about as many troops in its ranks as General Smith had at Hagaru. The Marine general was willing to supply such air support as he could spare, but Faith and his men were going to have to get themselves out of their predicament.

Though the full burden of directing air support for the Army battalions fell to Stamford and his enlisted Marines (the Air Force forward air controller had been killed), Stamford himself remained calm in the midst of growing hysteria and even retained his hearty appetite. Stamford: "At one point I was looking around for a place to sit down so I could eat a can of C-rations and I saw the corpse of a Chinese soldier. He was in a kneeling position, resting on his elbows. The top of his head had been blown off. As the body froze, the brain expanded and rose up out of the cranium, looking like a piece of pink coral on a Pacific reef. The hoar frost that fell during the early morning hours covered the top of his brain and was now sparkling in the sun. I opened the can and, using the 'coral' as a sort of centerpiece, sat down on the corpse and wolfed down my meal."

A Marine helicopter sent by Hodes landed inside the inlet perimeter late in the afternoon to evacuate the wounded battalion commanders, Reilly and Embree. Before nightfall a Marine L-5 liaison plane, also sent by Hodes, dropped a supply of morphine. These two acts were about all the assistant division commander could do to help Faith and his beleaguered troops.

Colonel Alpha Bowser: "General Hodes was quite embarrassed

about asking us for help in extricating the Army troops. He recognized that what he was asking was impossible. Any Marine force from Hagaru strong enough to blast its way through to the GIs would have left our perimeter dangerously vulnerable."

Task Force Faith was going to have to fight its way out on its own—with Marine close air support—if it could.

43.

COLONEL LEWIS B. PULLER—
called "Chesty" by most, but not to his face—was a living legend
in the Corps. An authentic character, Puller had for nearly three
decades led troops in many of the Corps's toughest battles. A
bandy-legged man with a pugnacious face and the chest of a pouter
pigeon, Puller was regarded as an ideal troop commander because
he won battles and took good care of his men. In the march from
Hamhung to Koto-ri he gave first priority to tentage so that warming havens could be set up immediately for his riflemen. This led
indirectly to a shortage of small-arms ammunition in the early
phase of the campaign, and when a Division staffer questioned him
about it, Puller replied, "Frozen men can't fight. If we run out of
ammunition, we'll go to the bayonet." Puller could hardly open
his mouth without delivering a quote. Soon after the onfall he said,
"We've been looking for the enemy for some time now. We've
finally found him. We're surrounded. That simplifies things."

Unlike Litzenberg and Murray's regiments, the three infantry
battalions of Puller's 1st Marines were separated from one other.
Lt. Col. Donald Schmuck's First Battalion (1/1) guarded the railhead and supply dump at Chinhung-ni, on the south side of Funchilin Pass, ten miles down the line; Lt. Col. Thomas Ridge's Third
Battalion (3/1) was at Hagaru—minus Sitter's George Company,
still hung up at Koto-ri. Puller thus had only one battalion with
him at Koto: Lt. Col. Allan Sutter's Second Battalion (2/1), plus an
artillery battery and about 300 engineers, medical personnel, military police, communications and transport troops.

Koto-ri itself was a modest affair—"a few huts," according to
General Smith. "The plateau region in the vicinity was windswept
and bleak. Small planes and helicopters had considerable difficulty
in surmounting the pass south of town; the arctic air from the
north flowed down over the pass, causing fishtail winds and tur-

bulence. In the recollection of the troops, Koto-ri was about the coldest and most disagreeable spot encountered during the course of the Chosin operation."

Puller knew that to defend Koto-ri properly he would have to hold the commanding terrain around the village; but, like Ridge at Hagaru, he was far short of the troops needed to set up that kind of defense. The only alternative was to establish a tight perimeter and carefully coordinate the fires of all supporting weapons. By the morning of November 28, Chinese troops in mass were plainly visible in the mountains north, south, and west of the village. Marine artillery broke up one concentration after another, but the encircling movement continued, and Puller was worried about his overcrowded perimeter. Every warming tent was packed to capacity. A single round from an enemy mortar tube, not to mention a series of coordinated barrages, could do great damage.

The single road was closed to both the north and the south. A spotter plane reported eight Chinese roadblocks between Koto and Hagaru to the north and at least three along the road to Funchilin Pass to the south. Wire contact in both directions had been severed by the enemy; communication between Puller and General Smith was uncertainly maintained by radio. Ten miles to the south, patrols sent out from Chinhung-ni by Schmuck's 1/1 had sighted formations of Chinese on the skylines to the west.

General Smith now ordered Puller to mount a major effort to open the road between Koto and Hagaru—as major an effort as could be mounted from the 2,100 men at his disposal. Puller was grateful that Sitter's George/1—along with Army Captain Charles Peckham's B Company/31 and Lt. Col. Douglas Drysdale's 41 Royal Commando—had reached the perimeter safely before the enemy shut down traffic.

41 Marine Commando was an interesting outfit. Trained for amphibious reconnaissance, the three-hundred-man unit had arrived in mid-November, requesting service with its Yank counterpart. Drysdale was ordered by Admiral Turner Joy to report to Colonel Litzenberg. This was the second time the U.S. and British Marines had campaigned together, the first being the Boxer Rebellion in China at the turn of the century. Since then, cordial messages had been traditionally exchanged on the respective birthdays—October 28, 1664, and November 10, 1775—and toasts raised on either side of the Atlantic. The American Marines admired the comman-

dos' jauntiness ("Well, chaps, what's next on tap?"), their spit-and-polish appearance even in the worst weather, and their green berets. (Drysdale had decreed that anyone who lost his beret would have to wear a bare steel helmet such as the American GIs wore, the ultimate disgrace; replacement berets were simply not to be had. Soon after 41 Commando arrived at Koto, a diminutive private named John Stock lost his, swiped perhaps by a souvenir-hunting Yank. Stock confessed the loss at once to his troop commander, Lt. Peter Thomas, who gave him a severe roasting but then generously loaned him the spare he happened to have in his kit.)

Puller now appointed Lt. Col. Drysdale as commander of the breakthrough force, which was composed of troops not integrated into the perimeter: Sitter's company, Peckham's company, 41 Commando, and assorted Headquarters and Service personnel. All told, the force was the numerical equivalent of a battalion, roughly nine hundred men. There the similarity ended, for there was no structure to the conglomerate formation. Before midnight a third of these troops would either be dead or prisoners of war.

Task Force Drysdale jumped off at 9:45 A.M., November 29, moving past the spotter-plane strip on their right amid flurries of snow and swirling mist. One could sense the undercurrent of competition between the British and American Marines as 41 Commando took the first objective, a hill just north of Koto, against light opposition. George/1 took the next, a hill further up the road on the other side. Drysdale's plan was to leapfrog in this manner all the way to Hagaru, with Peckham's B/31 in reserve.

PFC Francis Newbold, George/1: "We were still within sight of the huts of Koto-ri when we ran into trouble. We watched the commandos take the first hill, their green berets looking good against the snow; but they were taking hits. Then it was our turn. As for the doggies, I don't recollect them going against any of the objectives."

Corporal Ron Moyse, a blunt-featured commando squad leader, found the U.S. Marines a praiseworthy lot but thought they made too much noise in the field and used up more ammo than the situation called for. The American Marine, he observed, was "a less rational, more excitable animal than his British cousin. One thing we had in common, though: we always regarded ourselves as vastly superior to any Army mob. . . . Not far out of Koto-ri our sickberth attendants began to be very busy, rushing about from wounded to wounded, and we finally came to understand that there were a lot of Chinese bastards shooting at us from every conceivable angle and that we were all in the same bloody boat."

Captain Norman Vining, Marine forward air observer, recalls that there were far too many targets and not nearly enough Corsairs. Yudam-ni and Hagaru had priority, but he was able to call in three air strikes. Just as the fourth came into sight above the ridge, his ground-to-air radio went out. Vining: "You can imagine the frustration of *that*, since the ridges were fairly crawling with Chinese."

Three hours after jump-off, Task Force Drysdale had advanced only two miles, with nine more to go. Around noon Drysdale contacted Colonel Puller on the radio and explained the situation. Puller told him to sit tight; he would send tanks from Koto. When they arrived an hour later, Drysdale requested that they be fed into the column in pairs; but the tank commander, Captain Bruce Clark, USMC, wouldn't hear of it, insisting that his tanks should remain together. Since Puller had not placed Clark under Drysdale's command, the British officer had to accede to the tanker's wishes. The subsequent breakdown of Task Force Drysdale can be attributed in part to this misjudgment of the use of available armor. As S. L. A. Marshall pointed out, the survival of thin-skinned trucks and jeeps in the column depended largely on their ability to keep moving rapidly, while tankers tend to stop and shoot back when fired on. By stopping so often to return fire, the tankers continuously blocked the road, rendering jeeps and trucks vulnerable to small arms and mortar fire. Drysdale virtually pleaded with Captain Clark at one point to cease firing and move his tanks out smartly, but the tank officer was too enthralled with the wealth of targets to grasp the sense in Drysdale's plea.

Task Force Drysdale gradually became paralyzed; unit cohesion, not strong to begin with, began to slip away as infantry troops mingled with headquarters and service troops. By 4:30 in the afternoon the column, now halfway between Koto and Hagaru, was stalled in the road. Clark advised Colonel Drysdale that the tanks could get through the curtain of enemy fire, but that it was probably not safe for the truck convoy to press on.

What Drysdale needed now was a command decision. Contacting division headquarters in Hagaru, he asked whether the task force should continue an advance that was becoming costlier in dead and wounded with each moment. The message was delivered to General Smith as he was visiting casualties at 'E Med,' one of two Navy hospitals established at Hagaru. For Smith it was a decision that was paradoxically painful and easy, for without reinforcements it was likely that Hagaru would fall that very night. Captain Sitter was standing beside Drysdale when the order from Smith came in over the net: "Press on at all costs."

The two men exchanged somber glances. Drysdale nodded and said, "Very well, then: we'll give them a show."

And so the word was passed up and down the column: We're going to make a run for it. Corporal Ron Moyse recalls it this way: "The message that came down to us was: Imperative we get through to Hagaru. Absolutely necessary."

In one spot along the line of vehicles, the Chinese were already so close they could throw grenades with effect. One of these landed in the back of a truck as the troops were dismounting. PFC William B. Baugh, a rocket-launcher gunner attached to Sitter's company, shouted "Grenade!" and deliberately took the force of the explosion with his body. He died a short time later. His posthumously awarded Medal of Honor citation reads, "Baugh, by his superb courage and valiant spirit of self-sacrifice, upheld the highest traditions of the United States Naval Service. He gallantly gave his life for his country." Baugh was twenty at the time of his death, but he looked younger. Born in Kentucky, his home of record was Harrison, Ohio. (On September 22, 1984, Mrs. Opal Couchman, his sister, broke the traditional bottle of champagne against the portside of the Navy cargo ship *William B. Baugh*.)

Captain Sitter was beating on the side of a tank with his carbine. Finally a face appeared above the turret. "There's a railroad embankment on the right," Sitter shouted. "I want you to fire along there." The tanker answered, but in the din Sitter couldn't understand what he was saying. He shouted back: "Give us whatever fire you can so we can get this column rolling."

Thus the head of Drysdale's column, with D Company tanks leading George/1 and the commandos, gathered steam and rolled out of sight at dusk, unaware that they were leaving Peckham's B Company and most of the Headquarters and Service troops behind.

Ron Moyse: "The running of the gauntlet to Hagaru was positively hellish. The Chinese had taken up position in roadside ditches and were letting rip most effectively. On my left, as we sat in the back of a Marine truck, Captain Leslie Marsh was hit in both legs by a burst of fire. On my right Corporal Tanky Webb was shot through the left eye. And seated on the other side of him a young commando named John Woodward was shot through the head and knocked off the truck. At the same time the Marine driver was shot and killed. Fortunately for us our troop second-in-command took the wheel and drove on, remaining in the driver's seat for the rest of that nightmare journey, himself being wounded in the process. . . . Hagaru was about five miles farther ahead and we pressed on as fast as the trucks could carry us.

"Finally we saw the glow of the engineers' floodlights on the airstrip, and when we came around a curve, there in front of us was a cluster of pyramidal tents, and I figured we were home free." But these were the tents Captain Kulbes's X Corps engineers had erected before being ordered to join the fight on East Hill; and after the engineers departed, a number of Chinese had moved into them. These troops now rushed outside and opened fire on the convoy. Sitter and Drysdale's survivors scrambled out of the trucks once more and drove the Chinese into the hills.

Major Edwin Simmons: "I well remember Drysdale in his green beret, dripping blood from a wound in his arm, by the light of a Coleman lantern in our operations tent saluting and reporting 41 Commando present for duty."

Lt. Col. Ridge asked the tall British officer for an estimate of the number of Chinese opposing the task force. Drysdale thought it over, then said, "A minimum of three battalions." Ridge directed that George Company and 41 Commando spend the rest of the night in perimeter reserve. Sitter recalls that his troops were tired and disorganized after the running fight on the road; it took him until one o'clock in the morning to get the company settled down.

The phone rang shortly after he fell asleep. It was Major Joseph Trompeter, Ridge's operations officer. Sitter: "He told me to look outside the tent flap to my immediate front. 'See that hill?' he asked." Within an hour Sitter and his men were on their way up the slippery slope of East Hill, joining Kulbes and the other assorted units which had been holding back the enemy.

Private John Stock, the small commando who had lost his beret, now discovered that the one loaned him by his troop commander had a bullet hole in it. His survival was a miracle; nevertheless, he dreaded having to face the wrath of Lt. Peter Thomas; but Thomas smiled and said, "Keep it as a trophy of a very near miss."

Ron Moyse: "My personal low point in the campaign came that night, on learning the facts of life and death while counting corpses in the trucks. The loss of several friends manifested itself. A trivial note: I lost my personal kit in the scramble. Among the items lost was a cherished pair of boot brushes issued to me in 1943. Funnily enough I considered this my greatest loss among all the bits and pieces a soldier normally carries. Such was the quality of these brushes that they are probably doing sterling work on the odd pair of boots in China to this day. Aside from the clothes and equipment I was wearing, and my weapon, all I had left was the ring my eventual and still extant wife gave me in 1949."

PFC Fred Hayhurst, 41 Commando, had been shot in the leg during the run. On arrival at Hagaru he was carried into the first shelter at hand, a hut without a lantern in it. Hayhurst: "I discerned several other men stretched out in the dark and began jabbering away at them, failing to notice that none of them responded; then a head popped through the entrance and when I asked for something to drink, the poor fellow gave a little cry and backed out. Two medics showed up and took me to the proper hospital, by which time I had figured out that the hut where I had been temporarily parked was a morgue."

Thus the survivors of the attack in what was later called Hell Fire Valley—so dubbed by Drysdale himself—reached the dubious safety of the Hagaru perimeter. Captain Sitter, in his headlong rush to reach Hagaru, had assumed he was being closely followed by the rest of the column; but some sixty Royal Marine Commandos, most of Captain Peckham's Army company, and almost all Marine headquarters and service troops had been left behind and were now stranded in no man's land, at the mercy of the Chinese.

44.

IT WAS KOTO'S TURN. DURING the final moments of daylight, November 29, the Chinese unleashed their first attack against Puller's tight perimeter, swarming off the high ground near Captain Jack Smith's Easy Company and penetrating his defenses. In the melee that followed, seventeen Chinese were killed behind the Marine lines. Throughout the rest of the night Smith's men reported seeing flashlights out front as Chinese medics moved about, tending the wounded. In the morning Smith's men counted 175 corpses in the snow. No other Marine unit at Koto was molested that night.

In Hell Fire Valley a Chinese 82-mm mortar round hit an ammunition truck, destroying it and a jeep nearby, effectively blocking the road. Thus the Chinese began to carry out their tactical plan of fractionalizing the column. The next step would be to destroy the fragments. Some of the left-behind members of Task Force Drysdale gazed longingly down the road to Koto, wondering when, and if, reinforcements would arrive.

As George Company, the commandos, and Clark's tanks disappeared around the bend, the troops left behind were subjected to a more concentrated volume of fire. The shallow ditch beside the road provided little cover, leaving them vulnerable to plunging fire from the hills east of the road. Darkness put an end to air strikes, and the Chinese became bolder, pushing across the road to divide the remnants into even smaller segments.

Eventually the commandos, the Army's B Company, and various Marine headquarters and service troops shook down into three small clusters and one relatively large one. The latter, at the north end, consisted of 135 men under Major John McLaughlin, a Marine liaison officer with X Corps. Three hundred yards to his south was a group made up mostly of Captain Charles Peckham's B Company, 31st Infantry Regiment. Fifty yards below that was a small perimeter that included Captain Michael Capraro, a former San Francisco newspaperman who was the Marine Division's public information officer. Another hundred yards still further south was another group under Major Henry Seeley, the Division's motor transport officer. The four groups, about 380 men in all, covered a stretch of road roughly two-thirds of a mile long. There was no radio contact between them.

The overall setting was distinctive: the narrow road, a railroad embankment paralleling it to the east, and beyond that a shelf of ground rising into low hills set back from the road. Most of the Chinese machine guns and mortars had been set up on the hills, giving the enemy an excellent field of fire. On the west side of the road was the Changjin River, and beyond that a patchwork of rice paddies stretching away to a line of treeless hills. The Chinese appeared in no hurry to press their attack against the weak, vulnerable, poorly organized Americans.

Captain Capraro: "During all the stops and stalls earlier in the day, most of our energy was taken up with trying to get warm: flailing our arms, stamping our feet, and so on. We had no idea how serious the situation was until after dark when waves of Chinese suddenly hit the column from the east side of the road and, in a moment, breached and divided the convoy. It happened so fast I didn't have time to be scared; instead I experienced a feeling of disbelief and then disgust that we had let this happen to us. Funny thing, I served in China in '47 and was familiar with the crowds in Shanghai, and this reminded me of that.

"Time seemed to stand still as I waited for someone to shoot me, and at the same time I was fretting over the loss of my worldly possessions in the jeep: my passport, my typewriter, my *toothbrush*. Then the Chinese swarmed off the road like lemmings, and they were gone. I still don't know what all that was about. By then me and General Craig's aide, Lt. John Buck, were jogging in the opposite direction. We stopped at the bank of the river. We could hear bugles echoing back and forth in the distance."

It was going to be a long night. Their only hope was to organize themselves and try to hold out in some kind of perimeter until daylight, when Marine air would be available; then ground troops at Koto-ri could come to the rescue. Sometime around 10 P.M. the moon came out and Capraro could clearly see the outlines of the two perimeters north of him and the one to the south. By midnight the moon was behind clouds again and it was snowing a little.

Staff Sergeant James Nash, Marine military policeman: "Everything was so quiet you could almost hear the snow falling. Then the bugles started up again—the enemy's way of telling us we were surrounded. Then silence again. Then police whistles, much closer, and the firing started up once more. Some of us tried to use the trucks as cover, but we ended up in the ditch beside the road. Warrant Officer Lloyd Dirst walked from one end of the line to the other, a pipe between his teeth, passing out ammo, encouraging the men, directing their fire. Gunner Dirst was a steadying presence, which was what we needed. This was a panic situation if there ever was one. The Chinese were encircling our positions, like Indians around a wagon train, getting ready to close in and wipe us out. Gunner Dirst told us that if we stuck it out till daylight, the Corsairs would chase these people back into their rat holes. What we didn't know—and it was well we didn't—was that none of the radios were working."

A piece of shrapnel caught Gunner Dirst in the head. Sergeant Nash, who was wounded himself, crawled onto the road from the ditch, locked Dirst's arms around his neck, and dragged him back. Gunner Dirst died a few hours later, in the hands of the Chinese.

Sergeant Nash: "They closed in steadily on us. There was no rush, no storming of our positions. We kept knocking them down like ducks in a shooting gallery but they kept coming."

In McLaughlin's group at the north end, Army PFC Franklin Jack Chapman, eighteen, an ammo carrier in a 75-mm recoilless rifle squad, distinguished himself. He received his first wound, shrapnel in the left arm, in the early evening of the twenty-ninth. An hour later he was hit in the right leg. When he showed up again at the aid station he saw that the corpsmen were busy with more seriously wounded men, so he turned around and went back to the crew.

It was around nine o'clock when the gunner, a sergeant, jumped down from the weapon because enemy fire had gotten so heavy. Captain Peckham told him to resume his place at the gun, which was mounted on a weapons carrier. The sergeant refused to obey and proceeded to get down on his knees and start praying in a loud voice: "O Lord, protect us." Captain Peckham told him he was going to recommend a court martial, but this had no effect. The captain tried to find someone else to take over the gun and PFC Chapman finally volunteered. "You are to be commended," said the captain, "and cited for valor." With help from the rest of the crew, Chapman began firing at the enemy machine-gun and mortar positions.

Ammunition was almost gone now; Major McLaughlin personally collected rifle rounds from the dead and wounded and distributed them, two or three at a time, to those who seemed the most composed.

Another Marine MP, Sergeant Guillermo Tovar—son of a Mexican gold miner—was struck by a bullet while in the act of arming a grenade. "A slug passed through my left earlobe and buried itself in my neck. It spun me around and put me flat on my back. What worried me most was the grenade: I wasn't sure if I had armed it or not and was expecting an explosion any second. A British medic came over and I asked him to look for the grenade, but he couldn't find it. He pushed me under a truck and gave me a shot of morphine. After a while I heard the bugles again. I was flying high because of the morphine, but those bugles scared me because they sounded like men talking and I thought they were saying 'Kill!' and 'Victory!' By about 0100 the dope had mostly worn off and the bleeding had stopped, probably because of the cold. I was feeling exposed there under the truck and decided to see if I could crawl over to the ditch. When I got there I found a radio, which I used to shield my head. At one point I got myself together enough to try contacting Whiskey One—Koto, that is—but couldn't raise a soul."

It was around two in the morning when three Marines and an Associated Press photographer named Frank Noel decided to try and escape straight down the road. (The Marines were hospitable to Noel after they saw that his published photos were of actual combat, taken during the Inchon-to-Seoul campaign.) The four men climbed into one of the jeeps, promising to return with a full load of ammo, and went careening down the road in the direction of Koto. They had gone less than a hundred yards when several soldiers in white materialized like ghosts on both sides of the road. The driver braked quickly, keeping his hands visible on the steering wheel. An English-speaking officer stepped forward and instructed one of the Marines—identified in the official record as "PFC Spain of the MP company"—to return to the perimeter and inform the senior American officer there that he was to surrender his command at once.

Corporal Calvin W. Williams: "They ordered us out of the jeep after Spain took off on foot. I sat down on a rock, and some old guy who had been shot up came over and started kicking me, but another guy made him cut it out."

When PFC Spain reported to the major and explained the situation, McLaughlin called for a volunteer to carry his response to the Chinese. At that time Sergeant Guillermo Tovar was lying near Sergeant Nash. "Maybe I'll volunteer," he mumbled.

Nash said, "Tovar, if you go down there you won't come back."

Tovar climbed slowly to his feet and stumped over to the major. McLaughlin's instructions were startling and soon became one of the nuggets of Chosin lore: "Tell them I'm prepared to accept their surrender."

"Sir?"

"And tell them they'll be treated according to the Geneva Convention. I know they're going to scoff at this, Tovar—but try and sell them the goods. Tell them we'll feed them hot chow."

"Aye, aye, sir."

"And take Junior with you."

Accompanied by the reluctant Korean interpreter, Tovar set off down the road, holding his hands above his head to show that he was unarmed. Tovar: "After we proceeded about a hundred feet, some Chinese soldiers emerged from the shadows and surrounded us. They stood perfectly still, just watching us, until an officer showed up with an interpreter." Tovar gave him McLaughlin's message, patiently spelling it out until the interpreter understood it, then waiting patiently while he translated it. The officer looked at Tovar, his face expressionless. Then he spoke. When he was finished, Junior translated: "He say: Go back, tell major he have ten minute to surrender."

Tovar and Junior trudged back to the perimeter. Tovar was to make several of these trips before it was over. On the second trip the message from McLaughlin was: "I will surrender at 0630, not before. I need time to care for my wounded." Tovar: "The idea was to stall as long as possible, in hopes that dawn would bring some Marine air cover and none of us would have to surrender."

When Tovar delivered this message, the Chinese officer gave him the same blank look, then said through the interpreter: "You have five minutes." He raised his hand, displaying all five fingers in case the American had failed to grasp the meaning. On the third trip Tovar was joined by Major McLaughlin himself. While the major was talking with the Chinese officer, Tovar took the opportunity to visit with Major James Eagen, the division's assistant supply officer, who had been wounded in both legs. Several shivering Chinese soldiers kept watch on them as Tovar asked the major's views on the surrender.

"There must be a *regiment* of Chinese out there," said Eagen. "We've got a snowball's chance in hell of holding them off."

A moment later Major Henry Seeley appeared out of the darkness, only a short distance down the railroad track from the parley site. Seeley was the senior officer in the southernmost perimeter. "We're not surrendering," he told Tovar and Eagen. "We still have some ammo and none of us is seriously wounded." He turned to the MP sergeant. "Tovar, you want to come along with me? I'm going back now."

Tovar said no; he intended to stick it out with his own group. Besides, he was an important member of the negotiating team.

"Good luck, then." Seeley turned and disappeared into the darkness. (Seeley: "I never saw Jim Eagen again, and I've often wondered at the fortunes of war that doom one man and spare another.")

Returning to his perimeter, McLaughlin sought the counsel of Lt. Col. Arthur Chidester, the division assistant G-4, who had been wounded early in the fight. "The Chinese have assured me that if we lay down our arms they'll let us send the wounded back to Koto."

"You think we can trust them?"

"It's a chance we'll have to take."

"How much ammo have you got left?"

"Damn little."

"I don't see what else you can do, Mac."

"I've got our wounded to think of," said McLaughlin. "They can't survive very long out here in this weather."

Tovar: "The Chinese must have lost their patience at this point, because one of their officers spoke a single short phrase and it seemed as if every Chinese soldier within a hundred yards stood up and started to close in on us. They knew we had been stalling for time. Major McLaughlin and I were standing side by side when this happened, and I found myself saying out loud: 'We better shit or get off the pot, Major.' "

Using his forefinger and thumb only, McLaughlin gingerly lifted his .45 automatic from the hip holster and handed it, butt first, to the Chinese officer. "I'm not surrendering because you beat us," he said. "I'm surrendering to get our wounded cared for."

The order to cease fire was passed down the line from man to man, even though there had been no firing for half an hour. Some of the men now took the precaution of slipping C-ration cans into their parka pockets, anticipating the moment when they would pass under Chinese authority and enter the rice culture.

Sergeant Charles Dickerson: "The Chinese either took our weapons directly or told us to lay them down on the road. This one fellow came running up to me and I thought he was going to sock me or something; but he patted me on the back and said I was friend."

Tovar: "The agreement was that our wounded would be allowed to return to Koto. We began carrying them from the ditch over to the trucks, but the Chinese stopped us. That was the moment when I understood we were all going to end up in a prison camp—those of us who survived."

The Chinese began organizing their captives into groups, each guarded by two soldiers. The bag: about forty U.S. Marines, twenty British commandos, one hundred U.S. Army infantry and service troops. Tovar began to experience the claustrophobia of confinement, and, as he and McLaughlin were being herded across the railroad tracks, he muttered, "These people aren't going to keep me."

"Don't try anything yet," said the major. "They're watching too closely."

Tovar: "Just then I happened to see a dead Marine, his right arm frozen in an upraised position. It gave me a sense of dread, and I knew the major's advice was sound."

Captain Michael Capraro, of Major Seeley's group: "About halfway through the night I had a hallucination: a snow-covered rock out front came alive and began to move toward me, followed by others, and I actually called out for the riflemen nearby to help me meet the attack. I was not only fearful of getting killed, I was afraid of being captured. Having served in China in 1947 as an intelligence officer, I knew that capture meant complete degradation and exploitation for propaganda purposes; it meant severe hardship and what we now call brainwashing. It meant being paraded from village to village like some carnival geek with your arms tied behind you. So I was immediately agreeable to the idea of striking out toward the hills as soon as Major Seeley suggested it. When he came back from his meeting with McLaughlin and Tovar, he talked it over with us. Warrant Officer Dee Yancey pointed out that there was no enemy fire coming from across the river, and that the river at this point was frozen over. 'We ought to head out,' he said, 'before it gets light.'

" 'It'll be light in half an hour.'

" 'We should go now.'

" 'Come on, then,' said Major Seeley.

"There were about twenty of us in the group."

Major Henry Seeley: "Two GIs in our small perimeter had crawled behind a log before midnight and either froze to death or died of wounds; we had no choice but to leave them there. We crossed the river and headed across the paddies toward a ridge we hoped would give us some cover, and by daybreak we were out of sight of the valley floor. We had been moving south for about ten minutes when we heard voices behind us. Then a bugle sounded, and it was obvious that Chinese were on our trail. At that point I sent the group back down to the river, for the following reason: the terrain in the hills was somewhat confusing and I was having trouble keeping us oriented to Koto-ri; I knew we couldn't get lost if we followed the river."

Seeley, a former team shooter with trophies from the annual marksmanship matches at Camp Perry, Ohio, remained behind momentarily, adjusting the sights of his Springfield '03. When the first Chinese soldier appeared on the skyline, he dropped him with one shot, then scrambled down the slope to join Capraro and the others heading toward the river.

Capraro: "A fantastic thing happened as we made our way along the riverbank. Around the bend came a column of Chinese soldiers—about forty men in all. They had their heads down in the wind, each man just following the man ahead. Some of them must have seen us, but they took no action. We just kept going, holding our breath. Then another fantastic thing happened. A Marine helicopter appeared over a ridge to the south, making a terrific racket.

The Chinese in the column deployed, raised their weapons, and fired at it. The chopper had slowed to a hover above the paddy; but now, reacting to the rifle fire, it rose up sharply and banked away. All this action drew the enemy's attention away from us. I considered it a God-sent diversion."

Seeley and his group staggered into Koto-ri at about 9 A.M. While Seeley was off finding rations and arranging for shelter, Captain Capraro, representing the group, gave a verbal report to Colonel Puller. Capraro was then handed a cup of hot cocoa and a shot of whiskey. "What else do you need?" he was asked.

"Well, I could sure use a toothbrush."

Within two minutes, reports Capraro, a toothbrush, in its brand new glass tube, was handed over, much to his amazement.

Puller's regimental sergeant major, whom Capraro knew from the Guadalcanal campaign ("and who happened to be my daughter's godfather"), grabbed the exhausted officer and took him into his tent for a "home-cooked" meal. "Would you believe spaghetti and meatballs, and waffles with strawberries for desert? I didn't ask how he came up with such a menu; I just wolfed it down in silent gratitude."

Captain Bruce F. Williams's tankers had arrived in Koto-ri at about 3 P.M. on November 29, the last cohesive unit to enter the perimeter from the south. Puller sent them up the road with the notion of either reinforcing or rescuing the Drysdale column; but they ran into heavy opposition north of the perimeter, the enemy firing from the very hills so laboriously cleared by Sitter and the commandos that morning. The tanks pushed on slowly, and it was after dark when Williams and crew rounded a curve and saw the unholy mess up ahead.

Corporal Eugene A. McGuire, tank gunner: "Total chaos is what I saw through the scope. Tracers flying all over the place. Muzzle blasts, flames, smoldering fires, shapes of vehicles all askew, troops running back and forth across the road. No way to distinguish good guys from bad."

Listening in on the radio net, McGuire heard Captain Williams tell his platoon leader, Lt. Robert Gover, that it would be impossible to provide tank support due to lack of communication and the problem of distinguishing friend from foe. Williams directed the tanks to turn around, then contacted Major Robert E. Lorigan,

Puller's operations officer, alerting him that B Company tanks were returning to Koto. Moving southward a short distance, the tankers ran into a scorching wall of mortar fire. After sustaining some casualties, Williams decided to stop, circle up for the night, and await the Corsairs in the morning. Colonel Puller came on the net, suggesting but not ordering that Williams might make another try at returning to the perimeter. Captain Williams answered that it was now impossible to move, that they were well established, and that with some artillery support he thought they could get through the night. Puller didn't respond. Lorigan's voice informed Williams that 105-mm rounds were in short supply.

Williams: "We went over to the arty frequency and requested a white-phosphorous round three miles north and a hundred yards east of the road. This registration round landed very beautifully, and with little waste we registered six concentrations, three on each side of the road. Enemy fire decreased while we were adjusting these fires, but there was still plenty of action."

The tank next to McGuire's was holed in the stern by an antitank projectile, and a Chinese soldier got close enough to slap a satchel charge on top of the engine compartment. The explosion set fire to the transmission fluid. The tank commander, Sergeant Earl Swearingen, radioed that he and his crew were about to evacuate after removing the crystals from the radio and the firing mechanism from the gun. McGuire's tank commander, Sergeant Don Bennett, then told the assistant driver, Corporal Morgan, to open the emergency escape hatch on the bottom deck. Morgan tried but he couldn't crack it. (McGuire: "I think maybe a certain person had taken a piss through the hatch and when he replaced it the lid froze on.")

Word came that Swearingen's crew was in the act of bailing out. Corporal McGuire committed a tanker sin at that point by opening the loader's hatch and popping up with his Thompson at the ready while Swearingen was making his way over. A Chinese soldier standing beside the tank shot the submachine gun out of his hands, one round catching him in the wrist. McGuire fell back and secured the hatch. Just then Corporal Morgan managed to get the escape hatch open by banging on it with a box of ammo, and Swearingen and crew started climbing inside as fast as they could. McGuire was bleeding, but he put on a tourniquet and held his arm up against the turret wall until it stopped.

McGuire: "We had no ground Marines around that night and it was damn lonely. One brave gook climbed atop the tank and I saw him in the dim turret light. He fired through the thick sandwich of prismatic glass, but the round didn't come all the way through."

Captain Bruce Williams: "After midnight they stopped bothering us. It was crowded as hell with two crews in one tank but no one complained about claustrophobia. Every man was glad to be inside, out of the wind, with those Chinese all around."

At dawn Captain Williams and his tanks clanked unchallenged back to Koto, having contributed little to the salvation of the left-behinds of Task Force Drysdale. It had been a tough call for Williams, and he was later criticized for it. The question remains: What good could he have done by committing his tanks to the clogged mess of Hell Fire Valley? Strung out on the road south of the already-shattered Drysdale column, only the first tank or so could have brought its 90-mm gun to bear on enemy positions, assuming such targets could be located in the dark.

Of the 900–plus men who set out on the morning of the twenty-ninth, in rounded figures 150 had been killed, 150 had been wounded, and many others had been taken prisoner. Of the 141 vehicles in the convoy, at least seventy-five were destroyed. And yet two-thirds of Sitter's George Company and two-thirds of 41 Commando had survived the mad dash to Hagaru.

General Oliver Smith: "The casualties of Task Force Drysdale were heavy, but by its partial success the task force made a significant contribution, vital to the division. To the slender infantry garrison at Hagaru were added a tank company and some three hundred seasoned infantrymen."

Whether this reinforcement would make any difference remained to be seen. Reports flowing into division headquarters during the day indicated that another major attack could be expected soon against the southwest quadrant of the Hagaru perimeter. Hagaru remained the key to survival. At Hagaru was the C-47 airstrip, close to completion. At Hagaru was a defended perimeter, where the 5th and 7th Marines could reorganize, resupply, re-equip, and evacuate their casualties—assuming, that is, that the two regiments could fight their way fourteen miles down the road from Yudam-ni. At Hagaru, too, it would be possible to receive the remnants of the hapless Army task force east of the reservoir, evacuate those who could no longer fight, and re-equip those who were able-bodied. At Hagaru, finally, was the Division's head-quarters.

General Smith: "I am confident that RCT [Regimental Combat Team] 5 and RCT 7 could have fought their way out of Yudam-ni, regardless of the fate of Hagaru; but had Hagaru fallen, these two regiments would have faced a bleak prospect. They were burdened with fifteen hundred casualties, short of supplies and ammunition, and, under these circumstances, would have had to recapture Hagaru, reestablish contact with the outside world, reopen the airstrip with limited equipment, wait for resupply by air while their casualties were being evacuated, and then continue down the long road to the sea."

45.
THE DESTRUCTION OF TASK
Force Drysdale was a small-scale version of what was happening at that very moment to a U.S. Army division on the other side of the Taebeks, a hundred miles to the west. Lt. General Walton Walker's Eighth Army was reeling backward in retreat, and the 2nd Infantry Division, trapped by the Chinese on the road between Kunu-ri and Sunchon, had lost all cohesiveness and fighting power in a hurricane of mortar rounds and machine-gun fire. The division's commanding officer, Major General Laurence Keiser, had issued the informal How Able (Haul Ass) order to his regimental commanders, and at that point a disorderly retreat turned into a mad scramble and finally into an every-man-for-himself struggle for survival. Three thousand GIs of the 2nd Division were lost on the morning of November 30.

(Chew-Een Lee's younger brother, an Army platoon leader, was part of the dreadful scene. Lt. Chew-Mon Lee lay helplessly beside the road, a bullet hole in his chest, his lungs filling with blood, until someone from his battalion recognized him and loaded him aboard one of the still-operable trucks. Lee later told his Marine brother that he had seen tanks rolling over wounded men in the drivers' panic to get away.)

General Keiser, at the wheel of a jeep, arrived at the north end of the bloody gauntlet at mid-afternoon, only to find a gothic junkyard of wrecked vehicles with zombielike GIs slogging past them, stepping over the dead and wounded as they headed south. The general dismounted and strode among them, barking questions and demands, trying to shock them out of their collective trance.

"Who's in command here? You! What outfit do you belong to?" Finally, in a kind of hopeless resignation, he asked, "Can't any of you do anything at all?"

Abandoning his jeep in the middle of the clogged road, Keiser walked the entire six-mile stretch without being wounded, but by the time he reached the southern end of the massive ambush he was exhausted. As he started to step across still another body in the road, his boot struck the man's stomach and the body came alive, indignant. "You damn son of a bitch."

"My friend," said the general, "I'm sorry," and walked on.

More than a third of the Second Division was lost, along with almost all of its weapons and equipment. No less than sixty-two artillery pieces were abandoned along with thousands of rounds of ammunition. (The *New York Herald Tribune* inexplicably commended the division for a stand that would rank, the December 9, 1950, editorial said, as "one of the greatest holding actions of the war." The Marines, ever scornful, called Eighth Army's retreat the Great Bugout.)

News of the Eighth Army's disastrous rout and the crisis facing the Marines at the Chosin Reservoir was of course widely reported in the United States; stark headlines featuring the words *encircled* and *trapped* were seen on newsstands from coast to coast. (*The New York Times*, December 1, 1950: "U.S. Marines Encircled Near Reservoir in Northeast Beat Off Attacks by Chinese.") At Marine headquarters in Arlington, Virginia, the switchboard was flooded with calls from worried parents, wives, children, and friends. Marine spokesmen assured callers the situation was serious but not hopeless; Marines had been in tough situations before and always managed to fight their way out. That was true, but never had a Marine division been in a worse fix than this one, not even at Guadalcanal or Tarawa.

The massive Chinese intervention in Korea caused a world-wide tremor of fear that World War III was about to erupt. President Truman exacerbated that fear in his November 30 press conference when he indicated, in answering a routine question, that he might authorize MacArthur to use the atomic bomb.

Truman: "We will take whatever steps are necessary to meet the military situation, just like we always do."

Question: "Will that include the atomic bomb?"

Truman: "That includes every weapon we have."

Question: "Do we understand you clearly that the use of the atomic bomb is under active consideration?"

Truman: "Always has been. It's one of our weapons."

This casual rattling of the nuclear sword caused much international apprehension. In London a passionate debate erupted in the House of Commons, and Prime Minister Clement Attlee drew cheers by announcing that he would fly to Washington to obtain assurance from the president that he had no intention of using the bomb in Korea.

At mid-morning, November 29, a two-seater Marine helicopter landed briefly in the center of Fox Company's position at Toktong Pass with a small delivery of medical supplies and a battery for the 610 radio, allowing Lt. Donald Campbell, the artillery forward observer, to maintain contact with Captain Read's battery at Hagaru. A sniper, firing from the slopes of Toktong-san, scored a hit on the helicopter, just missing the pilot, Lt. Floyd Englehardt. When two more rounds struck the fragile craft, Captain Barber decided to wave the chopper away rather than wait for the loading-aboard of a desperately wounded Marine.

Toward dusk an Air Force C-117 dropped a load of supplies by parachute, but far off target. "They're supplying the enemy!" cried Barber as he watched the bundles coming down in the distance.

PFC Peter Holgrun: "Our hearts turned cold as we watched the big plane drop the stuff several hundred yards to the west. Some of the chutes failed to open and cases of grenades could be seen striking the frozen earth, breaking open, scattering everywhere. I couldn't help wondering how many of these grenades would be thrown at us that very night."

In short order a volunteer work-party under Lt. Peterson ventured outside the tightened perimeter, with company mortars firing salvos to cover them. Most of the volunteers went out unarmed, leaving their hands free to carry the ammunition that was more important to the Marines on Fox Hill than food or water.

Morale was generally high among the Fox Company survivors as daylight came on, even though half the men of the company were battle casualties and most everyone was suffering from frostbite and dysentery.

Harrison Pomers recalls Captain Barber entering the crowded aid tent to explain that he was short of warm bodies and needed volunteers to come back to the line despite their wounds. "Several wounded men forced themselves to get up and go outside. I don't recall any of their names right now, but they were all heroes." Pomers was too badly hurt to join them, but he was ready to fight where he lay if it came down to that. "I had my M-1 beside me, even though the corpsmen kept trying to take it outside. One of them pointed out that I couldn't even use the right side of my body. 'True,' I said, 'but I can use the left side.' Sometime before dawn I felt this wet sticky sensation on my back, and one of the corpsmen opened up my clothing when I complained about it. 'You got a hole as big as your fist,' he says, 'and your spinal column is exposed.' And that's how I found out why my right side wasn't working. (I have only partial use of my right arm and leg today.)"

X Corps had issued no plans or directives to the Marine division for two critical days—which did nothing to improve the Marines' opinion of the U.S. Army and its ways. General Almond had returned from the Tokyo conference to find an increasingly dire situation in his zone of command. The 5th and 7th Marines were cut off and surrounded at Yudam-ni on the western arm of the sprawling Chosin Reservoir. At Hagaru, at the foot of the reservoir, a lone Marine battalion was surrounded but holding on by its fingernails. Task Force Drysdale, attempting to reinforce Hagaru from the south, was in danger of annihilation. Puller's perimeter at Koto, eleven miles south of Hagaru, was under siege. On the east shore of the reservoir, not far above Hagaru, Task Force MacLean was dangerously exposed.

Early on the morning of the twenty-ninth, General Smith received a radio-link message from X Corps directing him to deploy one regiment from Yudam-ni to Hagaru, extract the cut-off Army battalions east of the reservoir, and open the road between Hagaru and Koto. Operations Instruction No. 19, as the order was called, reached Smith's headquarters at 10:19 A.M., confirming the telephonic message. It was a desperate order, quite impossible to carry out, and revealed once again how woefully disconnected from reality the corps commander was.

Smith had no intention of separating his two regiments at Yudam-ni. "It is superfluous to point out," he later wrote,

> that no RCT could be redeployed from Yudam-ni without first dealing with the three CCF divisions which surrounded RCTs 5 and 7, and that no forces would be available to open up the main supply route from Hagaru to Koto-ri until RCTs 5 and 7 had fought their way to Hagaru. The garrison at Hagaru had been attacked in division strength on the

night of 28–29 November and had suffered about 500 casualties. It was due to be attacked again in division strength on the night of 30 November–1 December. It was not feasible to dispatch an infantry force from this garrison to extricate Task Force Faith.

General David Barr, the 7th Division commander, was in Hagaru at the time, and agreed with Smith that no Marine units could be spared from the Hagaru perimeter. The Marine general had shown Barr his tactical map of the defenses, and Barr understood how precariously thin they were at every point except perhaps where Corley and Fisher's lines were. Nothing could be done for the beleaguered Army troops until the 5th and 7th Marines fought their way down from the north. With the help of Marine air support, Task Force Faith would either have to hold in place or fight its way to Hagaru.

On the twenty-ninth Major Henry Woessner, Litzenberg's operations chief, came up with the notion of forming a composite battalion and going to the rescue of Fox Company. Litzenberg approved the idea and assigned a company each from Davis's and Harris's battalions, plus one from the 5th Marines, putting them under the command of Harris's executive officer, Major Warren Morris. Litzenberg's instructions to Morris were simple: Push through to Toktong Pass, relieve Fox/7, and continue on to Hagaru. Morris gathered his force at the southern gate of the perimeter and set out. It was a brave but futile effort. A few minutes after Baker/7 led the way—as usual—the battalion ran into a squall of machine-gun fire from the ridge lines and gorges on either side. The road, which rose steadily toward the pass through a narrowing defile, became more dangerous with every step. Lt. Joseph Kurcaba, commanding officer of Baker Company, finally advised Major Morris by runner that further advance would be foolish. In a now-familiar sequence, as the point fire team was approaching Turkey Hill, a light observation plane swooped down between the ridge lines on either side of the road and dropped a hastily scrawled message warning Kurcaba of large numbers of Chinese deployed along the high ground. At 1:15 P.M. Litzenberg directed Morris to return to the perimeter.

It was General Smith's understanding that Army troops would take over responsibility for the road between Koto-ri and Hamhung; he had been told, specifically, that elements of the 3rd U.S. Infantry Division would be employed for that purpose. At 2:10 P.M. on the twenty-ninth Smith sent a message to Almond informing him that he wanted to move Lt. Col. Donald Schmuck's First Battalion, 1st Marines, from Chinhung-ni to Koto by noon the thirtieth; Smith requested that the 3rd U.S. Infantry Division take over responsibility for the railhead and the supply dumps at Chinhung-ni. The message went unacknowledged, and the 3rd Division remained far south of Koto.

Around noon, Almond, according to his command diary, directed his staff to begin preparing a new order concentrating X Corps for the protection of Hamhung/Hungnam. It was nine hours before his staff presented him with an actual plan of withdrawal. Thus was the X Corps offensive at last canceled.

At this time the 5th Marines at Yudam-ni, oriented toward the north, were holding the upper half of the perimeter, while the 7th held the southern half. Late that afternoon, General Smith issued an order that changed the complexion of the entire campaign: the 5th Marines were to take over responsibility for the defense of Yudam-ni, while the 7th Marines were to prepare to clear the road to Hagaru—"without delay, employing the entire regiment." As Litzenberg's regiment blasted its way southward, Murray was to pull back slowly, the two regiments staying in contact, ready to provide mutual support.

The withdrawal from Yudam-ni—or to put it another way, the attack southward—was about to begin.

Alpha Bowser: "Two prayers were in order at this point. First, that the 5th and 7th Marines would reach Hagaru quickly, with their fighting ability intact. Second, that we could hold on to Hagaru as they fought their way toward us."

46.

ACCORDING TO COLONEL AL-pha Bowser, General Smith invited General Barr to borrow his helicopter and "Go see for yourself" when the 7th Division commander indicated that he found the report on the situation at Pungnyuri Inlet hard to believe. When Barr stepped out of the helicopter at the inlet, some of Faith's officers came forward to greet him, but the general responded with a brusque gesture and stalked off to confer with Lt. Col. Faith. Few specifics have filtered down through the years about Barr's brief visit, but one can fairly surmise that the general informed the task-force commander that his troops were now under the authority of General Smith. On his return to Hagaru, Barr told the Marine general that Faith's wounded numbered around 500, and that bringing them out would be his biggest problem, aside from the Chinese.

On the morning of November 30, Colonel Edward H. Forney, a Marine amphibious expert attached to X Corps, briefed General Almond on the situation up north. This briefing constituted an important moment in the campaign, for it enabled Almond to grasp the brutal truth at last. His immediate reaction was to head for Hagaru in the L-19 light plane. There is no question that Forney's report alarmed the general—who is described in Roy Appleman's *East of Chosin* as "an entirely different man from the one who had visited the troops there two days earlier. He knew now that the survival of X Corps itself was at stake."

Almond met with Smith, Barr, and Hodes in a tent set up near the edge of the airstrip. In his customary direct fashion he informed them that as soon as the Yudam-ni Marines and the Army troops east of the reservoir were concentrated at Hagaru they would all head for Hungnam on the coast. (Privately, Smith objected to the corps commander's repeated use of the phrase *fall back* and the word *withdraw;* the reality was that the Marines and attached

Army troops were going to have to fight their way out of the mountains.) Almond told Smith that he would resupply his division by air drop if the Marine general would agree to destroy all encumbering supplies and equipment.

Smith: "I told him that my movement would be governed by my ability to evacuate the wounded, that I would have to fight my way back and could not afford to discard equipment."

Almond then instructed Smith to submit a plan with a time schedule for the extraction of Task Force Faith.

Smith: "[After Almond departed] Barr and I agreed that under the conditions a time schedule didn't make sense. [Captain Michael Capraro's comment: "Imagine General Crook sending a dispatch to Custer during the battle of Little Bighorn asking for a time schedule pertaining to the withdrawal of the 7th Cavalry!"] The two battalions would just have to do the best they could to get back to us. If they were still isolated by the time the column got back from Yudam-ni, I would send one RCT to extricate them."

General Smith now instructed Hodes to write an order directing Faith to fight his troops to Hagaru. When Hodes had done so, Smith signed it. He then called his operations chief over to his bungalow and vented his disgust over Almond's suggestion that the Marines should destroy their heavy equipment and burn their excess. He said that Almond had lost all effectiveness as a corps commander. According to Bowser, Smith then "expressed in no uncertain terms that we were pretty much on our own as of now, that anything X Corps had to say would be taken with a grain of salt, and that we were going to have to fight our way out without relying on X Corps support."

47.

AFTER MIDNIGHT ON NOVEMBER 30, the Chinese unleashed their third major assault against the Marine positions at Toktong Pass. Three Chinese infantry companies, armed with automatic weapons, satchel charges, and hand grenades, crossed the small valley south of the road and closed in on the base of Fox Hill. PFC Lloyd O'Leary, now the most senior among able-bodied mortarmen, hung a brace of illumination rounds in the sky, and in the glaring light the Marines watched the gnomish silhouettes creeping across the road. Some of the Marines had stretched white blankets taken from enemy dead over their holes; partly hidden by these and a light coat of falling snow, they watched as the specterlike figures moved tentatively up the slope, apparently unsure of the location of the Marine lines.

PFC Donald Childs: "The element of surprise was priceless."

The sudden volley delivered by the men on line awakened every exhausted, off-duty Marine on the hill, and within seconds their rifles and machine guns were adding to the storm of fire. The few Chinese who managed to cross the road on the flank of Peterson's platoon scurried to the retaining wall, desperately seeking cover from the grenades Peterson's men rolled down on them. Captain Barber limped about, steadying the line.

Veterans of the Chosin Reservoir campaign, old men now, still brood about comrades who died at the reservoir. Graydon Davis often thinks of his friend from Florida, PFC Claude Peoples. "One day during the summer campaign we were riding in the back of a truck and Gunnery Sergeant Kalinowski remarked that we all looked alike, even Peoples who was black, because our faces were covered with dust. We *were* all alike; we were Marines! He was hit on Fox Hill, defending a gun position. . . . You held your ground, pal, like a good Marine. *Semper fidelis*."

Lt. Larry Schmitt recalls how Peoples lingered in stoic silence in the aid tent before death overtook him. "I know he was conscious right up to the end because he gave me a smile about five minutes before he passed." Schmitt also remembers a private named Asa Fitzgerald who, wounded in the chest, could only speak in gasps, slowly weakening until the corpsmen carried his body outside; and a wounded Marine named Darryl Heberling, who gave up the ghost as he was complaining about the loaf of salami sent from home that he had lost along with his pack in the fight. None are forgotten.

Ten miles due east across the ice of the reservoir, the GIs waited passively for the next thing to happen. Lt. Col. Faith had set out no outposts, content to huddle with his weakened force in an open field along the south shore of Pungnyuri Inlet. His position could no longer be called a perimeter, strictly speaking; it was more like a number of scattered groups warming themselves around fires. November 30 dawned cold and windless. The fog began to dissipate around eight o'clock and by ten the skies had cleared. Captain Stamford kept his eye on the Chinese on the heights as he waited for the Corsairs to report on station. (His AN/prc-1 radio was capable of tuning in any frequency used by U.S. forces and could have been employed by Colonel Faith to establish communications with 7th Infantry Division headquarters; apparently these options never occurred to Faith or his staff officers.)

Captain Harold Eisele, Corsair pilot: "We flew several missions under Captain Stamford's control that morning. When he announced that I appeared to be on target, I could see as many American troops in my gunsight as Chinese; so I went around for a second pass, but once again I was unable to fire because the two forces were so close to each other. I told Ed we had seen large masses of enemy troops in the hills nearby, and he set us to work on them instead. F4Us carried twenty-mm cannons, and every third round was high-explosive ammunition, which was very effective against concentrations of troops; with these, plus our five-inch rockets and napalm, we killed many Chinese."

Around noon Stamford's high-frequency radio went dead. Recalling that the Air Force forward air controller—killed in the first night's attack—had lost his radio early on to enemy fire, he wondered if perhaps the needed parts could be cannibalized. The ruined set was a quarter mile from the Marine TACP's position. Two of

Stamford's men, Corporal Myron J. Smith and PFC Billy E. Johnson, volunteered to find it and bring it back. Four hours later, after the two young Marines had worked on the radio with bare hands in the freezing weather, it came alive, and once again the dark gullwinged planes were swooping down on the enemy like prehistoric birds of prey. (Neither Corporal Smith nor PFC Johnson would survive the campaign.)

Lt. Col. Faith assembled the handful of officers and told them that the crippled task force—assuming it survived the coming night—was going to break out of the encirclement next morning, December 1, and somehow negotiate the relatively flat seven miles of road between the inlet and Hagaru. Contrary to everyone's expectation, the night of November 29–30 had been quiet except for the distant rumble of artillery at Yudam-ni. Occasionally the GIs could hear buglers signaling in the hills to the east. A bright moon briefly illuminated the barren landscape, but the sky clouded over and it began to snow. Once again the troops on the ground began to worry about the availability of Marine air cover in the morning. The cold wind was particularly harsh that night. One of the company commanders reported that every one of his Browning automatic rifles was inoperable; another reported toward morning that one of his men had frozen to death in a sitting position in his foxhole.

The Army battalion that Colonel Allan MacLean had so longed to see was still far out of reach. Lt. Col. Richard R. Reidy's Second Battalion, 31st Infantry Regiment, was now halfway up Funchilin Pass, three miles below Koto-ri. According to Oliver Smith's aidemémoire, Almond had actually seen the convoy from his L-19; it was stalled in the rugged pass, several vehicles wrecked, discarded equipment strewn about. Smith says that General Almond wanted to "fix responsibility for the 2/31 mess" by relieving Reidy but that Barr objected, pointing out that only the commander on the ground knew what the situation was. Almond settled for sending a liaison officer to determine why the battalion was stalled and get it moving again. Army Major Joseph I. Gurfein was dispatched from Hungnam as Almond's personal representative, charged with ordering Reidy to get his outfit in hand and continue the march. Gurfein arrived at Reidy's position at dusk, November 30, and delivered the message in blunt language. Reidy was oddly reluctant to comply.

Captain Richard Mitchell, 2/31 operations officer: "Reidy tried to point out the importance of having some force occupy the terrain that controlled Funchilin Pass. Gurfein just kept saying, 'The Corps commander wants you to move to Koto-ri.' Reidy said he understood that, and would do so, but didn't anyone recognize the need to hold the terrain his battalion was now occupying, to keep the road open? Gurfein replied to the effect that this wasn't Reidy's problem and that he was to move out, now. Reidy then said something like 'The recommendation of the commander on the ground is worth nothing to the corps commander, then?' Gurfein replied to the effect that such was the case and that Reidy was to get his battalion moving, *right now*. At this point Reidy became unglued; he looked like a man who had been hit over the head with a baseball bat. He was totally stunned."

It wasn't until 7:15 P.M. that Reidy issued an order for the march to resume; the movement itself did not begin until four hours later, as the snowfall began. To all intents and purposes, Major Gurfein had now assumed command of 2/31.

Richard Mitchell: "Gurfein instructed Reidy that the battalion would move out in a column of twos. The troops were instructed to build up their small warming fires just before pulling out, to make the Chinese think we were still on the hill."

After moving a short distance to the crest of the pass, the point team encountered a roadblock that, as soon as a single GI started to clear it, turned out to be booby-trapped. Light debris from the explosion blew back over the soldiers near the head of the column. Mitchell: "Some of the troops took cover or hit the ground and a few moved rearward. Gurfein and I stepped onto the road and held out our arms to stop them. There was no panic, no rout, just some troops ducking."

Gurfein tells it differently. "Within ten seconds a near rout had started, with the lead company turning to the rear and starting to overrun the battalion command group. Not a single NCO [noncommissioned officer] or junior officer raised his voice to stop it. The battalion commander, pushed aside by his own troops, stood there silently. I had to personally step in and stop the men and turn them around. Not a single shot had been fired by the Chinese."

The battalion finally began straggling into Koto-ri at around 2:30 A.M. When Reidy reported to Colonel Puller, he was informed that the battalion was now attached to the Marines and assigned a section of the Koto perimeter to defend.

In his bland, understated way, General Smith had this to say about the episode: "The performance of the battalion was not impressive."

That same day, November 30, Colonel Bankson Holcolm reported to Smith that his intelligence staff had now confirmed that six Chinese divisions were operating against the Marines. By this time no one but the Marines themselves believed they could make it all the way back to the ships, seventy-eight miles south of Yudam-ni. Newspapers in the States were predicting their doom. Government officials acknowledged that there was little hope for the Marines. The director of the Central Intelligence Agency, Walter Bedell Smith, was quoted as saying that only diplomacy could save MacArthur's right flank.

The 31st Rear Command Post at Hudong, where Drake's tanks were parked, was four miles south of Lt. Col. Faith's inlet position. If Faith could break contact with the Chinese and pull back, Hudong would be his first destination. While hardly the haven Hagaru was, it was more defensible by far than the position at the inlet.

At about 4 P.M. the senior officer at the schoolhouse, Lt. Col. Barry K. Anderson, responding to an order from Hagaru, passed the word that everyone in and around the command post was to pack up and prepare to withdraw. Anderson's assistant S-3, Captain George Rasula, recalls the frenetic and unseemly haste of the decampment, commenting that it was "more like headlong flight than withdrawal." The evacuation of Hudong was rapid and total; the rearward move included 324 men from the 31st headquarters staff and company, the Fifty-seventh Battery Company, and Captain Drake's tankers. By six in the evening the schoolhouse and environs were deserted.

There was one intriguing footnote. A survivor of the I & R patrol, ambushed moments before the general Chinese onfall of the twenty-seventh, now appeared out of the dusk and climbed over the tailgate of the last truck as it was starting to pull away. In the darkness a few hundred yards behind Sergeant James Arie came soldiers of the Chinese 80th Division, who soon occupied the schoolhouse and the fields around it—the very position Lt. Col. Faith was planning to fall back on. Though neither Faith nor any of his men knew it, what remained of the task force was now hopelessly cut off.

The question of who gave the order to withdraw from Hudong has been debated for years. Appleman concludes that it came down from General Barr, who had apparently written off Task Force Faith because "he could not see any good coming from losing more men in behalf of those already lost." Thus one U.S. Army unit abandoned another U.S. Army unit to its fate. Within the hour, Colonel Anderson's convoy was tucked safely—relatively speaking—inside the Hagaru perimeter. Drake's tanks were soon occupying strategic points along the northern arc, guns outboard.

48. THE SECOND MAJOR ATTACK

against Hagaru began with a noisy demonstration in front of Corley's How Company. For several minutes the Marines heard an exotic concert of cymbals, chanting, and horns; then a 76-mm gun opened up against the command post—a mud and straw shack—and was silenced by a direct hit from an 81-mm mortar round. The expected infantry assault did not materialize. In the adjoining sector Fisher's Item Company was solidly dug in behind concertina wire in sandbagged gun pits. At 8:15 P.M. a bugle blared in the frigid darkness, a green flare arched into the sky, and small groups of enemy soldiers began to probe the Marine lines, seeking the location of automatic weapons. As the official history trenchantly has it, "The enemy could scarcely have chosen a less rewarding area for such research." Once again, as on November 28, the enemy had chosen to launch his major assault against Marine strength.

It was twenty-five degrees below zero when, around midnight, the main assault began in concentrated ferocity. Warrant Officer Willard Downs: "They came in wave after wave, dying almost in windrows, and there was a continuous roar in our ears."

Rounds from Marine tanks set a couple of huts in front of the lines on fire; enemy soldiers veered off-course to congregate around them, forgetting combat, forgetting mortality, caring only to feel the heat from the fire. The clusters of Chinese infantrymen provided excellent targets for the dug-in Marines.

After the attack on the twenty-eighth, Corporal Alan Herrington had scrounged a couple of inoperative .50-caliber machine guns from the artillery as well as a truck to bring them and their ammo over to his position. He and his gun-section mates were able to assemble one functioning weapon out of the two, and they mounted it on the edge of the pit where one of his .30-caliber Brownings was already set up. Herrington: "During the second attack the Chinese seemed to have no fear of the thirties and just kept coming on. When they got too close we would switch to the fifty and really clean house." Though the idea was ridiculed later, many of the line Marines were convinced the Chinese soldiers were "doped up." General Smith: "A great many . . . carried benzedrine pills and opium."

The all-or-nothing assault continued until first light, and when the Chinese gave up and pulled back they left a new harvest of corpses as evidence that several waves had shattered themselves against a wall of fire. This time most of the bodies were dressed in nonquilted olive drab uniforms. Among them were several men in black, identified later as political commissars and security officers. According to the official history, the Chinese left between 500 and 750 fresh dead on the field of battle that night. The cost to Fisher's company was two dead and ten wounded.

The situation on East Hill was still unsettled. PFC Francis McNeive, George/1: "The snow turned to ice as we ascended the slope. Guys would lose their footing and go sliding back down the path. Halfway up we found that some unit that had gone before us had tied long ropes to tree stumps and bushes and by hanging on to these we were able to make it to the top—where we immediately came under fire. PFC Tommy Wilcox was the first of our company to die on East Hill. I didn't see it, but I heard it: the crack of a rifle as he disappeared over the crest, then a sort of gurgle coming out of his body. The Chinese had us pinned down pretty good and we just wiggled around the rest of the day, each of us trying to find a deeper depression in the ground."

After dark the Marines of George Company were able to slip backward into slightly better positions; but later that night the Chinese began to lob grenades down on them and then, surging over the crest, forced them even farther down the slope.

PFC Robert Greene: "Following Marine Corps tradition I brought one of the Marine dead down the hill with me, dragging him by the ankle the way a child pulls a Flexible Flyer through the snow. His head kept bobbing up and down as if acknowledging and approving what I was doing for him. When we reached the bottom, someone came forward and took him off my hands—a Graves Registration guy. Then I just stood there and thanked God I was still going."

Two Marine engineers, manning a listening post on another part of the hill, reported seeing a mass of Chinese materialize in the dark, heading their way. The password and countersign that night were *Abraham* and *Lincoln;* but the two Marines, already bounding down the slope like mountain goats, did not wait for the customary exchange. Instead they yelled the sixteenth president's full name over and over, causing laughter down below despite the menace at their heels.

PFC Francis McNeive: "Each platoon has a weak link, even in the Marines, and ours was a PFC whose name I won't mention. This guy had been in the Army—which meant he was already a suspicious character. He was about thirty, pudgy, balding, lazy, a con man, a cheat, an all-around rotten person. When those grenades started coming down, he just turned and slid headfirst like a toboggan all the way down the slope. And he never came back. Later on someone spotted him skulking in one of the ruined buildings on Hagaru's main drag. We just let him be; we certainly didn't want the son of a bitch back in our ranks."

Around midnight the Marines heard the unmistakable sound of horses on the other side of the hill. The general reaction was an anxious mixture of bravado and humor, with jokes about Cossacks and Communists; but then a green flare arced up from behind the ridgeline and the wisecracks ceased abruptly. There were bugles and a strange sound like a hundred gongs ringing in different keys. The Marines strained their eyes to detect the first movement on the crest. Then the red flare popped overhead and the action started. The skyline was crawling with movement. You could see them crossing the full width of the saddle like a great shadow moving across the snow. PFC Janek Gruening, George/1: "It was a hell of a sight—like butterscotch syrup sliding down vanilla ice cream. We watched without firing, as our mortars and artillery punched big holes in the mass; but each hole would fill up quickly."

The survivors of George Company, 41 Commando, and the Marine engineer groups had set up a new line of defense at the bottom of the hill. Service troops, deploying along the railroad tracks, provided backup. The scene was bright as day after a mortar shell set fire to a seventy-drum stack of high-octane fuel. Lt. Col. Charles Banks, commanding that segment of the perimeter, brought small arms, tanks, and artillery fire to bear against the lines of enemy soldiers descending the slope, few of whom survived.

Warrant Officer Lionel S. Reynolds: "At times there was nothing but arms, legs, and assholes flying in all directions. I couldn't believe the slaughter I was seeing."

General Smith watched the nightmare scene from the doorway of his bungalow across the river, puffing placidly on his pipe. Smith: "Colonel Banks dropped by at one point to see me. He was full of beans. He said, 'If you give me a battalion, I'll drive the Chinese off the entire ridge.' We of course had no battalion to give him."

Francis McNeive: "In the morning, 41 Commando climbed up to our ledge, and together we made a counterattack that pushed the Chinese back over the crest. It was typical of the Marines that we paid no attention at all to the Chinese corpses strewn about; and it was typical of the commandos that they didn't allow such a situation to continue. They were tidy, industrious chaps, and they didn't approve of the way we left all those corpses sprawled everywhere. They proceeded to stack them on the top of the hill, and they ended up with a very large and squared-away pile. It was so prominent that everyone used it as a landmark or orientation point. Guys would huddle against it, using it as a windbreak. You'd see these dead faces looking over someone's shoulder. When some kind soul sent a warming tent up to us, we rigged it like a big lean-to against the stack, on the leeward side. That stack, it must have been a good seven feet off the deck, made up of sixty or seventy dead gooks to start with; and it kept growing, because every time there was a Chinese attack the bodies would be dragged over afterward and added to the stack."

By 9 A.M. a weak sun had burned away the morning mist, Marine air was on station, and the only Chinese to be seen on East Hill or in front of Fisher's and Corley's companies were dead ones. In his estimate of the night's carnage, General Smith put the official figure at 930. Probably twice that number were wounded, and most of them died soon enough. Marine intelligence established that the attackers on the night of November 30–December 1 had belonged to the 58th and 59th Divisions.

A little later Lt. Col. Thomas Ridge stopped by the division command post. Smith later recalled that the Hagaru defense commander was "pretty slow from the strain and loss of sleep, and concerned over the possibility of another attack and his ability to meet it. He couldn't see how he was going to hold both the air strip and East Hill. All I could tell him was that they had to be held with what we had until the 5th and 7th Marines fought their way south to join us."

By now Smith had another major problem to deal with. He received a report that the Chinese had destroyed the bridge at the penstock station in Funchilin Pass. The 1st Marine Division was now truly trapped, as Stateside newspapers had been saying all along.

A bright moon stood over Toktong-san until close to midnight; then a blanket of cloud was drawn across the sky, bringing with it flurries of snow. PFCs Donald Childs and Norman Jackson were standing watch in a foxhole overlooking a section of the road; the stretch immediately below them was hidden from view by a hump in the terrain. The two Marines were stunned to hear an amplified voice suddenly boom out from the blind spot: "Men of Fox Company, this is First Lieutenant Robert C. Messman of King Battery, 11th Marines. . . . I was captured two days ago by Chinese Communist Forces. Men of Fox Company, if you surrender now, the Chinese will treat you according to the Geneva Agreement. They will feed you. They will provide you with warm clothing. They will treat your wounds."

Childs and Jackson held perfectly still, lest they reveal how close they were to the speaker and the escort that was doubtless guarding him.

PFC Peter Holgrun: "This Messman sounded like he was reading some crap from a propaganda script. A Marine behind us yelled out, 'Send up a flare so we can see the bastard.' When it popped overhead, we got a look at the road. There was a small spring down there. Even though the temperature was below zero, the spring was still trickling across the road. That was our water supply. Anyway, there was nobody there! One of the machine gunners got off a short burst just to say 'Fuck you.' "

The Chinese hit Fox Company at half past two in the morning, crossing the road again with burp guns and satchel charges. PFC O'Leary, well supplied at last with illumination rounds, turned night into day and used high-explosive rounds to chop the attackers to pieces, joining the distant How Battery and Fox Company riflemen in the slaughter. Lt. McCarthy later wrote that he believed three Chinese companies took part in the assault. He heard one of his men joke that his rifle had gotten so warm he didn't even need his gloves.

When dawn broke, the Marines were still holding on.

49.
SERGEANT GUILLERMO TOVAR, Major McLaughlin, and the other prisoners of war, herded into the hills east of Hell Fire Valley, found themselves in a farmhouse a mile off the road. Tovar recalls it as a one-story affair with four rooms and a porch. The officers and enlisted men were separated there, and Tovar never saw Major McLaughlin again. Warrant Officer Lloyd Dirst, mortally wounded, remained in one of the rooms with Tovar and the others.

Tovar: "Gunner Dirst was unable to speak because of the head wound. I helped feed him and pushed a little snow into his mouth from time to time."

A tall Chinese captain appeared in the doorway and spoke to the prisoners in English. Tovar asked him what his name was.

"You may call me Francis."

"Can you get us some medical help, Francis?"

The officer explained that his convoy had been attacked by American planes; rice and medical supplies had been destroyed.

"Will you allow me to go back to the road to collect some first-aid packets from the dead?"

"Perhaps."

Tovar: "*Perhaps* was his response to many of our questions. He told us that the able-bodied wounded were going to have to walk to Manchuria. Though I had been shot in the head—at the base of the skull, actually—I got in line the following morning; but my Korean friend, Junior—we had been together since the Inchon landing in September—said, 'If you go north you'll never come back.' The interpreter advised Tovar to pretend he was incapacitated by his wound. Tovar heeded the advice and went staggering back to the farmhouse where he remained sprawled on the floor until the Chinese had taken the group away, Junior too.

From time to time Francis would come in for a chat with those who remained behind. He said he hoped to visit San Francisco some day. "Take us back to our lines," said Tovar, "and I'll show you around personally. I live near San Francisco."

Francis smiled. "Perhaps," he said.

Tovar: "The GIs in the farmhouse weren't the kind of men I'd ever want in my outfit. There were seven of them, and they were undisciplined and whiny, always fighting and arguing among themselves. On one occasion they started throwing potatoes around the room, acting like little boys who needed their nap. These representatives of the U.S. Army really embarrassed me with their behavior. One of them kept wailing and telling me his feet should be amputated. I wasn't the senior noncom present, but no one else was taking a leadership role. I was very conscious of being a Marine among doggies. I finally told them that I might have a hole in my head but my arms and legs were fine and if they didn't settle down I was going to drag their miserable asses outside and leave them there in a snowbank."

In the morning the Chinese were gone. Tovar and two others decided to try and reach Koto-ri. As they walked outside and moved away from the farmhouse, they expected someone to appear to stop them, but no one did. When they reached the bottom of the hill, an observation plane appeared low in the sky and they waved at it. They then proceeded along the left side of the road, heading south. Up ahead was a thatch hut; a Chinese soldier came out of the door and proceeded to urinate in the snow. He stared at them and they stared back. None of them were armed.

Tovar: "What we had experienced so far, I think of it as the entry to hell; but what we were *about* to experience was hell itself. While we were still in sight of the hut, a flight of Corsairs came overhead with a terrific roar and wheeled around as if to launch a strike at us, obviously mistaking us for Chinese. We ripped off our parkas and flapped them like crazy, but the planes launched rockets at us and one of them let loose an object like a big football, which fell end over end and gushed into billows of flame as it hit the ground. And I thought: 'I've come this far to get fried by napalm dropped by a fellow Marine?'

"We felt the heat, but it wasn't close enough to burn us, thank God. I was the only one who felt the effect of the rockets: a piece of metal struck between my shoulder blades, but all the layers of clothing stopped it. The Corsairs wheeled around again, and this time they fired fifty-caliber rounds at us. There was nowhere to hide. Shell casings tinkled and clinked all around us. It was obvious the Corsairs had been called in by the observation plane we waved at. They didn't hurt us physically, but speaking for myself, I was psychologically squashed. After they departed, my mind began playing tricks and I saw armed Chinese in every fold in the ground. By now we were moving along the bank of the frozen river, and when we went around a bend, there was the village of Koto-ri about a mile away."

A jeep appeared, barreling down the road toward them, with a plume of snow behind it. The driver took them straight to the aid station. Tovar's overriding desire was to get word to the Air Wing not to shell that farmhouse that was occupied by American prisoners of war. Several days later he was operated on and the .45-caliber slug was removed from the base of his skull.

By dawn, December 1, the problem of casualty pileup had become acute. The Division surgeon, Navy Captain Eugene R. Hering, paid an urgent call on General Smith at this time. Hering reminded the general that there were 600 wounded men at Hagaru who needed more sophisticated medical treatment than he could provide; that the Marines at Yudam-ni, assuming they could fight their way south, would bring at least 500 casualties with them; and that the Army troops on the east shore of the reservoir, assuming *they* could reach Hagaru, would also have about five hundred. Hering's estimates would prove conservative, but they were alarmingly high at the time, and it was obvious that Smith had to take action. "Casualties are going to keep piling up," Hering continued, "and before long we're not going to be able to handle them."

The only possible solution—a long shot—was to try and open the airstrip, even though it was less than half finished. Smith decided to request a test run. Within the hour, in one of the campaign's most suspenseful moments, all hands at Hagaru watched as a C-47 appeared over the southern skyline, descended slowly, touched down safely on the washboard strip, and shuddered to an engines-reversed stop. The time was 2:50 P.M. Half an hour later, with twenty-four casualties aboard, the plane was gathering speed on the rough ground, and it seemed for a moment as though the runway wasn't going to be long enough; but at the last moment the tail lifted, the wings took hold, and the plane cleared the hills.

Everyone recognized it as a turning point in the campaign, and troops on the ground broke into shrill cheers.

Four transports landed at Hagaru that afternoon, three of them returning to the air with a load of wounded. The fourth, hauling ammunition for Ridge's troops, collapsed its landing gear as it set down on the bumpy strip; the plane was quickly unloaded and pushed off the runway. By now the sky was darkening and airlift operations had to be suspended for the night.

Lt. Col. John Partridge's engineers had done a great thing, hacking an airfield out of the frozen earth. Veterans of the action at Hagaru would carry with them forever the sound and image of the five bulldozers at work by floodlight, their operators serving as riflemen when the occasion demanded it.

Hagaru was now tenuously linked to the outside world by air. One of General Smith's first decisions after the airstrip opened was to ask that replacements be flown into Hagaru. In rear areas such as Hamhung-Hungnam and Wonsan, hundreds of combat-trained headquarters and service Marines were available, and though the road up the mountain was closed by enemy roadblocks, the airstrip at Hagaru was now an open door. When the call went out, Marines down in the coastal plain began to line up immediately, eager to help their brothers in the mountains. Before long some 500 of them, many still recuperating from wounds received in battles from Obong-ni Ridge to Sudong Gorge, had provided a little more muscle to the ravaged infantry companies of the 1st Marine Division.

50.

AT THE PUNGNYURI INLET, AF-
ter dark on November 30, word was passed from hole to hole that
if the troops could hold out for one more night, everything would
be all right.

PFC Donald W. Chandler, E Company, 31st Infantry: "To those
who died so that we might live, I salute you. And a special blessing
to Sergeant Leonard Wilkens, who held us eighteen-to-twenty-year-
olds together with simple words that meant so much: 'Cheer up,
men. It's going to be better tomorrow.' Soon after that he was
killed by mortar fire."

After midnight, December 1, the Chinese launched an attack that
penetrated the east side of the sector, defended by the Third Battalion, 31st Infantry. It was by no means certain that the rest of
the GIs could hold out until dawn. The penetration gave the Chinese control of a knob overlooking the rest of the perimeter; it was
situated close to a concrete bridge that crossed the ice of the inlet
itself. Lt. Col. Don Carlos Faith, recognizing that the enemy had
to be driven off this commanding position, called on D Company
for the job. 1st Lt. Robert D. Wilson volunteered to lead the mission.

"Come on, all you fighting men," he called out. "We've got a
counterattack to make." Wilson was able to round up twenty soldiers, a pitifully small force for such a task. With only three grenades and a few rounds for their rifles, they shoved off at daybreak
in skirmish formation. As Wilson started upslope in front of his
two squads, he was struck in the arm by a bullet and knocked
down. He rose and continued climbing. A second bullet hit him in
the chest, but he did not stop. "That one bit," he was heard to
say. A third bullet hit him in the head and killed him. Sergeant
Fred Sugua assumed command, leading the ragged remnant a few
yards further until he too was shot to death.

*   *   *

Major Wesley J. Curtis, Faith's operations officer, later recalled the macabre scene that terrible dawn. "The dead, concentrated in central collecting points, had to be used as a source for all supplies, including clothing, weapons, and ammunition. Everyone seemed to be wounded in one fashion or another. Frozen feet and hands were common. The wounded who were unable to move froze to death." Medical supplies were now exhausted. There was no morphine left, and no more bandages.

A lone Corsair appeared over the inlet around 9 A.M. Establishing contact with Captain Edward Stamford, the pilot reported that, weather permitting, a flight of four would return to the position around noon. At that moment the sky was solidly overcast, but the prediction was for broken clouds and intermittent sunshine in three hours or so.

Faith had been discussing options with Major Curtis and his executive officer, Major Crosby Miller. Both majors believed that the inlet position would probably be overrun that night. Finally agreeing with them, Faith called in the rest of his officers and told them that on his own initiative he had decided to try and reach the Marine perimeter at Hagaru. "We have no communication with division," he said. "We'll be on our own except for Marine air support, which may show up around noon if the weather clears. My battalion will lead the way out."

Chinese soldiers, standing boldly in the open now, watched the exhausted, demoralized American soldiers prepare for the move south. Sergeant Chester Bair: "They loaded my truck with dead bodies, stacking them crossways, four high, and we had to break a few arms and legs to make them fit. Later on, so many wounded men showed up that we had to throw the corpses off to make room. We just let them lay where they fell."

Each vehicle carried from fifteen to twenty wounded men. There were about thirty trucks in all. As the vehicle column began to form up on the road, the Chinese came down off the slopes and took up positions along the breakout route. PFC James Ransone: "The day was dark and dreary. Able Company was supposed to take the lead, and we were busy lining up all the trucks. Here comes Colonel Faith in his shiny helmet and new parka and riding pants. He had a grenade attached to each side of his backpack harness and was holding a .45 in his hand.

Really, I thought he looked too sharp, too West Point, compared to the rest of us."

One of the staff officers suggested to Faith that instead of trying to go overland he might try taking the trucks across the ice of the reservoir. It was a sensible suggestion, but Faith feared that the heavily laden vehicles would break through.

Nearly 3,000 American soldiers, 600 of them wounded, and one Marine officer with his small enlisted crew waited tensely for the arrival of the Corsairs. During the interval a Chinese mortar barrage wounded several more GIs. The newly wounded men were somehow crammed aboard the overcrowded trucks.

At about one o'clock the gull-winged aircraft appeared in the southern sky and began to circle above, awaiting instructions from "Boyhood 14" on the ground. Captain Stamford was sitting in his radio jeep, idling just to the rear of Able Company.

"Are we ready to go?" called Colonel Faith. He then gave the order to move out. The trucks began to roll—and immediately encountered enemy fire. Chinese riflemen were shockingly close.

The air support began with a terrible miscalculation by the lead pilot, who let loose a napalm canister a millisecond too early. It landed in front of the point of the column, striking the ground in a billowing gush of flame that engulfed a dozen GIs. Lt. George E. Foster, his clothes vaporized, his skin blackened, remained on his feet, naked. He asked someone for a cigarette, then walked away, never to be seen again.

Stamford: "The main part of the napalm splashed onto the Chinese—they were that close. It was only the tail end that caught our people. I saw many Chinese rise up out of their holes and die."

Several of the American victims were members of PFC Ransone's squad. "I felt the heat but it didn't burn me. Men I knew well were rolling around in the snow, looking the way they usually looked even though they were dying, while others were burned to a crisp, their skin peeling back like big potato chips. Still others just blazed away like torches. There I was, practically in the middle of them, and I couldn't do anything to help. Somebody hollered, 'Keep going, the medics will take care of them.' But there wasn't anything the medics could do. The worst thing was when a couple of them begged me to shoot them. . . . Maybe shooting them would have been the best thing to do."

Major Curtis recalls that the troops then "flooded down the road

like a great mob, and tactical control broke down immediately."
Faith rushed forward with his .45 thrust toward them and got a
few of them to halt and face the enemy. The napalm incident was
a crushing blow to morale. Until then the platoons and companies
had maintained a semblance of their organizational structure; but
now, because of panicky intermingling, the units disintegrated into
leaderless clusters of what the Marines would scornfully call "individuals."

Stamford: "As soon as the column started moving again, Colonel
Faith grabbed me by the arm and ordered me into the ditch beside
the road. 'I don't want you killed,' he said. The trouble was, the
ditch had brush in it; and that, along with the slippery ground,
made it hard to negotiate. I came to a log ramp and saw the lower
legs and feet of a Chinese soldier and a gun barrel starting to swing
in my direction. I climbed the ramp and waved to my radio man,
PFC Myron J. Smith, pointing between my feet at the barrel, and
Smith fired a burst from the burp gun he had captured, and that
was the end of *that* Chinese. We then proceeded around a curve,
with the ice of the reservoir on our right, then climbed back to the
road. When Colonel Faith saw me, he again ordered me into the
ditch. I told him I couldn't keep up with the column that way, and
he said all right."

The column moved on in fits and starts, the Corsairs swooping
down from time to time to drive the Chinese away from the road.
General Smith was generous with close air support for Task Force
Faith; that day, approximately half the planes assigned to provide
support were involved with the protection of the motor column
east of the reservoir. If the column was going to make it all the
way to Hagaru, however, it would have to keep moving briskly to
reach the Marine perimeter before the planes returned to base at
dusk.

Wounded men in the trucks were now being wounded a second
time, a third time, or killed outright, and truck drivers were being
hit. For a while it seemed the Chinese were concentrating on the
drivers. Finding replacements was difficult; agreeing to get behind
the wheel was like agreeing to commit suicide. Crowds of Chinese
were plainly visible now on the east side of the road, yet few of
the GIs even bothered to raise their rifles, let alone fire them; that
would be too provocative, too dangerous. There was hardly any
fight left in Task Force Faith.

One of the Corsair pilots, Lt. Thomas E. Mulvihill, recalls that the Chinese on the ground reminded him of "picnic ants going across a big frosted cake. There were so many targets to shoot at you didn't know where to start." (At one point Mulvihill saw large animals below and, to his astonishment, recognized them as camels. Mulvihill says he was reluctant to report the sighting because "I figured they'd cart me off." Later, at a routine debriefing at Yonpo airfield, he hesitantly asked a fellow pilot if he had seen any strange animals up on the plateau. Lt. Turk Swinford responded, "Well, I wasn't going to say anything, but now that you mention it—yes, I saw camels.")

The column continued to lurch forward, while more and more GIs were struck by bullets. A massacre was in progress.

Sergeant Richard Luna of B Company was helping load newly wounded soldiers aboard the trucks. "It was impossible to get them all on. I don't recall now how many were left behind."

The rear guard, under Captain Robert J. Kitz, had deserted the task force, fleeing from enemy fire onto the ice of the reservoir, leaving the trucks entirely unprotected. Lt. Thomas J. Patton, A Battery, Fifty-seventh Field Artillery, was with one of the first groups to move out onto the ice. "We were about five hundred yards out when the Chinese began coming after us. But they didn't fire their weapons. . . . I saw a C-47 circling in the distance, approaching closer to us with each pass. I stopped and stamped in the snow the words WHICH WAY. Eventually the pilot saw it and flew down to Hagaru and began circling above it. Then he came back and dropped a canteen containing a note: 'Keep to center of reservoir. UN troops holding Hagaru. Good luck fellows.' "

Near the head of the column, Stamford was doggedly running air strikes; but there were too many Chinese now, pressing ever closer to the trucks. At around three in the afternoon the head of the column reached a bridge spanning a marshy stretch of ground; the bridge had been blown out by a Chinese demolition team. Trying to force a bypass, the first truck's wheels broke through the marsh ice and bogged down. Lt. Hugh May, the Headquarters Company motor officer, led a successful effort to get most of the trucks through by means of a winching operation, using up two precious hours of daylight. The ground was rough, studded with hummocks of swamp grass, and the trucks bounced heavily in their passage. Captain Richard Swenty: "As the trucks were running the bypass, you could hear the screams of wounded men in back. Many had broken bones, and I'm sure several died from the shock of crossing that frozen swamp."

Sergeant Chester Bair: "Toward dusk I looked toward the end of the column and saw Chinese closing in on the rear, and there were already some GIs walking up to them with their hands above their heads."

PFC James Ransone: "All discipline and control was gone, and everyone just took off on his own. There wasn't nobody to follow. My reaction at the time was to save myself." Ransone ran into a field between the road and the ice, seeking refuge behind a large corn-stalk, only to find a cluster of soldiers already there. Moving on, he became the target of intense enemy fire. One round went through his canteen, another struck his ammunition belt, another pierced his parka, a fourth cut off his bayonet scabbard, and a fifth went through his left arm. Returning to the road, he spotted his company commander and asked him to take a look at the wound; but the captain ignored him, acting as though the distraught private wasn't there at all. Another officer, an artillery observer, looked at the wound and said, "It's not bad. It's stopped bleeding. You'll be all right."

Ransone wandered off, heading across another field, and almost ran into a Chinese machine-gun crew trying to unjam their weapon. "They couldn't have been more than twenty yards away. When they noticed me they grabbed their rifles and I just turned and ran, zigzagging, until I came to a bank that dropped to the ice, and I went sliding down it. Out on the ice I kept slipping and couldn't make much progress until I took off my boots and then, in my stocking feet, I got away from the shore. The Chinese stood there watching me go but they didn't fire. I just kept going across the ice until I got exhausted and fell down and passed out."

The situation was rendered even more dreadful by the wounded crying out for help as bullets continued to slam into the trucks. Dozens of GIs huddled abjectly beside the vehicles in the lee of wind and bullet, ignoring the commands of the handful of officers and NCOs still active. Lt. Col. Faith had worked himself into a frenzy trying to induce his troops to fight. As dusk came on, Stamford, Captain Erwin Bigger, and several others saw Faith striding along beside the trucks, shouting at the huddled, beaten soldiers, brandishing his .45 threateningly at them. They watched as he paused beside one truck where two Korean soldiers were evidently trying to tie themselves to the undercarriage, the idea being—so it was later speculated—that they hoped somehow to ride the vehicle to safety, like Odysseus escaping from Polyphemus. With gestures and angry barks Faith ordered them to drop what they were doing and come out into the open. One of the men was heard to respond in Japanese: "I'm hurt." He said it over and over. Stamford and the others watched, agog, as Faith extended his right arm toward the cowering man and pulled the trigger, then shifted his aim and shot the other one as well.

"Shoot anyone who tries to run away," Faith shouted into the wind.

It was a sad and outrageous moment. Faith did not shoot any of the American soldiers who were equally demoralized—and who had received far better training than the hapless ROKs. Only by a stretch of the imagination could these two victims be characterized as military men.

Major Crosby Miller had been wounded in the left leg and left hand; a bullet had clipped off three fingers, taking away his Virginia Military Institute class ring and his wedding band. "I removed the glove from my right hand," Miller recalls, "and pulled it down over the wounded hand to stop the bleeding. The soaked glove soon froze and effectively closed off the flow. . . . I lay in the ditch taking stock of a very sorry situation."

Captain Stamford came along and loaded Miller across the hood of the radio jeep. At this time Miller informed the Marine officer that two members of his tactical control party were dead. (Corporal Myron J. Smith and PFC Billy E. Johnson were the two who had volunteered to find the Air Force air controller's radio, brought it back, and successfully cannibalized its parts.) Stamford had seen Myron Smith only a short while before, after the corporal was wounded; he had taken the radio from him, put it on his own back, then lifted the young man into another jeep. Sometime within the next hour, Smith's friend PFC Billy Johnson had climbed into the jeep to keep him company; both faithful Marines were killed a little while later when the Chinese pressed close to the column. Major Miller told Stamford that he had seen their side-by-side corpses in the jeep.

It was dark by the time the last truck was winched over the

frozen marsh. Marine pilots Thomas Mulvihill and Edward Montague recall Stamford's high-pitched voice in the deepening gloom: "It's all over."

Stamford's contribution had been invaluable. Without the Marine captain and his team, Faith's tattered mob would probably not have lasted beyond the second day. Air strikes aside, his leadership on the ground was a major factor in the survival of those who came through the ordeal east of the reservoir. One who observed this closely was Dr. Vincent J. Navarre, the surgeon attached to Faith's battalion. Navarre later wrote a letter to the commander of the 1st Marine Air Wing, Major General Field Harris, conveying his appreciation. "It is difficult to express the value of this man's leadership in that dark hour when leadership was needed so badly. Only those who were there can understand its worth."

The head of the column now came to an abrupt halt four and a half miles north of Hagaru, as the drivers of the first two trucks were shot to death. All momentum had finally dissipated and, in the purple shadows of dusk, everything was breaking apart. The Chinese, aware that there would be no more air support, came down from the barren hills and began raking the trucks and the GIs inside them with direct, up-close burp gun fire. Uninterested in taking prisoners, the Chinese were killing the Americans as a tactical measure—eliminating potential trouble behind their lines. As this began to happen, many GIs down the line turned toward the reservoir and made their way to the ice as fast as they could. A full moon hung over the painful scene, and the Chinese had no trouble finding targets.

Lt. Col. Faith was struck in the chest and went down hard.

Major Robert Jones, battalion adjutant: "When Faith was hit, the task force ceased to exist."

A mortar officer, Lt. Fields E. Shelton, tried to assist Faith in reaching his jeep but was too weak from his own wounds to do so. He put the mortally injured officer down on the road and staggered off to find help. After he had disappeared in the dark, a group of enlisted men that included Private Louis J. Grappo came trudging down the road and heard the fallen officer calling for help in a weak voice. They lifted him into the cab of the truck at the head of the line, next to the dead driver.

Captain Stamford was rounding up GIs, almost all of them wounded, to help him push the stalled and inoperative trucks off the roadway so that the vehicles behind them could get rolling. It was heavy work, and many of the soldiers reopened their wounds in the exertion. Taking a break, the Marine captain sought shelter in a hut crammed with GIs. One of them, he noticed, was a lieutenant colonel from the artillery battalion. Other officers were present as well, none exercising command authority. Stamford finally became impatient with them. "I walked out of the shack and up to Colonel Faith in the lead truck and asked him if he wanted me to try and continue on to Hagaru that night. He gave me a very weak 'Yes.' He could barely talk and seemed to be in extreme pain and on the verge of losing consciousness."

Through the sheer force of his bullying, Stamford managed to get several trucks moved a bit farther down the road; but they came to a permanent halt at a hairpin turn not far from the abandoned sawmill. In the rear of the column the Chinese were methodically slaughtering the wounded men inside the trucks. At the head of the column there was an incongruous air of calm under the lofty moon.

Major Wesley J. Curtis, First Battalion operations officer, using a tree limb for a crutch, limped up to the lead truck and spoke with Faith.

"How are you doing, Colonel?"

Faith's response: "Let's get going."

Moving on down the road, Curtis came upon Major Crosby Miller stretched across the hood of the radio jeep.

"You're going to have to walk."

Miller shook his head. "I'm hurting too bad."

Curtis limped slowly down the road. Looking back, he saw the smoke of white-phosphorous grenades toward the rear of the column.

It was about ten o'clock when PFC Glenn J. Finfrock, a wounded machine gunner, woke up on the road after having passed out from lack of blood. Rising slowly to his feet, he joined several wounded men trying to build a fire beside the lead truck. Faith's frozen body, says Finfrock, was slumped in the passenger seat of the truck.

In later years Wesley Curtis, then a retired colonel, wrote down the following answers to a set of questions he had often asked himself since the campaign:

"You were aware that Faith and Miller were seriously wounded. Were you not then, by law, custom, and tradition, in command?"

"Yes."

"Were you aware of it at the time?"

"Yes."

"Was it right, then, for you to cut out—to abandon the command?"

"No."

"What should you have done?"

"I should have remained with the truck column—regardless of consequences."

"Has this bothered your conscience?"

"Yes, for the past thirty-five years."

"If you had to do it over again, would you do the same thing?"

"Probably, yes."

Curtis then refers to the "Victorian concept" that a soldier's duty is to do or die and says it will not stand up under scrutiny. "A soldier's role is to fight—and live to fight another day—under conditions that favor success."

He describes the scene at the end. "There was no resistance left in the column . . . motors in the trucks were not running—drivers were not in the cabs of the trucks. The only sound was the moaning of the wounded and dying. I claim that neither a Patton in a Tiger tank nor a MacArthur on a white horse could have reversed the situation."

Curtis kept going, having decided to try for Hagaru by crossing the ice. Out in the middle of the huge manmade lake he became momentarily disoriented, but, using the Big Dipper and the North Star as guides, he regained his bearings. Before dawn he reached Marine lines at the point where Captain Benjamin Read's How Battery was sited.

Not far south of the Hudong schoolhouse, Stamford was suddenly surrounded by Chinese soldiers. He remained a prisoner for only a few minutes, however, dashing away when his guard was momentarily distracted. Stamford crossed the railroad tracks and walked to the sawmill, from which point the lights of Hagaru, two miles to the south, became visible. ("It looked like New York City to me.") Like Major Curtis before him, Stamford reached Marine lines at How Battery's position. He had come through the ordeal with nothing worse than a twisted ankle.

Back on the road to Hudong, Sergeant Chester Bair watched the Chinese approaching and decided that he did not want to be taken prisoner. "There were craters on the road from mortar round explosions, and I chose one that was crowded with dismembered and shattered GIs. I got down and burrowed in under them, covering myself as best I could, trying to appear as dead as I could."

Later, after the Chinese had left, he climbed out of the grisly tangle and made his way across the ice to Hagaru. He tried to explain to the Marine officer who met him what had befallen Task Force Faith and was stunned to learn that the Marines were now trying to get out of a trap themselves. Bair: "You could see that everyone was packing up, tearing down tents, getting ready to move out."

PFC Myron B. Holstein, Heavy Mortars, 31st Infantry, was one of the last GIs to cross the ice. "We could see the glow of the fires in the sky behind us. The Chinese had set fire to all the trucks and jeeps on the east shore of the reservoir."

51. EIGHT MILES WESTWARD ACROSS

the ice, the two Marine regiments at Yudam-ni were getting ready to break out of the trap. Litzenberg and Murray knew that Ridge's meager force had beaten off the enemy at Hagaru; but, as Murray put it, "Hagaru was fourteen miles down the road, and there was a hell of a lot of Chinese between us and them."

There had been plenty of action at Yudam-ni, but nothing as hot as the first night of the onfall. Many of the Marines now feared the enemy was merely holding back to await reinforcements. The 5th and 7th regiments had done well defending their perimeter; the question now was, how well would they operate on the offensive, weakened as they were?

The medical situation at Yudam-ni was even more critical than at Hagaru; there were so many wounded Marines that some had to be laid out on straw, underneath tarpaulin but otherwise exposed to the elements. Among the 500 wounded Marines at Yudam-ni was Lt. John Yancey, who had lain uncomplaining in a cheerless tent for two days. Yancey: "Every so often a corpsman would come over, reach into my mouth, and dig out a mass of coagulated blood. My lowest moment was when there was an enemy attack nearby: The corpsman had taken away my carbine and I felt naked. Most of the time I just lay there worrying about my platoon, pining away because I wasn't up there on the hill with them." What he didn't know was that Easy Company no longer existed as such: its remnants had been filtered into the ranks of Dog Company. (Korea was Yancey's last war, though he later volunteered for duty in Vietnam. The staffer who passed along the Defense Department's rejection cited among other reasons Yancey's lack of upper front teeth. "Colonel," Yancey is said to have replied, "I wasn't planning on *biting* the bastards.")

Litzenberg and Murray were now grappling with the problem of how to turn their regiments around—not an easy maneuver with the enemy pressing in on all sides. General Smith had told them what to do but not how to do it. Litzenberg: "Our situation at Yudam-ni was not a pleasant one. We were in a valley with five Chinese divisions around us. There were eight thousand of us and perhaps fifty thousand Chinese, with a sixth division in the offing— we were not sure of its location. We knew that the Chinese had the only road well blocked. We felt that simply to try and bull our way down this road, with the enemy staying ahead of us on both flanks and strong forces pressing on our rear, would keep us pretty well boxed in. We had to find a way to take them by surprise and throw them off balance."

Some time during the afternoon of November 30, Litzenberg conceived the notion of sending one of his infantry battalions across country to relieve Fox Company at Toktong Pass and, he hoped, at the same time disrupt enemy plans for the capture of Yudam-ni. The road from Yudam-ni to the pass described a bow-like curve; Litzenberg was wondering if he couldn't send Raymond Davis's battalion straight across the chord of the arc—along the bowstring, as it were. Such a cross-country trek, if Litzenberg decided to order it, would constitute the Marines' first major offensive move since the Chinese onfall.

While Litzenberg thought it over, the combined staffs spent the day working out a plan for turning the regiments around and placing the strongest battalion from each in a position from which to effect the breakthrough on the road. The plan was essentially as follows: Harris's 3/7 would seize blocking positions on the commanding ground south of the village while Davis made the overland trek to the pass. Stevens's 1/5 would hold a blocking position just south of the western tip of the reservoir while Roise's 2/5 defended ridges south and west of Yudam-ni, poised to serve as rear guard when the moment arrived. Taplett would then proceed down the road through Harris's positions, leading the main breakout. Ideally, Davis would reach the summit of the pass at Fox Company's position at about the same time Taplett reached it by road, with the other battalions strung out behind him. Once the breakout had been achieved, it was vital that momentum be maintained, otherwise the enemy could reencircle the breakthrough force. The battalions behind Davis and Taplett were therefore to be prepared to relieve them when it became necessary, to keep the tactical ball rolling.

Many matters needed tending to before the plan could be put into effect. Provisional infantry platoons had to be formed, mostly by cannibalizing the 155-mm artillery battalion. (The big howitzers had proven almost useless at Yudam-ni, with the enemy pressing so closely, because of their long range.)

Litzenberg's command post—a small tent—was now located at the southern edge of the village. Major Francis Parry, commanding one of the 105-mm artillery battalions, happened to stop by as Litzenberg was informing Davis of his new assignment. The regimental commander was sitting on his cot, Parry recalls, the battalion commander on the ground, holding a map. Parry started to back out but Litzenberg invited him to come in and sit beside Davis. Parry thus witnessed a scene that looms large in Marine Corps history: the moment when Colonel Homer Litzenberg directed Lt. Col. Raymond Davis to strike off with his entire battalion across the mountaintops, plunging into a trackless no-man's-land in the dark to attack the rear of the Chinese regiment surrounding Barber's company.

"The enemy assumes we're road-bound," Litzenberg was saying, "with our trucks and artillery and engineering equipment. We have a good chance of catching him by surprise with an overland move. I want you to work up a plan and bring it back as soon as you can. We've got to get going on this."

Parry: "I was impressed with the matter-of-factness of the briefing, even though Litzenberg was taking a terrific gamble. He was sending Davis off into the frigid gloom away from the main body, thus splitting the undermanned, tired-out force that was already heavily burdened with wounded. If this force bogged down, the fate of the 5th and 7th remained in doubt. The chances of mishap were everywhere. Davis's map was primitive. Maintaining companies in close contact and headed toward the objective through snow, ice, darkness, and treacherous mountain slopes would require a heroic effort. He could count on little artillery if he got in trouble. He was on his own."

It didn't take long for Davis to devise a plan. According to the map, his battalion would have to move about 7,000 yards, as the crow flies, to get the job done—a straight shot of four and a half miles. In actual distance, because of the steep slopes, the troops would have to climb about twice that far.

Years later Davis reconstructed from memory the briefing he delivered to his company commanders within the hour. "Surprise will be our essential weapon. Marines don't ordinarily attack at night, so the Chinese won't be expecting us. We'll move out in single file, along an azimuth of one hundred and twenty degrees. Every three minutes a star shell will burst along the azimuth to guide us, fired from a howitzer back at Yudam-ni. The success of the attack depends on complete silence until we meet resistance. Have your riflemen and gun crews secure their weapons so there's no clinking or rattling on the trail. Go heavy on the ammo loads but have them leave everything else behind except their sleeping bags and weapons. We'll carry extra ammo on stretchers—machine-gun and mortar ammo—and the stretchers will be available for our wounded if we get into a fight. The sick and walking wounded we'll leave behind at Yudam-ni, and they'll bring up the battalion vehicles after Taplett opens the road. We're not going to be able to stop and warm up a meal in the usual way, so have your men bring quick-energy food that won't freeze and can be eaten quickly: canned fruit, crackers, candy."

Today Davis says that the plan was simple because the situation was simple. "Some fellow Marines were in trouble. We were going to rescue them and nothing was going to stand in our way. Marines instinctively know they'll never fail to get support, that they'll never be abandoned or let down in any way by their fellow Marines, and they respond in like manner; it's automatic. Everyone knew this was an important mission. By seizing the pass we would unlock the gate and hold it open for the rest of the Marines in Yudam-ni."

Corporal Roy Pearl, Davis's radioman, recalls that when word got around that 1/7 was going to the relief of Fox Company, the troops were elated. "We had perfect confidence in Colonel Davis."

The Marines of Lt. Chew-Een Lee's Second Platoon, filing past the command post, were each handed an extra grenade by Gunnery Sergeant Henry M. Foster, the machine-gun platoon's senior NCO. A tall slender man with a mustache, Gunny Foster spoke a quiet word of encouragement to those he thought might need it. Lt. Lee observed the scene in hawklike silence.

PFC Robert P. Cameron: "It was about nine o'clock when we

got started. How Company was about half of what it was on Hill 1403, and our fire-and-maneuver tactics lacked the maneuver part because we were so few in number. The temperature was a major factor in the failure of our attack. It's damn hard to move, let alone attack, when you're frozen stiff. How can you be expected to charge up a slope when both feet are like blocks of ice? Colonel Davis finally had to send up Able Company to help get us to the top."

Turkey Hill barred the way. It lay directly in the path of Davis's projected route to the pass. Litzenberg sent up How Company, but they too got stalled. The colonel decided that Davis's First Battalion would have to help out. That was bad news for Davis, because it meant casualties for 1/7 even before the trek began, not to mention the depletion of ammunition and fighting energy.

Marine platoons used brightly colored "air panels" to mark their ground positions to pilots. Lt. Chew-Een Lee occasionally draped one of the garishly colored strips around his neck and shoulders. "I wanted my men to know where their platoon leader was at all times. I made the air panel into a kind of huge scarf or cape. It was a nauseating pink. So I was even more conspicuous than usual. . . . Yes, the enemy could see me as well as my men, but I didn't care about that. I wanted my men to be able to refer to me instantly for direction, correction, encouragement, and instruction."

The youngest Marine in Lee's platoon was a Private First Class named Basil W. Gewvelis, a Greek-American from New York. His fellows called him Chicken because of his extremely youthful look. Gunny Hank Foster, teasing him, threatened to turn him in for being underage. During an interval between air strikes, Lt. Lee spotted a line of Chinese on a high ridgeline. He wanted to show his men where the enemy was by firing a burst of tracers at them, but to do that it was necessary to elevate the barrel of the machine gun. He called for a Marine and PFC Gewvelis volunteered immediately. Lee asked him to get down on his knees and elbows so that the gun could be placed on his back. When that was done, the lieutenant crouched behind it, sighted in on the enemy, and got off a couple of well-aimed bursts. The enemy returned fire—from several hundred yards away—and one round somehow found its way to Gewvelis, drilling him through the head. The round did not go all the way through: the point of it was visible under the skin near the left ear. Lee: "I had used his living body as a kind of sandbag, and he had been killed while performing this strange role. His death was extremely painful to me."

PFC David Koegel, Baker/7: "We put [Gewvelis] into a nylon litter and took him over to an ambulance jeep on the road. He hung on for a day or two." (In a letter to Lee written in 1992, Koegel remarked, "I can understand your feelings about losing him, but there's nothing to regret about the immediate circumstances. He was a fine Marine, and though all those we lost were too young to die, he happened to be the youngest of all. But when he took that bullet in the head, he was no more exposed than anyone else at that moment.")

Lee: "I wrote the boy's mother a letter when I had time. I recall that her name was Pearl."

PFC Theodore B. Hudson, Headquarters and Service Company, 7th Marines, was recruited to go along on the night march to Tok-tong Pass. Gunny Foster, seeing how frightened the youngster was, came over to him and inquired if he had ever served with a rifle company before.

"No, sir,' " said Hudson. "Uh, Sergeant."

"I'll keep an eye out for you."

"Thank you, sir . . . uh, Sergeant."

Hudson remarked years later that no matter what was going on around Gunny Foster, the man remained calm, and his calm was catching.

Lt. Col. Davis was getting ready for the jump-off when Foster came by lugging an institutional-size tin of peanut butter. The fighting was still going on atop Turkey Hill, and Hudson was impressed with the way the gunnery sergeant repeatedly exposed himself to enemy fire while passing out blobs of peanut butter on the end of a stick. When the shooting got hotter, Gunny Foster lay down next to Hudson and a conversation ensued that Hudson later characterized as important.

"Where are you from?" asked the Gunny.

"North Chicago." Hudson explained that he wasn't referring to the North Side of Chicago but to a small town on Lake Michigan, up toward the Wisconsin border.

Foster just smiled and said, "You don't have to explain; I'm from Waukegan."

Theodore Hudson tried to tell an interviewer years later how amazing that was. There they were, the two of them, a white sergeant and a black private, stretched out under the sky on a snowy mountainside 10,000 miles from home with people shooting at them, and the sergeant was telling the private that his hometown was right next to the private's hometown; side by side, just like the two of them were at that moment.

"Waukegan, *Illinois?*"

He nodded. "My wife is waiting for me in an apartment above the Rialto Theater on Genesee Street."

"God! I've seen lots of movies at the Rialto!"

By the time they had to saddle up again, the two of them had made a solemn pact: Whoever got home first would pay a call on the family of the other one and pass along the news.

It took until dusk to drive the Chinese from the summit of Turkey Hill. Having now seized the jump-off point, Davis reorganized his unit with all possible speed, lining up the companies as follows: Kurcaba's Baker Company would lead the way, with Lt. Lee and his point team out front; the command group would come next, followed by Hovatter's Able Company and Morris's Charlie Company.

Lt. Col. Raymond Davis: "I got in touch with Litz and found him in an impatient mood. He said we had to go *now*. He pointed out that it was so cold, and getting colder, that if we let our men sit around much longer they'd freeze to death. I figured out later that the wind-chill factor made it around fifty degrees below zero. So I called the company commanders together and told them, 'We're going now—we're just *going*.' I was trying not to worry about the weakness of the battalion's tactical radios or about how we were going to deal with casualties on the steep icy slopes in the dark."

Litzenberg had told Davis to take along whatever was left of How Company to help make up for the losses of the day. This development came as an unpleasant shock to the nearly exhausted troops of Lt. Minard Newton's small band, who until that moment thought they had been relieved by Able and Baker Companies.

PFC Robert P. Cameron: "There were about twenty of us left. That's half a platoon. After we got word that we were going along, Lieutenant Newton assembled us and made a little speech. He reminded us that we were United States Marines and not doggies. At the end he said something funny and sad: 'The next man in this lash-up who gets himself killed—I'll personally *murder* the bastard.'"

At the last moment the regimental surgeon, Navy Lieutenant Peter E. Arioli, showed up. "Hello!"

"What are you doing here, Doc?"

Arioli explained that Davis's battalion surgeon was ill and he had volunteered to replace him.

"Glad to have you along."

Before Davis gave the signal to move out, he had the men double-time in place to check for noisy gear. There was no longer any putting it off: Davis turned to Lt. Lee and said, "Move out smartly."

And so the trek began. It was about 9 P.M. As historian Lynn Montross felicitously phrased it, the battalion tail was then pulled up the mountain, and the last physical tie was broken with the other Marine units at Yudam-ni. Davis was on his own.

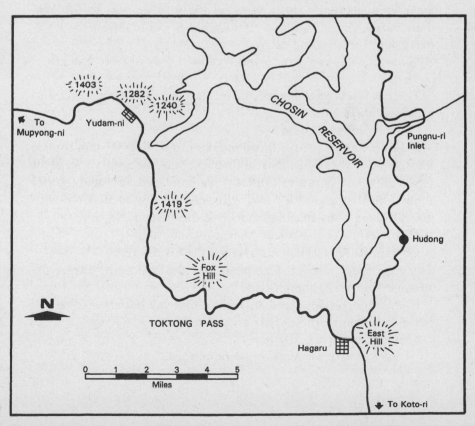

52.

THE TEMPERATURE WAS HOVER-
ing at twenty degrees below zero as Fox Company's third full day
at Toktong Pass drew on toward dusk. Under cover of a light
snowfall the Chinese moved four heavy machine guns onto the
rock-strewn ridge across the way and, after the snow stopped, began raking Fox Hill with long bursts of fire. Lt. Donald Campbell,
the artillery forward observer, transmitted the map coordinates of
the guns to Captain Read seven miles away in Hagaru. PFC Lloyd
O'Leary, the mortar chief, was instructed to stand ready: the moment How Battery's shells were on the way he was to lob two
illumination rounds aloft so that Campbell could adjust the howitzers' aim for a second salvo.

"Four guns at your command," came the word from Hagaru.

"Fire."

There was a distant boom, and a rumbling among the peaks and
valleys to the south.

"Four rounds on the way."

O'Leary's mortar shells lit up the sky just as the 105-mm rounds
impacted on the ridge. No adjustment was necessary. Sergeant
Clyde Pitts, of Sergeant Audas's platoon, had his field glasses
trained on the target area and witnessed the spectacular oblitera-
tion of four enemy machine guns and their crews.

"Wonderful," he shouted. "Beautiful shooting!"

Captain Read, in Hagaru, awaited the formal report.

"Cease fire," said Lt. Campbell into the handset. "Target destroyed. Mission accomplished."

It was difficult for Read to believe that his battery had wiped
out a target on the first salvo at such range.

"Say again after 'Cease fire' . . ."

"Target destroyed. Mission accomplished."

* * *

In the early light of dawn a Marine machine gunner on the left flank of Fox Hill saw a strange sight: two Chinese soldiers, both wearing fedoras, sauntered up the road from the south either ignorant of Fox Company's presence or unconcerned. When they were within twenty yards of the gunner he yelled "Halt!" The two men foolishly if instinctively reached for their pistols, and with a short burst the Marine gunner bagged himself two enemy officers. Lt. McCarthy recalls that for the rest of the campaign the Marine in question wore a bullet-holed fedora perched incongruously atop his parka hood.

During the daylight hours of November 30 there were more air and artillery strikes, and another visit by a helicopter. Once again the spindly craft was driven off by enemy fire, but not before dropping off fresh batteries. A late-afternoon airdrop from a C-47 ensured an adequate supply of ammunition. Hand grenades and mortar shells were now plentiful for the first time. The machine guns were heavily supplied, and every rifleman had three bandoliers, with more available at the command post.

Even after all that had happened at Toktong Pass, the survivors of Fox Company were feeling cocky. Captain William Barber: "I was no longer worried about the outcome. I was sure that Colonel Litzenberg would not leave us alone on that hill."

No one on Fox Hill had any inkling that Davis was on his way across the mountains.

The night of November 30–December 1 was dark, but toward the south a few stars glowed dimly above the soaring skyline.

Chew-Een Lee: "Lt. Kurcaba had come up to me before we shoved off and said, 'Battalion wants you as the lead platoon.' *Battalion.* That was his way of saying *Lt. Col. Davis.* I was of course honored but hardly surprised. He knew the Second Platoon was the steadiest, operating under the best leadership. And so we moved out. I was, as always, directly behind my scouts, in position for an immediate estimate of the situation, followed by direct action, as soon as we encountered the enemy."

There was general gladness about Lee taking the point. In later years Lt. Joseph Owen paid the following tribute to Lee in a letter to the writer: "He was a by-the-book officer who lived by time-tested rules. He was hard as steel, tough as nails, cold as ice—all the clichés apply. He was a natural-born battle leader. The men appreciated him greatly, and underneath that appreciation was the unique love a foot soldier has for a trustworthy platoon leader. He was a stickler for detail and discipline, certainly, but everyone knew he was constant and reliable as time itself. No one who served with Baker/7 can deny that he was the outstanding man in the company. Thank God we had Chew-Een Lee, wounded wing and all!"

Kurcaba had instructed the slight lieutenant to aim toward a certain star over the southern horizon that glowed a bit more brightly than the rest. "That's your heading," he said.

Lee nodded curtly and moved away.

Half an hour later the column of 500 Marines, a few Navy corpsmen, and Dr. Arioli—a file that stretched half a mile—was picking its way laboriously across the slopes, ridges, valleys, and saddles of a rocky wilderness. Star shells fired from Yudam-ni popped softly in the sky at regular intervals but somehow failed to perform their orienting function. The point of the column, descending into a ravine, lost sight of the brighter star and began drifting to the right. This was dangerous because the column would eventually butt up against the rear of the Chinese dug in on the ridges overlooking the road. Davis sent a word-of-mouth order up the line to correct the axis of advance, but because ears were muffled by scarves and parka hoods, word traveled only a short distance. Meanwhile, Lee's point team was drifting farther and farther off course.

"Come on, Pearl," said Davis to his radioman. "We're going for a little stroll." Lugging the heavy radio, Corporal Pearl followed him into the darkness.

Davis: "I made quite a racket thrashing through the snow, and that drew complaints. 'Quiet! Knock off the noise!' I could hear Corporal Pearl behind me explaining that it was the battalion commander who was making all the commotion."

In the meantime the column was stalled in place while Lee checked his compass, and some of the Marines in the rear began to lose patience. The grumbling was low in volume but high in feeling.

"Goddamn it, let's move the fuck out!"

"We're fuckin' freezing to death!"

"Pipe the fuck down!"

"Shut the fuck up!"

"Stand the fuck by!"

Lt. Kurcaba moved over to Lt. Owen and quietly asked him to find out what was holding them up. The mortar officer trudged forward until he came up beside Lt. Lee, who was standing motionless, seemingly impervious to the cold. Owen could see nothing in front of Lee but darkness. Lee was still wearing his arm sling; he had taken the glove off his good hand to better grip the compass. He told the mortar officer there hadn't been a star shell for a long time and he was having trouble adjusting the line of march. Turning to go back, Owen collided with a Marine churning furiously through the snow, and both men went down. As they climbed to their feet, Owen recognized the battalion commander.

"What's the holdup, Lieutenant?"

"The star shells aren't much good for orientation, sir."

The Marines seemed to have the desolate area all to themselves. The wind was erratic; sometimes it blew fiercely, sometimes it was still. When it was still, a cough sounded like a mortar shell exploding. After Colonel Davis conferred with Lee, the column began to trudge mindlessly forward again, in snow that was often knee deep. PFC Leroy Martin, How/7: "I think everyone was exhausted even before we left Turkey Hill. We hadn't had much sleep for days, had expended loads of energy in firefights, slogging up and down that terrain in bone-chilling cold; so this was a column of Marines in piss-poor shape. We were like a chain gang of zombies, blindly following the man in front."

The trail became icy, packed down by the boots of those ahead. Men in the rearward platoons slipped to their knees and staggered to their feet, only to slip again. The thud of their falls and their involuntary grunts of pain and frustration grew louder. The icy downhill passages were even more treacherous, especially for machine gunners and mortarmen with their cumbersome loads.

Chew-Een Lee's scout fire team was composed of three Marines. After correcting the line of march, Lee maintained tight control over their progress, keeping an azimuth bearing by the light of the flares whenever he could. Often it was necessary to hold up the column to let the scouts carry out a reconnaissance of the ground ahead and thus avoid leading the column over a precipice or into a stream if they were in a gorge. Lee: "This was not exactly a Sunday afternoon stroll in Central Park, I can assure you."

Lt. Col. Raymond Davis: "Up there on one of the ridges we ran into an especially harsh wind and it was just devastating. We all became absolutely numb with cold. [Davis has experienced both extremes of weather in his military career. When he commanded 1/1 on Peleliu in the Pacific, the temperature had reached 110 degrees.] At one point I got myself all hunched down in an abandoned Chinese hole with my map and flashlight and compass. Naturally, we didn't want the enemy to know we were there, so before I turned on the flashlight I made sure I was tucked in under a poncho. I then got oriented to the azimuth in relation to the next hill mass, turned off the light, and climbed out. The three company commanders were standing there shivering, waiting for orders—and suddenly I couldn't recall what I had done down in the hole! So I had to go back under the poncho and start all over."

PFC Allard Johnson: "When the wind died down we heard Chinese soldiers talking in low tones. I got the impression they didn't know we were there, or if they did know, they assumed we were Chinese."

Lee: "I was personally leading the column in a wide skirting motion when I heard a voice say very clearly, 'Ni ting dow ma?' You heard something? A different voice said, 'Shih.' Yes. A moment later: 'Da-luh!' We attack! And the shooting began. A PFC in Hank Kiser's platoon got shot in the ass—which he deserved, quite frankly, for having such a large ass. The enemy was about a hundred yards away but seemed much closer. At night the enemy always seems much closer."

Lee signaled his squads into skirmish formation and led them upslope on hands and knees. There was a torrent of oaths and firing as the Marines overran the position. An enemy squad had been sleeping on a wide shelf of rock that jutted out from the mountainside; most of them were shot to death in the brief action, but one or two Chinese scampered up the slope to safety.

The column had been moving slowly but without letup for three hours, and now, a long time after midnight, the point reached a spot that seemed to be the highest in the area, the top of Hill 1520. The long column again came to a halt.

Davis realized that his troops were virtually in a state of collapse; they began toppling over like so many dominoes, as if their loads had become too much for them. When he asked a rifleman which company he belonged to, the young man couldn't even answer.

Davis started shaking individual Marines bodily, trying to rouse them, and ordered the other officers to do the same.

After a few minutes of this he decided it was time to take a major break. Having no communication with Fox Company, he figured the safest thing to do was to hold still until daylight; otherwise the relief force would probably get fired on by Barber's troops if the column continued to move toward them in the darkness.

Davis had the TBX pack radio set up on the spot, and for the first time in several hours he was able to contact Colonel Litzenberg. He recalls the colonel saying, in a brief, businesslike interchange, "What's the situation? Over."

"Quiet, but the troops are worn out. Request permission to halt and grab a rest."

"Granted. Get back to us when you need to. Out."

Sergeant Schaeffer came up and told Davis he had something to show him. The colonel went off a short distance with Schaeffer and watched him reach down and pull up a large icy object that turned out to be a Chinese soldier. He was still alive: Davis could see the eyes moving. There were several others nearby, wedged tightly in holes for warmth, most of them dead. It had been some kind of outpost and the weather had all but wiped it out. Davis: "The men of Baker Company had already taken care of the ones still hanging on."

Davis deployed his troops in a tight perimeter as fast as he could and organized two-man patrols to make certain the men on twenty-five-percent watch were alert.

PFC Theodore B. Hudson: "When we stopped for our break I got chilled pretty bad and started shaking all over. There was no way to get out of that wind. Along comes Gunny Foster on his rounds, checking on every man's welfare as usual. When he saw the way I was shaking, he said, 'I'll be right back.' A couple of minutes later he shows up with a blanket. 'Wrap yourself in this,' he says. It was his own blanket, I'm sure. In those days I was convinced that gunnery sergeants never slept, so I accepted the offer since he didn't need the blanket anyway."

The Marines were pretty well hidden in the darkness, but Colonel Davis was already worried about their exposure in the broad light of day. There was no question that the mountains were crawling with enemy troops. Davis had just climbed into his bag and was zipping it up from inside when he noticed a Marine with an entrenching tool working nearby; as he sat up to caution the Marine to get off the skyline, there was a distant burst of machine-gun fire. One of the rounds brushed across Davis's forehead. It left a mark, but Davis wasn't seriously injured.

Major Thomas Tighe was the Marine standing nearby; he was trying to dig a hole for himself. Now came a second burst aimed in their direction, and Colonel Davis drolly suggested that the Chinese were trying to tell them Tighe's digging was keeping them awake. Tighe: "Needless to say, I stopped digging. Colonel Davis turned over on his side and, in that nerveless way of his, fell asleep immediately."

Silence settled over the wilderness of ice, snow, and rock.

53.

DAWN WAS JUST AROUND THE corner; it was time to saddle up and move out.

A young Marine in PFC Ralph Boelk's machine-gun section of Weapons Company, 1/7, decided that he couldn't go on. Boelk: "This was a six-foot guy from Texas, eighteen years old. You don't need to know his name."

" 'I'm not going any farther,' he said.

"We thought he was joking at first. He just lay there while the rest of us were rolling up our bags and fixing to move out. I tried joshing him. 'Listen, pal—in two or three days we'll be back aboard ship, bound for Japan and some of that good R and R.'

"He acted like he didn't even hear me. 'I've had it. I'm not going any farther.'

"I sat down beside him and offered him a chunk of our moldy C-ration chocolate. He wouldn't take it. Lieutenant Ed Shepherd and Platoon Sergeant Mount came over and tried to talk to him, but all he would say was 'I've had it, I'm not going any farther.' This guy, he just gave up. The spirit had gone out of him. Finally the lieutenant says, 'We gotta go.' He asked for volunteers to carry him and I ended up being one of them. We must have carried the poor bastard a good mile across those peaks."

The sky was glowing in the east when the column began moving toward the pass once again, this time with Kiser's platoon leading the way. The movement stirred the Chinese, who opened fire, and soon Kiser's troops were pinned down. Chew-Een Lee, hypervigilant as usual, moved forward to check on the situation, and told his runner to bring the platoon up.

Lee: "The fire was coming from a rocky hill mass off to the right. I didn't have to wait for orders from Mr. Kurcaba; it was automatic. The Third Platoon was not returning fire, which really annoyed me. I had long disapproved of Hank Kiser's laid-back, low-pressure style of command. *My* platoon *always* returned fire when fired upon."

Lee deployed his platoon in attack formation and began moving upslope under the supporting fire of two machine guns. The slope became steeper and steeper and Lee was nearly exhausted by the time he reached the crest. "My thighs were like pillars of lead; I had to will myself forward. I recall thinking how easy it would be for an enemy soldier to have toppled me backward merely by tapping me on the chest."

Despite the exhaustion and his wounded right arm, Lee still had enough strength to raise his carbine and fire at two soldiers who rose out of the snow before him. Behind them other Chinese broke and ran, and Lee directed his men to pursue them with fire. "I was appalled to note that our rounds were falling ten to twenty feet short in the snow. I made a mental note to have my men adjust their battle sights to compensate for the odd effect this misleading terrain had on one's aim. On the whole, though, I never felt more exhilarated than I did at that moment, reveling in the flush of a clear-cut Marine victory."

Lt. Col. Raymond Davis wasn't yet certain of his position in relation to Fox Company, but after the column moved a few hundred yards farther he recognized a rocky promontory that he had noticed on the march north in late November. "I was greatly relieved when I spotted that landmark, because it gave me a definite fix on our location. The bad news was that we had sustained a dozen casualties, including three dead, in the firefight at first light. We buried the latter in the snow and brought the wounded along on stretchers and canvas fold-up litters. We had no choice but to leave the dead behind."

Corporal Joseph Finn, How/7: "I was so dogtired that when a gook rose up out of a hole and took aim at me I didn't have the strength to raise my nine-and-a-half-pound rifle to shoot him! Staff Sergeant Maxie Pierson took care of him with his Winchester sniper rifle and saved me. Right there was the lowest point in the whole night for me, because until then I hadn't grasped how many gooks were out after us. This gook Maxie shot was just one of a whole lot who were swooping down on our rear."

Lt. Col. Raymond Davis had just reached the crest of yet another ridge when he saw the Fox Company perimeter ahead of him. "There it was, plain as day, about eight hundred yards off."

The Marines of the relief force stopped and stared in awe. The snowfield leading up to Fox Company's lines was covered with the bodies of Chinese soldiers in padded green, khaki, and white uniforms. There were hundreds of them. General Smith later estimated in his official report that probably 1,000 Chinese troops had been killed in action at Fox Hill or died of a combination of wounds and exposure.

Lt. Joseph Owen: "The bodies got thicker as you got closer to Fox Company. I swear to God you could have walked all the way around Fox Company's position without touching the ground, using those bodies as a carpet. Every one of them died a brave soldier, facing the enemy. When you're a young Marine you never think such thoughts, but I think them now."

Davis knew it would be dangerous to move closer to Fox Company without establishing radio contact; Barber's 81-mm mortars and heavy machine-guns could chew them to shreds if they were mistaken for Chinese.

Corporal Pearl's voice rang out: "Colonel—I have Fox Company!"

Pearl later reconstructed the interchange:

"Hellfire Six, this is Delegate Six. How do you read? Over."

"Delegate Six, this is Hellfire Six. Read you loud, read you clear! What's your position? Over."

"This is Delegate Six. We're close—real close. Just over the rise from you. Can you put Fox Six on? Over."

"Roger. Wait one."

Pearl recalls that he and the other radioman were in a state of high elation. "I was overwhelmed at bringing our two units together on the radio, knowing that Fox Company wasn't going to have to go it alone any longer. The colonel just stood there smiling. I held out the handset. 'Sir, Fox Six is ready to talk.'

Davis took the handset. "Fox Six, this is Delegate Six. Over."

"Delegate Six, this is Fox Six. Welcome aboard. Over."

Davis later admitted that he had choked up at the sound of Barber's voice, and said he was moved by his business-as-usual manner.

"Fox Six, we are approaching the ridge preparatory to entering your sector. We will show ourselves on the skyline in five minutes. Will you alert your people to that effect? Over."

"Delegate Six, this is Fox Six. Message understood."

Five minutes later: "Fox Six, can you see us?"

"We can see you, yes. Stay right where you are, Delegate Six— I'm going to send a patrol to guide you in."

"Negative on that, Fox Six. Keep your men in position."

Across the intervening distance the men of Davis's battalion saw the survivors of the Battle of Toktong Pass stand up and wave vigorously with blue, red, yellow, and white strips of parachute cloth. As Davis's men moved closer, weaving their way through the corpses, they noticed that many of the Marine positions had been fortified with grisly barricades of bodies. Several of the defenders—most of them walking wounded, their arms in slings, bandages and gauze wrappings hiding various wounds, the whole company looking ragged and filthy yet radiantly smiling—rose behind the grim stacks to greet Davis's troops.

It was 11:25 A.M., December 2.

"People," said one of Barber's men, noticing the general air of exhaustion, "you look like shit." Everyone within earshot laughed.

PFC Walter Klein of Fox Company heard one of Davis's Marines ask, "What the fuck hit this place anyhow?"

As Colonel Davis was introducing himself to the crippled company commander, Corporal Pearl approached, holding out the handset again.

"Sir, I have regiment."

Davis: "I informed Colonel Litzenberg that we had arrived on Fox Hill. 'Good work,' he said. The colonel was a man of few words."

Colonel Litzenberg: "When I received word that Davis had reached the pass, I no longer had any doubt about our ability to come out of Yudam-ni with our wounded, our vehicles, and our guns."

Pearl: "I stood around with a grin frozen on my face—until I saw a sight that wiped it off real quick: the stack of dead Marines between the aid tents."

Five days and nights of battle had left Fox Company with 118 casualties: 26 dead, 3 missing, 89 wounded. (A search was made for the missing Marines, but they were never found.) Six out of seven officers had been wounded. Almost every survivor, wounded and unwounded, suffered from frostbite and digestive ills.

Lt. McCarthy: "But we still had one hundred twenty-two effectives, by God, and we still held the pass."

The eighteen-year-old Texan who had refused to take another step was carried into one of the medical tents. The corpsman who examined him found no wounds or injuries; the young man had simply lost his will to live. To the lifelong astonishment of everyone involved, he died within three hours of reaching Fox Hill.

Boelk: "We were stunned. We didn't know what to do with him—this kid who was now a dead body. One of the Fox Company guys showed us where the dead were and we carried him over there and put him at the end of the row. I think the poor son of a bitch was literally frightened to death."

PFC Robert P. Cameron, looking around Fox Company's position, was impressed by two aspects. "The first was that Fox had held out so long against such odds. I couldn't help but compare their stand with our weakness on Hill 1403, which was more defendable terrain. But something went wrong with us on 1403 that didn't go wrong with Fox Company at Toktong Pass. You can't put it into words except to say the morale of each company was high, but How's morale wasn't high enough. The other thing that impressed me was the bravery of the Chinese soldiers. You could see them still in their ranks, sprawled in a kind of fan shape, every one of them facing Fox Company's guns."

Lt. Ralph Abell, learning that his old friend Larry Schmitt had been wounded, hunted him up in one of the aid tents. Schmitt was in a lot of pain because of wounds to the leg and abdomen. He hadn't known about the relief of Fox Company until he saw Abell's face, and then he let out a gasp. "Thank God, Abe," he said. "We're gonna kick the shit outta those bastards now."

When Abell stepped outside, he saw Colonel Davis crouching beside Captain Barber, who was now on a stretcher. At that moment Dr. Peter Arioli, the surgeon who gallantly volunteered to accompany Davis's battalion into the unknown, came outside the other aid tent. They all heard the flat crack of a distant sniper's rifle, and Abell saw Arioli go down. "I was only a couple of steps away from him. He didn't suffer; he was gone in seconds. One of the corpsmen examined him, pronounced him dead, and we added his body to the pile."

Major Thomas Tighe, Davis's operations officer, recalls that there were two Chinese prisoners on the hill when the relief force arrived. "They were docile little fellows, sitting patiently in a grove of trees, hugging their knees in the wind. When he asked Chew-Een Lee to interrogate them, the lieutenant was surprisingly reluctant to do so. Lee, very proud of being an infantry officer, did not want to be identified with any other kind of duty such as interpreting for the Intelligence Section. He tried to beg off by saying that the prisoners probably spoke a dialect unfamiliar to him. After discussing all this with Lee, Major Tighe finally came to understand the reason for his bristling reluctance. "All I had to do was assure him that we were not about to turn a good infantry officer into an intelligence staffer. That seemed to satisfy him, and he went over and hunkered down in front of the two prisoners."

PFC Leroy Martin was taking a nap nearby at the time. "People started talking Chinese right next to me! I woke up with a start and grabbed my rifle. 'As you were,' says the lieutenant."

Chew-Een Lee: "These people were former Nationalist soldiers who had fought under Chiang Kai-shek. They did not parrot the usual boring Communist propaganda. I asked them if they knew why they were fighting against American troops, and one of them answered with a catch-all phrase common in China: 'Mei yu fa-tzu.' It means, roughly translated, That's out of our control, or C'est la vie."

54.

LITZENBERG: "IN OUR ORDER for the march south, there were no intermediate objectives: 'The attack will start at 0800 on 1 December. Objective: Hagaru.' "

Only Taplett's and Stevens's battalions remained north of the village now. Pulling them out, as the official history says, "was to prove the equivalent of letting loose of a tiger's tail." One of Taplett's company commanders, Captain Harold Schrier, later told Taplett that the withdrawal from 1282 was the toughest fight he had ever been in. Taplett was impressed by the statement, coming from a man who had led troops at Iwo Jima. Schrier's company expended more than a thousand grenades during the pullback from 1282. Taplett: "When you need a grenade, nothing else will do. We kept him well supplied."

The bulk of the two Marine regiments was eventually withdrawn to positions south of the village, and soon Taplett's battalion was advancing down the road to Toktong Pass, flankers out, a lone tank leading the way. This M-26 Sherman, sent up from Hagaru to test the roadbed, was the only tank to reach Yudam-ni. It was placed at the head of the column with two bulldozers, the idea being that if the tank got knocked out, a dozer could push it off the road so it wouldn't block the motor column. If one of the dozers was disabled, the other one could then push *it* off the road. There was also a platoon of engineers up front, under Lt. Wayne Richards, ready to deal with roadblocks and any repairs needed on the roadbed.

Major Henry Woessner: "The troops felt badly about pulling out. The general attitude was that we should stay where we were and inflict more death and destruction on the enemy. Word got around that after we reached Hungnam on the coast, we were going to regroup and come back—and then really give the Chinese a shellacking. That was entirely different from the Army attitude, believe me. The Marines resented having to give an inch."

Lt. John Yancey was still pining away for his platoon, unaware that it no longer existed as such: the survivors of Dog/7 and Easy/7, both down to a handful of shaky Marines, had been combined into one unit called Dog-Easy Company and attached to Taplett's battalion. Major Maurice Roach: "The morale of Dog-Easy, as you can imagine, was not of the highest order."

Corpsman James Claypool: "When Yancey was with us, his people had a kind of Valhalla complex; but once he was gone, death was just stark and ugly and final."

There were several critical moments during the pullback from the northern hills, but the moment that gave Colonel Litzenberg the most concern occurred when the enemy surged over the crest of a hill north of the village, on the heels of Stevens's First Battalion. "We could see them streaming across the skyline and down the forward slope. Our artillery gave them a temporary body check, but they came on again. Then they all stopped—and began looting the houses of the deserted village."

The exit from the Yudam-ni valley began about a mile south of the village, marked by hills on either side of the road. Lt. Col. William Harris's 3/7 was to occupy one of them, Hill 1542. Taplett thought Harris was moving too slowly. After watching with growing impatience all the milling-about at the bottom of the hill, he finally contacted Lt. Col. Frederick Dowsett. "Fred, I want permission to advance down the road without waiting for Harris to take that hill."

"Sure," said the regimental exec. "Go when you think it's right."

Taplett took up his role as spearhead for the two regiments at about 3 P.M. on December 1. With the Sherman tank in the lead, the column moved rapidly for a mile before the Chinese opened up from the high ground. Lt. Denzil E. Walden's platoon of How Company sustained fourteen casualties at this time, about half of what was left, and the attack was temporarily halted. Aggressive and impatient as always, Taplett decided that regiment was not honoring its agreement to give 3/5 priority artillery support. He complained to Colonel Murray that every time he called for artillery the priority was elsewhere. "Goddamn it," said Taplett, "if you guys want to get out of Yudam-ni, it's *us* who will get you out—but we can't do it without arty!"

Corpsman Claypool: "You recall my telling you about George Fisher, the young corpsman who did such an outstanding job on 1282? We had been working together for three days now—he was always at my elbow—and I got to appreciate him, even though he gave every appearance of being timid and tearful and ready to bolt. Anyway, we were moving down the valley floor, getting ready to leave the valley, and I was saying something unimportant to him. When he didn't answer, I turned to look, and there he was lying in the snow. A bullet had struck him and he had died instantly. If there's a better way to go, I don't know what it is. I picked him up—he wasn't very big—and carried him toward the rear. A couple of Marines offered to help but I wouldn't give him over until I found a space in one of the overloaded trucks. I don't know why it's always a shock when someone you know gets killed in a campaign. You'd think a person would get used to it."

After dark, the temperature dropped. Captain Harold P. Williamson's men were exhausted. He called Taplett on the radio and recommended that How/5 hold in position for the night. Schrier called in with the same request on behalf of Item/5. Taplett checked with regiment and came back with this: "Murray says 'Hell no.' Continue the attack."

Before midnight, Schrier's company was moving against the enemy on Hill 1520, beyond Turkey Hill. Schrier himself was wounded a second time in the attack and became too weak to continue; 2nd Lt. Willard S. Peterson took over and the battle raged on. Staff Sergeant William G. Windrich, with a squad of Marines, held off an enemy counterattack long enough to permit Item Company to reorganize in the darkness, seven out of twelve of his men becoming casualties in the process. Wounded in the head by grenade shrapnel, Windrich refused evacuation, then led the First Platoon forward until he was hit again. He waved away an approaching corpsman. "There isn't time," he said. A few minutes later he was dead.

PFC Palmer S. Braaten, of Schrier's company, was an acting squad leader in the machine-gun platoon. Moving from gun to gun, he distributed ammunition, made emergency repairs on two of the guns, and helped evacuate the wounded. When the order was given to pull back, Braaten volunteered to cover the withdrawal by manning one of the guns alone. He was killed by a grenade as he was firing off his final belt of ammunition.

PFC Fred Davidson, George/5: "Care to hear why I joined the Marines? It was for a silly reason. Mary Jane McCleod was the daughter of the prison warden at McAlister, Oklahoma, and I had a terrible crush on her. Mary Jane was fifteen going on twenty-six and she had a figure out of West Hell. I thought I could impress her in Marine dress blues. Ha! She never even saw me in uniform."

Davidson had been burned by a white-phosphorous round on the night of the onfall but was carrying on despite the pain. "George Company was on some high ground south of Yudam-ni. The spot where I was was a small snow-covered plateau. The moon was up, bright enough to read *The Marine Manual* by. I remember shoving a big rock over to the edge so I wouldn't roll over it in my sleep. It took me a long time to crawl into the bag because of the burns on my back. Next thing I knew, here's all this shouting and shooting. I clawed my way out and grabbed the rifle, which was propped against the rock. I saw white blurs running past on the right. I raised the rifle but it wouldn't fire. I yanked the bolt back and shoved it home and tried again. *Pow!* Then someone headed straight at me and I had time to swing the rifle hard, catching the left side of his head. He fell on his knees and I got another purchase on the rifle—around the muzzle—and gave it to him good. The stock broke in two and the gook went down flat. There was yelling and gunfire on all sides, and at this point I just fell on my face in the snow and lay there without moving until it was over. There was silence for about five minutes and then a voice from somewhere like Alabama says, 'Okay, how the fuck did them bastards git so fuckin' close without nobody spottin' the fuckers?'

" 'Get a corpsman up here, we got wounded.'

"That's when I raised up from the snow and felt a sting on the right side of my waist. I picked up the broken M-1, put a round in the chamber, stuck the muzzle up against the gook's head, and squeezed the trigger. Just wanted to make damn sure he wasn't pretending to be dead, like I had. His rifle was in the snow beside him, and when I saw the bayonet on the end of it I knew he had done more than poke me with the muzzle. I unbuttoned my clothing and stuck my hand in where it hurt and there was blood. It was like syrup because of the cold. The wound was under the rib cage on the right side. I couldn't believe the son of a bitch had bayoneted me! At daylight I took a close look at the man's rifle and found out the reason he went to the trouble of bayoneting me instead of shooting me: he was out of ammo." The doctor at the aid station couldn't immediately tell how deep Davidson's wound was, or whether the steel had penetrated internal organs.

By noon George/5 had shoved the Chinese off Hill 1520—not far from Fox Hill—but at considerable cost. Captain Hermanson was among those knocked out of action. Lt. Charles Mize was now in command of a company that was the size of an understrength platoon, as Taplett's battalion continued to slug its way toward Fox Hill.

The vehicles in the column were packed solid with wounded and dead Marines, and with critical supplies. Litzenberg and Murray now made a hard decision: the rest of the dead would be left behind at Yudam-ni. Bulldozers gouged out a long pit about six feet deep. Trucks with working parties picked up the corpses from collection points and brought them to the pit. A total of eighty-five bodies, wrapped in parachute cloth, were laid out in a mass grave just south of the village.

PFC Robert Pruitt, Able Company Engineers, was one of the two TD-18 drivers who pushed frozen clods over the eighty-five bodies that were left at Yudam-ni. "It was hard duty. The dirt that had been gouged out to make the pit had frozen up again, so what we had to deal with was big frozen clods. All we could do was push them into the pit and sort of nudge them around and try to spread them evenly. There came a moment when we had to drive the heavy equipment across the ground with the bodies underneath. I had to run my dozer over a Marine whose arm was sticking up like he was waving, and that has bothered me ever since. I probably should have stopped and climbed down and tried to push the arm down, but I would have had to break the bone." Down through the years, Pruitt kept thinking about those bodies, and in 1957 he wrote to Headquarters Marine Corps inquiring about them. He felt better when he received a letter explaining that the remains had all been brought home after the cease-fire in July 1953, in accordance with the terms of the Korean armistice.

Sergeant Robert Gault, 7th Marines Graves Registration, stood beside Captain Donald France, Litzenberg's intelligence officer, as

Chaplain John Craven read a few verses of scripture at the edge of the mass grave. Gault had personally supervised the retrieval of many of the bodies. "Me and my helpers tramped all over those slopes, and sometimes we had to go forward of our lines to pick someone up and we got mighty darn close to the Chinese. They never bothered us, though. They just stared. Sometimes there were crowds of them. Some of them had probably never seen a Negro before."

"We'll be back," said Captain France.

"I hope so," said Gault.

55. AS THE VEHICLE COLUMN BEGAN

its ascent into the pass, Lt. Col. Raymond Murray turned for a final look at the village, the flat, snow-covered western arm of the reservoir, and the tall columns of smoke billowing skyward. Five days earlier Yudam-ni had been nothing but a name on the map; now it was a place Marines will remember as long as there's a Marine Corps.

PFC Jack Wright, George/5: "By mid-morning our company had relieved Item on Hill 1520. We didn't know it was called 1520 at the time, of course; it was just another hill. Anyway, it was there I saw a demonstration of what can happen if you allow your people to bunch up. We were waiting to move out, everyone nicely spread out except for these two pals crouched side by side. A sniper nailed both of them with the same round. One of them died instantly, but the other died real hard: grabbed himself, rolled over, grunted, rolled some more, grunted again, got up on all fours, crawled in a circle, flopped over and over, and finally just croaked. It was the ghastliest thing I ever saw. When it was all over, the platoon sergeant said, 'Okay, people, listen up. There's a lesson in this. Wright, tell us what that lesson is.' Before I could clear my throat to answer, everyone within earshot said—singing it sarcastically—'Don't bunch up!' After that, some of the guys crawled up to the body. One took his ammo, another his rifle, another his bayonet and scabbard, another his grenades. Then they did the same with the other body. Whenever a guy got hit, the others just took whatever gear they needed. It was understood."

When Wright and his squadmates reached the hilltop, they found only one Chinese left. His feet had frozen and burst open, and according to Wright's recollection, he was crying and growling at the same time. The corpsman took one look at him and shook his head. A moment later there was a shot. Wright: "This was the first time I knew a prisoner had been killed out of mercy and not out of necessity."

Wright was having trouble standing up. His squad leader came over. "What's wrong with you?"

"My feet are asleep."

"Let me see you stamp 'em."

"Hurts too much."

The platoon sergeant came over and told Wright to turn himself in at the medical tent.

"Aw, hell, Sergeant—my feet are asleep, is all."

"Get your ass down to the road, Wright."

At the medical tent the corpsman examined his feet, filled out a tag, and tied it around his left ankle. "You got a case of frostbite," he said. "Consider yourself evacuated." He pointed to the long line of vehicles. "Take your choice."

Nearby was a jeep and three wounded Marines in a trailer. "One of them beckoned me over and told me to climb in," Wright recalls. "I'll never forget him. He looked like he had been born at Tun Tavern in 1775. 'Take your boots off, and your socks too,' he said. I wasn't about to argue with this guy. When I pulled off my socks a layer of skin came off with them. The old guy unbuttoned his parka and pulled up his sweater and unzipped his vest and unbuttoned his dungaree jacket and lifted up his undershirt. Then he grabbed my feet and pulled them up on his bare belly so they could thaw out. He didn't even flinch. I wish I had bothered to ask his name."

From the top of the pass Lt. Col. Davis watched a sizable force of Chinese moving down a snow-covered ridge to the north. Crews were pulling heavy machine guns on two-wheeled carts. Davis speculated that they were headed his way, in response to the smoke from the campfires on Fox Hill, but more likely they were trying to keep ahead of the 5th Marines, who were coming down the road behind them.

The Chinese soon found themselves trapped between Davis's troops on the hill and Taplett's depleted but still ferocious battalion advancing along the road. After the overcast lifted at mid-morning, several hundred of these troops were caught in the open by a flight of Corsairs, the planes smothering the enemy with napalm while Taplett's and Davis's men poured fire into their ranks. Major Thomas Tighe: "There's no defense against napalm. When it touches padded quilt, the victim turns into something resembling the wick in a Coleman lantern." It was the most concentrated slaughter of the Yudam-ni breakout. General Smith later reported that an entire Chinese battalion was "eliminated" during the action.

Lt. Col. Harold Roise's battalion—the rear guard—was about two miles south of the village now, just north of the gateway hills where the valley floor ends and Toktong pass begins. Harris's battalion was a mile down the road, along with Stevens's battalion in the vicinity of Hill 1520. The many provisional platoons formed from artillery, headquarters, and service personnel provided close-in protection for the vehicles strung out along the road. A number of drivers had already been struck by sniper fire, and it was obvious the enemy had singled them out as a priority target. Marines from the escorting units were hastily recruited to replace them. It was not an assignment anyone welcomed.

The convoy was stalled between Toktong Pass and Hagaru. The wait was unusually long, and Lt. Col. Murray finally climbed out of his jeep, determined to learn what was holding them up. He was worried about gaps opening up in the convoy, because a gap would give the Chinese an opportunity to move riflemen and machine-gun crews down close to the road. He walked forward three or four hundred yards until he came to the lead truck. The driver was slumped over the steering wheel. Murray figured he had been shot by the Chinese. But no: the man was sound asleep, snoring peacefully, the engine idling away. Murray: "It was a wonder the truck didn't roll off the road and down into the chasm. Well, I roared like a lion and scared the daylights out of this poor fellow. The look on his face was priceless."

Captain Franklin B. Mayer: "I still don't know how those Marines on the ridges managed to stay on their feet. Down on the road, whenever we stopped it seemed to me that everyone just fell asleep on the spot. I would flop across the hood of the nearest jeep if there was any room there."

One of the jeep-hood wounded was PFC Fred Davidson. His burns were stinging badly and the pain from the bayonet puncture was even worse. He had learned by now that it takes about twenty minutes for morphine to go to work, and he timed each request to the corpsman carefully. Out there on the hood, whenever a firefight broke out nearby he felt naked. After one particularly close exchange of fire, he told the corpsman that he wanted to be helped out of the bag and off the hood immediately.

"I'll try and find a spot for you aboard one of the trucks," said the corpsman, "but you won't be any safer."

"Then I'll walk!"

"No you won't. That would agitate the wound and start it bleeding again. Let's have a look at it."

Davidson peeled up the dressing and they both examined it. It was nasty looking: there was some blood oozing, and the edges of the puncture were puffed up and white. The corpsman and a couple of able-bodied Marines found Davidson a spot in a truck, and he felt a little better.

It began to snow again, and by dawn the bleak terrain was covered with two or three inches.

Lt. John Cahill: "When we moved beyond Hill 1520, we spotted some folks on a ridgeline east of the road. We thought they were gooks. We were all set to open fire when we noticed the rolled-up sleeping bags bouncing on their asses, and there was no doubt they were Marines, either Davis's men or Barber's. We were damn glad to see them. We waved and they waved back. Some of the guys climbed down to shake hands with us. It was a big moment: the Yudam-ni folks and the Toktong Pass folks had made contact."

Davis was standing on an overlook when he spotted the Sherman trundling around a curve to the north. It was a great thing to see that tank and the Marines stretched out behind it. He climbed down to the road and held up his right hand like a traffic cop, and the tank ground to a halt. A minute or two later Colonel Taplett appeared. The two officers leaned against the tank and, shouting back and forth above the din, reviewed the situation. As far as Davis's battalion was concerned, a bold rapid plunge down the road was very much in order. His troops were fairly well rested by this time, whereas Taplett's troops were obviously wrung out. (Taplett's battalion, once nine hundred strong, had been reduced in three days of fighting to just under two hundred.) But Taplett expected to keep going, leading the way to Hagaru.

Taplett: "This became a sore point between me and Murray, the regimental commander. I actually pleaded with him over the radio net. My main argument was that the morale in my battalion was high and the troops had been on the go without letup and would freeze in their own sweat if they had to stop. 'If you pull us out now,' I told him, 'I'm going to have lots of weather casualties right away.' "

Murray answered: "Colonel Litzenberg and I have decided that 1/7 will take over the attack."

"A lot of my men are going to freeze up tonight," said Taplett, seething with resentment.

It was after dark when Kurcaba's Baker Company was ordered to saddle up again. Davis told him to gather his men and bring them down to the road. "Glory be," said Kurcaba, "we're going to travel by road at last!" Until then, Baker Company had operated strictly as ridge runners. Kurcaba told Lee to form his platoon into a skirmish line and, as it descended the slope, to look for surviving Chinese soldiers.

Lee balked vigorously. "Goddamn it, Joe!"

"What?"

Lee delivered a brief lecture. "The first principle of night combat is to maintain control. In terrain like this, the only way to do that is to move in a column."

"Battalion wants a skirmish line."

"Aye, aye, sir," said Lee angrily.

As he turned away to comply with the order, a voice issued from the darkness behind them. "Just a minute, Mr. Kurcaba."

"Sir?"

"Have the men move down in column."

A Marine chopper was circling Fox Hill. The pilot began doing rolls and other aerobatics—or so PFC George Crotts assumed—but then plunged straight down into the trees, flopping over and over in a sickening, spasmodic manner, like a big insect dying. Crotts was shocked; he had thought the pilot was being playful.

The crash had a sobering effect on the union of Taplett's and Davis's troops. There were no flames. Corporal Roy Pearl watched as the pilot's corpse was carried over to the stack of dead men; he still wore his leather flight jacket with the gold wings clearly visible. Pearl: "To this day I can't understand why the crash upset me so much, after all I had seen."

56.
THE POSITION AT TOKTONG PASS was originally occupied by 237 Marines and Navy corpsmen. There were eighty-six left. According to what Barber today considers a low estimate, more than 2,000 Chinese had died before the combined fires of Fox Company, Read's How Battery, and the Corsairs. Barber believes that at least 4,000 Chinese were committed to overrunning his position. The numbers weren't important; what mattered was that Fox Company, 7th Marines, had indirectly prevented the enemy from closing the circle around Yudam-ni.

Barber: "I'll never get over how close we came to not digging in that first night. It seemed almost foolish at the time, because we expected to move off the position early the next morning. But something made me order them to break out those entrenching tools and turn to, even though it was growing dark and we were all dogtired. . . . We would have been wiped out. We would not have survived the first night."

After Davis's battalion had moved well down the pass, Captain Barber began to pull his ragged survivors off the hill.

PFC Kenneth Benson: "We were glad to be leaving that place."

Private Cafferata, turning fretful, asked Benson to make sure they didn't leave him behind.

"Nobody's going to leave you behind, Hector. You know I wouldn't go without you." Cafferata was so big that his feet hung over the bottom of the stretcher, and it took four strong men to carry him to the road.

Davis's battalion was followed by about 800 walking wounded, most of them carrying weapons and ready to fight if called on. There were at least 1,000 more wounded and frostbite cases aboard the trucks. The problem was, where were they going to put the Fox Company casualties? Colonel Litzenberg detailed the regimental S-1, Captain John Grove, to halt each truck at the bottom of

Fox Hill and try to squeeze one more man on board. Litzenberg: "There's no record of the total number of casualties at that time, but eighteen hundred is close. I know this: There were hundreds of Marines who walked through that pass who should have been riding in ambulances."

All the wounded survivors of the Battle of Toktong Pass were eventually loaded aboard vehicles and disappeared down the road. That left the dead to deal with. A number of Marines were buried at the Fox Company position, and some of the others had to be buried along the road, but the numbers are not known.

Lt. Col. Dowsett: "There was no room for them aboard the trucks. We already had bodies on fenders and tied to howitzer barrels and anywhere else we could think of. We would collect the dead man's identification and personal effects and make some sort of grave for him, even if it was only a matter of covering him with rocks. In *The Marine Manual* it's called a hasty field burial. Sometimes you can only do so much."

Captain William Barber had been ordered to turn the remnant of Fox Company over to Lt. John M. Dunne, the company's one remaining unwounded officer; but Barber was reluctant to let go. Finally he called the young lieutenant over. "It's all yours, John."

Barber stumped down the road for a few hundred yards, falling farther and farther behind the company. After a while, the tail end disappeared around the bend and he couldn't see his men any more.

"It was a good rifle company. It was a company of Marines with guts and hope."

Between breaks in the snow flurries, the Marines on the road could see long columns of Chinese on the ridges, making their way southward ahead of the convoy. They were falling back before the Marines' advance, aiming to regroup near Hagaru, where the Marines expected to fight even bigger battles.

There was a stretch of road where the ground fell away sharply to the right, recalls Fred Davidson, and the Marines on the road had a clear view for a thousand yards across a series of sloping fields. There was a farmhouse down there, about 800 yards away. During one of the delays on the road, one Marine took an idle shot at the farmer working around his thatch-roofed house. The farmer started to run, and other Marines raised their rifles instinctively, took aim, and fired. By the time the farmer had staggered out of sight, a machine-gun crew had set up their weapon and were almost ready to cut loose. Davidson: "It wasn't a shining moment in Marine Corps annals. We were acting on instinct, and the instinct of your average Marine is to shoot gooks."

Major Thomas Durham: "We had some prisoners with us in pitiable condition. The ears of one of them had frozen through completely, becoming so brittle that they snapped off when he rubbed them. Others had frostbitten feet so bad that the swelling blisters forced them to remove their shoes. You would occasionally see a prisoner walking by in his bare feet. Bare feet in that temperature!"

Lt. Patrick Roe: "Toktong Pass was a brutally windy place, the wind funneling through, opposing our every step. When we got to a certain spot I remembered something I had seen on the march north: a bunkered dugout where we could get out of the wind for a few minutes. Sergeant Mitchell and I climbed up the slope, and there it was. Mitchell crawled inside with a flashlight and found two Chinese soldiers in the dark. One was dead; the other's whole body was frozen, including his head, which looked like a block of ice; but you could still see a thin puff of vapor as he breathed, and his eyes followed the beam of the flashlight. Mitchell and I backed out, I suppose to get some help dragging them outside; but by the time we returned, someone else had done the job for us: the two Chinese had been pitched into a snowbank and the bunker was now too crowded for us to enter."

To the front of the motor column and off to its flanks, Corsairs swooped down repeatedly to hurl rockets into enemy concentrations. Many Marines regarded a well-laid napalm strike as a spectacle of great beauty: orange flames and billowing black smoke against the snow. After the napalm splashed, there was usually a moment of stunned silence.

Lt. Chew-Een Lee: "Personally, I *chafed* whenever someone called in an air strike, unless it was intended for a large group. Too often it was only a sniper. What the hell were those Marines trained for if not to take care of a simple task like that! You don't need to bring in the whole goddamned Air Wing to deal with a sniper!"

On the road between Toktong Pass and Hagaru, word came

down to watch out for infiltrators. In most cases these were half-frozen, demoralized individuals who wanted to get close to the warm-up fires lit whenever the convoy stalled. Several Chosin veterans claim they recall seeing unarmed Chinese soldiers come in out of the darkness, stand by a fire among Marines, get warmed up, then go back up the slope.

PFC Theodore Hudson: "I'm afraid I got a little spooked when I first heard the warning about infiltrators. Somewhere south of the pass I noticed this short person plodding along in the dark. Actually, all I saw was his face by the light of a mortar-round explosion, but it was enough to give me a shock. Here was one of the very infiltrators we were supposed to watch out for! My first impulse was to shoot first and ask questions afterward; but I had enough sense to go over and tell Gunny Hank Foster we had a Chinese infiltrator walking down the road in our midst, and that he was armed. Well, Gunny Foster went over and took a look at the silhouette I had pointed out.

"That's Lieutenant Lee," he said. "Try not to shoot him, Theodore."

"Sorry, sir . . . uh, Gunny."

Lt. William J. Davis, Able/7 mortar officer: "Lee looked so little in that big parka."

Hagaru was not yet in sight, but Marines at the head of the long column could now see pillars of smoke from the smoldering fires there, evidence of the battle the night before.

It was close to seven o'clock, the evening of December 3, when they came within sight of the checkpoint at the north end of the Hagaru perimeter. There was a feeling of tension and excitement in the air.

"They're coming!"

General Smith: "From the command post I could plainly hear the noise of the approaching vehicles."

At the very point of the long column walked two lieutenant colonels, Davis and Dowsett. The latter had just received a radio message from the operations center in Hagaru, stiffly warning him to halt outside the checkpoint and identify himself properly, giving the correct password and waiting to be properly recognized before advancing. Dowsett replied coldly, "I have no idea what the password is. We're coming straight in. Don't get in our way."

As word of the imminent approach of the 5th and 7th Marines

flashed around the perimeter, the remnant of the Royal Marine Commando darted out in perfect order to drive the Chinese off the hill nearest the checkpoint, lest the reunion be marred by additional casualties. Lt. Patrick Roe: "They looked so neat and clean and militarily shipshape that some of us were embarrassed by the way *we* looked. We were all filthy, with ripped parkas that had lard all over the front from spilled C-rations. Our hair was all matted, our faces bearded and grimy, our lips cracked. Washing and shaving hadn't been a big priority over the last several days."

Five hundred yards north of the perimeter, the trucks ground to a halt. Those of the wounded and frostbitten who could do so climbed down to the ground and formed up on the bleak, snow-blown roadway.

"You people will now shape up and look sharp," shouted Davis. "We're going in like United States Marines."

One of the sergeants began calling cadence in the distinctive Parris Island manner, a haunting, stirring sound to anyone who has been through Marine boot camp. There in the early dark they began to march forward, haggard and hard, their shoe-pacs pounding in slow, relentless rhythm.

Colonel Bowser stuck his head in the doorway of the bungalow and invited the general to come outside. "It's quite a sight," he promised. A moment later Smith was standing on the step, puffing his pipe, watching the column approach.

Davis: "By the time we reached the checkpoint we were parade-ground Marines—stepping smartly, backs straight, heads up, marching in perfect unison, singing the Marines' Hymn."

PFC George Crotts: "Later on, a guy told me some of us looked like zombies. I told him that was because some of us *were* zombies. The dead Marines on the trucks, you see, when they heard that sergeant calling cadence, they came back to life and climbed down to join the ranks. *Semper fidelis* is strong medicine; it means 'Always faithful.' Tell you one thing: you could definitely feel the spirit of those who had gone ahead, as we like to say. They were there with us."

57.

CORPORAL ALAN HERRINGTON: "We were feeling good because we had held the door open for them at Hagaru. Many of us stood there at the roadblock looking for friends and acquaintances. When I saw this certain outfit going by, I asked after a sergeant I knew and the guy jerked his thumb toward the rear of the truck and said, 'Dead.' For a while I just stood there staring at all the frozen corpses going by. You would recognize an occasional face. Most of them were strangers, but every damn one of them was a personal loss to me. I can still see the icicles of blood."

Lt. Col. Randolph Lockwood: "I was at the roadblock to greet Colonel Litzenberg. The colonel, sitting in the back of a jeep, looked very grim as his driver pulled up. I went forward and welcomed him to Hagaru and informed him that I had twice attempted to comply with his order to proceed to Yudam-ni but that it had proved impossible. He climbed down from the jeep very stiffly and walked away without answering or even looking at me."

Many of the Yudam-ni Marines appeared dazed and confused at first, wandering about aimlessly with blank stares; but, as the official history puts it, "There were few who suffered any psychological disturbances that could not be cleared up with a good night's sleep and some hot food." Galleys had been set up to feed the incoming troops, who were now lining up for coffee, stew, and pancakes.

PFC George Crotts: "The smell of those pancakes drew us like a magnet. Escorts took us to the chow line, but they weren't really necessary. I made a discovery that day: plain bread will stick to the side of a field stove and fall off when the side turns to toast. We feasted all day on toast and pancakes and syrup and coffee and evaporated milk and sugar. This was living, man."

Lt. Col. Olin Beall, commanding officer of the division's Motor

Transport Battalion, took Raymond Davis into his tent and fixed a hot meal of C-rations for him. Davis: "They were just ordinary rations, but to have them served hot on a warm mess tray—it was like a brief visit to heaven."

For many of the incoming Marines, Hagaru seemed like an untroubled haven after all the dangers they had survived at Yudam-ni and on the way down. They soon learned something most of them hadn't even suspected: Hagaru had been cut off, just as Yudam-ni had been, and they were going to have to fight their way out of Hagaru as well.

PFC Fred Davidson, with his burns and bayonet wound, was taken by truck to the airstrip and loaded aboard a transport plane. The wounded were stacked four deep on both sides, with a narrow passageway in between. Davidson: "Then I saw her: a live female in that godforsaken place. An actual *woman* in uniform and hairdo and lipstick. We all just lay there staring at her cleanliness and neatness and feminineness. She understood. She didn't blush. She gave me a wet cloth to suck on, because I wasn't allowed to eat or drink anything." (Davidson underwent exploratory surgery at a hospital in Japan: no damage to inner organs; five months in hospital; complete recovery. When he heard later there were no nurses aboard the transport planes, he said, "Well, she must have been a ghost, then!")

Lt. Col. Thomas Ridge was among those watching at the roadblock. One can reasonably assume that he experienced a profound sense of relief. His weakly defended, shrunken perimeter was now massively reinforced; no longer would he bear the responsibility of holding it with one understrength infantry battalion.

General Oliver P. Smith: "I was considerably relieved to have RCTs 5 and 7 rejoin us at Hagaru. Quite an emotional experience."

The 5th and 7th Marines—bringing hundreds of wounded with them, enduring repeated attacks on a fourteen-mile march—had completed what military analyst Drew Middleton calls "the first stage of what must be considered one of the most masterly withdrawal operations in the history of war."

58. THE MAIN BODY OF THE DIVI-
sion was still to come. By mid-afternoon there was a gap of two
miles between Harris's blocking position near Turkey Hill and Lt.
Col. Harold Roise's rear guard, which was still in Yudam-ni. Roise's troops were beginning to notice signs of enemy encroachment
in the intervening space. It may have been nothing more than Chinese reconnaissance patrols, but the sightings were ominous and
unsettling.

Captain Franklin B. Mayer, Roise's headquarters commandant,
was keeping his eyes glued to Lt. Col. Roise, who sat in his jeep
smoking one cigarette after another. Late in the afternoon an artillery forward observer came up and said, "The arty's pulling out.
Better tell Colonel Roise." When he did, the colonel merely nodded. A bit later a radio operator came up and said the main convoy
was already moving through the pass. The two of them were standing within earshot of Colonel Roise, and Mayer couldn't resist saying, "Maybe we ought to get started, huh?" The colonel took
another drag on his cigarette. It was at this point that Mayer began
to wonder if 2/5 had been written off—appointed the sacrificial
lamb to hold the enemy's attention while the rest of the regiment
got away. (Mayer: "This was a sudden loss of faith on my part,
and I don't like admitting it even today.") Then the air–ground
liaison officer came up to inform Mayer that the head of the column had reached Hagaru. "Isn't it time to pull up stakes?" he
asked.

Over toward the river, the Marines of Captain Uel Peters's Fox/5
watched as the Chinese advanced slowly toward the village from
the north. For the moment, they were out of range of the company's small arms.

"War leaves no soft options," as General Smith said later. Before
the howitzers and their crews had pulled out with the main

convoy, all the outlying hamlets around Yudam-ni had been obliterated by artillery fire, a mission accomplished by Lt. Col. Harvey Feehan and his First Battalion, 11th Marines. It was well known by this time that the Chinese had expelled the civilians in the neighborhood and crammed themselves into the empty structures; but there was no more shelter in the outlying areas, and enemy troops were heading for the abandoned buildings of Yudam-ni. Just south of the village, the men of Roise's battalion, virtually alone now, watched them stopping to root through the smoldering debris.

Mayer: "We were all pretty rattled by this time. We were also worried that the Chinese were moving between us and the tail of the main vehicle column down the road toward Hagaru, which was already miles away. Harris's battalion, 3/7, was this little bitty lash-up of maybe three hundred Marines—less than a third its normal strength. The point is, there weren't too many Marines around our neck of the woods, and the Chinese surely knew it."

PFC Richard Seward, Easy/5: "I nearly jumped out of my skin when I heard a Chinese bugle sound nearby, but it turned out to be this poor old ox that wanted to be let out of its shed."

PFC Patrick Stingley: "I was looking around for Private Gomez when *pow pow pow* made me jump a foot in the air. Here's that darned Andy Gomez, and what's he doing but shooting at the entire Chinese army. 'Andy, cut that out!'

" 'Huh? But they're gooks.'

" 'Yeah, and you're gonna get 'em pissed off, too. There must be a *million* of 'em.'

Dr. Henry Litvin: "The psychological implications of the situation were quite beyond description: intense loneliness, a feeling of despair—as you might feel after being thrown into a lion's den. All through the day we had watched one Marine battalion after another file past us and disappear down the road to Hagaru. By the time dusk fell, all of us in the aid station were beginning to act like men who were doomed. There was no conversation. None of us ate a bite of anything. It all seemed so utterly hopeless. The two Marine regiments had had their hands full of Chinese for days on end. What was our little chopped-up battalion going to do against such a huge force? We were agonizingly aware that the Chinese could swallow us in a single bite."

When Litvin ventured outside for a moment, a voice called out: "Hey Doc, want to see something?"

It was Colonel Roise himself, sitting placidly in his jeep. Handing Litvin his binoculars, he directed the surgeon's attention to a certain hillside. What Litvin saw didn't make him feel any better about the future. Litvin: "The Chinese were pouring off the slopes. I wanted to turn to him and say, 'Colonel, can't you take us out of this awful place before it's too late?' "

Litvin then witnessed another stunning sight. A group of Marines, led by Lt. Thomas Alvah Anderson, went by, heading north. Once again he had to restrain himself from speaking out. "I wanted to shout, 'Lieutenant, don't you realize you're headed in the wrong direction? That's the way to death!' But it turned out—as I should have realized, if I hadn't been so emotionally flummoxed—that this group was the rear guard of the rear guard, headed toward their assigned position. I'll never forget the look of determination on their faces, and not a whimper among them. They were going the 'wrong way' to *fight*, for gosh sakes! And leading them was that skinny, happy-go-lucky Lieutenant Anderson."

At dusk Captain Franklin Mayer saw the last Corsair bank low over the valley of Yudam-ni, before heading south; he watched the gull-winged aircraft disappear over the mountain, wishing he could go with it.

Colonel Roise tossed his cigarette in the snow, stretched his arms over his head, arched his back, and climbed slowly out of the jeep. Every man within a hundred feet had his eyes fixed on the battalion commander.

"Wounded all ready to roll, Doc?"

"Yes, sir. Everything's all set."

Litvin watched him cup his hands to his mouth and yell: "Second Battalion! Saddle up!"

The order bounced from platoon to platoon; five minutes later, Easy Company was leading the way down the road, moving fast.

2nd Lt. Jack Nolan, Easy/5: "I took one last look. The Chinese were running to and fro through the smoke that was rising from all the burning piles of gear and supplies."

Franklin Mayer: "My memory of our exit from Yudam-ni is blank except for one thing. In the dark I stepped on the stomach of a dead Chinese soldier and nearly had a stroke because my weight pushed some residual air out of his lungs and he made a sound as though he was yelling at me: *'Yawwp!'* "

Roise's men moved through Harris's position at Turkey Hill, Harris's 3/7 now becoming the rear guard.

Lt. Patrick Roe, 3/7: "It was only with the greatest effort that we were able to keep the troops in place. They were like racehorses waiting for the gate to open.

"Settle down, Marines. Settle down."

1st Lt. Thomas M. Sullivan, Item/7: "We had a sergeant in the company who looked like he belonged on a recruiting poster. Six feet tall, broad shoulders, handsome tough-guy face, perfect posture. But this fellow couldn't stand being under fire. As soon as a firefight started he would volunteer to go to the rear for ammunition or supplies. Everyone understood that he simply couldn't stomach combat, and even though he wore the label COWARD on his forehead, none of the NCOs or officers thought to turn him in. His cowardice wasn't the result of deliberation or conscious thought; it was involuntary. He couldn't help himself. Anyway, the poor fellow turned white as a sheet when we took over the rear guard. I felt sorry for him. . . . At the other extreme was Private Jose Orosco from California, who was fearless. I was considering writing him up for a Silver Star, but then I got to thinking that he didn't deserve a medal since he had no fear to overcome. Isn't that what bravery's all about?"

The Chinese closed in on the very tail of the convoy as it neared Hagaru, in the neighborhood of the gold mines. There was a delay because several prime movers hauling howitzers ran out of diesel fuel. The stall occurred around 3 A.M. on the morning of December 4 as the troops were waiting for the engineers to repair a small bridge. Major Angus J. Cronin, operations officer of the 155-mm artillery battalion, formed a scratch unit of cannoneers and drivers and launched a successful counterattack, but the Chinese came back, pressing hard, and the situation began to look dire.

Because of an imminent threat that the howitzers might be captured, Major William McReynolds, commanding the Fourth Battalion, 11th Marines, ordered the recoil-piston nuts to be backed off so they could be removed and the guns fired if need be, which would cause the tubes to recoil off their carriages. If there was enough time, the breech block was to be destroyed with a thermite grenade. As it turned out, the guns were so loaded down with frozen bodies strapped on them that all this was impracticable, and several guns had to be abandoned.

PFC Arthur Koch recalls how cold he was during the delay at the bridge. "It was nasty cold. It numbed your brain as well as your body. It was so cold it made you want to cry, and there was no relief from it. When I finally got hit—a chunk of shrapnel in the leg—it was Gunny Barnett who took care of me once again. Down in the Pusan Perimeter, in the summer campaign, we took a pretty good licking in some of those firefights with the North Koreans, and I was in shock over it. I didn't think it showed, but I felt a tap on my shoulder and Gunny Barnett says, 'Here you go, Koch,' and hands me a small bottle of hundred-proof brandy. 'Have a nip of this.' I took a swallow and gave it back. 'You're a veteran now,' he says. When I got wounded at that bridge outside Hagaru, he showed up right away. 'Koch, you picked a lousy time to get your million-dollar wound.' He stood there chatting with me while the corpsman did his stuff, then patted me on the back and walked away. All this may seem like nothing, but it meant a lot to me. There's nothing finer in the world than a good Marine gunnery sergeant, and you don't get to be one unless you know how to handle Marines."

Doc Litvin was walking up and down the road exhorting individual Marines to keep moving about in order to prevent frostbite. "At dawn I had a chance to admire the magnificent Corsairs again. They were like dark guardian angels. God bless those valiant young pilots who shepherded us to Hagaru. In later years I bought a Revell model kit of a Corsair and assembled the parts with Testor's glue and mounted it on a little pedestal. It's still on a shelf beside my desk at home, and I must have looked at it a thousand times over the years."

Lt. Col. Raymond Davis's notion of marching into Hagaru "like United States Marines" was infectious; the 5th Marines came in on the same proud note.

Litvin: "Along with all the other military training I missed, no one ever taught me how to march; but I figured that if you kept your head up, your shoulders back, and strode forward as if you weren't tired, *that* was the way to march like a military man."

The tail of the great column pulled into Hagaru in the early afternoon of December 4. It was appropriate and fitting that the last vehicle to enter the checkpoint was a jeep carrying the forward air-controller who had directed the last strike against the Chinese in the fight at the bridge.

Soon after passing into the perimeter, Doc Litvin reported to the division surgeon, Navy Captain Eugene Hering, who was busy working on the tremendous backlog of casualties. (Litzenberg and Murray had come in with 1800 casualties, a third of them frostbite cases.) Hering nodded and said, "Good to see you, Lieutenant." Litvin was far too tired to be of any use, but he felt guilty as he crawled into his bag. He was asleep before his head touched down.

Major Thomas Durham's most vivid recollection of Hagaru revolves around corpses and food. "I was startled to see huge mounds of what appeared to be not merely hundreds but thousands of Chinese soldiers. This was the first time I realized that Hagaru had been under serious assault. Our battalion spent the day applying itself industriously to the true mission of the Marine Corps, which is sleeping and eating. I recall starting off with a can of Campbell's asparagus soup, which, in its frozen state, I pretended was ice cream. It took me a while to realize I was back in the land of hot chow."

The first thing Doc Litvin did on awakening was to write a letter to his parents. Litvin: "My parents had been reading the Philadelphia *Evening Bulletin* and knew the reality of the situation at the Chosin Reservoir, but I didn't know they knew. The letter I wrote them from Hagaru while half awake was the usual cheery travelogue, extolling the magnificent Oriental scenery, the picturesque villages, the quaint behavior of the natives, and so on. Many weeks later I learned that local newspapers all over America were spelling it out: the 1st Marine Division was surrounded and in danger of annihilation. One of the Philadelphia columnists used the phrase 'sliced to ribbons,' and I was told later that my mother collapsed when she read that. That wasn't the worst of it, though. I gave one of my upbeat letters home to a wounded Marine officer to mail from Japan, where he was about to be medevacked. It turned out that he had an undetected wound—a wound other than the one I had treated—and the letter delivered to the little mailbox beside the front door of the Litvin household was actually stained with blood."

When PFC Arthur B. Koch was having his wound re-dressed in Hagaru, the doctor inquired, "Think you can get around okay?"

"Sure, I can get around fine."

"Good. We need every man we can muster."

But when Koch reported back to his platoon in Easy/5, the lieutenant said, "What the hell you doing back here?"

Koch told him about the conversation with the doctor.

"Follow me," said the lieutenant, looking annoyed.

At the aid station he asked Koch to point out the doctor.

"That one right there, sir."

The lieutenant explained to the Navy surgeon that when Koch's wound stiffened up it would take four able-bodied fighting men to carry him on a stretcher. "I'm going to need those four men for the fight ahead of us," he said. The doctor sighed, nodded, and tagged PFC Koch for evacuation. Outside the tent, the lieutenant and Koch shook hands.

"Take care of yourself, Koch."

"Good luck, Lieutenant. Thanks for everything."

59.

EDWARD E. SMITH, A LIEUTEN-
ant in the division's Motor Transport Battalion, was helping to
defend the northern perimeter at Hagaru. He had been informed
by Colonel Beall's acting exec, Major Martin Roberts, that the
Corsairs reported Army survivors out on the ice. Smith was tied
into the machine-gun positions by EE-8 phone, and in the early
evening the left flank gunners reported movement to their front
and requested permission to commence firing. Smith told them to
hold up until they were certain they were about to be attacked,
because it was possible the movement in front was caused by Army
survivors. Smith then called Major Roberts and the two of them
worked their way over to the gun position. Sure enough, human
figures were visible out on the ice. Major Roberts shouted for them
to identify themselves. The answer was in English but hard to understand. Lt. Smith requested illumination and got one 81-mm
round, which enabled the two officers to see a crowd of U.S. Army
soldiers standing in the middle of a minefield.

"Don't move," called Roberts.

The GIs' spokesman explained that they had two Chinese soldiers with them. Major Roberts instructed them all to get down
flat in the snow and then send one of the Chinese through the
minefield. The man came all the way through without setting off
any explosions. After the second Chinese soldier came through, the
GIs followed their footprints through the snow. 2nd Lt. Edward
Smith: "Next morning I raised hell with our engineers about their
so-called minefield where two or three hundred men had walked
safely through. Some minefield! They said it was probably the
weather."

Diary entry, December 2, General Oliver P. Smith: "Quite a rescue operation has been in effect today in which Lt. Col. Beall has
been the principal actor. The condition of these frostbitten men is

pitiful. Some were crawling, some were hobbled, and some had lost all sense of direction and were walking around in circles."

Lt. Col. Olin Beall of Texas, fifty-two, was one of the great characters of the Chosin Reservoir campaign. His former driver, Ralph Milton, recalls that the colonel "had a very short fuse. Everybody tried to stay out of his way. All he was interested in was getting the job done, and he was good at that. Like Chesty Puller, he was a man of few words, and he hated paperwork. He carried all his paperwork in his pockets."

Captain Michael Capraro: "Beall was the ideal Marine commanding officer who did his job, took care of his troops, and didn't need to be loved."

Historian Roy Appleman: "He was a hard-bitten, no-nonsense officer of the old breed, but, as his performance at Chosin showed, he had a big heart and much humanity."

The windswept ice of the reservoir was dotted with GIs both alive and dead, still and moving, upright and prone. Beall, accompanied by PFC Milton and Navy corpsman Oscar Biebinger, came under enemy fire as they approached the shore near the abandoned sawmill. Milton put on the brakes and brought the jeep to a sliding stop. To indicate their peaceful intent to the Chinese on the shore, the three men climbed out and put their weapons—Beall's '03 sniper rifle with scope, Milton's Garand, Biebinger's .45—down on the ice. At first the Chinese allowed them to roam freely in their brave errand of mercy. Moving from man to man, the three found that some of the GIs had died of wounds and exposure, or both. Many of those still alive were in such poor condition that Milton remarked later it might have been better to shoot them. "They were like human vegetables. I was sure most of them were dying."

The three men found that they could carry six or seven GIs in the jeep and on the hood, ferrying them back to a collection point at the perimeter where a large bonfire had been built to thaw them out. They were shot at from time to time, but no one was hit. Toward dusk they spotted a squad of Chinese coming out onto a small peninsula that jutted into the lake. The two Marines and the Navy corpsman were working so close to shore that the squad was actually in their rear, between them and Hagaru. "Well, it's getting dark," said Colonel Beall. "We better get out of here."

Early the next morning, Beall returned to his self-appointed task. His helpers now included 2nd Lt. Robert Hunt, Corporal William

Howard, and PFC Andrew Contreras. As PFC Milton steered the jeep across the ice, a machine gun opened up from one of the coves, the rounds raising small puffs nearby.

When Milton brought the vehicle to a sliding halt, the gun ceased firing. "From here on we walk," said the colonel. "Leave your weapons in the jeep."

Milton: "They could have killed us any time they wanted. I figured sooner or later they were going to turn their guns directly on us."

"Let's go to work," said Beall.

A powerful wind was sweeping across the ice, making it difficult to maintain footing. ("It made you skate," says Milton.) There were at least two hundred GIs on the ice and a few yards inshore. The rescue team used their parkas like sleds to drag the soldiers to the jeep.

Milton saw some strange sights. He saw a Chinese soldier give a GI a cigarette, then light it for him, both of them cupping their hands around the lighter. Milton was so close to them he could tell it was a Zippo, probably lifted off a dead GI. He also saw two GIs in a rowboat that was frozen in the reeds near shore. One of them called out to Milton as he approached, "Go back! They'll kill you!" The two of them became garrulous as Milton helped them out of the boat, complaining bitterly about their officers, who, they said, didn't lift a finger on their behalf.

Around noon on December 3, Colonel Beall returned to the jeep to find a stranger in unfamiliar clothing standing beside it. The man nodded by way of greeting.

"I don't want too many people out here," Beall told him bluntly, "because it draws fire. What's your rank?"

"I'm a civilian."

"What are you doing out here?"

"I'm the Red Cross field director in this area. Name's LeFevre. Everybody calls me Buck."

Milton recalls that Colonel Beall was curt with the man because he was a civilian. (Captain Michael Capraro: "Marines tend to think of civilians as disorganized, inefficient, unfocussed beings of a lower order who get in the way on the battlefield.") Milton: "Mr. LeFevre was probably insulted but didn't show it. He turned out to be a big help, and the colonel finally gave him the task of directing the walking wounded to a collection point where our trucks picked them up."

So far the rescuers had ventured only a short distance inland; no one had as yet climbed all the way to the blackened hulks of the burnt-out convoy standing in funereal silence on the road. Late in the afternoon of the third, after all the survivors had been retrieved, Colonel Beall told Milton to get behind the wheel of the jeep, parked just offshore, and stay there.

"I watched him climb the slope and walk right up to the line of trucks," Milton recalls. "It was the bravest act I ever saw. He walked from truck to truck, inspecting every one of them. Then he came back and said, 'They're all dead.' At first I didn't understand, but he explained that every truck and jeep and trailer was filled with corpses. The colonel estimated there were three hundred bodies in the convoy."

Colonel Beall stood beside the jeep and took one last look around. "I think we've got everybody out who's still alive," he said, then climbed into the passenger's seat. Milton put the jeep in gear and they rolled back to Hagaru, heading toward the bonfire clearly visible in the dusk. Beall and his helpers had rescued some 300 wounded and frostbitten GIs. The 385 able-bodied soldiers who managed to reach the Marine perimeter under their own steam had already been organized by Ridge's command into a provisional battalion and provided with Marine equipment. (At least one Army man took part in the rescue mission, independent of Beall and company. Lt. Hodges Escue of the 31st Regiment's operations section was assigned to coordinate the passage of lines by GIs coming in from the east side of the reservoir. On his own, Escue drove to the sawmill site and brought back several loads of exhausted GIs.)

Shortly before nightfall, under a heavy overcast, a flight of Corsairs, on orders from Almond's headquarters, dropped pods of napalm along the length of the column, incinerating the vehicles and the bodies in them.

Beall personally reported to General Smith the results of the rescue operation that evening. Smith has left us a fleeting glimpse of this hero in his account of the meeting: "Beall was a very robust man who prided himself on his physical condition. He was always in training, and he did not drink tea, coffee, or liquor; he didn't smoke either. This evening he was beaten down and stated that he was feeling his age. (He enlisted as a private in the Marine Corps in 1917.) He asked for some hot water. The aide, thinking that Colonel Beall wanted to wash up, brought in a pan of hot water; but we found that, as part of his Spartan regime, he only wanted a drink of hot water."

Lt. Col. Don Faith was posthumously awarded the Medal of Honor for his actions east of the reservoir. Lt. Col. Beall received a Distinguished Service Cross. Captain Stamford was awarded a Silver Star. (Captain Michael Capraro: "If anyone should have received the Medal of Honor it was Beall. He risked his life repeatedly, especially when he climbed up to the road and looked into each of those trucks. Lieutenant Colonel Faith received it for simply doing his duty, and not very well at that.")

The demoralization of the Army troops was now total. Lt. Col. Barry K. Anderson, the senior Army officer at Hagaru, was directed by General Smith "to get some semblance of control over the Army personnel straggling into the perimeter." This was prompted, Smith wrote later, "by a report from Doctor Hering that malingerers had succeeded in having themselves extracted [flown out of Hagaru]." Lt. Col. Anderson, according to the general, "had great difficulty in arousing the men to any activity. They apparently considered that as far as they were concerned, the war was over."

Just before the great onfall on November 27, Chinese political commissars of the Ninth Army Group had distributed to the troops a pamphlet containing a lecture by one Captain G. Doidzhashvili of the Soviet Navy. Entitled *The Bloody Path,* it consisted mostly of the familiar obtuse, mendacious Communist propaganda; but there was one brief passage that was right on: "[The U.S. Marines] adopt a haughty and scornful attitude toward American soldiers." It was true—the Marines had long believed they did everything better than the Army. Whether or not this was the case, there was a distinct difference in their battlefield tactics. Army operations tended to be measured and sure (slow, the Marines would have said), with elaborate "softening up" of enemy positions by artillery barrages and aerial bombardment, much attention being paid to the minimization of friendly casualties every step of the way. The Marines, on the other hand, pursued the shortest, most obliterating campaign possible, believing that an all-out assault resulted in quicker victory and fewer casualties. While the Army aimed to push the enemy back by the incremental application of force, the Marines sought to annihilate him from the start.

Haughty and *scornful* are perhaps too gentle to characterize the Marine attitude toward the Army and its methods; *contemptuous* would be more accurate. When news of the Eighth Army retreat reached the Marine sector, an anonymous lyricist came up almost immediately with a scathing paraphrase of Hank Snow's "Movin' On" that has achieved immortality. It was called 'The Bug-Out Boogie:'

> Hear the pitter-patter of tiny feet,
> It's the U.S. Army in full retreat,
> They're movin' on; it won't be long.
> It's gettin' cool and they're movin' back to Seoul.
> A thousand gooks comin' down the pass,
> Playin' burp-gun boogie on a doggy's ass,
> They're movin' on; it won't be long.
> It's gettin' cool and they're movin' back to Seoul.

PFC Ralph Milton: "These so-called professional Army officers weren't doin' shit for their troops. They should have been court martialed. They left their weapons and their wounded behind. Is there anything worse?"

Army PFC Thomas F. Marker, mortars, 31st Regiment: "The Marine officers didn't hide in trucks or under bridges like ours did."

Army Lt. Col. William J. McCaffrey, deputy chief of staff, X Corps: "When the stuff hits the fan, by all means get in the middle of a Marine outfit, because they will hold together."

Lt. Joseph Owen, Baker/7: "They were a rabble, those doggies. There was no unit integrity. They were just a mob looking for shelter and safety. None of this surprised us; the GIs had behaved this way all through the southern campaign in the summer. 'Fuckin' doggies' was a phrase you heard often in those days."

Corporal Alan Herrington: "Accounts of the Army action east of the reservoir have since been inflated by the Army itself over the years, with the soldiers turned into heroes and Faith into an outstanding leader."

George Rasula, who served as the 31st's assistant operations officer, has tried over the years to look on the bright side. "We held out against a whole Chinese division, killing thousands of them. They would have raised hell in Hagaru if we had not held our position."

Historian Roy Appleman is probably correct in saying that if the Chinese had launched a coordinated three-division attack that first night, Hagaru could hardly have survived. In the final analysis, "the 7th Infantry Division troops who fought on the east side of the reservoir probably provided the narrow margin that enabled the 1st Marine Division to hold Hagaru, and this in turn made possible the completion of an airstrip from which several hundred wounded men were evacuated." But the Army's performance was in no way commendable; by default, they played the part of sacrificial lamb, and the lamb was slaughtered.

Army PFC James Ransone: "If it hadn't of been for the Marines, those of us who survived the massacre wouldn't be here today. You'll never hear me say a word against the Marines."

60.

CHINESE CASUALTIES OVERALL had been staggering, at least ten times those of the Marines; but General Sung still had 40,000 men at his disposal in the mountains between Hagaru and Chinhung-ni. It was clear to General Smith that his troops at Hagaru could not afford to dawdle; the longer they remained there, the stronger the enemy would become. The most important priority was the evacuation of the wounded from the Hagaru airstrip. Dr. Hering had discovered that the Air Force loading officer at the strip was not screening evacuees and that many survivors of Task Force Faith were feigning wounds or frostbite in order to get aboard the C-47s. This was stopped immediately and a system was set up whereby frostbite cases were screened three times: by the battalion surgeon, the medical company, and finally a team consisting of the division and regimental surgeons, plus a line officer from each regiment. As a working criterion, Hering referred them to the 5th Marines' regimental surgeon, Lt. Comdr. Chester Lessenden, who despite painfully swollen feet refused to be flown out and was working around the clock. The screening process was abrupt, arbitrary, and efficient: "You fly . . . you walk . . . you ride. *Next.*"

PFC George Crotts stood by as piles of gear and supplies were burned. He spotted a stack of clothing on fire, the flames licking close to a brand-new pair of socks. When he reached in for them, the Marine private in charge said, "You can't have those."

"Why not?"

"Because I'm supposed to burn everything."

"That's so the *gooks* can't use it. I'm not a gook, you blockhead."

"Still," said the private. "The lieutenant says burn it all, and that's what I aim to do."

Crotts reached in and pulled out the socks. He also saved a parka and a carton of Lucky Strikes. The private followed him the whole time, protesting. Crotts ignored him. "I was now ready for the big breakout to Koto-ri, with a new parka, a fresh pair of socks, and a carton of Luckies." Crotts would not take part in the breakout to Koto-ri, however; at the aid station where he went to have his feet looked after, he learned he had a serious case of frostbite and would have to be evacuated to Japan for treatment.

Casualties were being flown out as quickly as the planes could land, load, and take off. Captain Paul E. Fritz, Air Force transport pilot: "The cold air was stunning when we opened the side hatch after landing. Conditions at the strip were primitive. The 'control tower' consisted of a jeep with a radio in it, the radio operator stamping his feet beside the vehicle while he talked to the planes. Lines of wounded men were waiting, motley bandages and compresses covering their wounds, makeshift arm and leg splints, crutches made from tree limbs. After they were loaded aboard, there was the smell of fresh and dried blood, filthy combat dungarees, unwashed bodies, spent gunpowder, and vehicle exhaust fumes, all combined into one pervasive stench."

At the airstrip a sergeant noticed that PFC Alfred Bradshaw was still clutching a Thompson and asked could he have it; Bradshaw gave it to him. When he arrived at the Army hospital at Osaka, Japan, the medics were beginning to cut away his clothing when he remembered there was a grenade in one of his cargo pockets. It took him a long time to get it out because of his wounds, the medics waiting tensely until he handed it over. "The first thing I did after getting settled in the ward was to scribble a few lines to Jeanne to let her know I was okay. A few days later she received an official telegram with the worst message any wife can ever get.

Deeply regret to inform you that your husband Private First Class Alfred Paul Bradshaw was killed in action 28 November 1950 in the Korean area in the performance of his duties and service to his country. No information available at present regarding disposition of his remains. Temporary burial in locality where death occurred probable. You will be promptly furnished any additional information received. Please accept my heartfelt sympathy. Letter follows.
C. B. Cates, General U.S.M.C., Commandant of the Marine Corps

"Thank God my wife got my letter before the telegram arrived!"

When his plane took off, Army PFC James Ransone had no idea where it was headed, but he figured anything was better than Hagaru. His troubles weren't over yet: the engines lost power a few seconds after takeoff. Out the window, when the plane touched down, Ransone saw the propeller hit the snow and fly off, skipping across the snow; and when the fuselage hit the ground the wounded men were thrown forward because none of them were strapped in. When the plane finally stopped sliding, everyone was afraid that the high octane fuel—the air was heavy with the smell—was going to explode and burn them alive. "We were about two miles from Hagaru, in a hell of a fix. We helped each other out of the plane and moved away from it slowly while the Marines covered us with their Corsairs and sent trucks out for us. Then we were put aboard another plane. An hour later, when I looked down and saw the sea below, I was really glad to be out of the fighting and all the horrors of war."

PFC John Gallagher: "In Hagaru I had a chance for the first time to take off my boots and examine my feet, which had been bothering me plenty, and I was shocked: my big toes were burned black, as though charred. The corpsman tagged me for evacuation and I never saw my squadmates again. I still miss them."

As his C-47 took off, PFC George Crotts choked back tears and said a prayer for the Marines on the ground. "I really felt lousy leaving all those great guys behind."

When a man was wounded there was usually no time for goodbyes, and many a Marine evacuee experienced a feeling of melancholy at being torn so abruptly out of the hide of his outfit. For more than a few, the feeling has persisted down through the years, softened somewhat by attendance at division reunions. Some have never gotten over it.

Crotts: "At Yokosuka Naval Hospital we were treated like royalty, with officers' wives handing out coffee and donuts from welcome wagons. They gave each of us a rack in a huge auditorium that had been turned into a hospital ward; there were racks on the stage and in the balconies. I ran into Jean Bartels there, and after we shot the shit a bit I remembered about my father's watch and mentioned it to him. He smiled, took it off his wrist, and handed it over. End of *that* story."

From a hospital in Fukuoka, Lt. Lawrence Schmitt wrote another letter to his wife.

My dearest Evelyn:
I hope you got my brief note advising I was wounded. Things have worked out fine. I just saw the X ray and the break is not bad at all. It's just one bone in my calf. You should not worry. I am in good hands and am feeling fine. Please remember that this may be one of the luckiest "breaks" I could get.
Your loving husband, Larry

In the end more than 4,000 Marines and Army troops were flown out of Hagaru in a four-day marathon of evacuation. General Oliver P. Smith: "I believe that the story of this evacuation is without parallel." Many of the dead were flown out as well, including men from Fox Company killed in the last stage of the march from Toktong Pass. The X Corps chief of staff, Major General Clark Ruffner, objected to this practice as soon as he learned of it; General Smith ignored the protest.

Smith: "The Marines have a particular reverence for comrades killed in action. They will make every effort, even risking casualties, to bring in the bodies for a proper burial. We felt it was an obligation, so that these men would not be buried in some desolate North Korean village. It wasn't asking too much of the pilots and it didn't interfere with the evacuation of the remaining wounded. The extreme cold eliminated any problem we might have in regard to the preservation of the bodies."

On his final flight from Hagaru, Captain Paul Fritz's plane became an aerial hearse. The loaders had neatly intertwined the arms and legs of the dead and secured the stacks with rope for stability. "I wanted to make this particular flight with dignity, but how do you do that? I just tried to fly as smoothly as possible."

Time magazine called the disaster that had overtaken Eighth Army "the worst defeat the United States ever suffered." *Newsweek* called it America's worst military licking since Pearl Harbor. "Perhaps it might become the worst military disaster in American history. Barring a military or diplomatic miracle, the approximately two-thirds of the U.S. Army that had been thrown into Korea might have to be evacuated in a new Dunkerque to save them from being lost in a new Bataan."

From the official Marine Corps history:

> The situation in west Korea was depressing enough. But at least the Eighth Army had a line of retreat open. It was with apprehension that the American public stared at front-page maps showing the 'entrapment' of the 1st Marine Division and attached U.S. Army units and British commandos by Chinese forces. Press releases from Korea did not encourage much expectation that the encircled troops could save themselves from destruction by any means other than surrender.

PFC Robert P. Cameron: "The rumor was that the Division would hold Hagaru until spring; then the 2nd Marine Division would arrive from the States and together we would push the gooks toward the Yalu while President Truman dropped a couple more atomic bombs—to show the Japs we didn't discriminate. Despite the upbeat rumor, I was convinced it was only a matter of hours before I got killed in a firefight. It's funny. A week before that I was convinced I was immortal; but in the meantime I had seen so many Marines die and so many corpses going by on trucks that plain old common sense told me what any fool knew: It can happen to you and probably will."

The air evacuation would be completed by nightfall of December 5, and Smith planned for the Hagaru breakout to begin on that date; but Colonel Litzenberg advised him the 7th Marines would not be ready until men from other elements of the division were reassigned as infantrymen, to make up for some of the losses. Even after Smith furnished 300 officers and enlisted men from artillery units, the antitank company, and various headquarters and service units, the regiment was still at less than half strength. The same was true of Murray's 5th Regiment. Marine replacements were still arriving on the medevac planes. Clean-shaven, freshly dressed, eager, and alert, they seemed incongruously out of place to the grungy-looking veterans.

PFC Richard Suarez: "Some Marines were in trouble at a place called the Reservoir. That's all we knew. After I got off the plane, they assigned me to Item Company, 7th Marines, which had maybe fifty guys left out of a hundred and sixty original. I was shocked when I found out how many of them didn't think they were going to survive the campaign. That's why, looking back, I admire them so much today: they fought just as well and kept their discipline even though they figured their individual situation was hopeless. As for me, I had no doubt I'd get out. That's one thing the training did for me. I believed all that wonderful bullshit: one Marine really *was* worth twenty gooks. When they surrounded the 1st Marine Division at the Chosin Reservoir, it was *them,* the poor bastards, that was in trouble."

61. ENSIGN JESSE BROWN, TWENTY-

four, a native of Mississippi, was the first African-American aviator in the U.S. Navy. A Corsair pilot operating from the flight deck of the carrier *Leyte,* Brown was a hero to the handful of black seamen only recently integrated as the result of an order by President Truman. On the afternoon of December 4, as the last of the Yudam-ni Marines were closing on Hagaru, Brown took part in a four-plane sortie, searching out targets of opportunity in and around the reservoir.

It was mid-afternoon when Brown reported that he was in trouble. "I think I may have been hit by ground fire," he radioed. "I'm losing oil pressure."

He had already turned south, but it was evident that the stricken Corsair, now losing power, could not carry him all the way to the airstrip at Hagaru.

Lt. (jg) Thomas Hudner: "We tried to help him by going over the crash-landing checklist with him."

Too low to bail out, Brown picked out a clearing on a mountainside and said he was going to attempt a belly landing in the snow. Turning into the wind while his wing man (and roommate), Lt. William H. Koenig, circled nervously above, Brown brought his smoking plane in for the wheels-up landing. An unseen object under the snow turned a textbook crash landing into a spinning junk pile as the engine tore loose, hurtling through the air for a hundred yards. As the plane came to a shuddering halt, Koenig and Hudner could see that the forward fuselage was jammed upward at a sharp angle, pinning Brown's legs under the hydraulics panel. It seemed impossible that he could have survived such violence, but the two airborne pilots saw him slide back the canopy and wave. Hudner, swooping low a moment later, saw Ensign Brown rip off his gloves and release the latches on his parachute harness. But, ominously, he remained seated. He had landed into the wind, and Hudner could see smoke blowing back over the cockpit as Brown struggled to free himself.

Hudner then made a brave decision. "I felt that with relatively little risk I could drop onto the field where Jesse landed and make a wheels-up landing. I felt it was necessary to do so because the fire might spread and endanger his life."

While the division leader, Richard L. Cevoli, radioed for a rescue helicopter, Hudner circled the area at low altitude, seeking to assure himself there were no obstructions where he planned to set his plane down. He jettisoned his remaining fuel and ordnance, lined up his Corsair on the forest-encircled clearing, and landed, flaps down, on a twenty-five-degree upgrade about 200 yards upwind of Brown. Hudner was shaken and bruised in the rough landing, which broke his windscreen, but he climbed down and hurried over to Brown's smoking Corsair.

"The first thing I did was make Jesse aware of my presence. He was conscious but in a lot of pain. In view of the tremendous force of the crash, I figured he must have suffered severe internal injuries. It was miraculous that he had survived at all."

It was brutally cold. Hudner ran back to his own wrecked Corsair, radioed Cevoli to ask when the helicopter was expected to arrive, and requested that the rescue pilot bring a fire extinguisher and an ax. He gathered up a scarf and a wool watch cap and, returning to Brown, wrapped the scarf around his stiff hands and pulled the cap down over his head and ears. Hudner then tried repeatedly to free Brown, interrupting the struggle from time to time to pack handfuls of snow into openings in the front of the fuselage from which smoke was pouring. No matter how hard he strained to lift the panel off Brown's legs, Hudner couldn't budge it.

"Jesse refrained from voicing despair; in fact he made no complaint of any kind. It was an effort for him to talk. He was obviously in terrible pain, though he was stoic about it. All I could do was tell him that help was on the way. At one point he said that if we couldn't get him free he wanted me to tell his wife Daisy how much he loved her. I said I would."

The helicopter arrived at last, some forty-five minutes after Hudner's crash landing. 1st Lt. Charles Ward, the pilot, brought only a small fire extinguisher that soon fizzled out. The ax proved useless as well, bouncing off the metal plate that held Brown's legs in its grip. In addition to trying to help Hudner, Ward had to keep an eye on his helicopter, which had defective brakes, making sure it stayed put on the hillside in the wind.

Hudner: "The only way to free him was to cut off his legs with my hunting knife, but even that would have been impossible because we couldn't position ourselves to do it. It would have been a hideous butchering anyway."

Hudner and Ward, having tried everything they could think of to bend the panel off Brown's leg, now admitted to themselves it was hopeless.

Hudner: "We were terribly frustrated. To have gone this far in getting to Jesse and then not being able to do anything to help him . . ."

As daylight began to fade, Ward called Hudner aside and told him they had to get out before dark since the helicopter was not rigged for night flying.

"We both knew that Jesse could not survive the night. I went back and told him we were going to get more help. He must have known by this time that it was all over. We hadn't been able to accomplish a damn thing."

Before the helicopter lifted off, Hudner walked back to the smoking Corsair one last time to say good-bye and found Brown mercifully unconscious.

"I spoke to him anyway, in case he could hear me. I told him we would be back. There was no response. He may have been dead at that time. I like to think he was. If I got any satisfaction out of any of this, it was that we had remained with him until the end. One of the worst things I can think of is dying with the knowledge that you are all alone. At least Jesse wasn't alone. Just being with him, giving him as much comfort as we could, made the whole effort worthwhile."

Hudner spent that night with the Marines at Koto-ri. "I didn't sleep a wink, despite the exertions of the day, because it was so cold in that tent and because I kept thinking about Jesse up there in the mountains."

Back aboard the *Leyte,* Captain T. V. Sisson asked Hudner about the possibility of sending in a flight surgeon to help recover the body. Hudner explained that the crash site lay in enemy territory and that it would not be worth the risk. Ensign Brown, a professional, would have understood that every Corsair pilot was needed to assist "those poor guys on the ground," as he had called them only the night before in a letter to his wife. (The letter continued: "In the last few days we've been doing a lot of flying, trying to help slow down the Chinese Communists and give support to some Marines who are surrounded. . . . I will write you again as soon as I can. I'll love you forever.")

An alternate plan was developed. Pilots of VH-32 sortied a four-plane section of Corsairs, flew to the crash site, and, in a Valkyrian tribute to a fallen comrade, cremated him in a blaze of napalm. The site is at Latitude 40 degrees 36' N; Longitude 127 degrees 06.

Hudner: "Jesse was held in high regard by his mates in the squadron. He was a modest person, with a good sense of humor, and had many friends."

In 1973, at a ceremony in Boston harbor, Thomas Hudner stood beside Daisy Brown as a *Knox*-class destroyer escort was commissioned into the U.S. Navy as DE-1089. The USS *Jesse Brown* was the first naval warship to be named for an African-American naval hero. She serves today in the Atlantic fleet.

62. LT. JOHN Y. LEE, ROK LIAISON

officer: "The Japanese, when they occupied Korea—very harsh! In school they prohibit the Korean to speak his own language. I was seventeen when the Americans defeated Japan in 1945. The first thing that happen was the burning of the Shinto shrines in the mountains. My village was Yunbaik. not far from Panmunjom, where the peace talks were later held. It was a small farm village of one hundred houses on a hill with pine trees. A river in back of the village was full of fishes. My father was a scholar and farmer who taught the Chinese classics to young people. Their parents gave us sacks of rice as sons' tuitions.

"We had five years peace before the North Koreans attack in 1950. When war started I was living with my mother in Seoul, a sophomore at Korea College studying literature to be a teacher and poet. Every Sunday I attend Bible class taught by an American missionary, Mrs. Mabel Rittgers Genso. Mother and I lived in a rented room near the campus when we heard the war coming down from the north. I discovered I was no longer entitled to spend my days in serene meditation of the classics.

"Mother asked me firmly to flee. If the North Koreans capture Seoul, they will kill me or recruit me into their army by force. I gathered up a few belongings and said good-bye. The Han River was swift and brown, flooded with rains. The bridge had been destroyed by South Korean engineers. I took off my clothings and jumped in the water with my bag on my head. I believe it was thirty minutes swimming before reaching the other side. There I rested and watched the city burning. Then I walked for many miles and saw the South Korean army and American army retreating, saw them disperse like common mob and die. The American army was very bad, turning and running, not caring for their unit or each other.

"At Pusan I discovered United States Marines with spirits very high and different from U.S. Army. To my eyes who had seen only failures, retreats, and miseries, the sight of Marines with their weapons, joking and laughing and ready to engage in combat, was pleasing. The first time since outbreak of the war, I smiled.

"Because I spoke some English, I became interpreter and liaison for Marines. My name was Yi Jong Yun, but they called me Lieutenant John Y. Lee and gave me a carbine. I also carried a pen and notebook in my pocket to write poems. They were published in various literary magazines during the war. Many were expressions of sadness at the scenes of old helpless people leaving their villages behind. When the Marines went north in October, I, riding in back of a truck, saw a line of geese flying south across the moonlighted sky. In my poem I asked them to convey a message to my parents that I was well and thinking of them.

"Chosin was the coldest place in Korea, the only place where no rice grows because of the weather. Hagaru was on a plateau, with the Chinese watching us during daytime, to attack at night. Hagaru was like an island in a Chinese sea, and we were like fishes in a fishbowl. All the Korean civilians I met wondered how the Marines would escape the trap. They thought this was impossible.

"My work was recruiting villager labor, middle-age men, to help construct the command post and carry back airdrop supplies too far out, sometimes under enemy fire. Three of them were killed, several wounded. My loaded carbine was enough to keep them working, but I yelled a thousand times.

"In our work we built a wooden toilet for General Oliver P. Smith. After the carpenter hammered the last nail, he went in and sat down on the seat. I saw the general come out of his house and walk toward the head—the Marine word for toilet. I couldn't think what to do, frozen with fear for the carpenter. The general opened the door to see him sitting on the general's private seat. But General Smith told me to let the man finish his need. General Smith was a modest gentleman. What would happen to a Korean carpenter and Korean army lieutenant if this had been a Japanese general? Our heads would be cut off!

"I was object of envy to Marines who were stationary in the foxholes in bitter cold because I was moving around all day yelling at laborers for faster works. At times my nose bleeded out of exhaustion. At end of the day I dragged my body to the tent where the Marines received me with appreciative eyes, and with a few hours sleep I became a new man.

"Most Marines referred to Koreans and Chinese as gooks. Unless you came to know them you are treated as alien—you have no feeling, no knowledge, no individual. But Korean also treat foreigners as nonperson. It would be impossible to expect all mankind to be a sensitive individual. But some Marines came to know me in headquarters. First Lieutenant Charles Sullivan and Master Sergeant William McClung and other Marines shared our lives together. Attack on them is attack on me and vice versa. We formed eternal brotherhood at Chosin. In the evening by the stove, Master Sergeant William McClung told me of his life in Japanese prison during the world war. I remember most the part about his hands tied to a post one day while B-29 bombers were raiding and he had to bear the concussion of explosions of his own country's bombs.

"My work was also to maintain liaison with local authority. The Communist members of the village government fled before us, but their family was still behind. About three hundred people still hid in the village. There was the wife of the Communist party chief. I asked what she would do when the Marines go south. 'I will follow them,' she said. I asked her what good the Communists did for the people of Chosin. She could not think so. She was kind to me and my laborers and fed us with potato and corn cakes. They ate herbs from the mountain, Chinese cabbage and hot peppers, and kimchi made from radishes and cabbage. This woman was eight months pregnant. I always wonder what happen to her after we went south from Hagaru.

"My work was also Civil Affairs Officer. The Marines needed cooperation and friendship of the people. If they have any hostile element they could inflict damage to us, they could burn the ammunition dump, poison our water, or become spies against us. In visiting the people I used the most respectful language my father taught me. I told them the Marines were watching them, that one hostile act might bring massive machine-gun fire from the Marines because they could not divide Korean friend from Korean enemy. Otherwise, the Marines would protect them and not destroy their lives and properties.

"One evening I was visiting one house to another, and I observed about twenty people assemble silently. I worried why they were meeting, and I hid in a shadow until they all went indoors, then looked at them through the window. In their hands I saw old Bibles and hymn books they must have brought from deep hiding places. They began to sing with low voices, then prayed together. I saw their faces in torment for their souls, because they had suffered spiritually under Communist domination, denied to worship God and tortured for their belief. When the Marines came they regained their precious right to worship—but for how long? They knew the Marines were surrounded by the enemy and in a few days the enemy would occupy the village again. Their barns would be destroyed, they would have no food to eat and no place to go in the brutal winter. Through the window I saw many crying while the services were conducting. I knelt down in the snow outside the window and prayed for them. I asked God to witness their suffering and visit them in coming days when the Marines have departed.

"How can I express my admiration for the United States Marines? I wish I could be a Korean Homer for all those heroes. When I was first attached to them I was an outsider, stranger, an alien. For a while I watched them and saw they were a different type of people. By the end I was a part of them. I am an attorney now in Virginia. When the Chosin Few have their reunion, I am there to hold the hands of my brothers once more."

63.

THE AIRDROPS CONTINUED, with planes spilling a profusion of red, blue, yellow, green, and orange parachutes that delivered loads of rations, ammunition, and fuel into the perimeter. Though the airdrop operation was far from perfect, the outcome of the breakout would owe much to the dedication and skill of Air Force General William H. Tunner's Combat Cargo Command and the Marine Air Wing's twin-engine transports.

2nd Lt. Thomas Gibson, 4.2" Mortar Company, 5th Marines: "It was obvious that some of the stuff was packed by the Army because we got paper plates, paper napkins—and, so help me, *condoms*."

In happier days, when the North Koreans were being pushed toward the Yalu, Hagaru was regarded as a secure, rear-area base, and so the Division's post-exchange section had sent up loads of nonessentials aimed at improving morale, in case morale needed improving. Among these was a gigantic load of Tootsie Rolls, described in the official history as "a caramel confection much esteemed by Stateside youngsters for its long-lasting qualities." (General Smith: "In the fight from Hagaru to Koto-ri, these Tootsie Rolls were an important adjunct to the rations.")

General Tunner himself flew into Hagaru on December 4 and offered to send in planes as fast as the Hagaru strip could take them—and evacuate the encircled garrison by air. The notion might have seemed appealing at first, until it became clear that such an evacuation would finally reduce the perimeter to the tiny airstrip itself, and that the last few units would lack the military strength to defend themselves against a tightening noose of Chinese. It would also mean that the division would have to abandon all its heavy weapons and equipment. Smith, while expressing his appreciation of the offer, informed the Air Force general that instead of flying his men out, Marine R4Ds had already flown in more than 500 infantry replacements.

Tunner wasn't the only general who dropped in for a visit that day. Lt. Col. Carl Youngdale, C.O. 11th Marines: "All of a sudden there was somebody outside shouting for General Smith. The conference came to a dead halt as we cocked our ears. An aide was shouting that General Almond wanted to see General Smith. The general stood up very slowly, buttoned up his parka, cinched the belt around his waist, and stepped outside. I followed him and overheard part of their conversation. Almond was telling the general we had nothing to worry about and went on to paint a rosy picture of the division being covered by B-17s and B-29s. 'We're going to give you a safe escort,' he said, 'all the way back to Hamhung.' General Smith looked him straight in the eye and said, 'I think there will be sufficient fighting for all of us.' "

Almond found time during the visit to award Distinguished Service Crosses to Smith, Litzenberg, Murray, and Lt. Col. Olin Beall. An hour later, by helicopter, Almond was in Koto, pinning a DSC on Lt. Col. William Reidy, of all people, whose Second Battalion, 31st Infantry, had been led in disarray from Funchilin Pass up to Koto-ri by Major Gurfein. In the award document, Reidy is described as having "distinguished himself by extraordinary heroism . . . in keeping with the highest traditions of the military service."

The Army couldn't seem to do anything right as far as the Marines were concerned. Sergeant Asa L. Gearing recalls seeing an Army officers' mess tent in Hagaru that was stocked with canned delicacies and a wide assortment of liquor. "This stuff was intended for Almond's use after Hagaru became the X Corps forward command post. I'm not saying it was a sin for him to have stuff like this, but I couldn't help noticing that General Smith ate what the lowliest private in the division ate."

Sergeant Henry O. Feuer, Weapons 1/7: "Except for the metal spoon, everyone had quit carrying the aluminum mess gear, since there was no hot chow anyway except the occasional flapjacks. The spoon, though, was useful for prying loose chunks of frozen C-rations."

Sergeant Gearing: "The subzero temperature around the clock created some pretty awful effects with facial hair. Your nose seemed to run all the time, and the snot would freeze on the upper edge of your mustache. Residue from C-rations and some of your hawking and spitting would collect and freeze on your beard. Some guys looked like they could live for a week on the crap they had in their beards."

Brigadier General Edward Craig, assistant division commander, arrived in San Antonio on December 2. On the flight from El Paso—in an Air Force transport—a crew member struck up a conversation with him and mentioned the plight of the Marines at the Chosin Reservoir. Craig didn't know what the enlisted man was talking about. "General, your outfit's in bad trouble. I guess you haven't seen the headlines." General Craig: "It was a great shock when I did see them. 'Eighth Army in Retreat; Marines Still Trapped.' There was something of an uproar across the country because the American people had been led to expect the troops to come home by Christmas, and now the Chinese had created virtually a new war, and that war was going against us. My recollection is that the newspapers unanimously predicted the destruction of the 1st Marine Division."

The following day Craig received a phone call from General Cates, the Commandant, ordering him back to Korea without delay. Craig's reaction was a combination of frustration and sorrow: sorrow at having to leave his father's side; frustration at being ten thousand miles away from his true home, the 1st Marine Division.

Press correspondents were now arriving in the C-47s and R4Ds. The arrival of Marguerite Higgins of the *New York Herald Tribune* caused a general stir among the Hagaru Marines, who gawked openly at her as she swept by. Young, comely, and very aggressive, she expected to be treated on an equal basis with her male colleagues. It was not to be.

Corporal Roy Pearl: "What came out of my mouth when I saw her was 'My God.' I hadn't seen one of those in months."

General Smith, not prepared to deal with a female correspondent, ruled that "considering the possibility of enemy attack, she must leave the Hagaru perimeter by nightfall."

Higgins found Lt. Col. Raymond Murray concentrating on preparations for the breakout to Koto; she interviewed him briefly. She scribbled in her notebook that Murray was "a haggard ghost of the officer I met at Inchon." The breakout from Yudam-ni, he told her, had been possible because the Chinese were unable to observe one of the basic principles of war: they didn't concentrate their forces where they would do the most good. "If they had massed at our point of exit we would never have gotten out of there; but by trying to keep us encircled they diffused their strength."

Did the colonel think they would make the same mistake at Hagaru?

"We're counting on it," said Murray.

Corporal Alan Herrington: "I was waiting at the airstrip with my pal Curtis, who had been hit by shrapnel in the stomach and groin. He was on a stretcher, feeling a good deal of pain, when Miss Higgins came over and hunkered down with her notepad. She had a stuffy, snobbish way about her, and it seemed to me she was only interested in getting her story and didn't give a damn about the pain Curtis was in. But Curtis was game. She asked him what was the toughest thing he had to face in the campaign. Curtis thought it over. Then he smiled. 'The toughest thing,' he said, 'is getting three inches of dick out of six inches of clothing when I need to take a leak.' That was the first laugh we had had in a long time, but Miss Higgins was already interviewing the guy in the next stretcher."

Her view of the Chosin Marines—the survivors, she called them—was less than upbeat. In an article published in the *Saturday Evening Post,* Higgins admitted wondering if they had the will to make the final push to the sea. In describing the men themselves, she mentioned how ragged and woebegone they looked, their faces swollen and bleeding from the lash of the wind. Still, it is not entirely clear why the Marines resented her presence. Alpha Bowser suggests it was simply because of her arrogant manner.

General Smith was calm and confident as usual. Captain Michael Capraro, the division's public information officer—back on the job after his escape from Hell Fire Valley—heard the general tell a group of correspondents, "Nothing in the world can stop a Marine division with its massive air and artillery support, as long as the division is united."

Colonel Bowser was putting the finishing touches on his plan for the move to Koto when Lt. Col. Joseph Winecoff, the assistant G-3, said, "This is a new experience for Marines."

"What is?"

"Retreat. I'll have to look it up in the manual!"

General Smith, standing nearby, bridled at Winecoff's mild jest. "We have to attack in order to move," he explained. "You can't call that a retreat."

The Marine general was kept busy that afternoon with reporters' questions, many of them revolving around the word he objected to. The matter was more or less settled when a British reporter asked him directly if this was a retreat.

"Certainly not," said Smith. "There can be no retreat when there's no rear. You can't retreat, or even withdraw, when you're surrounded. The only thing you can do is break out, and in order to do that you have to attack, and that is what we're about to do."

Somehow Smith's explanation was turned into the ringing battle cry ever after associated with the Marines at the reservoir: "Retreat, hell—we're attacking in another direction!" Within twenty-four hours the line had appeared on front pages across America. (It echoed a World War I utterance that was already part of Marine lore. Moving up to the Belleau Wood sector in 1918, Captain Lloyd Williams was overtaken by a messenger bringing an order from the French commander to retreat. "Retreat, hell," said the Marine officer, "we just got here.") Captain Martin Sexton, the general's aide who was present during the exchange at Hagaru, is certain Smith did not use the word *hell*. And according to Alpha Bowser's recollection, what Smith said was, "Heck, all we're doing is attacking in a different direction."

Late in the morning of December 6, General Smith called a meeting of troop commanders and senior staffers and issued assignments for the Hagaru breakout. Litzenberg's 7th Marines would once again lead the way, attacking astride the road with all three battalions. Murray's 5th Marines would hold the perimeter (and, it was hoped, East Hill) until Litzenberg had progressed far enough down the road to permit Murray to follow. Except for drivers and the wounded, everyone was to move on foot on either side of the motor column, not only to furnish close-in protection for the trucks but to reduce frostbite casualties by keeping the troops active. One of his staffers reminded Smith that the regimental convoys would consist of more than 1,000 vehicles, and this led to a brief discussion as to the advisability of trying to bring them all out.

Smith: "I finally decided to leave to the Chinese the decision as to whether a vehicle was to be destroyed or not, but we were going to start out with all our vehicles."

64.

COLONEL ALPHA BOWSER: "ON December 4 we got some bad news. Our chief engineer, Lt. Col. John Partridge, came in to tell us that a twenty-four-foot section of the bridge at Funchilin Pass had been blown out by the Chinese. This bridge was about three miles south of Koto. My personal, private reaction when I heard the news was something akin to despair." The bridge, which spanned a gorge, was critical to the movement of the division's vehicles and tanks. There was no other way out, and—because of the steepness of the rocky slope above and below the bridge—no possibility of constructing a bypass.

General Smith: "The enemy could not have picked a better spot to give us trouble."

It was here that water coming through a tunnel from the reservoir was fed into large pipes called penstocks, which then carried it to a power plant in the valley below. The point where the water was transferred from the tunnel into the penstocks was covered by a substation containing the valve controls. The building was on the uphill side of the road, which at this spot crossed a one-way concrete bridge over a deep chasm. It was this bridge that the Chinese had destroyed.

Lt. Col. Partridge: "It was a damned serious situation, because there was no prefabricated bridging in Hagaru or Koto-ri, and it would take too long to construct a timber-trestle bridge. I proposed an air drop of treadway bridge sections at Koto-ri, which we would somehow transport to the site following the advance of our infantry elements. The trouble was, these sections weighed twenty-five hundred pounds apiece."

Partridge recalls his conversation with General Smith on the matter.

"How many sections do you need?"

"Four would be good."

"To your knowledge, have bridge sections ever been dropped by parachute?"

"Never heard of it, General."

"We'll have to do a test-drop then, so we can see the extent to which the sections get damaged."

"I've already thought of that, sir."

"Other sections could be brought up to Chinhung-ni from the south. If the drop at Koto-ri is unsuccessful, it might be possible for Colonel Schmuck's battalion to fight its way north, bringing the sections up the mountain from below."

Partridge had thought of that also.

The general then asked Partridge if he was planning to assemble bridge timbers at Koto in the event that all plans for installing the metal treadway went awry. (A trestle bridge might barely be strong enough in the limited time available, if the Marines were lucky, to support the division's tanks and heavy equipment.)

"General, we're already assembling bridge timbers at Koto-ri."

Smith could see that his chief engineer was becoming uncomfortable, even annoyed, by the questions. "He finally reminded me in no uncertain terms that he had gotten us across the Han River, had provided the necessary roads and the necessary airstrips, and that he could now be counted on to fix us a bridge. I told him to proceed with his plans."

The following day Partridge flew low over Funchilin Pass in a spotter plane and discovered a new and equally ominous development. Not far south of the substation and the downed bridge, the steel cableway trestle that crossed over from one side of the road to the other had been neatly dynamited off its concrete supports by the Chinese and dropped athwart the road. Even if the bridge at the substation was replaced, the downed trestle three quarters of a mile down the road would block all traffic most effectively.

One of the miracles of the Chosin Reservoir campaign, from the Marines' viewpoint, was that the Army's 58th Treadway Bridge Company had reached Koto-ri before the Chinese shut the gate in both directions. This tiny outfit consisted of four treadway bridge trucks and a handful of men under a lieutenant named Ward. The four trucks were loaded not with bridge sections, however, but with prefabricated building material to be used in the construction of the X Corps command post planned for Hagaru.

Partridge: "The air drop of the bridge sections was scheduled for 0900 on the seventh of December."

65.

EARLY ON THE AFTERNOON OF December 5, Lt. Col. Raymond Murray called a meeting of his battalion commanders and staff and delivered a stirring exhortation. "We're going to hold our present position until the 7th Marines clear the road to Koto-ri. When the time comes for us to march, we'll be coming out like Marines, not like stragglers. This is not a retreat. There are more Chinese between us and the sea than there are to the north of us. General Smith said it best: We're attacking in a different direction. Any officer who doubts our ability to break out had better catch himself a case of frostbite, and I'll see that he's evacuated. We're coming out like Marines."

After the meeting broke up, Murray had a visit from an old acquaintance, Keyes Beech of the *Chicago Daily News*.

"You should have been with us at Yudam-ni, Keyes. You'd have gotten a hell of a story up there."

Murray broke out a bottle of bourbon and poured them both a drink. The reporter asked him bluntly if he thought the Marines could get out of the trap.

"We got out of Yudam-ni, didn't we? If we could get out of there, we can get out of here."

Murray then revealed something to Beech that he hadn't mentioned to anyone else. "I didn't think we could do it," he said, and as he began to talk about the Yudam-ni breakout, he wiped tears away with the dirty sleeve of his parka.

It was almost dark. PFC James G. Collins, Able/7, was trying to scrape out a foxhole for himself when he saw a young Marine carrying a seabag and a brand-new BAR up the hill. He stopped to ask Corporal Buddy Jameson a question, and Jameson turned and pointed at Collins. "Up comes this clean-shaven kid with a big grin and I nearly had a stroke, because it was my own brother,

Edmon. After we embraced and pounded each other on the back, he told me he was AWOL. Instead of reporting to Baker Company, 1st Marines, he had climbed aboard a plane bound for Hagaru so he could be with me. I was very glad to see him, but this AWOL business worried me because I knew he was in serious trouble."

James took him over to his platoon leader, Lt. Bobby Bradley. "This here's my older brother, sir, and he's AWOL from the 1st Marines."

"Very good," said the lieutenant. "We need every man we can get. He'll join your fire team, Collins. You're short a man, aren't you?"

Collins asked the officer if he thought some kind of disciplinary action was in store for Edmon.

"I doubt it," said Bradley. "He didn't go AWOL in the face of the enemy, after all—he went AWOL *to* face the enemy. Big difference."

There was a fifty percent alert that night. Edmon stood James's watch without telling him; in other words, he didn't wake his brother up when it was time for James to relieve him. "That's the kind of big brother he was."

In later years Alpha Bowser admitted that, unlike General Smith, he had not been fully confident that the Division could extract itself from the trap. "For one thing, I kept wondering if Koto-ri would even *be* there in a few more hours. We knew by now that elements of the 76th, 77th, and 78th Chinese divisions were in position along the eleven-mile stretch between Hagaru and Koto-ri. We also knew that elements of the 89th and 60th Chinese divisions were deployed near Koto. And we still had the bridge problem to solve, not to mention the trestle below it. Tactically, the situation was not promising."

After dark, Colonel Bowser stepped outside, hoping to see a few stars, which would indicate the possibility of close air support in the morning; but all he found was solid overcast. From down the line of tents his ears picked up the sound of music. A group of young Marines was singing "Bless 'em All" with new lyrics: "So we're saying good-bye to them all, as southward our asses we haul; the Army's retreating, Marines are gum-beating, so cheer up, me lads, fuck 'em all. . . ." This was followed by a spirited rendition of "The Marines' Hymn":

From the halls of Montezuma to the shores of Tripoli,
we will fight our country's battles, on the land as on
   the sea.
First to fight for right and freedom and to keep our
   honor clean,
we are proud to claim the title of United States
   Marine.

Bowser: "It was quite remarkable to hear those youngsters singing their hearts out that way, despite the difficulties facing us down
the road."

Back inside again, Bowser remarked to General Smith, "If they
have the heart to sing like that at a time like this, maybe the Chinese don't have much of a chance."

The general took the pipe from his mouth. "Bowser, they never
had much of a chance."

There were a number of problems connected with replacing the
bombed bridge. No one knew if the special parachutes would be
big enough to do the job. The treadway bridge came in four sections, each weighing more than two tons. Eight sections in all were
to be dropped at Koto, enough for two complete bridges. Captain
Cecil W. Hospelhorn and ten enlisted specialists of the 2348th
Quartermaster Air Supply rigged and loaded the sections, each into
one C-117, the so-called Flying Boxcar. One of the sections was
then test-dropped in a field near Hungnam, floating to earth under
two forty-eight-foot parachutes. The section was badly bent when
it hit the ground, adding to the general apprehension at division
headquarters.

Major Henry Woessner, chief of operations, 7th Marines: "I recall thinking at the time: those bridge sections are an awfully weak
link for us to depend on for getting the division out."

The breakout began before dawn on December 6, the column moving steadily through Major Edwin Simmons's roadblock at the foot
of East Hill. The road from Hagaru to Koto-ri was relatively flat,
with the mountains set back some distance. Davis's 1/7 advanced
along the paralleling ridge to the right while Lockwood's 2/7
moved down the road itself with the remnant of Barber's Fox Company leading the way. At General Smith's direction, the senior

Army officer at Hagaru, Lt. Col. Barry K. Anderson, had organized a few GIs into a small provisional battalion. The unit, called 31/7 by the Marines, was now picking its way along the ridge to the left. Hungnam and the empty troopships lay at anchor fifty-six miles away.

PFC James G. Collins, Able/7: "We were taking ridge after ridge on the right to protect the convoy, running up against some pretty well-entrenched Chinese. Lt. Bradley called in the Corsairs, and one of the pilots got confused and opened up with his 20-mm guns too close to us, and a guy in our squad got his foot shot off at the ankle. My brother Edmon and me helped carry him down to the road. His name was Reinke and he kept saying, 'What'll my dad say?' A couple of hours later I unsnapped one of the flaps on my cartridge belt and found a piece of bone the size and shape of a cigarette frozen in there; it was a bone from Reinke's foot."

When Collins started back upslope, an Army lieutenant appeared out of the twilight to say he needed help taking out a roadblock. Edmon and the two other Marines were already halfway up the hill, gone from sight.

"Sir, I belong to Able Company, 7th Marines."

"That doesn't matter. You're coming with me."

After the roadblock was cleared, James decided it would be too dangerous to go wandering around in the dark, password or no password; he spent the night with the Army lieutenant and his GIs. Next morning he started hunting around for Able Company and the first man he recognized was Corporal Gilbert Holter of the third squad. When James asked him where he could find his brother, Holter burst into tears. Edmon, he said, had been killed late the previous day. He took out Edmon's wallet and his wristwatch and handed them over. He said Edmon had been shot by a sniper as he stood up to pitch a can of C-rations to another Marine. His body was never sent home.

James Collins: "I just hope and pray it was recovered and buried in Hagaru before we left."

Shortly before noon, December 6, Lt. Col. Randolph Lockwood, rounding a bend in the road two miles south of Hagaru, was confronted by a bizarre tableau. A dead GI with a bullet hole in his cheek was sitting upright behind the wheel of a jeep. The jeep was facing north; Lockwood presumed he had tried to make a run for it from the ambush in Hell Fire Valley. The vehicle had veered off the road, jumped the embankment, and landed on the gravel at the edge of the river. The Chinese had stripped him of everything but his long johns.

Lt. Col. Raymond Davis watched from the top of Hill 1276 as Lockwood's skimpy battalion resumed its southward march astride the road. Four hundred yards to their front, a wide ravine ran perpendicular to the road; the ravine was crammed with enemy soldiers. As soon as Davis spotted them he took Corporal Pearl's radio handset and alerted Lockwood to their presence. For the better part of an hour, Lockwood tried to direct mortar fire into the ravine, with little success. He later explained that the ground was icy and the mortar-tube baseplates slipped with each shot, resulting in a scattered pattern. He did finally managed to get some rounds on target, sending a few Chinese running.

Lockwood: "After we got moving again, enemy fire became so intense that Fox Company was virtually pinned down. I sent for Lieutenant Bey and told him to take his Dog-Easy Company down the ditch in column as close to the enemy's left flank as possible. Then I got Lieutenant Abell on the radio—he was now in command of Fox—and told him to prepare to assault the Chinese frontally as soon as Bey moved against their flank. I went with Bey. We negotiated the distance without being seen, hugging the embankment between the road and the riverbed. When we were in position I told Bey to have his men fix bayonets. I drew my .45, and we went scrambling up the embankment and over the top like a World War One assault, hitting the enemy with everything we had. When Lieutenant Abell launched Fox Company's attack, the whole affair turned into a textbook case-study, a splendid thing to watch unfold. The enemy was roundly beaten. Those not dispatched in the flank attack were eliminated by Abell's sharpshooters."

Lockwood was conversing with Abell shortly after the attack when a harried rifleman came up to them. "Sir?"

"What is it?"

"Mr. Dunne's been killed." The sergeant turned and pointed. "He's up there."

The two officers walked up the road and, as Lockwood puts it, "viewed the body in shocked silence." 1st Lt. John M. Dunne, the last of the original officers who formed Fox Company back at Camp Pendleton in July, and a close friend of Abell's, was stretched out on his back, his eyes open to the sky.

The roadblock had been breached, the Chinese driven back, and the way opened to Koto, at least for now. At that moment, in a sudden spray of snow and squealing brakes, Colonel Litzenberg pulled up in a jeep and climbed down to the ground.

"Why are these troops standing around?" he asked in the usual roar. "Move out!"

"We're in the process of re-forming, sir."

Litzenberg barked back, "I said *move out!*" and delivered a hard slap on Lockwood's back.

Lockwood: "He climbed into the jeep and snapped a peremptory command at the driver, who then spun the jeep around in reverse gear. I was literally knocked off my feet by the rear bumper and sent sliding across the road—unhurt but, let us say, disconcerted."

On the eastern ridgeline a group of 31/7 GIs under an Army captain captured over a hundred Chinese who had stood up, hands in the air, as the GIs approached. Not a shot was fired. The prisoners were ushered down to the road and turned over to the Marine MPs. At this point the Army captain decided to keep his troops on the road, thus leaving a segment of the convoy unprotected.

General Smith: "I had quite a time with the Army people—they had no spirit. We helped them as best we could. We even flew in weapons for them, as they had thrown theirs away. They expected us to take care of them, feed them, put up their tents. We disabused them of this idea. Eventually we salvaged three hundred eighty-five of these men and with other soldiers formed a provisional battalion, which I attached to Litzenberg. It was pitiful. Litzenberg gave them the task of guarding the left flank of the column in the breakout from Hagaru to Koto-ri. But whenever the Chinese attacked, the soldiers simply went through the column to the other side."

Lt. Ralph Abell watched another 31/7 unit taking some sniper fire on the left. The troops reacted by drifting down the slope and onto the road rather than returning fire. Abell walked up to the Army captain in charge and asked him what he thought he was doing.

"My men are freezing in the wind up there," he said. "They need a little break."

Abell remarked later that he couldn't bear it that the Army officer would leave the flank exposed like that and didn't give a damn. "Get your troops back upslope," he told the captain.

"You can't talk to me that way."

Of all people to show up at that moment, Colonel Litzenberg was suddenly right there between them, and when he got the gist of the exchange, he turned to the captain and said, "When a Marine lieutenant tells you what to do, you *will* follow his command, since he represents *me*." The officer turned away and reluctantly herded his GIs back up the slope.

Lt. Col. Frederick Dowsett, executive officer, 7th Marines: "But they came back down soon afterward. I sent word to the captain that I was going to send a Marine outfit to chase them up the slope and that if they refused to go we would open fire on them. Later that afternoon their leader, Lieutenant Colonel Anderson, appeared on the road and told me he had lost control of the provisional battalion."

66.

DURING THIS INTERVAL OF CON-
fusion and doubt, the Chinese were able to work their way in close
to the vehicle column.

1st Lt. Charles Sullivan, assistant headquarters commandant, 7th
Marines: "It was around 0200 when our segment of the convoy
got into trouble. The Chinese were close but not yet shooting. I
could hear them yelling." Having served in China from 1946 to
1949, Sullivan understood enough to know they were calling out
to the Chinese prisoners of the Marines, warning them that an
attack was about to be launched, telling them that if they got up
and ran in a certain direction when the shooting started they could
escape.

Sullivan didn't have time to take any tactical countermeasures
because the attack began immediately. About half the prisoners
scrambled away in the direction indicated, which was toward the
railroad embankment, while about a quarter of them did nothing,
probably because they were wounded or frostbitten. The rest dived
into the ditch. Many who stayed behind were shot to death by the
Chinese attackers. It was later speculated that the slaughter was a
kind of political mercy killing, that the prisoners were considered
ideologically contaminated by their brief contact with Westerners.
Sullivan: "Of the hundred and fifty or so prisoners we started with,
I'd say there were fifteen left alive when the firing died out."

Major Frederick Simpson, headquarters commandant, with the
assistance of Master Sergeant William McClung, deployed the
cooks, bakers, drivers, and bandsmen and drove off the enemy.
Captain Donald France, Litzenberg's intelligence chief, was killed
in the melee. Among those wounded were Lt. Col. Dowsett, the
regimental exec, and Chaplain Griffin.

Lt. (jg) Cornelius J. Griffin, U.S. Navy: "I referred to our silver-
haired colonel as Silent Homer because his voice carried a mile.

Would you care to hear about the first time I met him? It was at the railroad siding at Camp Pendleton. When he set eyes on me, he introduced himself in the usual tactful Marine manner. 'Jesus Christ,' he said, 'is this what I get for a chaplain?'

"Well, I was mortified. 'If the obviously prayerful colonel can devise a way to ameliorate the situation,' I said, 'the chaplain in question would certainly be gratified.' He came over and told me he would either make a Marine out of me or else get my ass shot off in the attempt. He then assigned me a clerk—Sergeant Matthew Caruso of Rocky Hill, Connecticut—and the two of us moved into an unused Quonset hut to hear confessions. That site today is occupied by a beautiful chapel known to Marines everywhere as the Caruso Memorial Chapel, in honor of the valiant young man who attempted to save my life on the night of December 6, 1950, and lost his in the bargain.

"Though a Navy officer, I was very happy with the Marines and greatly admired their indomitable spirit. Warriors all, there was not a warmonger among them. They were in Korea essentially for the purpose of stopping the war, of preventing the Northerners from conquering the Southerners, and they were experts at what they did. I thought of all this as a kind of homeopathic procedure, using war to stop war. . . .

"But I was telling you about my stalwart champion, Sergeant Caruso. We were in an ambulance somewhere between Hagaru and Koto-ri and had just picked up Sergeant John Audas, one of the heroes of the fight for Toktong Pass. He had been left in the ditch by mistake and was nearly frozen by the time we found him. Dr. Robert Wedemeyer was tending to him inside the vehicle when one of the corpsmen quietly informed me that the young Mexican-American Marine in the corner was dying. I hunkered down beside him, took his hand, and was administering the last rites of the church when there was a burst of fire outside, the bullets striking the ambulance even though it was clearly marked with a big red cross against a white background. Sergeant Caruso threw himself between me and the gunner outside and was instantly killed. One of the bullets caught me in the jaw and another in the right shoulder. After a corpsman stopped my bleeding I heard Dr. Wedemeyer tell him to remove Sergeant Caruso's body from the ambulance, and when I objected to this he said, 'This ambulance is for the living, Father.' So I had to watch in anguish as Sergeant Caruso and the young Mexican-American, who had also died in that squall of fire, were carried outside. . . . Your readers might like to know that Sergeant Caruso's wife bore a son less than a week after his death, and eighteen years later I received a phone call from Daniel Caruso: 'Father, I want you to be the first, after my mother, to know I'm joining the Marine Corps.'

"And if you'll permit me one more little anecdote? Several weeks after the Chosin Reservoir campaign, Silent Homer appeared in my ward at Oak Knoll Naval Hospital in California, grabbed my hand, and shouted, 'Well? Didn't I do exactly what I said?'

" 'And what was that, Colonel?'

" 'Why, I damn near got you killed, but I made a Marine out of you!'

"A high honor indeed. I now had the privilege—sealed in blood—of calling myself a United States Marine."

Sergeant Robert Gault, Graves Registration: "Yes, the enemy threw some devilments at us that night. Everything was a mess on the road, but Colonel Litzenberg got it straightened out with his wonderful yelling. It was always such a comfort to hear him. No, sir, the Army didn't do too good that night. If they had stayed on our flank like they was told, a lot of good Marines, like my friend Captain Donald France, would be alive today."

Lt. Charles Sullivan: "That was also the night we lost Master Sergeant William McClung. I was always bugging him to keep his chin strap fastened. He hated that helmet, and instead of wearing it he would usually carry it. I can see him now, standing there with the helmet under his arm. 'Put it on,' I'd say, and he would comply with a smile. 'And do the strap.' But the one order I should have given was for him to *keep* it on, with the chin strap fastened."

Lt. John Y. Lee and Lt. Sullivan, watching him drag wounded Marines off the back of a truck, saw the helmet roll off his head. A mortar round exploded nearby and a piece of shrapnel caught him in the forehead.

Lieutenant Lee: "We saw him killed. There was so much shooting and explosive, no one dared climb up to help wounded Marines in a burning truck of ammunition. Then I saw Sergeant McClung climbing into it with bullets all over, but he was not thinking of his life or death. I still cannot understand how he could work so much before he was hit."

At daybreak Lt. Sullivan spotted a group of Chinese heading in his direction from the other side of the railroad embankment. "They were so close," he said afterward, "that I had no time to do anything but attack." Nearby on the ground was a dead Marine's M-1 tipped with a bayonet. Sullivan snatched it up and hurled it like a javelin at the nearest soldier, skewering him in the chest. The others turned and fled.

Lt. John Y. Lee: "When the fighting was over I could not stop weeping over the death of Master Sergeant McClung, a fine Marine and humane person who cared for others more than his own life." In a letter to McClung's daughter many years later, Lee wrote this: "He was a father figure to many young Marines and one South Korean lieutenant. I will always think of this great man."

Colonel Davis appeared at Corporal Pearl's side to tell him he had to go down the road some distance and that the radioman was to remain where he was. Pearl sat down to rest on a stump, took out his wallet, and tried to extract a snapshot of his family; it took a long time because of his stiff fingers. He sat there staring at the photo by the light of a burning truck. "The people in the picture were like people I had known a long time ago."

Then a voice called out, "Hey, Pearl, you know what you're sitting on?" Pearl took a look. What he had thought was a stump was a Chinese soldier covered with snow and ice, seated with his trunk bent far over. Pearl was sitting on his back.

Colonel Davis had told the corporal he would contact him by radio, and he did. "Pearl," he said, "Colonel Dowsett's been hit and they've made me regimental exec."

"Congratulations, sir."

"Major Sawyer is taking over the First Battalion and I'm turning you over to him."

"Very good, sir."

"Where's my new radio operator?" asked a gruff voice behind him. Pearl was unhappy about the change in commanding officers; he had grown accustomed to Colonel Davis's ways and rhythms, and his calm, even temperament. "Major Webb Sawyer was a taller gentleman, for one thing, and I had to hustle to keep up with his long stride. And his personality was less friendly. He turned out to be a crackerjack battalion commander, but I sorely missed Colonel Davis."

* * *

Somewhere on the road between Hagaru and Koto-ri, Major Warren Morris, 3/7's exec, had a brief conversation with Major Maurice Roach, Litz's logistics officer. Morris told Roach that Colonel William Harris had been acting strangely ever since they left Yudam-ni—talking about how he would never allow himself to be taken prisoner again, keeping his backpack filled with rations and first-aid supplies, wearing it on his back at all times. "It was obvious he was shook," said Morris.

Captain William R. Earney, operations officer, 3/7: "He had taken to wandering around alone, so I didn't think it peculiar when I saw him standing by himself about a hundred feet up a ravine east of the road."

1st Lt. Thomas M. Sullivan's platoon had been firing from the side of the road away from the enemy, using the ditch as cover, when Colonel Harris showed up alone and asked him to identify himself and his unit.

"Sir, Lieutenant Sullivan, Second Platoon, Item Company."

Harris stretched out his arm, pointing to the east. "Move your platoon across the road and line up along the railroad embankment. I have a job for you."

Sullivan was sure the colonel was going to send his platoon up against a Chinese machine gun overlooking the road, "a mission that didn't have a whole lot of appeal to us. I was able to get the men in position without losing anyone. We lay there in the cold wind awaiting further orders, but the colonel never came back."

The last anyone saw of Lt. Col. William Harris, USMC, was around 6:30 A.M., December 7. Despite a painstaking and risky search by Sergeant Gault and his Graves Registration team, Harris was never found. Gault: "I asked everybody I met if they had seen the colonel. Lots of folks had seen him. One fellow said he saw him five minutes ago. Where? Down that way. We went down there, and farther too, but there was no sign of him. In our work, you understand, we always tried to work fast getting the bodies out, so the fellows wouldn't have to stare at them and worry about how many of their friends were gone. Often the fellows pestered us while we were working, wanting news about their friends, but nobody came near us while we were looking for the colonel. We looked behind rocks, under boulders, in ditches and Chinese bunkers—because when a man is wounded, he'll usually crawl someplace out of the wind and hide from the enemy. . . . You get a feel for it after a while, and I could tell we weren't going to find him. That man was just gone."

Litzenberg sent Major Roach back up the road with a platoon with orders to venture into the ravine where Harris had last been seen, calling out his name as loudly as he could. "If he's hurt, he'll hear you and answer."

Major Roach: "We climbed up that ravine farther than we should have. We went in so far that we passed a blazing fire with several Chinese soldiers huddled around it. They pretended not to see us and we pretended not to see them, and all the while I was calling out at the top of my voice: 'William Harris, this is Hal Roach. Answer me if you can. Are you there?' "

Captain William Earney, possibly the last Marine to see the colonel alive, was the one who later broke the news to his father, the chief of the Marine Air Wing. Major General Field Harris came aboard Admiral Doyle's flagship in Hungnam harbor that evening, seeking solitude. Doyle wrote later that he noticed Harris was unusually subdued.

"Anything on your mind?"

Harris told the admiral that his son Bill had been reported missing near the reservoir. "To my knowledge," says Doyle, "that evening was his only concession to grief. He was too conscientious a Marine, too aware of his responsibilities to those still fighting to slack off in any way—but it must have been hard."

67. COLONEL LITZENBERG: "IT WAS about this time we learned that two Chinese regiments, the advance elements of a fresh corps, had reached our area from Manchuria. Had we delayed another twenty-four hours to perfect all the details of the breakout, we would have been faced with fighting our way through a whole new corps rather than staving off two regiments on our flank. That might have meant the difference between victory and defeat on our march down the mountain."

At times the wind whipped the snow into blinding clouds, slowing progress on the road as effectively as the Chinese. Only about three miles had been covered by the time dusk fell on December 6.

Corpsman Claypool: "This section of the road and the riverbank beside it had been an assembly point for the Chinese in their assaults against Hagaru, and bunches of them had been caught by artillery and air. Bodies had piled up near a small bridge, eventually sinking into the snow; and then the snow had turned hard and what you ended up with was a strata of corpses encased in ice. From a bridge we watched a bulldozer working the road, smoothing it out for the convoy. The driver swept the blade across the ice and just severed any arm or leg or head that happened to be sticking up."

Lt. Patrick Roe: "You've probably seen cartoons showing a man flattened like a pancake by a tank; that's how these bodies ended up looking. It wasn't particularly messy because the cold weather kept everything frozen. In some spots the bodies were like a collection of multicolored ice cubes in the general shape of human beings."

In Hell Fire Valley, halfway between Hagaru and Koto, abandoned trucks and jeeps were lined up bumper to bumper on both sides of the road, either burned or shot to pieces. Some were still smoldering. Christmas packages with their bright red and green wrappers and ribbons were strewn across the mile-long site. There were clusters of dead Chinese here and there, and dead Marines sitting behind the wheels of the trucks. Footlockers had been pried open, mail satchels ripped apart, and the wind had blown hundreds of letters across the landscape.

Commando Ron Moyse: "Ian Woodward had been knocked off the lorry during the Task Force Drysdale breakout on November 29, but we found him on our southward march. The Chinese had laid him out among some others in a gully just off roadside. He was in a perfect state of preservation, like all the dead at the reservoir—refrigerated by the diabolically cold air."

Sergeant Asa L. Gearing, G/5, recalls the enemy fire between the Drysdale ambush site and Koto-ri. "It was a rainstorm of lead. The crack and whine of ricochets and near misses was constant. Guys kept dropping in the road, and the corpsmen could hardly keep up. I felt like a walking dead man and I was too damn tired to care. It was a miracle anyone survived."

Some managed to maintain the maniacal cheeriness in the face of death that is characteristic of Marines in the field. PFC Richard Grogan recalls PFC Allard Johnson's mock order at the conclusion of a short break, as the troops were saddling up to resume their march in the storm of lead. "All right, Marines, listen up. I want every man on the starboard side of the road to move over to portside, at my command. Those on portside will move to starboard at this time and vice versa. All Marines forward will go aft and all those aft will go forward. Ponchos and camouflage-covers with the green side out will be switched to brown side out and vice versa, at my order. Are there any questions at this time? *Hawrp!*"

Lt. Joseph Owen, Mortars, B/7: "We were always on the lookout for variety in our diet. Somewhere along the road I commandeered a can of mincemeat from one of the trucks and got it open with a K-Bar. There we stood passing that big institutional can from man to man, dipping into it and licking the mincemeat off our filthy mittens. I thought the stuff tasted as good as anything my mom ever made, which shows you the shape I was in. The young replacement Marines looked at us like we were nuts. They were totally disgusted. Actually, I felt sorry for these kids because they weren't acclimated to misery and confusion like the rest of us. I remember this one kid . . . he looked so bewildered that I just told him, 'Here are your orders: When you see a gook in padded quilt, shoot him. Got that?' "

Corporal Richard Bahr, Baker/7: "Lieutenant Chew-Een Lee had this cooking routine he'd go into whenever he had time. He would boil some rice and mix it with condensed milk. One day he beckoned me over and told me to help myself to a couple of spoonfuls. Guess he thought I looked peaked or something."

Lee says he cannot recall anything of the kind, and he doubts that he would have been so generous with his personal chow; but Corpsman William Davis testifies that Lee tendered the same invitation to him as well. "It was incredibly delicious, given the circumstances," says Davis.

One of the interpreters was a professor at Seoul University who went out on many patrols. Gunnery Sergeant Hank Foster decided that the man should wear a helmet, and gave him his. Lt. Lee was appalled when he learned of this, but it was too late to do anything because the professor was already out on patrol. During the attack southward from Toktong Pass, Lee came across a dead Marine beside the road and instructed Foster to remove the man's helmet and put it on. He did so, and the two of them walked into Hagaru together. It was to be was the last time Lee spoke with Gunny Foster.

Kurcaba's Baker/7 was leapfrogging with Able and Charlie Companies south of Toktong Pass, when a Chinese soldier appeared in Lt. Lee's path, pointing his rifle at him. Joseph Owen, following a step behind Lee, swung his carbine at the man, but PFC Lupacchini cut him down first with a burst from his BAR. The enemy soldier collapsed across a tree trunk, the rifle falling into the snow.

"We got him okay now, Lieutenant!" said Lee's self-appointed bodyguard.

"That's the kind of protection I'd like to get," said Owen to his runner, Corporal Robert Kelly.

"You'd have been dead a long time ago without me," said Kelly in his raspy voice.

"Yeah, Kelly. What would I do without you?"

*   *   *

Hagaru, Koto-ri, and Hungnam had been connected by a radio-relay system that, according to General Smith, "provided continuous, nonfailing, rapid, and reliable service. The progress of the breakout depended in no small degree on this linkup." At 2:40 on the afternoon of December 6, the relay equipment at Hagaru was dismantled—or secured, as Marines would say—and the station at Koto, with General Smith now on site, became the Division's main communications hub.

At six o'clock that same day the Hagaru airstrip was closed. In all, 4,312 wounded and frostbitten men had been airlifted out, plus 137 dead Marines. At the same time, more than 500 Marine replacements had been flown in, as well as several hundred tons of ammunition, rations, fuel, and medical supplies. The last evacuees from Hagaru were men who had been wounded in the final struggle to control East Hill; there were about sixty of them.

General Oliver Smith: "Colonel Litzenberg sent a message around 2 P.M that he had broken through and was making good progress. That was a good moment for me to move to Koto. It was a trip that required perhaps ten minutes by helicopter. The pilot followed the road at four or five hundred feet altitude, and as we passed over the leading elements of the 7th Marines, I could see there was considerable fighting going on."

Conferring with Colonel Puller on his arrival, Smith learned that the Koto-ri perimeter was well defended and that hot food and warming tents would be ready for the 10,000 troops now fighting their way toward the temporary haven. The road leading south from Koto was still blocked, however; the watergate bridge was still down, and Smith could see with his own eyes masses of Chinese on the skyline around the perimeter.

68.
THE 5TH MARINES' ATTACK
against East Hill was almost anticlimactic. Captain Samuel Smith's
Dog Company led the way, jumping off at 0830 on December 6,
and was relieved by Uel Peters's Fox Company three hours' later.
Chinese resistance appeared to collapse on the blood-soaked hill,
and 300 prisoners were taken. It appeared that the Marines now
controlled the heights overlooking the road leading south; but that
night the enemy returned in strength. By the light of the flares the
defenders watched as columns of Chinese trotted down the road
from the north, four abreast, then began climbing the hill. As they
approached the Marine lines, they fanned out and tried to penetrate, but the machine gunners cut them down like wheat.

For Dr. Henry Litvin, the East Hill affair was part of the overall
nightmare. "I recall lifting the helmet off a wounded Marine and
seeing his brains pour out like stew from a pot while his heart
continued to beat. I stood up and stepped back, overwhelmed by
the waste and horror of it, knowing I couldn't do a darn thing to
help him."

Just then a cheery young Marine came up and said, "Guess what,
Doc? We're rear guard again!"

Litvin stared at him dumbfounded. "But we were rear guard at
Yudam-ni."

"Yeah! Quite an honor, huh?"

The news filled him with apprehension. He was already a nervous wreck about the bullet holes that kept appearing in the canvas
of the medical tent. ("In the daytime, from inside, you'd think you
were looking at a starry night sky.") A moment later, Lt. Karle
Seydel, a machine-gun officer, stopped by for a visit. This young
man had been kind to Litvin on the troopship.

"How are things holding up, Doc?"

"Not too bad right here, but they don't look so hot in general."

"Don't worry, Doc—we'll beat the bastards."

Litvin didn't believe him. "I recall thinking, 'Why don't you give it to me straight, Karle Seydel?' As night fell, all I could think of was that we were about to be overrun. There was heavy fighting going on nearby. That was the last conversation I had with Karle Seydel."

PFC Jack Stefanski, Dog/5: "It was rocky where we were. We were ordered to move around the right side of some boulders but couldn't, because there was a steep drop-off just beyond. We were then sent around the left side, but that didn't work out either, because of enemy fire from across the ravine. I found a slit trench to dive into and there was a dead Chinese in it. When I got up to return fire, I put my right knee in his eye socket; it was convenient and I knew he didn't mind."

Stefanski spotted a group of Chinese moving down the ravine, and a moment later an impact on his left side toppled him. There was no pain; he climbed back to his feet. His squad leader, seeing that Stefanski was in a good spot for throwing grenades, began tossing his over to him; Stefanski pulled the pins one at a time and lobbed them underhand. "I heard a BAR working nearby and saw O. K. Douglas climb on top of a rock and hose down some gooks with a full magazine, reload, and spray another twenty rounds. He was good." Then the Chinese pulled back and everything was quiet.

Stefanski looked around, worried. There was nobody alive in sight, Marine or Chinese. He sat down on the ground, lit a cigarette, and tried to figure out what to do next. It seemed as though he was the sole survivor on East Hill; this was the lowest point of the campaign for Stefanski. The highest point occurred a moment later when 1st Lt. George McNaughton came crawling up behind him.

"I'm glad to see you, Mr. Mac."

"What're you up to, Stefanski?"

"Sir, I can't find anyone from the platoon. Are we the only ones left?"

"Don't be ridiculous," said the lieutenant. "Come with me."

A machine gunner, PFC George Howell, came up and said, "Hey, Stef, I hear you got hit."

"Huh? Not me."

"I saw it knock you over. Take off your pack."

With Howell's help he shucked it off and, sure enough, there was a hole in the canvas. The round had drilled through a tin of dry rations and punched a hole in his rolled-up blanket.

During the day, Stefanski volunteered to carry the dead and wounded down to the road. It was heavy labor; the trail was like a bloody toboggan slide. "One of the dead Marines turned out to be PFC Robert Shepherd. We had become friends aboard the *George Clymer*. I recall thinking when I found his body: 'Well, he's so little he'll be easy to drag, compared with these other bozos.' It was hard, though, finding Bob Shepherd there with no life in him. He wasn't the only one I felt bad about. A little farther upslope was Sergeant Larsen, and not too far off there was Lieutenant Seydel with his mustache all neat and trim."

The work was making Stefanski thirsty; he stopped and ate a handful of snow. "I kept seeing the faces of those dead Marines. A dead Marine is an awesome thing. Later that day I was sitting at a fire trying to thaw out some C-rations and this song kept going through my head, and I recall one line in particular: 'Looky there, ain't she pretty?' It made me think of the dead Marines, because they were like big wax dolls laid out on the snow. A few days earlier, Mr. Mac had warned that some of us wouldn't be here tomorrow, and sure enough he was right. Mr. Mac was always right."

Sergeant William S. Gerichten, a machine gun section leader, was near the lieutenant when he was killed. He recalls Seydel as an officer who took care of his men. "I remember one time my fingers were so cold I couldn't deal with the buttons of my two pairs of pants when I needed to relieve myself. He saw I was having trouble and stooped over and unbuttoned everything for me, said, 'Let me know when you're through,' and afterward did them all up again. It may sound like nothing, but it meant a lot at the time. . . . Anyway, I was nearby when he died. He took a step sideways and fell in the snow. It was so slippery up there that people were falling all the time, but it was clear he was dead and had died instantly, which is the best way. . . . We failed in our efforts to bring his body out of the mountains with us. I've thought about that for years, and I've never doubted that Lieutenant Johnson's decision to give him a hasty field burial at the bottom of the slope was correct, given the circumstances."

Lt. Richard M. Johnson, Dog/5 platoon leader: "You are probably aware that Lieutenant Colonel Roise's battalion was the last one out of Hagaru. As the battalion was getting ready to pull out, we were still busy bringing dead Marines down the hill and loading them aboard trucks." Johnson and his helpers had already carried down about ten corpses, sliding each one downslope on a poncho with a man at each corner. Because of the extreme temperature, the ponchos were brittle and tended to tear; the whole operation was very awkward and slow. The last body was Lt. Seydel's. There was only one truck waiting by this time, and the officer in charge told Johnson he couldn't wait any longer; the driver was gunning the engine.

Johnson: "I couldn't blame them for being nervous; you could see masses of Chinese heading our way at the north end of the valley. But I asked them to wait, and went back up the hill to help the four Marines who were trying to get Lieutenant Seydel down the slope." The truck was gone by the time they reached the bottom. They put Lt. Seydel beside the road and gathered some rocks and covered him as best they could, with the Chinese coming closer every minute. "At a certain point we just stopped, all of us agitated and frustrated and sad. We stood there and uncovered—that's Marine talk for taking your hat off—while I said a few words to our Maker. Then we hurried off to rejoin the battalion, which had already pulled up stakes."

Doc Litvin: "I wish I had been able to spend more time with Karle Seydel. He was a lovely young man and I miss him to this day."

69.

BY THIS TIME, ACCORDING TO Corpsman James Claypool, there wasn't anyone left who wasn't exhausted. "I had to grab some of these kids by the nape of the neck to get them back on their feet, but as I became more fatigued myself I became lazier, and sometimes I would just stand there and administer a mild kick to get a kid roused, then a harder kick if that didn't work, and harder still until he actually got up." One of the Marines became so angry that he threatened to shoot Claypool. "Fine," said the big corpsman. "Shoot me later but get on your feet now."

PFC Doug Michaud, 1/5, with two of his pals from Duluth, found an ingenious way to catch a few winks whenever the column was stalled. They would make a tripod with their bodies, leaning against each other, back to back. "It wasn't comfortable but I swear we got some sleep that way."

Army captain George Rasula saw a young Marine collapse from fatigue; he went over and offered a helping hand as the Marine struggled to regain his feet. The youngster was about to take hold when he noticed the Army insignia on Rasula's cap.

"No thanks," he said, pulling back his hand. "I'm a Marine."

Lt. Charles Sullivan: "Sleep isn't the word for it; we sort of passed out. Same with the prisoners. There was a trio of POWs more or less traveling with our group who shared a single blanket. Every time there was a holdup they would squat with their backs to the wind, the blanket partially covering all three, and go into a kind of trance. One time, when we started up again I saw that one of them had apparently frozen to death. The remaining two got up and moved on without even looking at him, and I suppose they made better use of the blanket after that. We didn't want to leave the dead man squatting in the middle of the road, so we dragged him over to the ditch. The next time we stopped, about a half mile farther on, I noticed that another prisoner had taken his place under the blanket. I wondered if by the time we got to Hungnam the only thing left would be the blanket itself."

Corporal Alan Herrington, Item/1, was slogging along on sore feet when he noticed that right next to him was a Chinese soldier carrying another prisoner on his back. "This was one rugged individual: he was moving down the road as fast as we were, even under that weight." Lt. Fisher decided he couldn't stand the sight of two enemy soldiers in their midst, even though they were unarmed and one was a casualty. He directed two of his Marines to escort the pair out beyond the flankers. For an hour or so, Herrington watched them climbing along the slope, the one man struggling under his load, until the pair disappeared in the mist.

Lt. Col. Raymond Murray was another who was impressed by the enemy's stoicism. Because of their inadequate footgear, the Chinese had much more trouble with frostbite than the Americans. "On the road between Hagaru and Koto-ri, I saw some of them walking on stumps this big around, like elephant feet. All these huge blisters had combined into one big clump and that's what they were walking on. Their feet made this special sound on the road: *clack . . . clack . . . clack.*"

The Marines were still leery of the refugees, fearing infiltration by armed Chinese; interaction with civilians was therefore rare. Lt. Ralph Abell recalls ordering his platoon sergeant to pick up and carry a baby he saw sitting behind a burning hut. "We gave her some powdered milk. That didn't go over too well. We gave her some licks of our C-rations, and that hit the spot. She was passed from man to man and finally turned over to the chaplain. She would be pushing fifty now. I've always wondered how she made out."

PFC Steven Spanovich, 11th Marines, found himself trudging along beside a young man and woman with a baby on her back. They nodded at him and smiled, then the man reached out his hand, offering a chunk of honeycomb. The artilleryman tried to refuse, but the Korean insisted. Spanovich: "I'll always remember them, wanting to share what little they had. I hope they made it down the mountain."

*   *   *

At daybreak on December 7 the column was abruptly halted by a concentration of enemy fire from the heights to the east. During a lull it became apparent that the Chinese were about to launch an infantry assault against a segment of the column occupied by the guns and crews of George and How Batteries. Major James Callender and Captains Ernest Payne and Benjamin Read lost no time unlimbering and preparing for action. Trucks were jockeyed back and forth so that the muzzles of the nine howitzers could be thrust between them, while crewmen passed boxes of shells over the tailgates and others carried them to the guns. The stage was set for an unusual confrontation: a fight to the finish between an infantry battalion and two batteries of artillery.

Now that it was broad daylight, the men of Sergeant Russell Rune's machine-gun section watched as Chinese troops began to mass on the other side of the railroad tracks. Captain Read ordered him to bring his crew back to the road, where Captain Payne was organizing truck drivers into a firing line. Major Francis Parry: "It was none too soon. Individual Chinese were already sticking their heads above the embankment or jumping up for a better look."

The gun crews began to fire shells straight across the railroad embankment, stopping the Chinese as they began to flow onto the tracks. There had been no time to dig in the gun trails, so the men of each howitzer's crew braced themselves against the gun shield, absorbing part of the recoil with their bodies and helping to keep the fieldpieces in position for the next shot. With each shot the guns would lunge backward a few feet, taking the crew with them. After every fourth or fifth round the gunners would push the pieces forward again and resume blasting away at the oncoming troops. There was no time to sort ammunition; crewmen were shoving whatever variety of shell was at hand into the breeches—high explosive, armor piercing, white phosphorous, canister—firing away at targets so close they were at times endangered by shrapnel from their own shells. Neither was there time to set fuses or count propellant charges; there was only time to shoot, clear, load, and shoot again. The scene was appallingly grim: a mass dismemberment or vaporization of human beings in padded quilt.

When it was all over the Marines counted more than 500 shattered corpses on the field of battle. How and George Batteries had fired more than 600 rounds. Three Marine crewmen had been killed, thirty-four wounded.

Major Parry: "Has field artillery ever had a grander hour?"

Lt. Abell's most frightening experience was the rescue of the abandoned American and British prisoners, reported by Sergeant Guillermo Tovar. "Fox Company had gotten safely to Koto and we were all crapped out when Major Lawrence, the battalion ops officer, shook me awake and said we had to go back up the road to pick up some of our people."

PFC David Teter, Fox/7: "They woke us up shouting 'Fall outside! Saddle up! Quickly!' They told us the Chinese had agreed to release some prisoners and we were to go back and collect them and escort them to Koto. There were maybe twenty of us in all. As we started back up the road, half asleep, we ran into Marines still coming down from Hagaru and they kidded us about going the wrong way. I figured the reason they sent us back up that road was because we had neglected to get killed and this time they wanted us to get it right."

They walked two miles up the road, then turned into a ravine off to the right. Abell: "It was hard on the nerves going back north, but the tension got much worse after we entered that wilderness, knowing that hundreds of Chinese were all around us and could easily cut us off. They were in plain view."

The twenty Marines followed a stream bed that opened out into a little valley with steep slopes. There were Chinese soldiers standing on the skyline looking down at them. Every one of the Marines had his rifle slung, signifying that they were on a peaceful mission; it also left their hands free to carry stretchers. PFC Teter: "My attitude was fatalistic. I had just come off Fox Hill, where half the company was either killed or wounded. It was just a matter of time before they got me too, and there wasn't a damn thing I could do to keep it from happening."

The rescue party climbed up to a one-story wooden house with a porch, where they found several GIs and two British commandos stretched on out the floor of a bare room. The abandoned prisoners were very glad to see them. One of the GIs was clutching a bag of mail and wouldn't give it up: he was determined to deliver the mail, even after all he had been through. Lt. Abell and his men loaded them, and the mailbag, onto stretchers and carried them outside. Abell: "We practically ran down the ravine under the gaze of the Chinese. The road seemed a safe place by comparison. It was like emerging from Hades."

70.

BACK IN HAGARU, ROISE'S AND Stevens's battalions were still holding the line, but the line was wavering.

2nd Lt. Nicholas M. Trapnell, Able/5, was one of those who sensed big trouble, even though he couldn't see or hear anything unusual out front. Hurling an illumination grenade into the darkness, all he could see when it exploded was a peaceful snowy scene, fit for a Christmas card. When he ran out of illumination grenades, Trapnell had a whispered conference with his platoon sergeant as to whether they ought to fire a burst from one of the guns so the tracers could light up the area. It would give away their position, but they decided to do it anyway, lest the enemy sneak up on them. "So the gunner cranked off a short burst," Trapnell recalls, "and what I saw turned my heart to ice: a wall of Chinese soldiers in white, creeping across the snow in total silence."

If the phrase "human wave attack" had not yet entered the language of the Korean War, it certainly did before the night of December 6–7 was over. From the official history:

> The struggle during the next three hours was considered the most spectacular if not the most fiercely contested battle of the entire Chosin Reservoir campaign, even by veterans of the Yudam-ni actions. Never before had they seen the Chinese come in such numbers or return to the attack with such persistence. The darkness was crisscrossed with a fiery pattern of tracer bullets at one moment, and the next the uncanny radiance of an illumination shell would reveal Chinese columns shuffling in at a trot, only to go down in heaps as they deployed. Marine tanks, artillery, mortars, rockets and machine guns reaped a deadly harvest, and still the enemy kept on coming with a dogged fatalism which commanded the respect of the Marines. Looking like little round gnomes in

their padded cotton uniforms, groups of Chinese contrived at times to approach within grenade throwing distance before being cut down.

Lt. Col. John Stevens's command post was set up in a warehouse a hundred yards behind his two forward companies, Able and Charlie. Hancock's Baker Company was in reserve close behind them. Stevens: "The warehouse was a place where you could get in out of the wind, so we had a lot of visitors, including the regimental commander, Colonel Murray. I happened to be talking with him when the attack started and received word that part of [Captain James B.] Heater's Able Company was being overrun. Colonel Murray obviously expected me to commit [1st Lt. John R.] Hancock then and there, but I decided to wait it out. Hancock himself was champing at the bit."

Among the Chinese troops that overran Lt. Edward Collins's platoon of Able Company were several unarmed stretcher-bearers. When a pair of them passed close by without seeing him, the lieutenant, obeying a mad impulse, pulled the pin on a grenade, plopped it on the stretcher they were carrying, and ducked back in his hole.

"Not exactly Geneva Convention," said Colonel Stevens when he heard about it later.

"But sir, they were carrying ammo on the stretcher."

"I'm glad you mentioned that."

After Baker Company—committed at last—broke up the attack and drove the enemy back, the gray light of dawn revealed innumerable moving targets for Marine sharpshooters. Marines are proud of their accuracy with the rifle, and this was a splendid opportunity to demonstrate their skills. Trapnell watched Gunnery Sergeant Orville McMullen slowly squeeze off eight rounds from a single clip and kill eight Chinese in a row.

Dr. Henry Litvin: "The tent flaps parted and they brought in Captain Uel Peters, Fox Company's C.O. He was a fiery, gung-ho kind of guy; the Corps was everything to him. He was sitting up on the stretcher, looking tense and impatient. 'Let's *go*, Doc,' he said. 'Patch me up pronto, will ya? I gotta get back to the company. Those goddamn gooks are all over the place.'

"I went down on my knees and took a look. Patch him up? Holy mackerel, one of his legs was flopped over at a ninety-degree angle, and part of it was *glowing*. What a mess. I didn't know what to do. I didn't know what to say. One of the corpsmen explained that what I was looking at was white phosphorous. They never told us about that at medical school. I learned later that white phosphorous takes the moisture out of your skin by sucking the oxygen from the water molecules. You can cover the burn but you can't extinguish it. It will burn down to the bone, until the oxygen is exhausted. The corpsman showed me how to daub it with copper sulfate. You had to keep doing this for a long time, and all the while Captain Peters is saying, 'Can't you hurry it up, Doc? I gotta get back to the company.' At one point I looked up, and there in the light of the Coleman lantern stood Colonel Roise with tears streaming down his face. After that I wasn't ashamed to let my own tears fall, and when Captain Peters saw that, he had to face the reality of the situation. He stopped chattering and just lay back on the stretcher."

At mid-morning, after all the shooting had died down, Lt. Col. Raymond Murray took a walk down the road leading through Stevens's position. In World War II he had participated in the Guadalcanal, Tarawa, and Saipan campaigns, but he had never seen so many bodies in one place as he saw that morning in Hagaru. They were piled up all the way from Heater's lines, across the supply dump by the railroad track, and halfway up the slopes of East Hill. Official estimates vary, but the consensus was that there were well over 1,000 dead Chinese in plain view. Stevens had lost ten killed-in-action and forty-three wounded during the night. When Murray returned to the regimental command post he learned that Litzenberg's column was already well down the road. It was time to get the 5th Marines rolling.

Taplett's Third Battalion once again led the way. Major Thomas A. Durham recalls that they came upon a pile of bodies just south of town, where an attack on Litzenberg's convoy had been driven off. One of the bodies stirred and climbed to its feet, about 400 yards away from where Durham was standing. The Chinese soldier couldn't make up his mind what to do next. Some of the Marines beckoned him to climb down to the road. He stood there among the bodies, bewildered, looking around. Finally making up his mind, he turned and started trotting toward the woods. Several Marines took snap-shots at him, but because of all the layers of clothing it was almost impossible to get the heavy M-1 rifle in proper aiming position for the medium-long shot, and the man got away.

Durham: "A little later the order came down that we were to inspect each body, and if a telltale vapor appeared at the mouth or nostrils, we were to finish him off. I happened to be standing near a downed Chinese soldier when I got the word. I discovered on close examination that he was breathing, and sent him to join his ancestors with a .45 slug through the temple. This was the first man I ever killed at close range. I took his belt as a souvenir. Being a good soldier, he had marked his gear. Later I had his name translated. I still have the belt." (Attention, Military Personnel Directorate, Peking: You can switch Han Hung Min from your missing-in-action file to your killed-in-action file.)

Taplett's depleted battalion was so aggressive in its attacks along the ridgeline south of Hagaru that Marines walking beside the convoy broke into cheers from time to time.

By mid-morning, December 7, there was no one remaining in the ruined town but Roise's battalion and a demolition team.

Doc Litvin: "We were now alone in Hagaru. It was like what happened at Yudam-ni all over again. This was definitely not the sort of thing I anticipated when I began my career in Navy medicine. I guess it was apparent to one and all that I was very tense, because Lieutenant Colonel Roise himself came over and steadied me. 'Don't fret, Doc,' he said. 'We'll get out of here.'

" 'Are you sure?'

" 'Yeah.'

"But how, I asked myself, could he be so darn sure?"

Captain Franklin B. Mayer was standing near Colonel Roise's jeep. The battalion commander sat calmly, as he had at Yudam-ni, cigarette dangling from his lower lip. After a while Mayer heard Roise make what Mayer today recalls as "a most amazing statement."

"You know something?" Roise said. "If I had plenty of air and arty I could hold this place all winter."

Mayer glanced over at Captain Sam Smith, who had also heard the remark; the two of them raised their eyebrows at each other.

Mayer could hear the forward air controller, Captain Davis Johnson, talking with Corsairs above the cloud cover. The flight leader reported that he was looking at the sunrise, and that the sun would soon dispel the clouds and the ground Marines would have air cover shortly. In the gray dawn Mayer listened to them circling with their loads of ordnance, and when they finally appeared the planes seemed very beautiful to him—the way their rockets drilled the hillsides, then the steep climb, engines booming and a whistle of speed; the way they swooped down again as Captain Johnson talked them onto a different target.

"All winter," said Mayer, shaking his head in disbelief. *"Jesus Christ!"*

PFC Richard Seward, Easy/5: "I was in Lieutenant Jack Nolan's platoon, and we were the last unit out of Hagaru, although I'm not going to argue the point. We had orders to dismantle, destroy, burn, and depart, and we did what we could—dumping fifty-caliber ammo down a well, for instance. The pillars of smoke were so high, I heard later, you could see them from Koto-ri, eleven miles down the road. Just before we left I walked around the corner of a shack to take a piss and came face to face with three Chinese soldiers sharing a tin of food. They stood up and we stared at each other. It was kind of a shock for me because I had never been so close to any live Chinese. But there was no fight left in these men. The nonexpression on the Oriental face, though—it can be unnerving! I just backed away, and they returned to their meal."

Seward thinks he may have been the last Marine out of Hagaru. One thing he's sure of: he was sitting on the last tank out of town. Shuffling along behind the tank was a large crowd of civilians in white robes, some with burlap wrapped around their feet, most carrying huge A-frame loads on their backs and bundles on their heads. Beyond them, not far off, Seward could see the Chinese coming down the slopes, on the lookout for food and warm clothing. "They were no threat to our column, but they spooked the refugees, who panicked like a flock of sheep—actually overrunning the last tanks in line. It was like a human flash flood. They ran a good quarter mile before we got them stopped, and some of the families got separated. From then on we used our bayonets to keep them a hundred yards back."

As the official history says,

> It is not likely that any of Roise's weary troops paused for a last sentimental look over their shoulders at the dying Korean town. Hagaru was not exactly a pleasure resort, yet hundreds of Marines and soldiers owed their lives to the fact that this forward base had enabled the Division to evacuate all casualties and fly in replacements while regrouping for the breakout to the seacoast.

The Chosin Reservoir campaign was replete with bizarre moments, and one of the oddest was the affair of the Caped Trio. Lt. David Peppin, Marine engineer, had reached a point three-quarters of the way to Koto when he realized that a large gap had opened between his group and tail of the convoy ahead. When he walked around a blind curve he saw three Chinese officers in the middle of the road, a hundred yards ahead. They were standing stock still, arms akimbo, staring at the Marines as they came into view. The three men were wearing tailored uniforms and capes lined with scarlet-colored silk. It seemed obvious to Peppin that they were officers of rank, probably observers from the high command. There were no bodyguards visible, just the three of them, standing like statues. Lt. Peppin knew enough Chinese to call out to them to surrender, but they continued to stand there unmoving.

Peppin: "We tried several times to get some kind of reaction out of them. Finally, one of my men, without asking, just blasted them out of the way with a long burst from his Thompson. Hell, we couldn't wait around all day! And we didn't want to approach any closer. They were armed with pistols, after all."

By midnight, December 7, the last troops of the division had reached Koto-ri. It had taken nearly forty hours for some 10,000 men and 1,000 vehicles to fight their way down from Hagaru. The new arrivals filled the perimeter to the bursting point, but Colonel Puller had made adequate preparations; hot food and warming tents were ready. There would be no layover as there had been at Hagaru, however; the enemy was massing in the mountains to the south and the advance would be resumed at first light the following morning.

(In a radio conversation with Colonel Puller that day, Lt. Col. Donald Schmuck at Chinhung-ni had inquired how things were going at Koto. "Fine," said Puller. "We have contact with the enemy on all sides.")

*   *   *

A short distance north of Koto, a machine gun overlooking the road began firing at the 5th Marines as they appeared around the bend. A detachment from Baker/7 was sent back up the road to deal with the matter. The gun was situated atop a hill in the shape of an inverted rice bowl. Lt. Chew-Een Lee: "Joe Owen and his mortar crew never shone more brightly than they did that day. They set up their tubes and began pumping out shells as I formed my platoon into a line of skirmishers. The mortar rounds were perfectly accurate, and when we swept over the top, the evidence was before us: the bodies of the wounded and dead machine gunners, and the gun itself: a heavy Maxim, manufactured in Russia, the kind with wheels."

PFC Daniel Kott, one of Lee's runners, appeared beside him, all out of breath, his cherubic face distorted. "Mr. Lee, Mr. Lee!"

"Well?"

"Gunny Foster, Gunny Foster!"

"What about him?"

"Gunny Foster's killed!"

"So what?"

"Sir?"

Lee turned on him and yelled. "So what! Get back to your proper position!" PFC Kott looked at the lieutenant strangely and backed away. Lee: "I tried to brush it off, you see. So many Marines had been killed by that time. How can you allow yourself to mourn for one man more than another? How can you mourn for *any* of them when you're so busy trying to keep the rest alive?"

The Chinese had cut the road below Chinhung-ni as well as above it. Lt. Col. Schmuck had already seen with his own eyes a large concentration of Chinese not far north of his position, cutting him off from the rest of the division (a sighting described in detail in Chapter 71). A Marine engineer platoon under Lt. Thomas G. Glendinning was encamped beside Changjin Power Station No. 2 in the Sudong Gorge, two miles south of Chinhung-ni. On December 6 an attack from a dominating ridgeline sealed off the camp and blocked the road to the north. The American flag flying from Glendinning's command post was shot down in an early volley. The lieutenant replaced it himself, then radioed Colonel Schmuck that he needed assistance. (The attack had come as a shock to the engineers, who assumed themselves to be far in the rear and reasonably safe.) The battalion commander dispatched a reinforced platoon, which soon had the ridge under covering fire, allowing Glendinning to lower the flag, shut down the command post, and extricate his small force.

With Glendinning's engineers back in the fold at Chinhung-ni, Schmuck's First Battalion, 1st Marines, became the most isolated, vulnerable, and endangered unit in the division. 1/1 was the last fresh battalion in General Smith's arsenal, and it was now time to bring it into action, clearing the road for the breakout from Koto-ri and protecting the bridge site by the watergate so that Lieutenant Colonel Partridge's men could replace the downed span. Schmuck and his men began preparing themselves to carry the fight to the enemy.

71.

ALL THREE OF GENERAL SMITH'S infantry regiments (minus 1/1) were now together for the first time since the Wonsan landing; but there was no opportunity to celebrate. Intelligence reports indicated the enemy was preparing his main effort in the ten-mile gauntlet of Funchilin Pass, between Koto and Chinhung-ni. General Smith: "From the standpoint of terrain, this was the most difficult defile through which the division had to pass. It offered an excellent opportunity for the Chinese to block our way." And there remained the matter of the bridge at the watergate; unless it could be replaced, the division's entire train of vehicles would be lost, and carrying the wounded south would become a problem with no solution. As the result of a bold reconnaissance patrol led by Lt. Col. Donald Schmuck, Smith had now determined that Hill 1081, dominating the bridge site, would have to be taken and held to allow the withdrawal of the division. Schmuck and his First Battalion, 1st Marines, was assigned the task.

It was clear to all hands that the troops at Koto had to get on the road as swiftly as possible, no later than daybreak the following morning. With some 14,000 men to accommodate, the perimeter was dangerously crowded; any sudden thrust by enemy infantry or the appearance of artillery pieces on the ridgelines could turn the perimeter into a slaughter pen. General Smith already had some 600 fresh casualties on his hands. They were being flown out, slowly, by a handful of obsolete Navy torpedo planes, landing and taking off on the short observation-plane strip north of the village; but a heavy snowfall on December 8 put an end to air operations, leaving some 400 wounded stranded on the ground for the moment.

Not only were wounded and frostbitten Americans waiting to be flown out, but whole families of refugees were ready to take to the road. It was a stark, disturbing scene: hundreds of Koreans, with their bundles and carts and cattle, had gathered outside the perimeter, waiting patiently in the freezing wind to follow the Marines down from the high plateau. Corpsman James Claypool: "We could do nothing to help these people. We had our own wounded to care for, our own dead to carry. I've wondered ever since whether a single villager actually made it all the way to Hungnam with us."

General Smith's marching order called for Litzenberg's 7th to lead the attack to the watergate bridge, followed by Murray's 5th, while Puller, with two of his three battalions, held the perimeter. Ten miles south of Koto, at the foot of the pass, Schmuck's 1/1 was keeping the back door open for the division and guarding the supply dump at the Chinhung-ni railhead. Schmuck had already anticipated that General Smith might employ his battalion to open the way for the division. On December 2—the day Raymond Davis's 1/7 linked up with Barber's Fox Company at Toktong Pass— Schmuck personally led a daring patrol to determine how far the Marines could proceed up the pass without opposition. Major William Bates, Weapons/1: "Colonel Schmuck was a good-humored, enthusiastic man of short stature who appeared to strut. He was boldly decisive in his leadership. This sortie up the pass was a typical Buck Schmuck venture."

The patrol was divided into two sections. The main party, led by the colonel himself, included Major Bates, an artillery forward observer team, and a squad of riflemen. The colonel sent the second section, a rifle platoon, down the railroad track that ran along the floor of the gorge. Acting as a decoy, the platoon was to make no attempt to conceal itself and would retire if fired upon.

Schmuck's party began its advance along the road soon after first light. The slopes were steep, the road winding; the patrol would probably be able to approach close to the enemy without being spotted, or so it was hoped. They proceeded north in two jeeps and a truck as far as the last bend in the road before the penstock station came into view. At this point they halted and climbed out. The three vehicles were turned around—not an easy task on that narrow road—and parked with their noses heading downhill. According to Major Bates, the motors were left running. Colonel Schmuck led them forward on foot, in single file, hugging the steep slope on his right, trying to stay out of sight of any observers who might be stationed on the peaks and ridges. The concrete building came into view and they moved past it (not crossing the bridge, obviously, since the bridge was gone, but picking their way across the slope on the uphill side of the building) and then continued on around a series of curves. Bates thought he saw movement on a slope some distance ahead. Peering through field glasses, he spotted a Chinese soldier shaking out his blanket some 500 yards away. Colonel Schmuck saw him at the same time, and both officers dived into a snowbank and lay still for a few moments.

The colonel insisted on proceeding even farther up the road, and as they rounded the next bend, a broad vista opened before them, and Bates saw what he regarded as the most spectacular sight of the campaign. "Right there in front of us, spread all across the slope, were hundreds of Chinese soldiers. At first we were certain they had seen us, but on close examination through binoculars we found that they were behaving like any troops would in reserve—walking around, cutting brushwood, cooking food, smoking cigarettes, napping, what have you."

Leaving the squad of riflemen to guard against an enemy approach on the road, the artillery forward observer team—2nd Lt. Robert G. Tobin, Corporal A. A. Hammon, PFC Anthony J. Caso—were sent up a gully that led to a commanding ridge on the right. When Lt. Tobin reached the top he saw a large contingent of enemy troops on the slope. About two miles beyond them, the perimeter at Koto lay in plain view. Tobin sent PFC Caso along the ridge to take a look in the other direction, just in case. Meanwhile he reported his sighting to the colonel down on the road. When Caso came back, about five minutes later, he was agitated.

"What did you see, Caso?"

"I found more gooks," he said. "All kinds of gooks."

"How close?"

"The closest is about a hundred yards from the top of the ridge there."

"Okay, go back and keep your eye on them. Let me know if they move this way."

Then Colonel Schmuck called in an artillery strike, in as great a volume as possible. Major Bates: "I had the honor of calling in the marking rounds. The first was short. The second was long. The third hit one of their ammo dumps. After that it was 'Fire for effect.' The Chinese were still milling about on the slopes when it came down. There was no cover on those slopes. We really hurt those people."

Lt. Col. Schmuck: "I enjoyed that day more than any I spent in Korea. It is very seldom that a battalion commander gets directly involved in such a mission."

Major Bates: "I've always been amazed that the Chinese failed to spot our approach, because we moved so close to them. After the barrage had been going on for a while, someone yelled and pointed, and when we turned to look, there was a body of troops moving toward our rear. We were in danger of being cut off unless we got out of there in a hurry."

Schmuck now ordered Lt. Tobin and the others to return to the road on the double. Tobin sent Hammon to bring PFC Caso in. At the same time, the colonel contacted the platoon in the gorge and told them to turn around and head back to Chinhung-ni.

Corporal A. A. Hammon found Caso sitting up there with his rifle across his lap. He was calm even though a Chinese sentry was walking back and forth only a short distance down the slope.

"We've been spotted," he told Caso. "Come on."

When they all got down to the road, they ran back to the vehicles and took off in a cloud of snow.

The excitement wasn't over yet. A Chinese unit, estimated to be of company size, was moving swiftly downslope on the cable-car right of way. Bates: "It was a close thing. We missed being intercepted by about one minute."

The patrol was a tremendous success, not only because of the artillery action, but more importantly because Colonel Schmuck had identified Hill 1081 as the key terrain feature in the pass. It was the one position that had to be taken and held to ensure the safe passage of the division in its move south of Koto.

"From that point on," Schmuck recalls, "I believed our battalion was in a good position to attack up the canyon and seize 1081. My orders to do so were received on December 7. We were to begin our northward move at 0800 the following morning."

That same day, four sections of M-2 steel treadway bridging were dropped into Koto from C-119s. One of the 2,500–pound sections fell into enemy territory and another was badly bent as it landed on frozen ground within the perimeter. Two of the four plywood center sections, designed to fill the gap between the parallel tread-

ways, were also lost to the enemy. The undamaged sections and
plywood inserts, recovered by the Brockway trucks, were turned
over to Lt. Charles Ward, U.S. Army, and his 58th Treadway
Bridge Company. This was one Army outfit the Marines were going to have to trust and rely on.

Lt. General Lemuel Shepherd, commanding all Marines in the Pacific, flew into Koto for an on-the-spot appraisal of the situation
and mentioned to General Oliver P. Smith in passing that he intended to accompany the division in its breakout from Koto-ri.

General Shepherd: "I had known O.P. since the end of the First
World War, and I thought he would welcome me as someone who
could take some of the responsibility off his shoulders. Well, I was
wrong. O.P. didn't like the idea at all. 'General,' he said, 'please
don't march down with us. We have no idea how many Chinese
are out there and we have a long way to go. We could still be
overrun. No one wants to see a lieutenant general of Marines killed
or captured.' Just as I was about to board the plane, my old friend
Lewie Puller showed up with a very irate Marguerite Higgins in
tow. It was clear he was quite interested in getting rid of her. 'General,' he said, 'would you take this woman with you?' Poor Maggie! She had already been chased out of Hagaru. Now she wanted
me to intercede and ask O.P. to let her stay. 'This is the biggest
story of the war,' she pleaded. 'I don't want to miss it, General.' "

Her pleas were in vain. She and Shepherd flew out together after
what the official history calls "a strong seizure of chivalry" on the
part of General Smith, who insisted that the trip down the mountain was too dangerous.

Lt. Col. Raymond Murray: "I was really sorry General Smith
felt Maggie had to go. It would have been good public relations if
she had marched down with us. Maggie may have been a woman,
but she was as good a journalist as any of the others we had with
us."

During the night, many Marines poked their heads outside to check
the sky, hoping to see stars, which would indicate that close air
support for the infantry might be available in the morning. It is
recorded that at 9:37 P.M., December 7, a lone star was sighted
above a mountain to the southwest of Koto-ri. The weakly shining
star was then obscured by flurries of snow, but its appearance and

reappearance throughout the night is remembered today by many survivors of the campaign as a symbol of hope.

The 7th Marines jumped off from Koto early on December 8, their first objective Hill 1328, west of the road. The 5th Marines followed, lunging forward against Hill 1457, east of the road. The weather had turned ugly again, and snow was swirling thickly, meaning that there would be no air or artillery support. And the temperature began to drop.

72.

LT. JOSEPH OWEN, BAKER/7: "Once again we had to climb the slopes and drive the gooks back so they wouldn't harass the convoy. When we weren't breaking through the crusted snow we were slip-sliding along icy trails, and it was windier up there than it was down on the road. Always, it seemed the next hill was higher and steeper than the one we were on. Whenever we got pinned down by enemy fire I had to give myself the same sermon: *You are a lieutenant in the United States Marine Corps. You are expected to provide leadership under fire. You have no choice in the matter.* Then I would crane myself up off the ground and stumble ahead in the snow. At about this time the entire People's Liberation Army surged into sight on the ridgeline and then disappeared behind a curtain of snow. . . . Those poor devils, jogging to overtake the head of our column! When they had to stop, they would freeze in their own sweat."

It was a gloomy gray morning, threatening snow. Baker/7 was a mile south of Koto when they ran into a squall of fire from the ridge. Lt. Joe Kurcaba came forward to check it out, then sent for his platoon commanders. He was standing just off the road with Joe Owen. Lead was flying everywhere. Lt. W. W. Taylor, one of the platoon leaders, approached the spot where they were standing, then sensibly took the precaution of flattening himself on the ground. "You guys are going to get yourself killed if you keep standing there like that," he said.

Kurcaba looked down at him. "Woody, if I get down I'll never be able to get up."

It began snowing now, hard.

Lt. Kurcaba was pointing out a route to Owen on the map, suggesting how Owen might outflank the enemy with his twelve-man "platoon." Owen: "I heard Woody's warning, and right after

that we had like a blinding whiteout of snow. Suddenly Joe Kurcaba slumped against me and I instinctively threw my arms around
him, lowering him to the ground. A bullet had pierced his forehead
just below the rim of his helmet. . . . This beautiful Polack with his
broad Slavic face, he was like a big brother to us. . . ."

After Owen had absorbed the initial shock of the company commander's death, he reached down, removed Kurcaba's map case
from his belt, and went off to find Lt. Lee, who was now in charge.
When he found him near the right side of the road, Owen informed
Lee that Kurcaba had died in the act of ordering Owen's platoon
around the left flank, an end-run attempt. Lee listened, blank-faced,
and said, "Carry on, then."

Everything became quiet as Owen and his men started the climb.
Within five minutes Owen was sure he had the Chinese flanked
because he could hear them talking off to the right. At that point
a runner came puffing up to tell him that Lt. Taylor wanted him
back down on the road pronto. Taylor was now the company commander, the runner announced, because Lt. Lee was down. "What
do you mean, down?"

"Wounded, sir."

"How bad?"

"Looks bad, sir. Can't tell yet."

PFC Attilio Lupacchini had continued to shadow Chew-Een Lee;
during their marches and firefights he always managed to stay close
to the lieutenant. Often out of the corner of his eye, Lee could see
Lupacchini turn his face toward him, keeping an eye out. Everyone
knew that he had appointed himself Lee's bodyguard. Lee never
asked what his motivation was ("Perhaps he regarded me as a good
luck charm"), but it was serious business as far as PFC Lupacchini
was concerned. He was there at Lee's side during the last attack
the lieutenant ever led.

Baker/7 had been ordered to pass through Able Company and
attack an enemy position off the right flank. Under heavy fire, it
became necessary for Lee to move among his dispersed Marines,
directing them one by one to places where they had some semblance of cover. He placed several of them in the ditch beside the
road. Lee: "I had to kick ass continually. This one replacement
kept his head in the snow instead of maintaining observation on

the enemy. I went over and shoved his face even farther in the snow, banged on his helmet with the butt of my carbine, and yanked him into a sitting position.

" 'Keep your goddamn head up. You're a rifleman now.' "

A few seconds later, the new man sustained a light wound: a bullet peeled a strip of skin off his hand.

"Lieutenant, Lieutenant, I got shot!"

"Everybody gets shot," said Lee harshly. "Go find the corpsman, get your goddamn bandage, and report back to me."

Lt. Lee then moved toward the tank that had just come up, preparing to adjust its fire on the enemy positions. At that moment there was another flurry of snow, and at the same time a machine gun opened up and he was struck down, one round striking his right arm, another ricocheting off the tank and grazing his face.

Corporal Gerald Hogan, Baker/7, recalls that Luppachini appeared instantly, as if by magic, and helped Lee over to the ditch. Corporal Hogan met them there and helped the lieutenant ease himself out of his pack straps. Luppachini broke out a compress bandage and applied it to the Lee's arm wound. When the lieutenant changed position to make himself more comfortable, Hogan was shocked to see that his parka was all bloody under the pack. Lupacchini sliced off Lee's mitten with a K-Bar and gently blotted the blood from his eyes with his scarf.

"Everything gonna be fine, Lieutenant."

Lee was able to walk unaided to the aid station. When Dr. Wedemeyer saw him, he said, "What, you again? This time we'll make sure you stay down."

("See the dimple on my cheek?" asked Lee recently. "The wound healed very nicely. It improved my looks, people say.")

That night on the stretcher, the night of December 8–9, was the coldest he had ever been or ever would be. Lee: "I lay there clutching my dispatch case—I still have it, with Chosin Reservoir dirt on it—with my good hand, getting colder with each hour. I could feel the energy draining out of me, and I assumed it was because of the loss of blood, and shock; but I learned later it was the coldest night of the entire campaign. Someone said it got down to thirty below."

The men he served with retain strong opinions of Lt. Chew-Een Lee. Corporal Gerald Hogan: "His leadership sometimes scared the hell out of me, but it was the kind of leadership that got the division out of there. The scaredest I ever got was when I saw Mr. Lee get wounded and knew he wouldn't be leading us any more."

Lt. Joseph Owen: "Chew-Een Lee was a combat leader nonpareil. He was a stickler for detail and discipline, certainly, but everyone knew he was consistent and dependable as time itself, and every Baker/7 survivor will tell you to this day that he was the outstanding man in the company. We held him in awe. Every Marine who fought alongside him tried hard to live up to his standard of service to his country and Corps."

Lt. Woodrow Wilson Taylor: "He was arrogant as hell and very conceited, but there was no foolishness in him. He was strict, demanding, very blunt—he had no tact at all. I liked him very much. He was a real fighter."

It was somehow sadly appropriate that PFC Attilio Lupacchini fell only minutes after Lieutenant Lee's departure from what he called the cutting edge.

Joseph Owen: "Lupacchini wasn't exactly a parade-ground Marine. He was small and had a hatchet face. You wouldn't want him in your outfit if you were running an embassy guard detachment. But he was a good field Marine, and he worked hard at protecting Lieutenant Lee. After Lee went down, Lupacchini didn't have anyone to protect, and he didn't do a very good job of protecting himself. At least he died fast, which was a blessing."

Corporal Merwin Perkins: "The two of us were lying next to each other. 'Cover me,' he said. He got up and ran a few yards, then dropped in the snow. Then he covered me while *I* ran forward. He said, 'I'm going up to those rocks. Cover me.' When he reached the rocks he dropped again. I ran up and flopped down beside him.

" 'Okay, Lupacchini.'

"He didn't say anything. I reached over and poked him. He was gone. Didn't even have a chance to say good-bye! It was right after that that I heard someone say, 'Joe's down.' "

Lt. Joseph Owen: "Corporal Robert Kelly was my runner, a tough kid from Chicago. Just before I got hit I had sent him to the rear to take care of some ammo problem or other. 'I can't do that,' he said.

" 'What do you mean you can't do that? Get going.'

"He shook his head. 'If I leave you alone you'll get hit.'

"He was really pissed off. He looked at me and predicted flat out that I'd get clobbered without him. We were standing in the middle of the road, mind you, bullets whizzing all around, and here's this kid yelling at me, all red in the face. He finally went stomping off, waving his arms and ranting."

Because of exhaustion and the deepening snow, it was becoming harder to zig and zag in the face of enemy fire. Owen actually saw the Chinese soldier who shot him. He was firing a burp gun and one of the rounds struck Owen in the left shoulder and another in the right elbow. Owen: "I was dismayed. I was perplexed. I thought a terrible mistake had been made. There was a tank nearby and I was worried that it would roll over on me. I was also worried that frostbite was going to take my toes. So I lay there on the snow, wiggling them like a good, well-trained Marine. Corporal Kelly didn't actually say 'I told you so,' but the expression on his face did. . . . It turned out that Chew-Een Lee and I were both laying on stretchers in the aid tent, freezing our respective nuts off on the coldest night of the year without knowing the other was right there in the same tent. After the blizzard subsided hours later, we both got flown out of Koto. I remember waking up in a big gymnasium in Japan with hundreds of wounded doggies yelling for a medic—a *medic,* mind you, not a corpsman; and that scared me because I was afraid they had mislabeled me as a doggie and I didn't want to be in the same administrative system with any fuckin' doggies. I had no confidence in their works in any way, shape, or form— not even in their medical department."

As soon as Lt. Taylor took command of the company, he disbanded Lt. Lee's platoon and filtered his men into the other two platoons. There were only twenty-seven Marines in the company now. Baker/7 had started out with about a hundred and eighty.

Corporal Frank Bifulk: "I thought, holy cats! There's an awful lot of disappearing going on. More and more faces were missing and you wondered where the heck they all went. It was like someone reached down and yanked them up and away into the sky. And them Chinese, they wasn't even that good of a shot!"

Baker/7 pushed on. After they reached the top of the pass, the snow stopped and the wind began to howl. There was no way to get out of that wind. The Chinese were everywhere, it seemed. From the spot where the company halted at dusk, Lt. Taylor and his men could see large numbers of enemy soldiers, just outside the range of small arms. Taylor watched them moving down the slopes, coming across the valley, picking their way along the ridgelines. They weren't shooting; they were moving into their nighttime positions. When the wind was right you could hear them chattering. It was the sound of a large crowd.

The 7th Marines were not moving as fast as Colonel Litzenberg desired. Major Warren Morris was now in command of the Third Battalion. "I was not satisfied with his progress in the hills," said Litzenberg later. At about eleven that morning Litzenberg had sent for Morris, instructing him to commit his reserve. Morris looked at the regimental commander, not sure whether to laugh or cry. "Colonel," he said, "all three of my companies are up there: fifty in George, forty in How, thirty in Item." That was it: a total of 120 Marines out of a battalion that at full strength would number a thousand.

73.

ALL EVIDENCE INDICATED THAT Funchilin Pass would be the site of the enemy's most determined stand. It was already known that elements of the Chinese Communist 60th Division occupied prepared positions on Hill 1081, overlooking the watergate breach from the southeast. Early on December 7 a prisoner had been brought to the intelligence tent at Koto; his name was Wu, and he was a regimental librarian in the 60th Division. Like all Chinese Communist soldiers he was well-briefed on the size, disposition, and intentions of Chinese units in the sector. He verified that the 60th Division had been assigned the job of blocking the Marines' march south of Koto, with support from the 58th and 59th Divisions. He said that the 178th Regiment of the 60th had been charged with attacking any American unit marching north from Chinhung-ni, further adding that the 179th Regiment of that division was presently located in and around the railroad tunnels below the village.

A battalion-size U.S. Army unit, designated Task Force Dog, had relieved Schmuck's 1/1 at Chinhung-ni that same afternoon, and Schmuck had immediately called a meeting of his company commanders. Captain Robert Barrow, commanding Able Company, was the last to arrive; he had been helping the Army captain who relieved him to get his bewildered soldiers into position. They were wholly inexperienced in combat, half of them GIs recruited from rear echelons throughout the Pacific and Far East, the others South Koreans conscripted off the streets of Pusan. Barrow: "The problems of discipline and control were insurmountable. I wouldn't have had that man's job for all the tea in China."

PFC Gordon Greene, 1/1, recalls that the Koreans paid no attention to their officers. "As soon as they arrived they built huge bonfires and the doggie officers had a hell of a time getting them to douse them as darkness fell. We were all uneasy about leaving the railhead and division dumps under their protection after we marched."

Captain Barrow had worked closely with Chinese Communist guerrillas operating against the Japanese during World War II. Colonel Schmuck now called on him to say a few words about the Chinese fighting man.

Barrow: "I told the troops that these were peasant soldiers accustomed to unusual hardships. They could march great distances with ease in the roughest terrain. They could exist on a diet so meager as to astonish you. They can outwalk us and outfast us, I told them, but they can't outfight us."

By two o'clock in the morning, December 8, Schmuck's fresh battalion had been assembled in a snowy field near Samgo Station. Two days' rations were issued, to be carried inside the parka where they were less likely to freeze. All hands were to carry two pairs of socks. Only one tent would be carried along: the first-aid tent.

Schmuck reported to Colonel Puller by radio that all his companies were present and accounted for, that the battalion was ready to move out. The regimental commander warned him that the weather forecast was unfavorable and that he should not count on getting air or artillery support.

Under a heavy snowfall, 1/1 began the six-mile approach march at half-past two in the morning, Captain Robert Wray's Charlie Company leading the way. There was no wind. The temperature was five degrees below zero. The battalion advanced in silence along a steadily ascending road, their footsteps muffled in the snow. At daybreak a wind sprang up out of the north, blowing powdery snow around the column. Thick clouds obscured the mountain that was their objective.

Captain Wray reported that he had reached the shoulder of 1081. "No enemy in sight," he told Schmuck. It was now Captain Barrow's task to attack in an easterly direction and fight his way to the summit while Captain Wesley Noren's Baker Company advanced on the left flank, moving along the slopes between Barrow and the road.

In their six-mile hike up the narrow road, the battalion climbed about 1,200 feet. Hill 1081 was now directly above them but invisible in the storm. The storm, as the Marines realized later, was a blessing. Leaving the road at this point, Barrow and Gunnery Sergeant King David Thatenhurst led the way up the slope. The climb was very difficult, for the slope was steep, rocky, and covered with ice. Those who carried the heaviest loads—the machine gunners and radiomen—had the hardest time of it.

Reaching the top of the first ridge, the two Marines stopped and listened. In spite of the wind, they could hear voices. The snow was falling in sheets but occasionally there would be a break, as if a curtain had been pulled aside, and they could see Chinese soldiers moving around bunkers a hundred feet or so higher up. When the platoon leaders and forward observers joined Barrow on the ridge, they all lay low and watched the Chinese for a while, trying to determine the extent of their positions as the rest of Able Company worked its way up the slope. The presence of the Marines was so far undetected.

PFC Gordon Greene: "We were crawling up the incline, sometimes on all fours, sometimes using the butt of our weapons as climbing clubs. Occasionally a man would lose his footing and make a clean sweep of an entire fire team as he plummeting downhill like a human toboggan."

Lt. Col. Schmuck, following on the heels of Noren's company, set up his command post in a large Chinese-built bunker close to the road. It was still fresh with signs of human habitation. There was a meal on the stove and the rice was still warm. Hanging laundry was still wet and just beginning to freeze.

Major William T. Bates, Weapons Company: "We set up the first-aid tent beside the road, on a ledge of ice made by a dammed stream. We spread some pine branches underfoot to make it a little more comfortable. There were no flat spots anywhere except on the road itself, but we couldn't block the road because the whole division with all its equipment was—we hoped—about to come through. None of us was worried about the bridge, by the way; we were confident the engineers would figure out a way to replace it."

Captain Barrow beckoned the 4.2-inch mortar forward observer, Staff Sergeant Myers, and asked if his tubes had been set up yet down below. "All ready, sir," said Myers. The mortarmen were surprised when Barrow said he was going to call in a fire mission. "Won't that tip our hand?" Myers wanted to know. Barrow replied that it would not, because the Chinese would never imagine that Marine infantry would be so close to the impact area of such big gear as 4.2-inch mortars. The snowfall continued to obscure the very top of the mountain.

Barrow: "We couldn't see the beaten zone, but the rounds landed close enough to shake the ground around us. How much good it did I can't say."

It was mid-afternoon when 2nd Lt. Donald Jones's platoon, with Sergeant Harry Spies's machine-gun section attached, rose up and moved directly against the enemy. Two of Jones's squads picked their way along the steep shoulder of the ridge while the third moved in column along the spine. About halfway to the bunkers, the snow curtain was swept aside by a gust of wind, the immediate presence of the Marines was revealed to the Chinese, and the fight began. Barrow: "The Second Platoon suffered heavy losses, but they would not be denied! As they closed with the enemy, they began to yell as if on signal. There was a crescendo of shouting, grenade explosions, and rifle fire, and when it was over I don't think a single Chinese was left alive in those bunkers."

The operation against 1081 was PFC Gordon Greene's first combat experience. He watched the Second Platoon disappear in the blizzard, heard the firefight, and watched the walking wounded come staggering back. Seeing them in that condition bothered him; it brought the reality of combat into focus. Later they brought down the dead, and that was much worse. Greene: "They dragged the bodies down as far as the shelf of rock where the wounded were, and after a few minutes all of them, the wounded and the dead, were covered with snow."

It had been a short, tough fight, but Barrow knew it was only the beginning. If the outlying defenders fought that determinedly, the battle for the main position on the knob was going to be even tougher. Meanwhile he brought up the other two platoons and, anticipating a counterattack, deployed them in a tight defensive perimeter and began evacuating the wounded. It took about five hours of slipping and sliding, falling and cursing, to get each man down to the aid station.

It was dark now. The snow had stopped falling, and in its place came an intense wave of cold air on a biting wind. The temperature plummeted. It was apparent that coping with the weather was going to be as big a problem as dealing with the enemy.

PFC Greene: "We were told to dig in, but that was impossible because the ground was nothing but rock. We were completely exposed to the wind. It was stupefying. Every so often you'd hear someone say, 'Jesus *Christ*.' "

The temperature got down to twenty-five below that night, and the wind channeled the frigid air through Funchilin Pass, straight across the slopes of 1081. Barrow: "We found out later that these two days and nights were the coldest of the entire campaign. I learned that only leadership will save you in such conditions. It's easy to say that a man should change his socks; but getting him to do so when the temperature is twenty-five degrees below is another matter. Boot laces become iced over, and it's a struggle just to get the boot off your foot. Most of the time you have to take off your gloves to do it. I found it was necessary to stay with the individual until he actually took off his boots and changed his socks and put his boots back on. Then I'd get him to walk about to restore the circulation." Barrow devoted himself to this task throughout the night but could not prevent the eventual loss of sixty-seven of his men to frostbite, seven of whom became amputees in the end.

Soon after midnight the Chinese launched their counterattack, a platoon-size assault designed to test the Marines' strength. Barrow's subsequent radio report to Schmuck sums up the action succinctly: "We killed them all."

Barrow's radio operator, Corporal Daniel Fore, had lost his sleeping bag on the climb up the mountain while juggling the SCR-300 radio, extra batteries, his weapon, and his gear. Barrow gave Fore his own bag, "not as a noble gesture," Barrow explained later, "but because I was damn sure that if I had no bag there would be no temptation to goof off. We needed all the alertness we could muster. I spent the remainder of the night moving from man to man and stamping my feet to keep the circulation going."

December 9 dawned gorgeously on the snow-covered mountain, the sky bright and clear, the air bitterly cold. Barrow studied the final objective through his binoculars: a semicircle of bunkers on the skyline. Clear skies meant that air support would be available. The Marines, test-firing their weapons, found that many of them had frozen up during the night.

Following a heavy dose of artillery and mortar preparatory fires, Captain Robert Robinson called in a series of air strikes that Barrow said was the most beautiful he ever witnessed.

Robinson brought the first four aircraft against the knob of 1081 proper, controlling the strike from the ground by backpacked VHF radio. The first pass was a dummy run; the next was a strafing attack, to make sure the pilots were oriented to the target. From that point on it was up to the flight leader to make his own runs with no further correction from the ground, unless he got off target. Robinson had previously marked the defenses by smoke, but it was unnecessary: sticking up from the very center of the knob was one of the twin-legged towers that carried the hydroelectric cables from power station to power station—a conspicuous landmark for the planes to guide in on.

After the preparatory fires had ended, Lt. William McClellan's First Platoon jumped off, with Staff Sergeant William Roach's Third Platoon close behind. In a series of leapfrog maneuvers, the Marines overcame the enemy with a flurry of grenades and had the knob captured by noon.

74.

TWO MAJOR OBSTACLES RE-
mained: the gap over the 2,900-foot chasm where the bridge had
been, and the railroad trestle that had been dropped directly onto
the road a half mile farther on.

Lt. Col. John Partridge was standing with the Brockway trucks
at the top of the pass, waiting for the infantry to capture the
ground by the watergate breach. Lt. W. W. Taylor of Baker Company, 7th Marines, had been assigned the task.

Taylor: "Colonel Sawyer showed up at around 0900 and told
me to send a platoon down to the building at the penstocks.

" 'Sir,' I told him, 'my whole company's about the size of half a
platoon.'

" 'Send whatever you can spare.'

"Well, I sent off about half the company—thirteen men under a
sergeant. They joined up with a small group from Charlie Company and after a short fight we took the shelf overlooking the gate-
house. We killed a few Chinese before we realized that none of
them was even attempting to return fire. They were half dead, their
hands and feet frozen. . . . Yes, it's true that I gave the order to put
the rest of them out of their misery. We couldn't give them medical
care, we couldn't carry them with us, and we couldn't leave them
unguarded in our rear. My men took twenty or twenty-five of them
out of this world, and frankly I've never regretted giving that order."

Majors Webb Sawyer and Thomas Tighe were standing in the
road talking when Tighe noticed a small man at his elbow. Tighe
did a double take, then grabbed him, exclaiming, "Why, the son
of a bitch is a Chinaman!" It was, however, an unarmed, nonbel-
ligerent Chinaman, one of many now turning themselves over to
the Marines rather than freeze to death.

The patrol Litzenberg had ordered Sawyer to send included Corporal Roy Pearl, who was very proud to be part of the leading element of the division at that important moment. The breach at the penstocks still had to be spanned by the engineers, which meant that the fourteen Marines had to climb up around the valve-control building to get over to the other side of the drop.

PFC Ronald J. Moloy, Baker/7, was the first man to enter the building; PFC Charles R. Keister, cradling his BAR, was right behind him. Moloy stepped over a Chinese soldier who was stretched out on the floor, thinking he was dead. He wasn't; Keister finished him off. There were others. After they cleared out the building, the two Marines continued down the road a short distance; then, deciding to take a break from the wind, they sat down with their backs against the cliff. Moloy: "Some unarmed Chinese appeared around the bend a moment later, and came ahead as if to walk right past us. Keister and I sat there bug-eyed at first, but then Keister motioned the man in the lead over to us and we went through his pockets. The rest of them apparently thought we were official searchers or something because they all lined up for a shakedown. Keister and I laughed about it later—how unprofessionally we had searched them. We were both so tired we didn't even bother to get up—did the whole thing sitting on our frozen butts."

Corporal Roy Pearl had been trying to follow Major Sawyer's order to stay in touch by radio, but because of the sheer cliffs, his signal didn't always carry. At one point he asked for and received permission from the patrol leader to run back to the last hairpin curve to send a message. Pearl: "Here's where my zigzag training came in handy: I ran all the way with the heavy radio while bullets went *zig* as I zagged and *zag* as I zigged. The funny thing was, when I raced around the turn I ran right into Colonel Litzenberg, who had just joined Majors Sawyer and Tighe and a Chinese prisoner they had.

" 'Sir! We have contact. There are gooks all over the building down there.'

" 'Very good. Return to your unit.' "

By the time the corporal got back, the Chinese in the building had been killed and there were a large number of enemy troops standing around outside, trying to surrender. Pearl: "It was kind of weird. We were surrounded by unarmed enemy soldiers. Finally, the shooting just stopped."

* * *

The way was now clear for the installation of the treadway bridge. The Brockway trucks, loaded with bridge sections, had left Kotori in a blinding snowstorm with an escort of military police, and the drivers were now laboriously working their rigs toward the head of the regimental column.

Lt. Col. John Partridge: "Along about mid-afternoon we took some incoming mortar rounds near the Brockways. The trucks, with their hydraulic operating systems, were vulnerable items of essential equipment; we had to get them out of there." It was at this point that Partridge began to wonder about their chances of transporting the bridge sections down to the breach. After a good deal of trouble and problem-solving, the engineers got the trucks back uproad and out of the line of fire; but as they were being parked, one of them backed onto what appeared to be a flat piece of ground—and went through the ice of a frozen-over pond. Partridge: "This was definitely the most harrowing hour in the campaign for me. It lasted until I learned that the truck in question was loaded with spare construction material and *not* with one of the bridge sections."

The time had come to deal with the breach itself, now or never.

The first thing to do was to check the length of the gap. Lt. David Peppin carried a roll of wire over to the other side by climbing along the uphill side of the mountain. Taking the measurement by stretching the wire across, he found that the gap in the roadway was twenty-nine feet. This meant that the bridge sections on the trucks were seven feet too short: each treadway section was twenty-two feet, end to end.

Everyone stood around pondering the problem, trying to work out a solution.

Lt. Peppin: "Then one of my sergeants pointed to a pile of railroad ties back up the road a ways. 'Why don't we build a crib on this little shelf?' he suggested. There was a ledge about eight feet below the surface of the road, on the north end of the gap. It was worth a try. There were no other options. We rounded up some Chinese prisoners and told them we'd feed them if they gave us a hand. I think every one of them went to work with frostbitten hands and feet, carrying those timbers down to the site."

Colonel Litzenberg showed up as the engineers were cutting the ties to length. "What's the delay?" he demanded.

"The bridge sections are too short, Colonel. We're constructing a wooden abutment on this side to make the fit."

"How long is it going to take?"

"A couple of hours, sir."

He looked at his wristwatch. It was 1218. "All right," he said, "I'll hold you to that."

Using sandbags as a foundation, the wooden cribbing was stacked in alternating layers. The Brockways were brought forward, and two of the bridge sections were laid down side by side, with a space between them. Plywood sheets, four inches thick, were then spread between the treadways, resting on the steel lips that ran the length of each girder. The tanks would be able to cross the chasm using the two parallel spans, one track on each treadway; the rest of the vehicles would cross with one tire on one of the spans, the other on the plywood center section.

Disaster struck when the first vehicle, a bulldozer, was making the crossing. With one of its tracks on the girder and the other on the plywood, the heavy machine broke through the wood with a loud crack and teetered precariously over the chasm. Moving slowly and carefully, the driver managed to climb back to the edge of the precipice. It looked as though the bridge was ruined beyond repair; but Sergeant W. H. Prosser dared to go out and climb aboard the canted machine and somehow got it backed onto the northern side of the gap. Wielding the blade delicately, he realigned the steel beams, spacing them the correct distance apart. The cracked plywood sheet was discarded and replaced. Prosser then drove the bulldozer to the other side as the onlookers' cheers echoed off the looming slopes.

The railroad overpass now had to be dealt with. This latticework trestle, on concrete abutments fifteen feet tall, had carried the mountain tramway across the road 800 yards below the bridge. Chinese sappers had set off explosive charges at both ends, dropping the trestle neatly across the road, blocking it completely.

Lt. Peppin: "This seemed to me a tougher problem, even, than replacing the bridge at the spillway. We were going to have to blow the thing apart piece by piece, which would take a long time. The tramway tracks, after crossing the trestle, continued up a sloping draw on the east side of the road. A small stream was flowing down the bottom of the draw, and where the water reached the road it sort of fanned out, and some of it was frozen in sheets underneath the trestle. Just for the hell of it, I told the bulldozer operator to butt his blade up against it and see what happened. Well, it was like opening a farm gate: the whole structure just swung aside, and he slowly skated this huge object right off the road."

The bridge was ready for use by 1530. Lt. Col. Partridge climbed into his jeep, drove it to the top of the pass, and told Colonel Litzenberg the convoy could come down. Partridge: "I can remember the way the wind was whipping across the shoulder of the hill at that moment. There was a good deal of drifting snow. It was one beautiful afternoon, bright and clear."

75.

IN THE HEAT AND RACKET OF the final assault on the knob, one of Captain Barrow's riflemen on Hill 1081 shouted and pointed excitedly downhill toward the road. "Look! Look!"

It was another great moment of the campaign. Troops and trucks of the division column could now be seen nosing around a switch-back curve far below. The bridge was in, and they were coming across it.

Lt. Col. Donald Schmuck: "We waved back and forth to each other and it was quite an affair."

The panoramic view from the top of 1081 revealed at a glance the destruction which would have been visited upon the oncoming Marines if Able Company's mission had not been successful. In short order Barrow's men cleared the mountain of the last vestiges of resistance, exhausting their supply of grenades, the weapon of choice in the mopping-up phase. Barrow: "We did better than the Chinese with grenades, not only because we were better throwers, but because we had a better grenade." By the time it was over, the crest was completely devoid of snow, barren and ugly from the bombing and shelling, with at least 500 dead Chinese scattered around. When Colonel Schmuck climbed up the mountain to in-spect, he expressed amazement at what had been accomplished and how difficult it must have been.

"I'll be damned," he kept saying, as he looked over the enemy's bunker-and-trench system.

After dark on the 9th, Barrow reported to Schmuck that of the 225 Marines he had led up the mountain, only 111 remained able bodied. He also reported that Able Company was out of ammu-nition. The colonel turned to Captain Hopkins, his Headquarters C.O., and issued a blunt order: "Get some ammunition up to Bob and bring his wounded down." Hopkins organized a group that

included cooks, supply personnel, wiremen—forty Marines in all—
and began climbing the slope in the moonlight, lugging boxes of
thirty-caliber ammo, grenades, and stretchers. It took more than
four hours to reach the top.

Hopkins: "On our way across the crest, numerous Chinese bodies lay in our path—more enemy dead than I had ever seen. The
look on some of their frozen faces reminded me of expressions
usually seen in horror films."

After delivering the ammunition, Hopkins and his men turned
to the wounded. The trip back was harder than the ascent, and the
wounded suffered greatly. At the bottom of the mountain one of
the bearers broke down when he learned that the wounded man
he helped carry had died during the descent. "I nearly busted my
fuckin' gut bringing the son of a bitch down, and now the fuckin'
bastard has gone and fuckin' died on me! Jesus!" The youngster
sat exhausted in the snow, weeping with frustration, disappointment, and sorrow.

That night Barrow slept with his legs partially inside a caved-in
bunker. His feet remained oddly comfortable throughout the night.
Next morning, Gunnery Sergeant Thatenhurst stuck his head inside
the bunker and said, "Introduce me to your friend, Skipper." Barrow took a close look. From the shadows came an occasional puff
of vapor, the breath of an enemy soldier. Barrow's Chinese foot-
warmer, already near death, died soon after the two Marines pulled
him out and exposed him to the below-zero weather.

The actual linkup was relatively undramatic. The patrol leader,
Gunnery Sergeant William H. McCormick, approached a group of
Marines standing by the Chinese bunker Colonel Schmuck was
using as a command post. McCormick's beard was slathered with
blood from a grazing wound across his cheek.

"Sure nice to see you guys," someone said.

"Nice to be here," said McCormick.

One of the headquarters Marines stepped forward. "Gunny,
there's an aid station around the bend. Let me give you a hand."

"As long as I've come this far on my own, I might as well keep
going. Thanks anyway."

Corporal Roy Pearl found a spot in the First Battalion command-
post bunker and took a nap. "I woke up around three in the morning and stepped outside to take a piss, and saw a beautiful sight:

a long string of headlights coming slowly down the mountain." Pearl stood there and watched the trucks go by for a while, then ducked back inside for his pack and radio and weapon, and joined the column. After marching along for about thirty minutes, a jeep pulled alongside and he heard a familiar voice out of the darkness:

"Is that you, Pearl?"

It was Lt. Col. Raymond Davis. Pearl hadn't laid eyes on him for a long time, and he was very glad to see him.

"How you been, Colonel?"

"No complaints. How's things with you?"

"Fine, sir. Just fine."

"That's good. . . . Take care, Pearl."

"Good luck to you, sir."

As Roy Pearl put it years later, "We had been through a lot together, Colonel Davis and me."

The tail end of the Division was about to pull out of Koto-ri. In the swirling snow, two bulldozers had excavated a pit the size of a basketball court near a row of miner's shacks; it was several feet deep with a ramp at one end, so that the trucks could back down and unload. Before noon the mass grave had received the corpses of 117 Marines, Navy corpsmen, British commandos, and U.S. Army soldiers, each wrapped in a sleeping bag or parachute. A chaplain read a few words of Scripture, and then the bulldozers pushed the clods of frozen earth over the fallen.

Sergeant Robert Gault, Graves Registration: "There was a wonderful turnout for the burial. General Oliver P. Smith was there. Colonel Litzenberg and Colonel Murray and Colonel Puller were there. We had a chaplain of each faith there. It wasn't like the burial down at Inchon, it's true, where each fellow had a white cross with flowers on them brought by Korean civilians. It wasn't as fine as that, no, but it had more true heart."

After everyone had left, a Graves Registration officer paced off the spot with compass and notebook in hand and drew a map in case the Marines should ever return. The bodies buried at Koto-ri on December 8, 1950, are still there.

PFC Ronald Compadre, U.S. Army: "I was watching some stragglers climbing aboard the truck ahead of ours. The truck started moving before the last man could get in, so he turned around and walked over to our truck. He was a Marine and his parka was crisscrossed with blood. I leaned over to give him a hand, but he pushed me away and climbed aboard very slowly. It seemed to take forever. When I asked him to speed it up he paid no attention. The reason I was in a hurry was because they told us Koto was about to be blown up. Sure enough, about five minutes after we started rolling there was this *boom,* like the opening of a drum solo, then another, and then a whole series of booms, until it became like one continuous roar. We sat in the back of the truck watching this enormous black cloud, streaked with orange flame, worrying about whether some of the debris was going to fall on us."

Few of the Marines spent any time worrying about the refugee situation, but Captain William Hopkins actually lost sleep over it. What bothered him most was the way members of families became separated from each other. He often saw children trudging by alone. He recalls watching a brother and sister pass by in a swarm of refugees, and a little later the girl, shivering and distraught, came back up the road, obviously looking for her brother. Hopkins recalls that she had bangs and reminded him of his own sister when she was nine or ten. As she passed the bunker, she fell over in the snow and lay there. Hopkins brought her inside and revived her with hot tea and C-rations and then, regretfully, sent her back outside after advising her to continue on down the mountain.

When Hopkins drifted off to sleep the night of the 10th, there was hardly any movement on the road; most of the Marine units had passed through to safety. "Only those outfits engaged in the rear guard action remained north of us," he said. At 0200, December 11, he was jolted awake by a loud explosion a few hundred yards up the road. It meant that the very tail end of the 1st Marine Division had crossed the newly installed treadway bridge, and that Colonel Partridge's engineers had then destroyed it. With that, Captain Barrow's Able Company was summoned down from the crest of 1081, and by dawn the entire First Battalion was headed south.

A mile or so below the trestle, Captain Hopkins caught sight of a frozen body beside the road and recognized the girl with the bangs who had reminded him of his sister.

76.

WITH A DEAD MARINE STRAPPED to the bumper of his jeep and two others on the hood, Colonel Puller was almost ready to depart Koto-ri. His driver, Sergeant Orville Jones, was still searching for bodies to carry out with them.

"Just make damn sure they're Marines," Puller told him.

He left Koto at about three that afternoon, shouting encouragement to a group of men on the road. "Don't forget you're United States Marines. All the Communists in the world can't stop you now."

Corpsman James Claypool: "Some of the tail-end Charlies were able to grab a ride on the last trucks out, but I was afraid to ride down the mountain because I had seen a six-by slide across the ice and go over the edge. Dead and wounded Marines came flying out of it, tumbling end over end in their sleeping bags." When the truck hit bottom, it had come to rest on its rear end with the headlights still on, shining straight up the canyon wall. Having seen that, Claypool decided to keep walking until the road flattened out, and only then would he try to catch himself a ride.

There was one more Marine-Army confrontation. Lt. Col. Robert Taplett was informed that a group of GIs assigned as flankers were trying to join the column down on the road. Taplett walked back to the treadway bridge and saw that it was true. "I thought you people were supposed to be guarding our flank," he barked. None of the GIs answered him; each soldier continued to follow the man ahead of him as they proceeded along the edge of the roadway. Finally their officer showed up. "I'm Colonel Anderson. Is there a problem?"

"Aren't you people supposed to be holding the high ground over there?"

The Army colonel complained that the wind was gusting sharply on the ridge and said he had decided to come down and cross the bridge "like the rest of you." Taplett called him a son of a bitch and said he would allow his soldiers to remain on the road for one reason: "I don't want troops as lousy as yours out there on our flank. We'll take care of it."

The First Marines' Catholic chaplain was celebrating mass as the last troops prepared to leave Koto. PFC Paul Martin, 1st Marine Reconnaissance Company, recalls that the sermon was about saints and martyrs who had died for their beliefs. "There was quite a crowd listening to him, including a few Marines I had always thought were atheists. After the service was over we got word to follow the division out of Koto; Recon was to bring up the rear. We were already at the south end of town. As the last of the column passed through our position, I became more and more aware of what a great honor it was to protect the division's rear, even though Recon was small in number and lightly armed."

Late in the afternoon, amid growing tension, PFC Martin listened to a bit of brave banter about being left behind.

"Hey, you guys—we're gonna have the whole town to ourselves."

"Lieutenant, you can be the mayor of Koto-ri!"

Major William Bates was manning the checkpoint by the cable-car overpass and planned to remain there until the last vehicle had gone by. At around 0200 on the morning of December 11 he received word that the entire division had cleared his position by the trestle. Bates secured the checkpoint and moved down the road with his men. What he didn't know was that the First Platoon of Recon Company and the tanks were still behind them, out of sight and earshot because of the steep cliffs and switchbacks.

Recon was an experienced and cocky collection of Marines, all volunteers, all Regulars. The eyes and ears of the division, as they were known, were to be sorely tested that night. The mission of 1st Lt. Ernest Hargett's First Platoon was to guard the last ten tanks, bringing up the rear of the division column. The idea was that if the treadway bridge proved incapable of bearing the Shermans, they would be the only element lost, since there were no other vehicles behind them. The tanks were now moving slowly down the road with their headlights on, dismounted crewmen acting as guides to keep the drivers from getting too close to the edge of the precipice. Following the last tank was a large crowd of civilians. The Recon Marines were having trouble keeping them at a distance.

After the tanks had passed between the two gateway hills south of Koto, the Chinese began to close in. The Recon Marines were not yet aware that the roiling mass of refugees had been infiltrated by armed Chinese who were even then working their way toward the front of the crowd.

PFC George Ziegler, machine gunner, spotted figures wading knee-deep in the snow off the road, barely visible against the white background. At first he assumed they were refugees—civilians were always dressed in white—but then some of them got close enough that he recognized their uniforms and weapons.

"Get ready to fight," said Lt. Hargett.

Ziegler: "Corporal Billy J. Paige was standing close by with his BAR. I had the machine gun cradled in my arms. I kept turning to look down the road at the tanks heading south, feeling lonelier and lonelier. A whole bunch of Chinese suddenly appeared on the east side of the road, closer even than the others, and Paige and I opened up at the same time. Between us we killed at least ten of them. They just sank out of sight in the snowbank."

During the next hour the engineers at the watergate carefully counted the tanks crossing the steel span and wondered what was holding up the last nine.

Some time after midnight, one of the tanks near the rear had a brake freeze-up. The disabled Sherman now blocked the road. The tanks ahead of it went clanking onward, disappearing around the bend, opening a gap that left the last nine tanks isolated about a mile above the treadway bridge. Several attempts to bypass the stalled Sherman failed, as did all attempts to push it over the edge of the road. Thus were the last tanks in line cut off and stranded.

Sergeant Pete Bland noticed a wave of excitement in the crowd beyond the last tank, people milling around, jabbering nervously. Bland didn't know what was going on until he heard a voice calling out in accented English. Someone was trying to tell him a group of Chinese wanted to surrender. The voice kept saying it over and over: "Chinese soldier surrender now." Bland went down the road to find the lieutenant. The action was just starting when they returned. Five figures emerged from the crowd and advanced in a file toward them. By this time a fire team of Marines had deployed across the road, weapons at the ready. PFC Ziegler had his machine gun set up on the right. The Chinese soldier in the lead approached closely enough for the Marines to see that he was unarmed.

Lt. Hargett moved out to meet him, his carbine set on automatic. Corporal George Amyotte covered him with his BAR as Bland and Ziegler stood by on either side.

"Look out, Lieutenant!"

Amyotte had determined that the other four Chinese were armed with burp guns. Hargett took aim and squeezed the trigger of his carbine, but the action was frozen. Without hesitation he charged headlong into the Chinese, swinging his weapon like a club, knocking the first two men to the ground, sending a third stumbling backward. A sputtering potato-masher grenade came sailing out of the mass of refugees. The explosion knocked Hargett to the ground. He lay in a daze, listening to the sound of Amyotte's automatic rifle as he killed all five Chinese before they had time to recover. The clashing echoes bounced around the slopes and gorges and finally faded out. A single civilian could now be heard shouting the word *balu* (many) over and over. Hargett later told an interviewer he was sure the man was trying to warn the Americans that there were many infiltrators among the crowd.

Sergeant Bland: "Just then a swarm of Chinese emerged from the mob, and at the same time we saw others scrambling up the embankment on our flank. Amyotte changed magazines and poured fire into them along with the rest of us, and in a matter of seconds the slope was littered with bodies. Some of them came rolling down like logs onto the road. One came to rest right by my feet."

Another grenade landed, exploding near Ziegler, and another group of Chinese sprang forward. Ziegler, momentarily stunned, watched helplessly as two enemy soldiers approached close enough to grab the machine gun by the barrel. Ziegler and the Chinese struggled for possession of the weapon for two or three seconds, until it was finally wrested from the hands of the dazed and wounded Marine.

A third grenade arced in, exploding as it landed on Amyotte's back. The young corporal happened to be wearing an experimental shrapnel-proof jacket of laminated fiberglass, which saved him from serious injury; but like Hargett and Ziegler he was stunned by the explosion.

The phone on the rear of the last tank had been shot away, and the Recon Marines, knocking on the hull with their rifle butts, had been unable to elicit a response. Hargett, having now recovered his wits, jogged down the road to try and bring up the next-to-last Sherman to join the action. As Hargett approached the tank, a Chinese soldier on the cliff above dropped a satchel charge; it exploded as it landed on the turret. For the second time in five minutes, Hargett was knocked down but not seriously injured.

Sergeant Bland: "The lieutenant returned just as the Chinese were beginning to overrun us. Two or three of them raced past and got as far as the last Sherman. We had shoved two of our wounded men under the tank for cover—Corporal Billy Paige and a Marine named Ferko—and we managed to kill the Chinese without hitting the two of them."

The enemy was now building up strength on the clifftop, and Hargett made a difficult decision. Common sense dictated that he withdraw his platoon, but his orders were to protect the tanks. Turning to the platoon guide, Sergeant Gerald A. Hansen, he said, "Go tell Major Gall we're holding but need help."

Hansen headed down the pass. Up to this point, he and everyone else in the rear guard assumed the division column was intact, waiting around the bend for the resolution of the fight by the tanks. Hansen was shocked to discover, as he turned the corner, that the tanks down the line had all been abandoned. The steel monsters squatted in the middle of the road, their engines still ticking over, their hatches open, with not a single crewman to be found. More shocking still, the rest of the division was not in sight. The tiny Recon platoon was in imminent danger of being cut off, surrounded, and destroyed.

Back at the point of contact, another satchel charge sailed onto the road, this one blowing PFC Robert E. DeMott over the edge of the precipice. His fall was miraculously checked by a narrow ledge near the top of the sheer drop. DeMott, unconscious, hung there precariously.

Sergeant Bland: "Nobody noticed DeMott was missing because we were so busy. One of my BAR men, PFC Richard Moore, ran out of ammo and asked if I had any extra. All I had was one clip of eight, plus four rounds in my M-1. Just then I saw four Chinese setting up a machine gun between us and the civilians. The civilians were stretched out flat on the roadway, trying to stay out of the line of fire. I took aim and fired all four rounds and watched the Chinese wilt into the ground, in slow motion. As I was loading the last clip, Moore informed me that he and I were the last two Marines to the rear of the tank. I went over and crawled under the Sherman and took a bandolier of ammo off PFC Leonard Ferko, who I'm sure was dead by this time. PFC Billy Paige lay beside him, badly wounded."

Just then a grenade exploded behind Moore and he said, "Okay, I think I'm hit." Struggling to remain calm, he addressed Paige as Sergeant Bland began stripping the ammo off Ferko's body.

"Got any extra mags?"

"Sure do."

Paige gave PFC Moore all he had left, two full magazines. Paige said, "Gimme a cigarette, Candy Ass." According to Bland, Paige and Moore were like brothers, each one always trying to outdo the other.

"I been hit too," said Moore. "Just now."

"Oh, yeah? Where they get ya?"

"In the butt."

"Ha! Figures."

Bland had the bandolier now, and yelled at Moore to come on, it was time to go. They both scuttled backward around the bend and ran into Lt. Hargett and Gunnery Sergeant Stanley LaMonte coming up the road. Bland: "Moore and me expected the lieutenant to grab some Marines and lead us back to get Billy Paige, but it turned out to be impossible. There were too many Chinese on the road by this time, and when we saw them we knew there was only one thing to do and that was turn around and get the hell out of there."

Lt. Hargett: "I wasn't sure what to do. It's hard for a Marine officer to pull back, withdraw, retreat."

He stood there undecided, until Gunny LaMonte, already wounded in the leg, limped over and yelled over the racket. "Lieutenant," he said, "the gooks have a machine gun going on our flank. Right now they're firing too high, but they'll soon correct that. Most of our wounded are headed down the road with Hansen. The tanks have been abandoned and there's no way we can make use of them. Either we pull out right now or we're dead."

Hargett ordered what was left of his platoon to head south. Paige is still listed as missing in action.

*   *   *

At the treadway bridge, Captain William R. Gould and his handful of engineers were becoming increasingly anxious over the nonappearance of the last few tanks and the Recon platoon. All other units of the division had long since disappeared down the road in the dark, leaving the engineers unprotected. Their feelings of isolation and vulnerability were becoming acute. Gould was sitting against the outside wall of the valve-control building, his carbine across his lap, when a column of men approached from the south. He counted thirteen, the number of a full-strength Marine squad. Just as it occurred to Gould that no Marine squad could contain that many men after what the division had been through, the point man was already stepping across Gould's outstretched legs and Gould could see the burp gun in his hands. The Marine engineer held perfectly still as the others stepped over him, not even daring to turn his head for a minute or two after they were gone.

A short time after that bizarre crossing of trails, Gould heard the sound of footfalls up the road, the soft clink of gear, and then a voice called out roughly.

"Hey!"

"Yeah?"

"You a Marine?"

"Yes."

"What outfit?"

"1st Engineers. Who are you?"

"Recon, First Platoon."

"Come ahead . . . Damn glad to see you."

At the south end of the bridge, a Recon sergeant named Ernest DeFazio recognized an old acquaintance in the darkness: Lt. Nicholas Canzona.

"We're the last, Lieutenant."

"You sure?"

"No question."

Canzona pulled him aside and, digging deep inside his clothing, produced a small bottle of Chianti his mother had sent. "I've been saving this for the right moment," he said. "This is definitely the right moment."

Canzona produced a corkscrew from his pack and wielded it expertly in the dark. They each took a swig, toasted each other, took another swig, and watched as the rest of the Recon platoon made it safely across the plywood.

A few minutes later a dull boom echoed around the peaks and canyons as Chief Warrant Officer Willie Harrison set off an 800-pound charge of TNT, the explosion dropping the treadway into the yawning chasm. The time was 0230, December 11, 1950.

The very last man out was PFC DeMott. Regaining consciousness some time after daybreak, he found himself perched terrifyingly on a shelf overlooking the power station far below. Moving slowly and carefully, his head aching, ears buzzing, DeMott climbed back to the road and headed south as fast as his wobbly legs would carry him, expecting every moment to hear the shot that would kill him.

Lt. Hargett: "That was one rough night, even for Marines."

The seemingly endless series of switchbacks eventually straightened themselves out as the Marines came down out of the mountains. There was a point, at dawn, when a panoramic vista opened up and they could see the countryside that stretched from Sudong all the way across the alluvial plain to the armada of troopships, still miles away, anchored and waiting off the port of Hungnam.

PFC William L. Gobert, Recon: "From there on we never had to fire a shot. We kept looking back to see if there were any gooks on our tail, and we kept our eyes on the ridges, too, waiting for an ambush that never happened. My one regret is that we had to leave PFC Leonard Ferko and Corporal Billy Paige behind. Marines are valuable. You hate to lose even one."

77.

DOC LITVIN BELIEVES IN RETRO-
spect that he found a way to sleep while marching. The layers of
clothing, stiff from dirt and cold, seemed to prop him upright as
he rested chin on chest and shuffled along. From time to time his
head would snap up and, lo, he would find himself a mile down
the road. Litvin vividly recalls the moment when he came around
a bend in the road and saw, spread out below, a beautiful vista in
the cold sunlight. Two or three miles more and he would be out
of the mountains at last.

Corporal Frank Bifulk: "When we hit the valley it was like going
from Minnesota to Florida. Boom, it wasn't cold any more. When
I caught the smell of that salt air and saw those ships in the distance, I knew we were okay."

"*I walk away,*" said Corporal Patrick Stingley, drawing tired
laughter from Marines slogging nearby who remembered the line
from the movie *Broken Arrow*.

Commando Ron Moyse: "But then we reached a point just south
of Sudong where we came under artillery fire, mortar fire, and
sniper fire! It turned out that most of it, possibly all of it, was
friendly—in manner of speaking."

Captain Michael Capraro: "When we were almost off the mountain we heard shooting down below and everybody thought, 'Oh,
God, more gooks ahead,' but it was only the damn doggies firing
at each other."

Colonel Raymond Murray: "The Army's 3rd Division was putting out plenty of firepower, all right, but what they were aiming
at was each other. And they were missing."

(The Marines' disgust and outrage over the Army's performance
at the Reservoir reached such a pitch that the secretary of the Navy,
Francis P. Matthews, sent an official message, ALNAV 126, to unit
commanders, directing that "no member of the naval service utter

any comment reflecting adversely upon or belittling the role of any other branch of the service. . . . Please assure that all Marine personnel returning to the United States are provided with thorough instruction on the contents of ALNAV 126 and its implications concerning interviews with press and radio.")

Doc Litvin: "When we got to Chinhung-ni, they put us aboard an ancient steam locomotive which tooted its whistle over and over. It was a wonderful, jubilant sound. The smoke from the engine's smokestack had sparks in it that blew back and burned holes in our parkas. Did we care? Heck, no!"

A tent camp had been set up at the edge of Hungnam for the Marines coming off the mountain. Many of the tents remained empty, poignant testimony to the division's losses.

When Jack Stefanski stopped by the battalion aid station to have his feet checked, he was told he had to be evacuated. He was oddly reluctant to depart. Hobbling back to his tent to pack his gear, he was met by Lt. George McNaughton. Stefanski: "Mr. Mac put his hand on my shoulder and said I shouldn't feel bad about leaving the company. He said I had done a good job. He said I was a good Marine. My voice failed me at that time. I couldn't even say thank you; I just nodded and tried to smile. It was one of the happiest moments of my life."

George Crotts: "I could have been, and should have been, a better Marine. Being a Marine is a privilege, and it behooves you to be as good a Marine as you can be."

The cemetery in Hungnam was situated on a small plateau at the edge of the city. An American flag hung at half mast. Snow-covered mountains loomed in the distance, and if the wind was blowing just right you could hear the faraway echo of bugles.

"May hate one day cease," the chaplain was saying to those assembled, "and be forever ended."

General Smith, cap at his side, stepped forward. The bleak winter sun shone on his snow-white hair as he turned and faced those paying their last respects.

"It is regrettable," he said, "that their resting place must be for the time being on foreign soil, so far from home. Wherever they lie, the memory of what they did, and their sacrifice, will be remembered by their brothers in arms."

On the morning of the December 12, the 1st Marine Division began boarding the troopships.

Doc Litvin: "When I reached the top of that ladder, those Navy boys just grabbed hold and shoveled me over the railing like a sack of potatoes. I've never been happier before or since, and I swore I would never be unhappy again."

Robert P. Cameron: "After I got settled aboard the troopship, I tried to unwind in the hot showers, letting my skin turn red, getting the chill out of my bones. Someone came by and told me an old pal named John Evans had been killed south of Yudam-ni. Because I was in the shower, I could just let the tears roll down my cheeks. I stood there remembering his face and the faces of others, and the tears kept coming. The way I figure it, tears like those—well, they're a kind of salute to all the Marines who have gone before."

Weeks later, recuperating in the Philadelphia Naval Hospital, Chew-Een Lee thought about Gunnery Sergeant Henry Foster, allowing his death to hit home for the first time. He wanted to contact Foster's widow to tell her how much he had meant to the men who served with him, but he had never taken down her address. He would also like to have told her that Foster had been looking forward to his retirement and had intended to take her on a delayed honeymoon. Some forty years later, as Lee was discussing all this with a writer, his voice suddenly changed as he said: "In a professional way, Gunny Foster and I were close. There are so many things I could have told his wife about him." Lee put his hand over his eyes and wept; and when it passed, he said in a quavering voice, "To this day I regret that I didn't open up to him a little. I would like to have known him better. He was an outstanding Marine."

Theodore Hudson spent several weeks at the Yokosuka Naval Hospital, recovering from frostbitten feet. Whenever he saw someone from the outfit, he would ask for news of Gunny Foster. They all said he was dead—shot and killed north of Koto-ri. Hudson couldn't accept that as the official word, however, because more than once during the campaign he had heard that so-and-so was killed in action but then the very next day he would see the man going about his regular duties. Even after four or five Marines told him Gunny Foster was dead, Hudson wasn't ready to accept it as fact. Hudson: "Being dead was a condition that didn't fit a man like Gunny Foster."

Eventually they transferred Hudson to the hospital at the Great Lakes naval base, which is close to North Chicago. On his first

liberty weekend, Hudson stopped by the Rialto Building on Genesee Street to honor the pact made on Turkey Hill.

It was a Saturday morning around ten o'clock. The apartment
was on the second floor. After Hudson knocked, the door opened
just a crack, a chain across it. The woman inside—who turned out
to be Gunny Foster's sister in law—closed it quickly when she saw
Hudson's dark face.

"Yes?"

"Hello. My name is Private First Class Theodore B. Hudson,
United States Marine Corps, and I'm a friend of Gunnery Sergeant
Henry Foster."

She unchained the door, let him in, and invited him to sit on the
couch. Hudson was nervously clutching his barracks hat in his lap
when Mrs. Foster entered the room in a nightgown, housecoat, and
slippers. The conversation began awkwardly. Hudson was tongue-
tied because he didn't want to make the mistake of referring to
Foster in the past tense if he was still alive. He told her how her
husband had come around that wretched night with a can of peanut butter, feeding his men gobs of it on the end of a stick; how
he gave PFC Hudson his own blanket; how he gave the interpreter
his helmet.

"That's just like him," said Mrs. Foster.

They chatted some more, and finally Mrs. Foster said, "I guess
you heard."

Hudson: "And that's when I started in, because there was no
denying it at that point. There we sat, me on the couch, Mrs. Foster
in the chair, and devoted ourselves to bawling for a little while.
When I got up to go, she asked me to call again so we could talk
some more about the Gunny, but I never went back. It would have
been too painful."

78.

NEWSWEEK CALLED IT AMERica's worst licking since Pearl Harbor. Secretary of State Dean Acheson called it the greatest defeat suffered by American arms since the Civil War battle of Bull Run. Of all the divisions comprising Eighth Army and X Corps, only one was singled out for praise. Historian Edwin P. Hoyt called the Marines' march from the Chosin Reservoir "one of the greatest retreats in the course of military history."

The Marines have never liked hearing the word *retreat* in connection with the campaign. Woodrow Wilson Taylor, the only Baker/7 officer to come through unscathed, says it best. "Hear this: It was an attack, not a retreat. The whole campaign was an attack. First we attacked in a northerly direction, up to Yudam-ni. Then we attacked in a westerly direction, a mile west of Yudam-ni. Then we attacked in a southerly direction, from Yudam-ni to Funchilin Pass. Where's the retreat in that, I ask you?"

Joseph Owen: "We kicked the shit out of the Chinese the first time we met them, which was at Sudong, and we were still kicking the shit out of them when we crossed the treadway bridge. They were surrendering to us, not the other way around. Retreat, you say?"

The Chosin Reservoir campaign was, in fact, a series of tactical victories within the overall context of a strategic defeat. Estimates of the number of Chinese divisions that engaged the Marines at the reservoir vary; it was at least six and probably more. (General Smith told the commandant that the division "cut its way through seven Chinese divisions and parts of three others.") In any case, the Marines rendered ineffective the greater part of Sung's Ninth Army Group, which suffered an estimated 25,000 killed in action and 12,500 wounded between October 15 and December 15. Marine casualties in round numbers: more than 700 dead, nearly 200 missing, 3,500 wounded, and more than 6,200 nonbattle casualties—mostly frostbite victims, of which one-third soon returned to duty.

President Truman, not trusting MacArthur's estimate of the situation, sent to Korea as his personal scout a man he had served with during the First World War, a retired Army major general named Frank E. Lowe. Quoting from Lowe's subsequent memo to the president,

> The close cooperation and coordination existing between officers and enlisted men exemplified the true "Esprit de Corps" that is so easily recognizable in a Marine unit. At no time did the Marines retreat or withdraw during this operation. They continually fought their way out of the trap, and effectively destroyed the combat effectiveness of two Chinese armies. Their casualty toll was heavy, primarily due to frostbite; but they succeeded in carrying their dead and wounded with them, and did not lose any of their equipment. Indeed, a magnificent performance.

Perhaps the most unexpected, though obscure, accolade came from General Edward Almond five years after the 1950–1953 Korean War ended, in the form of the war diary he donated to the Marine Historical Center with the following heartfelt inscription:

> To those gallant officers and men of the U.S. Marines who served in X Corps under my command in Korea, I dedicate this volume with high respect and great admiration. No more gallant men ever fought the battles of our country in any of its wars. My thanks to each of them. [signed] Edward M. Almond, Lt. Gen. Ret., Anniston, Alabama 3/12/58

In his later years, John Yancey often brooded over the action on Hill 1282. "I've played that game over and over in my head, especially when I've had a drink or two. Yassir, over and over . . . I shouldn't have put the machine guns on that ridge. They should have been up on the slope, where there was a better field of fire."

A year after the campaign, Yancey ran into the lieutenant who had lost his nerve on the night of November 27–28, 1950. Yancey was stationed at Parris Island at the time. "I saw him enter the officers' club and go up to the bar. It was apparent that his reputation had preceded him—everyone moved away. He stood there and had a drink by himself. Then he went into the dining room and sat down at one of the tables where several others were eating. They all got up and moved their dishes and silverware and glasses to an unoccupied table. I thought all that was stupid, but I could understand it. Anyway, I called him over and invited him to sit with me. 'So far,' said the lieutenant, 'you're the only officer on the base who has spoken to me outside of duty hours.' During the meal he told me he was trying to get back to Korea before the war ended so he could restore his honor. I never saw him again."

Charles Sullivan occasionally dreams that Master Sergeant William McClung is trying to wake him up to go on watch. "I can actually feel his hand on my foot, shaking me awake, and I'm always surprised when I sit up and there's no one there."

James Ransone sometimes feels a shock in his stomach as he recalls the napalm-scorched GIs begging him to put them out of their misery. "Maybe we should have done what they asked," he says. "It would have saved them a lot of suffering."

Alan Herrington says that every time it starts to snow at night, he finds himself listening for the pop of a flare overhead and the sound of Chinese bugles signaling an attack.

Doc Litvin: "The only way we got out of Frozen Chosin is because a lot of young guys knew how to fight. God bless the Chosin Marines. They are my brothers for life. . . . Every Memorial Day my thoughts go drifting back to those youngsters who never came home. I can still see them, exactly as they were then. They'll never grow old."

The survivors of the 1st Marine Division sailed from Hungnam harbor on December 15, 1950, bringing to an end one of the most memorable campaigns in the history of the Corps. By Christmas eve every U.S. soldier and sailor, all South Korean military personnel, and about 100,000 refugees had been packed aboard ship as Navy demolition experts prepared the waterfront for destruction. After the dock was cleared and the ships were headed out to sea, a gigantic explosion tore across Hungnam harbor in a thunderous shock wave of smoke, flame, and rubble.

Shortly thereafter, a message from the command ship USS *McKinley* advised General MacArthur in Tokyo that the last elements of X Corps had been evacuated from the beachhead. MacArthur relayed the message to Washington, where President Truman was heard to say that it was the best Christmas present he had ever had.

Patrick Roe: "We did a good thing. It is worth remembering."

1. Gen. Edward M. Almond, U.S. Army – Commanding General, X Corps, 1950; 2. Lt. Col. Olin L. Beall, USMC – Commanding Officer, 1st Motor Transport Battalion; 3. Lt. Col. Raymond G. Davis, USMC – Commanding Officer, 1st Battalion, 7th Marines; 4. Brigadier General Henry I. Hodes, U.S. Army – Asst. Div. Commander, 7th U.S. Division. (Photo taken in 1951 after his promotion to Major General.); 5. Col. Homer L. Litzenberg, USMC – Commanding Officer, 7th Marines; 6. Lt. Col. Raymond L. Murray, USMC – Commanding Officer, 5th Marines (*on right, with Gen. Smith*); 7. Col. Lewis B. Puller, USMC – Commanding Officer, 1st Marines; 8. Lt. Col. Harold S. Roise, USMC – Commanding Officer, 2nd Battalion, 5th Marines. Photo 1958; 9. Maj. Gen. Oliver P. Smith, USMC – Commanding General, 1st Marine Division; 10. Lt. Col. Robert D. Taplett, USMC – Commanding Officer, 3rd Battalion, 5th Marines; 11. Col. Allan D. MacLean, U.S. Army – Commanding Officer, 31st Infantry, 7th U.S. Infantry Division; 12. Lt. Col. Don C. Faith, Jr., U.S. Army – Commanding Officer, 1st Battalion, 32nd Infantry, 7th U.S. Division.

13. PFC William B. Baugh, USMC – George Co., 1st Marines; **14.** Capt. William E. Barber, USMC – Commanding Officer, Fox Co., 7th Marines; **15.** PFC Alfred P. Bradshaw, USMC – Dog Co., 7th Marines **16**. Ensign Jesse L. Brown, USN – Fighter Squadron 32, U.S.S. *Leyte* **17.** Pvt. Hector A. Cafferata, Jr., USMC – Fox Co., 7th Marines; **18.** Capt. Michael C. Capraro, USMC – Public Information Officer, 1st. Marine Division; **19.** Corpsman James A. Claypool, USN – Easy Co., 7th Marines; **20.** PFC Edmon A. Collins, Jr., USMC – Baker Co., 1st Marines; **21.** PFC James G. Collins, USMC – Able Co., 7th Marines; **22.** PFC George S. Crotts, Jr., USMC – Dog Co., 7th Marines

23. Gunnery Sgt. Henry Foster, USMC (*right*) – 1st Battalion, 7th Marines; **24**. 1st. Lt. Ernest C. Hargett, USMC – Recon Company; **25**. Lt. (j.g.) Thomas J. Hudner, Jr., USN – Fighter Squadron 32, U.S.S. *Leyte*; **26**. PFC Arthur B. Koch, USMC – Easy Co., 5th Marines; **27**. PFC Theodore B. Hudson, Jr., USMC – 1st Battalion, 7th Marines; **28**. Staff Sgt. Robert S. Kennemore, USMC – Easy Co., 7th Marines; **29**. Lt. John Y. Lee, Republic of Korea Army, attached to 7th Marines Headquarters – Liaison Officer; **30**. 1st. Lt. Chew-Een Lee, USMC – Baker Co., 7th Marines; **31**. Lt. (j.g.) Henry Litvin, MD, USN – 2nd Battalion, 5th Marines.

32. PFC Attilio Lupacchini, USMC – Baker Co., 7th Marines; **33**. 1st Lt. Lawrence J. Schmitt, USMC – Fox Co., 7th Marines; **34**. Master Sgt. William J. McClung, USMC – 7th Marines; **35**. Cpl. Ron Moyse, Royal Marines – 41 Independent Commando; **36**. 2nd Lt. Joseph R. Owen, USMC – Baker Co., 7th Marines; **37**. PFC James A. Ransone, Jr., U.S. Army – Able Co., 32nd Infantry, 7th U.S. Division; **38**. Capt. Edward P. Stamford, USMC – Forward Air Controller, attached to 1st Battalion, 32nd Infantry, 7th U.S. Division; **39**. Sgt. Guillermo H. Tovar, USMC – Military Police, 1st Marine Division; **40**. PFC Ray L. Walker, USMC – Able Co., 5th Marines; **41**. 1st Lt. John Yancey, USMC – Easy Co., 7th Marines.

SOURCES AND
RECOMMENDED READING

Aguirre, Emelio, *We'll Be Home By Christmas: A True Story of the United States Marine Corps in the Korean War.* New York: Greenwich Book Publishers, 1959.

Appleman, Roy E., *Disaster in Korea: The Chinese Confront MacArthur.* College Station: Texas A & M University Press, 1989.

Appleman, Roy E., *East of Chosin: Entrapment and Breakout in Korea.* College Station: Texas A & M University Press, 1987.

Appleman, Roy E., *Escaping the Trap: The U.S. Army X Corps in Northeast Korea, 1950.* College Station: Texas A & M University Press, 1990.

Beech, Keyes, *Tokyo and Points East.* Garden City: Doubleday, 1954.

Berry, Henry, *Hey, Mac, Where Ya Been? Living Memories of the U.S. Marines in the Korean War.* New York: St. Martin's Press, 1988.

Blair, Clay, *The Forgotten War: America in Korea, 1950–1953.* New York: Times Books, 1987.

Cagle, Malcolm W., and Manson, Frank A., *The Sea War in Korea.* Annapolis: U.S. Naval Institute, 1957.

Engle, Eloise K., *Medic: America's Medical Soldiers, Sailors, Airmen in Peace and War.* New York: The John Day Company, 1967.

Duncan, David Douglas, *This is War!* New York: Harper and Brothers, 1951.

Futrell, Robert F., *The United States Air Force in Korea, 1950–1953.* Washington: Office of Air Force History, 1983.

Geer, Andrew, *The New Breed: The Story of the U.S. Marines in Korea.* New York: Harper & Brothers, 1952.

Goulden, Joseph C., *Korea: The Untold Story of the War*. New York: Times Books, 1982.

Griffith, Samuel B., *The Chinese People's Liberation Army*. New York; McGraw-Hill, 1967.

Gugeler, Russell A., *Combat Actions in Korea*. Washington: Combat Forces Press, 1954.

Hammel, Eric, *Chosin: Heroic Ordeal of the Korean War*. New York: Vanguard Press, 1981.

Hopkins, William B., *One Bugle No Drums: The Marines at the Chosin Reservoir*. Chapel Hill: Algonquin Books, 1986.

Hoyt, Edwin P., *The Bloody Road to Panmunjom*. New York: Stein and Day, 1985.

Hoyt, Edwin P., *The Day the Chinese Attacked, Korea 1950*. New York: McGraw-Hill, 1990.

Hunt, George P., *The Story of the U.S. Marines*. New York: Random House, 1951.

Knox, Donald., *The Korean War: An Oral History, Pusan to Chosin*. New York: Harcourt Brace Jovanovich, 1985.

Leckie, Robert, *Conflict: The History of the Korean War*. New York: Putnam, 1962.

Leckie, Robert, *The March to Glory*. Cleveland: World, 1960.

Marshall, S.L.A., *Battle at Best*. New York: Morrow, 1963.

Marshall, S.L.A., *The River and the Gauntlet*. New York: Morrow, 1953.

Montross, Lynn, and Canzona, Nicholas A., *U.S. Marine Operations in Korea, 1950–1953; Volume III, The Chosin Reservoir Campaign*. Washington: U.S. Marine Corps Historical Branch and Government Printing Office, 1957.

Owen, Joseph R., *Colder than Hell: A Marine Rifle Company at the Chosin Reservoir*. Annapolis: Naval Institute Press, 1996.

Parry, Francis Fox, *Three-War Marine: The Pacific-Korea-Vietnam*. Pacifica: Pacifica Press, 1987.

Rigg, Robert B., *Red China's Fighting Hordes*. Harrisburg: The Military Service Publishing Company, 1951.

Toland, John, *In Mortal Combat: Korea, 1950–1953*. New York: Morrow, 1991.

"The Chosin Few" News Digest

Interviews and correspondence with survivors.

U.S. Marine Corps Historical files.

INDEX